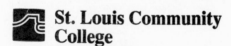

λ Unspeakable

λ Unspeakable

The Rise of the
Gay and Lesbian Press
in America

Rodger Streitmatter

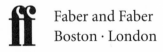

Faber and Faber
Boston · London

Library of Congress Cataloging-in-Publication Data
Streitmatter, Rodger.
    Unspeakable : the rise of the gay and lesbian press in America /
Rodger Streitmatter.
        p.   cm.
    Includes bibliographical references and index.
    ISBN 0-571-19873-2
    1. Gay press publications—United States—History.   2. Gay press—
United States—History. I. Title.
HQ76.95.U5S77 1995
305.9'0664'0973—dc20   95-21803
                                                                                            CIP

Jacket design by Darlene Barbaria
Jacket photograph appeared in the June/July 1970 issue of *Come Out!* newspaper.

Printed in the United States of America

I dedicate this book to the courageous women and men who founded a lesbian and gay press long before it was fashionable or financially profitable to do so. Those pioneers nurtured this new journalistic genre even though it meant being fired from their jobs, being shaken from sleep in the middle of the night with harassing phone calls, and having their bones crushed by baseball bats wielded by bigots who insisted that the material documented in the gay and lesbian press—and now in this book—had to remain unspeakable.

Contents

Introduction

In December 1969, two plainclothes police officers seized 15,000 homoerotic magazines, films, and slides from a Greenwich Village bookstore. Even though the officers boasted that their undercover operation had netted the largest haul of pornographic material in memory, New York daily newspapers opted to ignore the incident. Not so *GAY*. Indeed, in addition to reporting the arrest of three bookstore employees, the tabloid illustrated the news item with a five-by-twelve-inch photograph of one of those employees. *GAY*'s huge photo showed Rick Nielsen wearing a coy smile—and nothing else. The full-frontal nude photograph placed the handsome young man's genitalia squarely in the reader's face, allowing the gay weekly at once to inform and to amuse its readers, while thumbing its nose at journalistic convention.[1]

Welcome to the gay and lesbian press. Brash. Bold. Audacious. In-your-face. Defying the rules of American journalism—and proudly so.

But before pooh-poohing this little-known genre of publishing as nothing but a vehicle for smut, a critic is well advised to look beyond the dangling genitalia. Close reading of this particular issue of *GAY*, for instance, shows that the newspaper, though published a quarter century ago, addressed many of the same civil rights issues that are still making headlines today. One article reported that a gay voting bloc had helped sweep Mayor John Lindsay back into office. The editorial page condemned military officials for asking recruits if they had ever engaged in homosexual acts. The arts page panned a film for stereotyping lesbians as creatures of violence.[2]

For five decades, the lesbian and gay press has published a distinctive brand of journalism committed to affirming the values of the community it serves, while documenting a shocking record of society's homophobia. This particular genre of journalism is not mentioned in the standard histories of mainstream media, and only in recent years has it begun to receive a paragraph or two in the histories of alternative media. The attitude of derision many scholars feel toward

PAGE 10—DECEMBER 15, 1969

WAR RESISTER ANNOUNCES HE'S "QUEER"

New York, N.Y. In a "peace movement" publication called WIN, former Greenwich Village candidate and war resister David McReynolds has bared his homosexuality "for reasons that remain as mysterious... as the seasons." Describing his homosexuality as a "bed of nails" McReynolds gives lurid details of his encounter with a knife-wielding Marine and a good-looking black fellow both of whom meant to "roll" him.

"Gay is not good," says McReynolds, "it is boring." "I know faggot eyes too well," he continues, "tragic cows seated on bar chairs with smooth vacant faces." McReynolds expresses deep concern for persons who may be "driven into" homosexuality because they "groove on a certain guy." ▄▄▄

CORDUROY CLUB ASKS SUPPORT AGAINST POLICE ACTION

New York, N.Y. The Corduroy Club, a private 3-story social club at 240 West 38th Street, is asking for financial support from its members to cover legal expenses in its current court defense action against the city. Harrassed unnecessarily by police several months ago, the club, which was founded by prominent homosexual spokesmen, has provided its members with a variety of social outlets, including dances, card parties, movies, plays, and dinners. It is estimated that between $500 and $1000 will be required to cover legal fees. ▄▄▄

STUDENTS SEEK SPOT FOR GAY DANCE

New York, N.Y. The Student Homophile Leagues of New York University and Columbia University are exploring the possibility of sponsoring another All-College Gay Mixer. The last of such dances attracted an overflow crowd to The Church of the Holy Apostles (28th Street and 9th Avenue) where clergymen acted as chaperones for hundreds of young men and women. People of all sexual orientations were invited, and many were encouraged by the well-rounded turnout. "The first College Mixer was an historic occasion," said the Reverend Robert W. Wood, a Congregationalist pastor. The major problem now facing organizers is finding a dance hall large enough to accommodate the crowds that are sure to flock from colleges throughout the nation. "Last time," said one college student, "there were visitors from as far away as California."

The Studio Bookshop's Host: Rick Nielsen

bookshop employees ARRESTED

plainclothesmen CHARGE SALE of PORNOGRAPHY

Greenwich Village, N.Y. The Studio Bookshop, 500 Hudson Street, one of the city's largest and most popular "beefcake" shops has sustained arrests by two plainclothesmen who seized what they called "pornography" portraying homosexual activities "the largest haul of 'pornographic' materials here in many years." Magazines, color films, and 15,000 slides were included in the seizure, and two employees and a part-owner were charged with "sale and possession" of the materials. Sales of regular photos have not been hurt by the seizures, however, and customers are frequenting the shop as usual. ▄▄▄

doctor says HOMOSEXUAL EYES GROW large

Las Vegas, Nev. Dr. Eckard H. Hess told a convention of the American College of Medical Hypnotists that the pupils of homosexuals and overweight persons say something about their "condition." "The pupils grow larger," says Hess, a University of Chicago professor, "when the eye beholds something pleasant." He states that pupils provide a window to the brain so that "all the world is able to see it." Hess also stated that a "normal" man's eyes may grow to twice their usual size when the eye registers a picture of a nude woman. ▄▄▄

paul goodman SAYS: My HOMOSEXUAL NEEDS HAVE MADE ME A NIGGER

New York, N.Y. Well-known writer and educator, Paul Goodman, has once more clarified the fact that he is homosexually inclined. "Allen Ginberg and I once pointed out to Stokely Carmichael, how we were niggers," writes Ginberg in the November issue of WIN magazine, "but he blandly put us down by saying that we could always conceal our dispositions and pass. That is, he accorded to us the same lack of imagination that accords to niggers; we did not really exist for him."

Goodman's explicit avowal of his homosexual feelings has seemed to cause little stir among the educational circles in which he moves. "I say what I think right," he points out. "I make points if there is occasion. I have even made wit, which is more than I can say for conferees of SDS or Resistance."

Goodman admits that becoming a "celebrity" in the past few years has lent him sexually rather than helped him. "For instance," he writes, "decent young collegians who might like me and used to seek me out, now keep a respectful distance...perhaps they are now sure that I must be interested in their skin, not in them."

Goodman quotes gingerly from HAWKWEED, his book of poems in which his life style is often evidenced. "The ban on homosexuality," he states, "damages and depersonalizes the educational system. The student-teacher relationship is almost always erotic, if there is a fear and to-do that it might turn into overt sex, it either lapses or becomes sick and cruel....Needless to say, a functional sexuality is incompatible with our mass school system. This is one among many reasons why they should be dismantled."

GAY, *like many lesbian and gay publications, was fully committed to informing its readers—while also titillating them.* Courtesy of Jack Nichols.

the gay press was captured in the single sentence one of them used to dismiss it. In *The Underground Press in America*, published in 1970, Robert J. Glessing wrote: "Hundreds of mimeographed publications have sprung up over the past twenty years to defend fetishism, fags, teeny boppers, scatology. ..."[3]

The catalyst for the current book was my personal growth as a scholar. I began my career as a reporter for a daily newspaper. After ten years in the newsroom, I shifted to the classroom and became a journalism professor. And after earning a Ph.D. in American history, I began in earnest to contribute to our understanding of the evolution of American journalism. My scholarship has never glorified the establishment press, which I find increasingly undeserving of praise. My first book, *Raising Her Voice: African-American Women Journalists Who Changed History*, was a biographical study of eleven black women whose careers spanned the 1830s to the 1990s. To place my work in a larger context, I studied the scholarship on the various forms of alternative journalism that have developed as groups outside the mainstream of society have become dissatisfied with their lack of coverage in the establishment press. I studied the African-American press, the women's suffrage press, the women's liberation press... until the day it hit me: my scholarly life and personal life were out of sync. While I was *studying* a wide variety of alternative publications, every week I was *reading* a gay newspaper. Why wasn't I studying what I was reading? Why was the particular form of alternative journalism that increased the quality of my life not discussed in any of the existing scholarship? The day I asked those two questions was the day this book was conceived.[4]

Despite the fact that lesbian and gay publications have been slighted by scholars, they are neither small in number nor lacking in heritage. Early this decade, *Our Own Voices: A Directory of Lesbian and Gay Periodicals* documented the existence, either today or in the past, of more than 2,600 publications in this country alone. That bibliography laid the groundwork for the present volume, which seeks to illuminate the evolution of this intriguing form of American journalism.[5]

The guiding mission of this current work is to describe and analyze how we gay people have spoken to ourselves. I have, therefore, limited my scope to publications that have stated, forthrightly and without ambiguity, that they are aimed at lesbians and/or gay men. Further, I have looked only at publications created and owned by gay people. *Bachelor* magazine of the 1930s and *Tomorrow's Man* of the 1950s are not included because they never identified themselves as targeting gays, although their physique photographs attracted a large gay readership—or at least *viewer*ship. The *Village Voice* is not included, though it has published many gay-oriented stories, because most of its staff members have been straight. The *Gay Power* newspaper of the late 1960s also is absent because it was published by a straight entrepreneur interested only in exploiting the gay community for financial gain. Feminist publications born in the 1970s, such as *Ain't I a Woman* and *Off Our Backs*, have not been included because they were, and some still are, produced by collectives composed of straight women as well as lesbians.

Categories established in *Our Own Voices* have allowed me to focus on publications containing editorial substance of general interest to lesbian and gay readers, bypassing those that the bibliography identified as consisting solely of erotica or as being published as newsletters distributed exclusively to members of political, social, or professional organizations.

One challenge I faced arose because many writers and editors working for early publications did not use their real names, fearing—and rightly so—that their identification as homosexuals would lead to their being arrested or fired from their jobs. In fact, these realities destroyed the publication that, had it survived, would have been the subject of the first chapter of this book. In 1924, Henry Gerber, a Chicago postal worker, founded the Society for Human Rights and produced two issues of a publication titled *Friendship and Freedom*. When police got wind of the activities, they arrested Gerber, who was summarily fired from his job, and destroyed all copies of *Friendship and Freedom*.[6]

The earliest publication that has survived is *Vice Versa*, a lesbian magazine founded in Los Angeles in 1947; my first chapter is devoted to that historic magazine. Although I have interviewed the founder several times, she asked that I not publish her name. The reader will know her only as Lisa Ben, the anagram for the word *lesbian* that she created to conceal her identity. Such is the reality of documenting the voices of an oppressed minority that continues to be denied social and political justice.

On a happier note, one delight of this project evolved from the lesbian and gay press being a relatively recent phenomenon. I have, therefore, been able to track down many of its pioneers. They are introduced through direct quotations from their published articles and my interviews with them. On a personal level, talking with these women and men has allowed me to live the dream of the journalism historian: chatting with the Mary Katherine Goddards and John Peter Zengers of the lesbian and gay press.[7]

Some readers will cringe at my comparing the subjects of this work with such icons of American journalism. Certainly it is true that many of the women and men described in these pages are more accurately described as activists than as journalists. And yet, as early as the mid-1950s, the lesbian and gay press was attracting professionals who had journalism degrees from the Universities of Missouri and California, as well as some with experience on the *Kansas City Star* and the *San Francisco Chronicle*. For half a century, these and other talented and committed journalists have led one of the most important social movements of the twentieth century—in both their published words and their militant actions.

They have provided a lifeline for millions of men and women who have read their words as a first step toward understanding their own sexuality. Our newspapers and magazines have linked the drag queens and "dykes on bikes" at the head of the gay pride parades with the lonely and frightened individuals still deeply hidden in the closet. The publications have connected lesbians with gay men, as well as those of us who grew up in tiny towns such as Princeville, Illinois, with those from the gay meccas.

Russian revolutionary Vladimir Lenin observed that a newspaper is one of the best political organizers, and that is especially true with respect to the emergence of a self-conscious gay community. Because we exist everywhere but each of us must consciously identify himself or herself as a gay person, newspapers and magazines are uniquely important in our social movement. The writers and publications described in these pages have, in other words, served an oppressed minority first by helping gay people identify themselves and then by speaking up and striking back against the powerful forces of prejudice and bigotry. Journalism can fight no battle more noble.

Although this book nudges journalism history down a new path, the rich scholarship on the history of African-American, women's suffrage, and women's liberation publications have provided excellent road maps. That research has articulated important themes that helped me trace the emergence of the lesbian and gay press during the 1940s, 1950s, and 1960s. The foundation created by those themes then allowed me to identify the characteristics that distinguish this press as a unique genre of alternative journalism. For the scholarship of other advocacy media showed me that, by the late 1960s, lesbian and gay publications had indeed broken the conventions not only of mainstream journalism, but also of the various forms of alternative journalism.[8]

This book is intended to introduce readers to a little-known genre of journalism while also serving as a reference work for further study of it. The narrative and accompanying endnotes document locations and founding dates for each publication mentioned in the text. They by no means, however, encompass every lesbian and gay publication ever printed. To have included all 2,600 individual voices would have transformed this book into a volume of encyclopedic proportions, making it a bibliographical work rather than a narrative one. Therefore only representative publications have been included. Specifically, after the initial three chapters, I have selected a dozen publications to represent the lesbian and gay press of each era. Such selectivity ensures that the reader can gain a sense of the personalities of the individual publications rather than having to plod through mind-numbing lists of names and dates.

That selectivity does not mean, however, that this book concentrates only on the largest or wealthiest publications. I have consciously included newspapers and magazines with small circulations and brief histories, as these pub-

lications tell an important part of the history of an alternative press that has
had to struggle for economic survival. I also have been committed to representing lesbian publications and gay male publications on an equal basis.

The first chapter tells the story of a determined young woman who typed
twelve copies of a highly personalized publication during an era when copy machines were unheard of and homosexuality was unspeakable. The next three
chapters, which include details gleaned from 6,800 pages of material in FBI files
on gay groups, trace the emergence of a handful of magazines and newspapers
created to disseminate information that was vital to lesbians and gay men—
even though the mainstream media refused to discuss it. At the same time, the
publications encouraged readers to accept and celebrate their sexuality, an essential step in the genre's effort to mobilize political action aimed at changing a
society that reviled gay people as perverted and contemptuous.

Chapter Five begins a different story. For after the 1969 Stonewall Rebellion
ignited the modern Lesbian and Gay Liberation Movement, "wild and woolly"
tabloids and street newspapers erupted as never before. As the sheer numbers
of publications exploded, so did their variety of messages—and their decibel
levels. Later chapters chronicle the more recent stages of evolution. They show
how the proliferation of publications in the 1970s helped lesbians and gay men
define themselves and their culture, and then how publications transformed
themselves into outspoken advocates of civil rights for an oppressed minority
that was savagely attacked, first by venomous political and religious forces and
then by AIDS, one of the most devastating epidemics in the history of modern
medicine. The next chapter describes yet another distinct phase of this intriguing history as glossy gay magazines exploded to create one of the hottest stories
in the publishing world in the early 1990s. These chapters do not glorify the lesbian and gay press; they expose both its successes and its failures—which have
been legion—at living up to the standards established in earlier eras. The final
chapter discusses what the history and current status of the genre suggest about
its future.

Acknowledgments

Although only one name appears on the cover of this book, many people have donated their time and energy to help me research and write it. First, I am indebted to the dozens of men and women who allowed me to interview them about their work with the gay and lesbian press. In particular, I thank Jim Kepner, Joan Nestle, and Jack Nichols for repeatedly straining their memories in valiant attempts to answer the hundreds of questions that an obsessed journalist-turned-historian can come up with—"So what exactly *is* a double-crunchy lesbian?" to "So if you never hear about any *water* at gay bathhouses, why were they called *bath*houses?" Thank you for the education.

In addition, Joan is one of the many women and men who read and commented on this manuscript when it made far less sense than it does today. Don Henderson and Chris Delboni demonstrated their friendship by trudging through the earliest versions. Larry Gross and Susan Henry shared their wisdom and counsel by reading later iterations, helping me sharpen some points and smooth off the sharp edges of others. I thank each of them for making the final product a better one.

I also thank Barbara Cloud and Gerry Baldasty at *Journalism History,* Jean Folkerts and Peggy Blanchard at *Journalism Quarterly,* and Wally Eberhard at *American Journalism* for supporting both me and my work by publishing articles on the history and evolution of a genre of journalism that less professional scholarly journal editors would have dismissed.

On my own faculty in the American University's School of Communication, I thank Dean Sanford J. Ungar for being a stronger advocate than I deserve. Most bosses tell you what they expect of you; Sandy has awakened my own expectations.

Much of the information contained in this book could not have been unearthed without the assistance of individuals working in research institutions around the country. In particular, I want to acknowledge the generous help of

Pat Allen at the International Gay and Lesbian Archives in Los Angeles and Brenda Marston at the Cornell University Library in Ithaca, New York. My work also has drawn heavily on the materials in the Lesbian Herstory Archives in Brooklyn, the June L. Mazer Lesbian Archives in Los Angeles, the Rare Books and Manuscripts Division at the New York Public Library, and the Rare Books Room at the Library of Congress.

I thank my sister, Doris Boehle, and my children, Matt and Kate, for supporting me even though they don't always understand why I have such a passion for my scholarly work. And, finally, I save my deepest sense of gratitude for Tom Grooms. When he comes home from work each night and climbs the stairs to my third-floor computer room, he never knows if he will find me bouncing off the walls with euphoria because I found the right words or hanging irritably from the track lighting because I didn't. Even so, he keeps climbing the stairs each night to find out.

λ Unspeakable

λ 1

Breaking the Editorial Ice with "America's Gayest Magazine"

The 1940s represented a watershed decade in the history of gay and lesbian Americans. World War II sent throngs of young men into the military, while propelling young women into the labor force as never before. Millions of men and women who felt a same-sex attraction found themselves separated from their families and living in urban environments where they had the opportunity to express their homosexuality. The West Coast was at the center of this evolution, partly because of the region's concentration of defense-related industries and partly because soldiers and sailors returning from overseas assignments were discharged there.

For lesbians living in Los Angeles, one of the most popular nightspots was a dingy bar named the If Club. In the summer of 1947, a petite young woman with softly curled brown hair and a ready smile sashayed into the bar and began handing out packets of pages fresh from her typewriter. Each packet had been meticulously secured with a row of four staples along the left-hand margin. A statement on the top page read: "There is one kind of publication which would, I am sure, have a great appeal to a definite group. Such a publication has never appeared on the stands. Newsstands carrying the crudest kind of magazines or pictorial pamphlets appealing to the vulgar would find themselves severely censured were they to display this other type of publication. Why? Because *Society* decrees it thus. Hence the appearance of VICE VERSA, a magazine dedicated, in all seriousness, to those of us who will never quite be able to adapt ourselves to the iron-bound rules of Convention."[1]

Vice Versa contained no bylines, no photographs, no advertisements, no masthead, and neither the name nor the address of its editor. Indeed, in a profession where cynicism is a trait synonymous with the field itself, many journalistic graybeards would scoff at the suggestion that such typewritten pages could be classified as part of the Fourth Estate. True, *Vice Versa* looked more like a term paper than a newspaper, and it made no pretense of attempting to answer who? what? when? or where? regarding the news of the day. Yet it set the agenda that has dominated lesbian and gay journalism for fifty years, for the editor blithely introduced many of the characteristics that would define the myriad publications that would follow down the precarious path it created. Conceived and edited by a single woman and appearing monthly, the historic publication combined a unique editorial mix and a highly personalized style—much like the 'zines so popular today. But this particular magazine launched a whole new medium of communication that ultimately has helped to unify alienated readers while combatting their oppression.

So the creation of *Vice Versa* rightfully marks the birth of this country's lesbian and gay press. Jim Kepner, founder and curator of the International Gay and Lesbian Archives and himself a writer for dozens of gay magazines and newspapers, said: "*Vice Versa* established the basic format for the general gay magazine—with editorials, with short stories, with poetry, with book and film reviews, and with a letters column. It set the pattern that hundreds have followed."[2]

The charmingly rebellious voice behind the venture was that of Lisa Ben, the pseudonym of a secretary who was immersed in the euphoria of discovering her own sexuality. Neither Ben's real name nor the pseudonym, which she created by rearranging the letters in *lesbian,* ever appeared in the 136 pages of *Vice Versa.* But throughout its nine-month lifespan, the pioneering magazine reflected her boundless energy and wide-eyed optimism.

Lisa Ben Founds a New Genre

The story of *Vice Versa* is the story of Lisa Ben. Born in 1921, Lisa grew up on an apricot ranch in Northern California. An only child, she studied the violin for eight years and attended college for two, until her parents forced her to cease both activities because they insisted she must fit into their mold of a docile young woman. In 1942, she completed the six-month secretarial course her parents prescribed. After saving her money for three years, she defied her parents and escaped to Los Angeles.

Ben recognized she was a lesbian in 1946. She then began visiting lesbian bars, which offered the only refuge from a society hostile toward homosexuals. Ben did not enjoy the bar scene, however, and did not know many other lesbians. In fact, her isolation was the force that impelled the young woman to make her mark on the history of American journalism. She recently recalled: "I was by myself, and I wanted to be able to meet others like me. I couldn't go down the street saying: 'I'm looking for lesbian friends.' So this was the only way

By founding America's first lesbian magazine in 1947, Lisa Ben became the "mother" of the lesbian and gay press. Courtesy of Lisa Ben.

I could think of to do it. That's why I started *Vice Versa*. It gave me a way of reaching out to other gay gals—a way of getting to know other girls. I wasn't very comfortable in the bars. But when I had something to hand out and when I tried to talk girls into writing for my magazine, I no longer had any trouble going up to new people."[3]

In addition to helping Ben broaden her social circle, *Vice Versa* also gave her something to do at work. After arriving in Southern California, she had landed a job as a secretary at RKO Studios, then one of the country's most prestigious producers of motion pictures. She recalled: "My boss said, 'I don't have a heck of a lot of work for you to do, but if you don't look busy, people won't think I'm important. So I don't want you to knit or read a book. I want you always working at the typewriter. I don't care what you type, as long as you're typing something.'" With that invitation, Ben decided to create a typewritten magazine on the subject that was dominating her thoughts—being a lesbian.[4]

For a title, the creative young woman combined two concepts central to her magazine. Homosexuality was considered a "vice"; the lesbian lifestyle was the opposite—or "versa"—of most people's lives.

The production system Ben developed was simple, and the press run small: "I put in an original plus five sheets of carbon paper. That made a total of six copies from each typing. It was a big, commercial typewriter. So when I typed the pages through twice, I had my twelve copies. That's all I could manage. There were no duplicating machines in those days, and, of course, I couldn't go to a printer." Ben composed most of her writing at home in the evening and then took it to work to type during the day. "If anyone came around, I had to zip it into my briefcase real quick," she said. "I had my own office, so that didn't happen too much."[5]

Like most 1940s lesbians and gay men, Ben opted not to disclose her sexuality publicly. Besides, printing neither her name nor her address fit well with the editor's purpose. If a woman was interested in getting a copy of the magazine or writing an article for it, she had to contact the editor in person.

Although Ben socialized in lesbian bars, she constantly feared she would be arrested. She touched nothing but soft drinks, recalling: "I didn't want to be so addled that they would take me off in the paddy wagon and put me in the pokey." On the one occasion that she was involved in a raid, during which she was questioned but not arrested, the experience frightened her so much that she never returned to that particular bar. Her concern was well founded. Police routinely raided gay bars, arrested the customers, held them overnight, and published their names in the local newspaper. Numerous Los Angeles lesbians of the 1940s also were stalked and harassed when they left the bars, and some of them were raped—often by police officers.[6]

So Ben was cautious about the content of her magazine. In her first issue, she told prospective contributors: "Material must stay within the bounds of good taste." For Ben, that meant no four-letter words and no sexual material. Ben boasted: "I made sure that, in case I got caught, they could never show that *Vice Versa* was dirty or naughty." In addition to banning the names of contributors, she avoided publishing the names or addresses of bars or other businesses that catered to lesbians.[7]

In light of her care with editorial content, Ben was surprisingly cavalier with distribution. She mailed three of the twelve copies of the first issue to gay women in and around Los Angeles, giving the rest to women she met at the If Club. She recalled: "I would say to the girls as I passed the magazine out, 'When you get through with this, don't throw it away. Pass it on to another gay gal.' In that way, *Vice Versa* would pass from friend to friend." Ben estimated each copy reached several dozen readers.[8]

By her second issue, Ben began to sense that her free-wheeling method of distribution might be dangerous, begging her readers: "Puh-leeeze, let's keep it 'just between us girls!'" By her third issue, the naive young editor realized the magazine could be considered obscene. "I had no idea how daring or dangerous this was. I used to mail them blithely out from the place where I worked, until somebody said, 'Don't you know you could get in trouble for mailing this?'" After the warning, Ben never again sent *Vice Versa* through the mail.[9]

The editor kept her production expenses at a minimum by using the office typewriter and typing paper. These frugal steps allowed Ben to give copies away for free. "I never sold my little magazine because it was a labor of love. I felt that I should not commercialize it. That would be wrong."[10]

Lisa Ben was absolutely right, however, in thinking that creating a magazine would raise her profile within the *sub rosa* lesbian network of Los Angeles. Six months after she launched the magazine, she told her readers, "I never supposed that VICE VERSA would enjoy such popularity, or lead to so many pleasant and stimulating friendships as I have since found."[11]

Two months later, after the February 1948 issue, *Vice Versa* ceased publication because of a change in Ben's employment. When a new owner bought RKO Studios, her work assignment was changed. In her new job, she had neither a private office nor free time, and she could not type the magazine at home because she had no typewriter. Overarching these logistical problems was the fact that the young woman had accomplished her objective. Ben, with a coy smile, recently recalled: "I was getting a little social life, too—becoming a sly little minx. I was discovering what the lesbian lifestyle was all about, and I wanted to live it rather than write about it. So that was the end of *Vice Versa*."[12]

Creating the Prototype for the American Lesbian and Gay Press

The nine issues of *Vice Versa* varied in length. The first issue numbered fifteen pages, while later ones ranged from nine to twenty. Each was the size of a sheet

```
                              VICE VERSA

                         America's Gayest Magazine

          October, 1947                         Volume I, Number 5


                             TABLE OF CONTENTS


          THE HALLOWE'EN SPIRIT.................................1

          MASQUERADE -- Short Story............................2

          LYRICARICATURE -- New Version of Old Lyrics.........10

          MY FRIEND, THE NIGHT -- Idyllic Fantasy.............11

          UNUSUAL RECORDS -- A bit of chatter
                             about a rare platter.............13

          THE WHATCHAMA-COLUMN -- Wherein readers
                                  express their views
                                  and opinions................14
```

Although it looked more like a classroom term paper than a revolutionary journal,
Vice Versa *led American journalism in a bold new direction.* Courtesy of Lisa Ben.

of typing paper. Ben had to type each article twice to determine the number of
blank spaces she had to leave between words to maintain the flush-right margin
in the final typing. Despite this tedious work, every page of every issue was perfectly flush—and none contained a single strikeover. "I'm very meticulous that
way," Ben said proudly. "I was always very good at office work."[13]

The front page looked like the title page of a term paper. It contained the magazine's title, table of contents, date, and volume number. The front page of all but the first issue also contained the subtitle *America's Gayest Magazine.*

Ben's attempts at humor occasionally led to a sophomoric tone. In her first film review, she labeled the work "unsitthroughable." The headline for a January article urged readers to "Co-oper-8 in '48," and the headline for a February item, in honor of Valentine's Day, wished readers "Heart-y Greetings!" Ben's holiday spirit infected her articles as well. A December article began: "It was all that I could do to keep ahead of Santa and his perennial reindeer and get this magazine to you."[14]

While such frivolous language generally can be excused as the product of youthful enthusiasm, the tone sometimes trivialized substantive messages. An October editorial, for example, suggested that Halloween was a particularly important holiday for lesbians because discrimination forced them to mask their identities every day of the year. Detracting from the editor's insightful analysis, however, was her reference to the holiday's magical "atmos-fear."[15]

Vice Versa's lack of a professional tone did not dissuade readers from praising it, as their positive comments crowned the magazine an immediate success. Readers wrote: "I wish to thank you for the privilege of seeing this unique publication," "May your jaunt into journalesbianism prove to have the angels' support," and "There is really little room for improvement!"[16]

After one reader wrote that the magazine made her feel that she finally had found a group she belonged with, Ben responded that this was precisely the feeling she had hoped *Vice Versa* would engender: "Even though readers may never actually become acquainted with one another, they will find a sort of spiritual communion through this little magazine, which is written by and for those of our inclinations. As long as I know that my friends enjoy reading VICE VERSA, I shall try to keep on publishing it."[17]

Setting a Positive Tone

Vice Versa's editorial content was in harmony with the subtitle's emphasis on being the country's "gayest" magazine. In fact, the positive tone was one of the fundamental characteristics the publication contributed to the media genre that emerged from it. The vivacious editor created the positive tone to counteract the way gay people saw themselves covered in American newspapers. She said, "To every newspaper I ever read, we were the unspeakables." On the rare occasion gay people were spoken of, they were depicted as criminals or psychopaths. Ben recalled: "Every once in a while there would be an article in the newspapers like, 'Party of Perverts Broken Up at Such and Such,' and there would be a list of names. Or else you would hear thirdhand about a raid down at some boys' club, and they took in a certain number of—they didn't say *gay people*, they would say *perverts* or some unpleasant name."[18]

The youthful editor was determined to present her readers with a more up-beat view of life. Ben repeatedly told her readers not to feel ashamed of their sexuality. She wrote, "My feelings in such matters have always seemed quite natural and 'right' to me," and "I, for one, consider myself neither an error of nature nor some sort of psychological freak." Ben's acceptance of a favorable attitude toward her sexuality translated into an editorial philosophy of lesbian pride. Unlike mainstream newspapers and magazines, *Vice Versa* did not denigrate homosexuality. Nor did it apologize or communicate a sense of guilt or shame to its readers. Instead, it consistently encouraged lesbians to develop a positive self-image both as homosexuals and as women.[19]

Ben has insisted that neither she nor her magazine was political in nature. In 1978, she told an interviewer, "Politics just didn't exist for me." She repeated the sentiment in a 1993 interview: "I have never been a marcher or a political activist or screamed out about my rights or anything. I've just never felt that way. I just don't want to get up on a soapbox about it." And yet, by reflecting her positive attitude toward her lesbian feelings and lifestyle, *Vice Versa* made a powerful political statement two decades before gay people organized this country's first public demonstrations. Ben recently said: "I didn't think the things I said were political statements at the time. But now, yes, I can see that maybe they were."[20]

Ben's strongest endorsement of lesbian and gay pride came in a remarkably progressive editorial that, when its outdated jargon is stripped away, is strongly reminiscent of the militant rallying cry of the 1990s: "We're here! We're queer! Get used to it!" Ben's 1940s version about the "Third Sex," a label sexologists of the time used for homosexuals, read: "The Third Sex is here to stay. Homosexuality is becoming less and less a 'taboo' subject, and although still considered by the general public as contemptible or treated with derision, I venture to predict that there will be a time in the future when gay folk will be accepted as part of regular society."[21]

Rather than lamenting the difficulties of being part of a repressed minority, Ben urged her readers to celebrate their double good fortune of being women and also being women who appreciated feminine beauty. She wrote: "How much more beautiful, in every way, are women than men! I am glad that I was not predestined to be oblivious to and unattracted by feminine charm. How thankful I am to have been born in womanly form and yet to possess the capacity of appreciating to the fullest extent feminine beauty!"[22]

The editor often mentioned the new freedoms American women were securing, focusing specifically on how the changes could have a positive impact on gay women. With her rose-colored glasses firmly in place, she wished fond farewell to the days when the woman's sphere was restricted to marriage and children. Ben saw time-saving innovations such as frozen foods and electrical appliances as making it easier for women to live independently of men. She wrote, "Never before have circumstances and conditions been so suitable for those of lesbian tendencies."[23]

Politicizing Lesbian Fiction

Because a network for distributing news of interest to lesbians did not yet exist, *Vice Versa*, like the publications that would follow immediately in its wake, was composed largely of fiction. As the first of those publications, the magazine introduced a concept that would become a staple of the lesbian and gay press for the next two decades: using short stories and poetry to communicate political messages. Every issue contained at least one piece of fiction, most of them written by the editor.

Ben clearly used *Vice Versa*—although she continues to say it was unconscious—as a political platform from which to promote her particular set of values. One such value was gay separatism. Ben spent as much time as possible with other gay people. "It goes without saying that I loved to spend time with gay gals," she said, "but I had many gay men friends, too. They were like brothers or cousins to me. What I didn't have was straight friends, and I didn't really want them. I got along at work, but I didn't want to take them home with me. I was—and still am—very much what would be called a gay separatist."[24]

The longest item ever to appear in *Vice Versa* reflected Ben's separatist attitude. The ten-page short story told of a homophobic drunk who blacked out and then awoke to find himself in a twilight zone peopled entirely by homosexuals. The parody of how straights treat gays described the drunken man's encounter after he made a denigrating remark at a gay bar: "Harry Runk suddenly felt himself spun around as if he were a top. An irate girl with jet black hair and flaming green eyes faced him. 'I heard what you called my friend. Take that, you unspeakable outrage of nature!' Runk picked himself up off the floor. Two husky laddies in skin-tight bolero suits pinioned his arms to his sides. 'Somebody call the cops!' shrilled one. It didn't seem any time at all until Harry heard sirens outside. Badly frightened now, and with most of the fight knocked out of him, he stood there, awaiting his arrest."[25]

The story turned the tables and empowered lesbian readers, thereby communicating Ben's own anger toward straight America. In the same issue, Ben told readers she had written the story in response to newspaper articles in the mainstream press: "I was rather irked by recent sensational newspaper accounts containing derogatory remarks about us. Indulging in these fantastic ramblings provided a harmless release for my outraged feelings."[26]

Ben also expressed her values through publishing fiction written by her readers. A short story that depicted a lesbian wedding, for example, reflected Ben's own desire to become involved in a committed relationship modeled after heterosexual marriage. "I'm not a militant feminist," she said. "If I had my druthers, I'd love to stay home and have my partner go out and do the job." Though Ben's longest romantic relationship was in the 1950s and lasted only three years, she promoted conventional relationships through the fiction she published.[27]

Yet another political statement Ben communicated through fiction concerned masculine/feminine roles. Ben's personal style deviated from that of many lesbians. She said: "I was obviously feminine. I had my hair long, and I wore jewelry. I didn't look like a gay gal. I didn't have the close-cropped hair and the tailored look that was so prevalent in those days. I didn't do any of that jazz because I just didn't feel like it. And I was darned if I was going to do it just because everybody else did. I'm a girl and I've always been a girl. The only difference is, I like girls."[28]

On the topic of appearances, the five-foot-one-inch-tall Ben chose the medium of poetry to express her political support for feminine grooming and fashion. In "Protest," she wrote critically of masculine-looking lesbians:

How willingly we go with tresses shorn
And beauty masked in graceless, drab attire.
A rose's loveliness is to admire;
Who'd cut the bloom and thus expose the thorn?[29]

Initiating a Forum for Lesbian and Gay Issues

Using *Vice Versa* to reflect her own political beliefs did not preclude Lisa Ben from opening her magazine to other voices. For the editor, like many lesbian and gay journalists who would follow her, was eager to create a venue for public discussion of topics the mainstream media ignored. She recalled: "I realized there were a lot of good minds out there that could probably write a lot better than I could. And why didn't they all get together and contribute and we could have a meeting of the minds?"[30]

Ben initiated the concept of lesbian and gay publications serving as open forums for readers, saying, "This is your magazine. VICE VERSA is meant to be a medium through which we may express our thoughts, our emotions, our opinions." Every issue contained at least one item by a reader, and eventually half a dozen readers-cum-writers contributed letters, poems, and short stories—creating the first printed dialogue among American lesbians.[31]

The benefits of such an open forum were threefold. First, it aired lesbian issues as they had never been aired before, allowing readers to discuss topics they previously had had no means of talking about in print. Second, it encouraged and rewarded writers who otherwise might not have succeeded in publishing their work. Finally, although *Vice Versa* was aimed at lesbians, Ben hoped copies would reach heterosexuals as well. That meant the magazine could showcase lesbian writers, thereby helping to educate the public about the abilities of homosexuals. Ben used this potential benefit to encourage readers to submit quality work: "If VICE VERSA should be subjected to the glance of unsympathetic eyes, let us at least show that our magazine can be just as interesting and entertaining on as high a level as the average magazine available to the general public."[32]

Ultimately, however, Ben valued establishing an open forum more than she valued publishing high-quality material. She recalled: "There was no place else they could publish, but they just wrote the most below-par stuff—just Godawful. What can you do? I had to put it in." One piece Ben struggled with but finally published was the short story depicting a lesbian marriage. A passage from the melodramatic work illustrates why she was reluctant: "She placed one hand on the Bible, and with the other tremblingly slipped the ring upon your finger. 'As God is my witness,' she breathed, then encircled your neck with her warm arms and pressed a precious kiss upon your lips."[33]

In her second issue, Ben created a department especially for contributions. She stated, " 'The Whatchama-Column' heading was intended to indicate that this department was a potpourri, a sort of melting pot, to air opinions and exchange ideas on pertinent subjects." The column dramatically demonstrated its ability to attract diverse voices when its first contribution came not from a lesbian, but from a straight man.[34]

Although that first letter, the first ever written to a lesbian or gay publication, was unsigned, Ben later acknowledged it was the work of a man who has since become an international celebrity. Forrest J. Ackerman has been described, in the many newspaper and magazine stories written about him, as "Mr. Science Fiction." For during the last fifty years, Ackerman has amassed 300,000 pieces of science fiction, horror, and fantasy memorabilia to create the largest such collection in the world. Often described as eccentric, Ackerman is known for his boyish enthusiasm as well as his wit—he coined the term *sci-fi*. In the late 1940s he was working as a writer and literary agent in Los Angeles.[35]

Ackerman's letter in *Vice Versa* introduced what was to become a pervasive theme in lesbian and gay journalism: attacking the psychiatric community's position on homosexuality. "It might prove a helpful form of emotional therapy," he wrote, "if the gay-born would repudiate the phrase 'Nature's tragic mistakes' and speak instead, say, of 'Nature's interesting experiments.' One should refuse to consider him-or-herself one of a Legion of the Damned."[36]

Contributors generally were in concert with Ben's political beliefs. Only on one occasion did a reader take the editor mildly to task, challenging Ben's sweeping statement that conditions had never been better for lesbians. The contributor referred Ben to Greek and Roman times. The conciliatory editor responded: "She is quite right. I should have amended the statement."[37]

Creating a Bibliography of Lesbian Materials

During the 1940s, women and men who were unsure of their sexual identity had access to very little information about homosexuality. Ben recalled: "Even to get those dreadful psychology books from the library, which were terribly wrong but still the only thing available at all, we had to ask the librarian for the key, saying, 'I'm doing a paper on deviant behavior for my psychology class.' And still she would turn up her self-righteous nose and make you feel like the lowest creature on Earth."[38]

In hopes of helping her readers process their feelings without having to endure such humiliation, Ben transformed *Vice Versa* into a virtual card catalog for lesbian material. The magazine created a list of several dozen books, motion pictures, plays, and songs with lesbian themes.

Ben and her small stable of writers provided critical reviews of many of the works. Ben praised "Pervertida," a song composed by Augustin Lara, saying, "The lyrics are beautiful, as is the melody, suitable either for listening or dancing pleasure," as well as the 1944 novel *Diana,* saying, "Get acquainted with 'Diana.' You'll find her fascinating and informative company."[39]

The most notable of the critiques was Ben's analysis of *The Well of Loneliness*. Published in the United States in 1928, the lesbian novel sold widely and created such a scandal that it became the subject of obscenity trials. Written by

British lesbian Radclyffe Hall, the book reflected the now-outmoded view that homosexuality is the result of the soul of one gender being trapped in the body of the other. Although many readers today criticize the novel as depressing, in the 1940s it at least assured gay women that they were not alone.

Ben devoted eight single-spaced pages to her laudatory review, calling Hall's work a "most admirable novel" and gushing: "It is magnificently and intelligently written and tenderly expressed," and "'Well of Loneliness' should be heartily recommended for every reader of VICE VERSA."[40]

Readers were equally enamored of the novel. One wrote, "The 8 pages devoted to 'Well of Loneliness' were a masterful review of a fine book." Another suggested that Hall had performed such meritorious service for gay women that they should abandon the term *lesbians* and begin calling themselves *clyffes*.[41]

Ben did not always hand out bouquets. Her review of the motion picture version of the same novel, *Children of Loneliness*, for instance, was scathing. Ben wrote, "The references to homosexuality as a 'weakness' and an 'evil' are an insult and an abomination to any clear-thinking and right-minded person."[42]

The lengthiest compilation of lesbian-oriented materials included the titles, authors, and publishers of ten novels, followed by brief critiques written in Ben's shoot-from-the-hip style. Comments included: *We Are Fires Unquenchable*—"not so hot"; *Loveliest of Friends*—"hostile propaganda"; *Extraordinary Women*—"dull"; and *Trio*—"boring."[43]

Readers grew to depend on the mother of the lesbian press for her critiques. One woman wrote: "All of us around here are being seen with VICE VERSA on our knees, looking very pensive, and suddenly making brief comments like: 'You don't even need to read the books or see the plays—it's all here!'"[44]

Life After *Vice Versa*

After Lisa Ben's job responsibilities changed, she continued to work as a secretary for various Los Angeles companies for the next three decades. She did not, however, continue to work in the lesbian press. In fact, after founding and editing *Vice Versa*, she published only four more pieces—two short stories and two poems for *The Ladder*, the lesbian magazine founded in 1956. Nor was she an active member of the Daughters of Bilitis, the country's first lesbian organization. She joined DOB, which formed in 1955, but stayed on the sidelines. "I mostly just baked cookies for the meetings," she recalled. "I didn't wave the flag. Public demonstrations were never my style."[45]

Instead, Ben shifted to another unique form of lesbian activism. In the 1950s, she became frustrated with the negative comments female impersonators and other gay performers made about their sexuality. "As long as we debase ourselves for a laugh, we'll always be thought of as the scum of the earth," she said. "So I decided, 'Let's get something on the upbeat!' "[46]

So just as Ben had blazed a positive lesbian trail in journalism, she did the same in entertainment. She created lesbian-oriented lyrics for popular songs, such as, "I'm gonna sit right down and write my *butch* a letter, and ask her won't she please turn *femme* for me." When she sang her songs at a lesbian bar in 1958, she brought down the house with laughter. Spurred on by the bottle of wine she won that first night and the rise in popularity of folk music, she added more songs to her repertoire, including, "Always True to You, Darling, *In My Fashion*" and "I'm a *Boy* Being a *Girl*."

Ben's lyrics were humorous, but they did not vilify gay people. Her parody of "Hello, Young Lovers" included

Hello, young lovers, what*ever* you are,
I hope your problems are few.
All you cute butches lined up at the bar,
I've had a love like you.
I know what it means to wear customized jeans
And go cruising in high platform shoes:
You cruise right on by, and that glint in your eye
Speaks of hope you can never quite lose.[47]

Ben had offers to sing her parodies for straight audiences, but she declined, recalling: "I always remained a separatist." She sang in a few lesbian bars but preferred clubs for gay men. She said: "It was like being in a party with thirty or forty of the brothers I never had—and I was their kid sister. They always treated me like a little lady, and, in those days, I guess I was. And I guess I am still." She ended her musical work in 1962.[48]

Because Ben included no bylines in *Vice Versa*, it was not until she went on stage with her lesbian parodies that she created the pseudonym she continues to use today when discussing her journalistic work. When asked why she continues to use a pseudonym, Ben provides different responses at different times. On several occasions, she has expressed concern for relatives who might be shocked by the revelation. When challenged with the fact that both of her parents are dead and she has no other close relatives still living, the septuagenarian responded, "People give you such a hard time when you've done something like

I did. I don't mean they hurt you, but they come around and want to talk to you, pester you. I'm an old woman. I don't need that."[49]

After working as a secretary for forty years, Ben retired in 1980. She now lives in a small house in Burbank, California. As a pastime, she cares for her own menagerie of cats and feeds pets living at an elementary school near her home.

A Journalistic Foremother

Vice Versa merits close study, despite its brief duration and limited circulation, because of its historic significance as the earliest extant example of the lesbian and gay press in the United States. Analysis of this pioneering publication is singularly important because it spotlights some of the functions and characteristics that ultimately would come to define this overlooked genre of the American news media. When undertaken within the larger context of communication networks created to propel social movements, such an examination identifies *Vice Versa* as exhibiting a mixture of some unique and some common themes.

One distinct characteristic evolves from the fact that Lisa Ben founded *Vice Versa* to improve her own social life. Unlike the founders of African-American, suffrage, and women's liberation publications—and, indeed, unlike the founders of most of the lesbian and gay publications that would follow hers— Ben did not participate in overt forms of social activism. She never joined a single march, demonstration, or protest. She never held an office in a lesbian organization. She demanded no changes in the American social order. An isolated young woman who was discovering her sexuality, Ben created her magazine to improve her personal situation. Like millions of gay people, she felt a desperate need to communicate on a personal level, but initially she had no intention of boosting the quality of life of other lesbians. Only in her later years has Ben even acknowledged that her publication served to advance the cause of gay rights, and many contemporary activists would criticize Ben's continued use of a pseudonym as betraying the social movement they lead today. In the larger context, Ben's nonactivist orientation suggests the lesbian and gay press was to be a pluralistic genre that would not always follow in the path forged by the alternative newspapers and magazines that came before it.

Vice Versa also stands apart from other movement publications because it was the product of an individual rather than an organization. Ben did not produce her magazine as a vehicle to communicate the ideology of a larger group of people who had been drawn together because they adhered to a specific principle or were determined to correct a particular wrong in society. She alone founded and edited the magazine. This fact suggests that this new genre of alternative press would be highly personalized, sometimes representing the views of a single individual.

Further, *Vice Versa*'s appearance presents a vivid contrast to that of most social movement publications. The size of a standard piece of typing paper with a very formal format, it was painstakingly typed to perfection. This appearance communicates a strong sense of precision, far different from the nonconformist and rag-tag images common among movement publications. This highly conventional form suggests another distinguishing characteristic of the lesbian and gay press would be a strong commitment to form and appearance.[50]

Other aspects of the magazine are consistent with themes prominent in the publications of other social movements. The positive tone that permeated the magazine, for instance, is reminiscent of the early African-American press. Just as early black newspapers expressed their readers' hopes for a brighter future symbolized by freedom and justice, this lesbian magazine reflected the editor's rosy view that looked toward the day when lesbians and gay men would embrace equal rights as first-class citizens.[51]

Vice Versa also was similar to the early African-American press, as well as the women's suffrage and women's liberation presses, in its attempt to provide an open forum for diverse voices from within the community. Just as African-American and feminist journals allowed their respective audiences the voices the mainstream press denied them, this historic lesbian magazine welcomed readers to express themselves—even to the point of sometimes sacrificing writing quality. Ben never succeeded in attracting as many contributors as she would have liked, but her publication established, nevertheless, the open forum as a central element in the lesbian and gay press.[52]

Although Lisa Ben was able to sustain *Vice Versa* only for nine months and produced only a dozen copies of each issue, she broke the editorial ice for the hundreds of magazines and newspapers that have been published since the perky young woman carried her first armload of typed pages into that Los Angeles bar in the summer of 1947. Ben never anticipated that the tiny magazine she created to combat her own loneliness would play a singular role in a social movement that would help define the second half of the twentieth century. She said of her publishing venture, "I certainly didn't think of it as anything *courageous.*" Her written words did, however, express hope about the future of gay Americans—and, subsequently, the nascent press she founded. In one prophetic editorial, Ben wrote, "Perhaps VICE VERSA might be the forerunner of better magazines dedicated to the Third Sex which, in some future time, might take their rightful place on the newsstands beside other publications, to be available openly and without restriction."[53]

λ 2

Creating a Venue for the
"Love That Dare Not Speak Its Name"

Despite the emergence of small lesbian and gay networks in several cities, tolerance of homosexuality remained elusive in the 1950s as the Cold War defined one of the most regressive eras in the history of gay Americans. The era was set on its destructive course in early 1950 when Undersecretary of State John Peurifoy told a U.S. Senate committee that most of the ninety State Department employees recently dismissed for moral turpitude were homosexuals. That bombshell launched a Senate investigation that resulted in a final report—"Employment of Homosexuals and Other Sex Perverts in Government"—characterizing homosexuals as emotionally unstable and morally corrupt. Because of these weaknesses in character, the senators contended, homosexuals were vulnerable to blackmail by foreign agents. The investigation coincided with the beginning of Senator Joseph R. McCarthy's anti-Communist witch hunt designed to regain the White House for the Republican party. When the report was released, McCarthy expanded his hate campaign to homosexuals. And after Dwight D. Eisenhower was swept into the White House in 1953, he issued an executive order barring homosexuals from federal employment and military service.[1]

That America's first widely distributed gay and lesbian publications appeared in the shadow of McCarthyism attests to their founders being persons of strength and valor. And that the editors identified themselves in print further speaks to the pivotal role they played in the rise of a visible and courageous gay press. Scholars have lauded those founders for making a contribution of singular importance. In his history of the Gay and Lesbian Liberation Movement, John D'Emilio wrote, "The pioneering effort to publish magazines about homosexuality brought the gay movement its only significant victory during the 1950s."[2]

Like *Vice Versa*, the monthly publications of the 1950s were based on the West Coast. *ONE* was founded in Los Angeles in 1953; *Mattachine Review* and *The*

Ladder followed in San Francisco in 1955 and 1956. These magazines advanced beyond *Vice Versa* in several crucial respects. They were distributed nationally. They withstood attacks by the U.S. Senate, postal officials, and the FBI to win the legal right for gay-oriented materials to be sent through the mail. They also achieved longevity: all three were published for more than a dozen years.[3]

But their most important accomplishment was that the magazines did, indeed, *speak.* They created a national venue for homosexuals, forming an arena in which lesbians and gay men could, for the first time, speak above a whisper about issues fundamental to their lives. The magazines gave an oppressed minority the chance to express thoughts that previously had been barred from public discourse. Their readers appreciated the courage the editors exhibited. A Fort Worth, Texas, man spoke for many of the 7,000 men and women who subscribed to the magazines—as well as the tens of thousands who read the well-worn copies that circulated surreptitiously in gay and lesbian communities all over the country—when he told *ONE*'s editors: "My prayers (and I mean it literally) and my spirits are behind you." Finally, Lesbian and Gay America had a voice. In fact, it had three.[4]

ONE Becomes the First Widely Distributed Gay Publication

In the fall of 1952, a dozen Los Angeles gay men gathered for one of a series of secret meetings to discuss the problems they faced and to raise their group consciousness about homosexuality. Dale Jennings, one of those men, recently recalled: "I didn't have the patience to sit there night after night and hear everybody whine over and over again about how tough it was to be homosexual. It was all true, but talking about it didn't change anything—nothing but talk, talk, talk. So I said, 'We're talking to ourselves. That's not enough. We have to talk to more people. The newspapers won't print anything about us. So let's create a publication of our own. Let's start a magazine.' And that night, the gay press was born." In January 1953, the men created a magazine to expand their discussions to a larger audience. Though the men did not articulate it at the time, at some level of their consciousness they must have known that the transition from secret to public communication was a political act of profound importance.[5]

Don Slater, another of the founders, insists that creating *ONE* represented the birth of the Gay and Lesbian Liberation Movement. "A social movement has to have a voice beyond its own members," he said recently. "Before this time, homosexuals just spoke to themselves. They just talked—whispered, really—to each other. Talking to each other in little groups can't create a social movement, a mass movement. For the first time, *ONE* gave a voice to the 'love that dare not

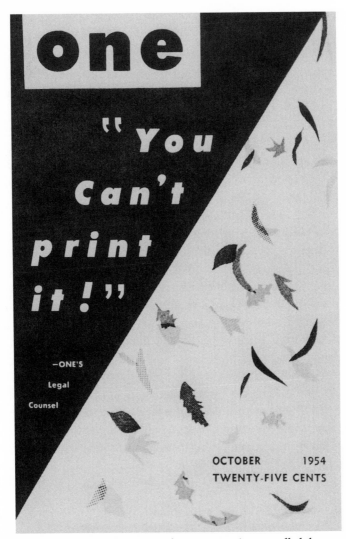

The content of the October 1954 issue of ONE *magazine propelled the gay and lesbian press to the U.S. Supreme Court—and a landmark decision in its favor.*

speak its name.' Nobody else had ever done that. The magazine was the beginning of the movement."[6]

The founders took their title from a quotation by Victorian essayist Thomas Carlyle: "A mystic bond of brotherhood makes all men *ONE*." The magazine would be aimed toward gay men who understood the kind of bond Carlyle spoke of and, indeed, such a bond already had begun to develop among the men through their discussion meetings. The founders defined the term *men* literally, largely excluding women from the magazine in the first instance of a gender conflict that would continue to plague the lesbian and gay press. By its second issue, the magazine was receiving letters complaining that the staff and editorial content were predominantly male.[7]

ONE's founders opted not to affiliate with the country's only existing organization of gay men. Jennings recalled: "Members of the Mattachine Society wanted the emphasis to be on the contributions that homosexuals had made to literature—to the culture. The editors did not agree. We wanted to focus on gaining equal rights." *ONE* was soon speaking assertively. One cover story carried the headline "I Am Glad I Am a Homosexual." Editorials stated: "Homosexual acts between consenting adults are neither anti-social nor sinful; legal attempts to regulate such behavior violate American principles of personal freedom," and "Solutions must be found for the present minority status of millions of American men and women who refuse any longer to tolerate suppression, subjection and abuse from every side. As citizens they have their rights."[8]

In reality, *ONE*'s historic first step toward seeking equality meant that it sought to provoke thinking rather than action. To defend itself against any charge of promoting political activism, it stated: "Let no one rashly assume that the Magazine is now going into politics. Nothing could be further from its intentions. It has its field: the homosexual and homosexuality." Nevertheless, publishing *ONE* was a momentous step, as the magazine adopted a much more assertive stance than the Mattachine Society, which hoped to achieve tolerance of homosexuality by accommodating to heterosexual America in action as well as thought.[9]

Mattachine Review Offers an Alternative Philosophy

After *ONE* opted not to promote the views of the Mattachine Society, members of that organization created *Mattachine Review*. This second widely distributed gay magazine reflected the beliefs of the Homophile Movement, the group of homosexuals who sought societal acceptance. Participants in the movement strived to establish communication rather than assert rights. They hoped to achieve acceptance through a conciliatory approach to society and by conforming to the dictates of the dominant social order. In the words of Hal Call, editor of the *Review*, "We wanted to show people that homosexuals were the products of ordinary, average families—that we weren't pariahs. The *Review* wanted to educate people so they would treat homosexuals with decency. We worked through *evolution* rather than *revolution*."[10]

During a time when the vast majority of Americans were repulsed by homosexuality, adherents to this philosophy believed accommodating to normative standards of behavior would defuse hostility toward them and ultimately lead to equitable government policies and just treatment in the legal system. Movement leaders coined the term *homophile,* a word that would remain in use throughout the 1960s, to encompass homosexuals as well as heterosexuals who were "interested in the study and/or support of homosexuality." More important, the term served to protect individuals involved in the movement from automatically being labeled "homosexuals." In their effort to attain acceptance and educate the public, homophiles relied mainly on heterosexual doctors, lawyers, and ministers to speak for them.[11]

The Mattachine Society had been founded in Los Angeles in 1950 as a secret society of gay men, many of whom had strong leftist leanings, who came together in private homes to socialize and build a community of support. The organization, which did not maintain a membership list and did not conduct public demonstrations, found an eager audience for its meetings, with as many as 200 men attending the sessions that were held nightly.[12]

After Call joined in 1953, he learned that some of the founders were members of the Communist party. Call, fearing the threat of McCarthyism, led a revolt within the society. He said recently that the Mattachine Society could not have grown if it had remained a secret organization, "But before we went public, we had to make sure we didn't have persons in our midst who were Communists and would disgrace us all. The Reds had to go." So Call wrested the leadership from the founders and moved the society to the right. Rather than raising the consciousness of its members, the Mattachine Society sponsored blood drives and collected clothes and magazines for local hospitals. The membership dropped slightly from the earlier days. Call, a professional journalist, recognized that communication would be essential for the growth of the fledgling organization. So in January 1955, he founded *Mattachine Review* to promote the organization's philosophy of conciliation.[13]

Although the *Review* was not at the forefront of efforts to secure gay rights, it reflected a distinct stage in the evolution of Gay America. In an item labeled "Aims and Principles of the Mattachine Society," Call stated that the magazine would act in a "law-abiding" manner and was "not seeking to overthrow existing institutions, laws or mores, but to aid in the assimilation of variants," a term the magazine used for gays. Call had no interest, however, in expanding the magazine to include female "variants." He said recently: "Lesbians were not un-

der fire the way men were. They didn't have the kinds of problems with the police that gay men had. Cops and other straight men felt very threatened by male
homosexuals; they didn't feel threatened by lesbians. They just thought a lesbian was a woman who'd never been fucked good."[14]

The Ladder Raises a Feminine Voice

In fact, although police entrapment of gay men received more attention, police
officers also were abusing the rights of lesbians. This abuse sometimes extended
to the officers—at once reviled and titillated by lesbianism—forcing gay
women to have sex with them. Beyond their continuing battle with the police,
lesbians struggled with other problems as well. One concern was whether a
married lesbian should divorce her husband and risk losing custody of her children, at the time a certainty if her sexuality became known to the court. It was
also a time when gender-based salary inequities created severe economic difficulties for unmarried women.

In 1955, four lesbian couples in San Francisco created the Daughters of
Bilitis as a social and discussion club for gay women, meeting three times a
week and soon attracting as many as fifty women per session. Because two of
the founders had journalism backgrounds, the group soon created a publication. In her first issue of *The Ladder,* editor Phyllis Lyon wrote: "We enter a
field already ably served by 'ONE' and 'Mattachine Review.' We offer, however,
that so-called 'feminine viewpoint' which they have had so much difficulty ob-
taining. It is to be hoped that our venture will encourage women to take an
ever-increasing part in the steadily-growing fight for understanding of the
homophile minority."[15]

The title of the publication was chosen because it was seen as a means lesbians could use to climb out of the "well of loneliness" that Radclyffe Hall's
popular novel had depicted as their plight. *The Ladder* provided the first public
forum in which large numbers of lesbians could express their feelings. Historian D'Emilio observed, "*The Ladder* offered American lesbians, for the first
time in history, the opportunity to speak with their own voices."[16]

Ideologically, *The Ladder* stood closer to *Mattachine Review*'s conciliatory
stance than to *ONE*'s assertive one. *The Ladder* sought to inform lesbians and
reduce their loneliness, but it did not propose to transform them into militant
activists. Assistant editor Del Martin said the thrust was "educating the lesbian
so she could cope with herself and society. We zeroed in on fear, trying to reassure our audiences with articles by attorneys and physicians mainly."[17]

Contradicting this accommodationist stand, however, *The Ladder* took the progressive step of capitalizing all uses of the word *Lesbian*. Lyon explained: "We weren't ready to storm the barricades, by any means. We were *not* militant; we sought only tolerance at that stage. But we certainly were eager to speak for lesbians—with a capital *L*."[18]

The magazine's contributions are best summarized in the words of the women who spoke through it. Playwright Lorraine Hansberry represented these women in a 1957 letter to the editor: "I'm glad as heck that you exist. You are obviously serious people and I feel that women, without wishing to foster any strict *separatist* notions, homo or hetero, indeed have a need for their own publications. Our problems, our experiences as women are profoundly unique as compared to the other half of the human race. Women, like other oppressed groups of one kind or another, have particularly had to pay a price for the intellectual impoverishment that the second class status imposed on us for centuries. Thus, I feel that *The Ladder* is a fine step in a rewarding direction."[19]

Striking a Pose

The groundbreaking magazines looked like scholarly journals, as they measured five and a half by eight and a half inches. This size was chosen as a cost-saving measure. A very inexpensive publication could be produced by simply folding standard sheets of typing paper in half and stapling them at the crease. Issues typically ranged from twenty to thirty pages.

ONE was the most dramatic in design. In keeping with the high level of taste and style many gay men possess, the founders insisted their magazine be typeset and printed rather than typewritten and mimeographed. This was a daring decision because the magazine had no consistent source of revenue beyond the pockets of the founders. But those men saw professional printing as essential for the proper reproduction of the strong, modern graphics that became the magazine's trademark. Those graphics reflected the audacious step the founders took in creating the country's first widely distributed gay publication. Typical was an issue that contained a report on police harassment in Miami. As a visual reflection of the article, the white cover featured bold black lines colliding around the words "Miami Hurricane." Inside artwork showed two frightened young men swimming furiously in a black ocean as a huge, menacing hand hovered above them.[20]

Although it is impossible to gauge the impact of the high quality of the magazine's design, at least some heterosexuals were impressed by it. In a 1954 front-page article blaming the rise of homosexuality for the increases in drug addiction and juvenile delinquency, the *San Francisco Examiner* made only one positive statement about gays. The newspaper quoted the city's district attorney as saying of *ONE*: "I've seen a copy of the magazine they put out. It was very artsy."[21]

ONE also took the lead in setting boundaries for images in this new genre of

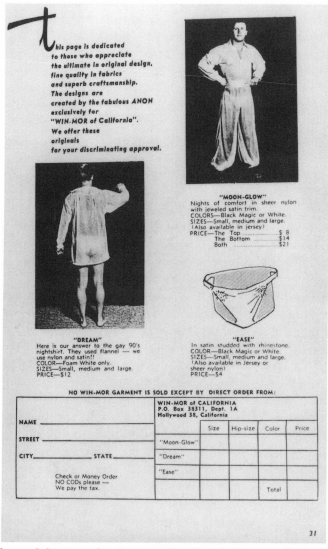

An ad for men's harem-style pajamas and satin undershorts studded with rhinestones launched the gay press into a love-hate relationship with advertising.

publishing. Initially, the editors barred any suggestive images, insisting, "*ONE* is not and has no wish to be an erotic magazine." But the editors began to bend this rule in October 1954 when the inside back cover carried a full-page ad. It promoted men's satin undershorts studded with rhinestones and harem-style pajamas made of sheer nylon, both modeled by a handsome and physically well-developed man. The model's genitals were fully covered with solid white briefs, but, when the images were combined with the copy accompanying them, the ad was suggestive. One caption read: "Here is our answer to the gay 90's nightshirt. They used flannel—we use nylon and satin!!"[22]

The ad elicited strong reader reaction. A Los Angeles man was outraged: "I can't see why you besmirch your format with an ad such as you have on the inside of the last cover. It is a perfect target for mockery!" A Pennsylvania man wrote: "The rhinestones inside the back cover make me sure I do not love you at all this month. Your judgment blew a fuse when you printed that." And a Connecticut reader expressed a sense of betrayal: "The feminine attire worn by the male model I find disgusting and against every principle of your fine work. Don't spoil it by cheap pictures."[23]

In their response, the editors first defended the images on pragmatic grounds: "For the first time in two years of our existence a genuine, commercial, bill-paying advertiser has appeared voluntarily." The editors then devoted even more space to a defense based on ethical principles: "It may be the day will come when those of us who do not care for rhinestones will become a little less self-conscious about those who do, and less ready to feel ashamed of them. *ONE* is, and must continue to be, dedicated to tolerance." After this watershed, the editors accepted more ads from the same company for swimwear and lounging pajamas.[24]

Mattachine Review also was printed. But, in keeping with its conformist philosophy, it was unimaginative in design. Only clip art of generic images, such as the U.S. Capitol and a television set, occasionally broke up the sea of type. Although *The Ladder* initially was mimeographed and similarly bland, later covers featured strikingly clean, simple drawings that sometimes carried strong messages. One of the most memorable depicted an attractive woman removing a tear-stained mask to reveal a contented face beneath.[25]

Filling the Pages

Personal essays dominated the editorial content of all three magazines. The longest article in *ONE*'s premier issue described Jennings's police entrapment a year earlier when the Los Angeles vice squad had charged him with soliciting a plainclothes police officer to commit a homosexual act. During the trial, Jennings acknowledged that he was homosexual but denied the specific charge. After the jury had deliberated forty hours, eleven members favored acquittal but the twelfth said he would hold out for guilty "till Hell freezes over." The city then dropped the charges. Jennings concluded his first-person account with an early call for a unified Gay Rights Movement: "Were all homosexuals and bisexuals to unite militantly, unjust laws and corruption would crumble in short order and we, as a nation, could go on to meet the really important problems which face us."[26]

Fiction had a strong presence in the publications. Short stories and poems not only showcased the literary talents of gay men and lesbians, but also provided readers with positive depictions of gay people. In this area again *ONE* took the lead, establishing an annual writing competition with winning entries being published in the magazine. *ONE*'s willingness to publish fiction attracted such major writers as Norman Mailer and Clarkson Crane, who both wrote original short stories for the magazine.[27]

Fiction contained in *The Ladder* created a bridge between the 1940s and 1950s lesbian press. Although Phyllis Lyon was not aware of the existence of *Vice Versa* when she founded *The Ladder,* she later learned of that earlier publication, came to know Lisa Ben, and reprinted poems and short stories from *Vice Versa.*[28]

The 1950s magazines also contained editorials, descriptions of research projects that pertained to gay men and lesbians, lists of recent books and articles about homosexuality, and a constantly growing number of letters to the editor. None of the material contained sexual terms or "four-letter" words.

News content initially was minuscule, as the editors had no national network of gay- and lesbian-oriented news to tap into. As the magazines became established, however, readers began sending in news items. Soon all three magazines carried monthly columns of news briefs—"Tangents: News & Views" in *ONE,* "Newsreel" in *Mattachine Review,* and "Cross-Currents" in *The Ladder.*

The columns documented the unjust treatment of gays as no publication had done before them. W. Dorr Legg, business manager for *ONE,* said, "At that time L.A. seethed with stories of police brutalities, of so-called 'entrapment cases,' of raids, of apartment doors being battered down, of officers hiding in the trunks of cars, of secret cameras and peep-holes, of tape recorders concealed in portable radios or behind draperies."[29]

The publications did not, however, limit their reports to California. Jim Kepner, who wrote consistently for *ONE* and *Mattachine Review* as well as occasionally for *The Ladder,* initiated something of a one-man news service.

While working full time at a milk carton manufacturing plant and collecting materials for the International Gay and Lesbian Archives he later founded, Kepner searched for gay-related news items in as many newspapers as he could get his hands on. He also urged readers to send him clippings of local news items involving gays, eventually attracting some two hundred contributors from around the country. The articles were, of course, uncompromisingly negative. Kepner used the clippings to compile, using the articles published in the three magazines, the first comprehensive record of gays being ridiculed, entrapped, and abused. The total mounted higher and higher as Kepner documented the victims of what he characterized as homosexual witch hunts: 11 in Phoenix, 6 in Salt Lake City, 40 in Dallas, 10 in Oklahoma City, 67 in Memphis, 162 in Baltimore.[30]

Kepner's task was not simply a matter of clipping and reprinting articles containing the keyword *homosexual.* In the 1950s, homosexuality was still such a taboo subject that newspapers did not speak about it directly. "You learned how to read between the lines," Kepner recalled. "They might not have mentioned the raid of a homosexual bar, but if several men were arrested and no women were mentioned, you assumed it was not a whorehouse. In the article, they might mention one man was dressed in a 'womanish' manner. You looked for those words."[31]

Typical was a *Miami Herald* item about twenty-one men being apprehended because police were concerned that the Twenty-Second Street beach had become a hangout for "males with a feminine bent." The article quoted Police Chief Romeo Shepard: "We had no charges we could book them on, but it's just a question of cleaning up a bad situation and letting undesirables know they're not wanted here." *ONE*'s item about the Miami event—in fine advocacy journalism style—concluded, "They may have looked 'feminine' and even confessed to being homosexuals, but you cannot be charged with homosexuality or criminality; it must be with a homosexual act."[32]

Such interpretations by the editors consistently supplemented the who, what, when, and where of the stories. Kepner began one item in *ONE* by describing a judge who had chastised two gay men for their "aggressive attitude" when defending themselves against charges of homosexual activity. Kepner then launched into an attack on the inequities of the judicial system: "Perhaps American citizens are supposed to supinely submit to the most vicious smears, be robbed of their freedoms and then meekly go to jail without protest. It may be that a wave of 'bad' courtroom manners would bring a little healthy respect for constitutional rights back into the picture."[33]

Struggling to Survive

By the end of the decade, the three magazines had far surpassed *Vice Versa*'s tiny circulation but certainly had not become titans of American journalism. Their aggregate distribution totaled 7,000. *ONE* dominated the field with 5,000— subscribers included sex researcher Dr. Alfred Kinsey. *Mattachine Review* followed with 1,000. *The Ladder* inched its way to a circulation of only 700, foreshadowing the low circulation figures of the hundreds of lesbian publications that were to follow it. Gay male publications, gradually attracting more and more revenue from advertising aimed at affluent gay men with large disposable incomes, were destined to achieve higher circulations; lesbian publications, struggling to provide a communication forum for their economically limited readers, would never—even today—match the circulation figures of their male counterparts.[34]

Readership for the journalistic triumvirate was, of course, much larger than circulation. With *The Ladder,* for example, one Washington, D.C., woman subscribed and then each month invited friends to her home to read the magazine out loud to a room filled with thirty or forty lesbians. Such "*Ladder* parties" occurred in towns and cities all over the country. Letters flowed in from women near and far. A Pasadena woman wrote, "I join the ranks of those quiet followers who find you a light in the dark night and a warm fire for alien souls." A woman in Brunswick, Ohio, concurred: "However silent or distant we may be, there are many, many friends of yours back here in the East. Although I wish my spine, backbone and courage could be as great as yours—it isn't."[35]

The fear felt by gay people was not misplaced. *ONE* reported in 1954 that the day after the first self-identified homosexual American had appeared on television, he was summarily fired from his job. He did not even bother taking his case to court. People were understandably hesitant about placing their names on a mailing list of homosexual-oriented material. The editors tried to reassure readers that subscribing to the magazines would not destroy their careers— publishing articles titled "Attorney Stresses Nothing to Fear" and "Your Name Is Safe!"—but fear of exposure continued to impede subscription growth.[36]

Readers were more willing to purchase individual copies, which were sent in envelopes containing no return address, than to subscribe. But the magazines also faced a major problem with single-copy sales: newsstands refused to sell them. The only place staff members initially could sell their magazines was in the gay bars of Los Angeles and San Francisco. Martin Block, founding editor of *ONE*, said, "I would take a stack with me into the bars and 'ply my trade,' so to speak." Only after the bar sales proved that the magazines could make a profit did a few newsstand owners agree to stock copies. As soon as they did, 90 percent of sales were by single copies rather than subscription. By the end of the decade, the three magazines were selling at dozens of newsstands and adult bookstores around the country, with *ONE* boasting that it was selling copies in every state.[37]

Despite their occasional bragging, the magazines constantly teetered on the edge of financial collapse. Subscription sales combined with the twenty-five cents charged for single copies covered half the expenses. For the *Review* and *The Ladder,* the other half came from membership dues for the organizations the publications represented, along with out-of-pocket contributions from staff members. *ONE's* founders created their own corporation founded as an educational enterprise that conducted classes and sponsored lectures on homosexuality, but the magazine never made a profit. Don Slater said: "*ONE* never paid for itself. It wouldn't have survived if we editors hadn't put our own money into it continually. We wanted it to work. So we all just pitched in."[38]

The Ladder was in the worst financial shape because its circulation was the smallest and its founders, being women, were paid lower salaries than their male counterparts. Fortunately, one of the women who helped produce the earliest issues, Helen Sanders, worked in the office at Macy's department store in San Francisco. So, after the other women typed the mimeograph masters at home, Sanders surreptitiously duplicated the copies on a mimeograph machine at Macy's.[39]

The magazines could not depend on advertising, traditionally the major source of revenue for commercial publications, because businesses refused to be identified with homosexuality. The first issue of *ONE* carried three ads, but all three—for a bookstore and design service—had been placed by staff members at no charge to the businesses. Neither *Mattachine Review* nor *The Ladder* carried any advertisements whatsoever. Martin Block, who served as *ONE's* editor for the first five issues, recently recalled: "We absolutely talked our heads off trying to persuade stores to advertise, but the owners adamantly refused. They insisted that their businesses would be destroyed if their customers saw they were advertising in a gay magazine. It was ridiculous. We gay men *were* those customers!"[40]

Initially, no staff member received any payment for his or her work. That changed—up to a point—in April 1953 when *ONE* hired Legg as the first full-time employee to work for the Gay and Lesbian Liberation Movement, paying him a salary as business manager. He recalled: "I was offered twenty-five dollars a week, when available. It was generally not available. A year later, that salary skyrocketed to a hundred dollars a week, which was virtually *never* available." Legg survived on a private income. In June 1957, Call left his job at a trade magazine to work full-time as editor of *Mattachine Review*. He was paid no salary for editing the magazine but eked out a livelihood by doing job printing on a press several members of Mattachine Society bought for $1,000 to print the magazine. Call said, "It was a very poor livelihood. I had to borrow money from my mother just to pay my rent."[41]

Pioneering in a New Journalistic Genre

The nascent lesbian and gay press soon attracted talented professional journalists. By the mid-1950s, staff members had brought a solid record of education and experience to the fledgling movement press. Del Martin of *The Ladder* spoke for many early staff members when she said: "I was drawn to the process of collecting information and then translating it for my readers, but it wasn't until I began writing for the lesbian press that I had what I would really call a *passion* for reporting. And why not? We were creating a whole new form of journalism."[42]

Hal Call was the first professional journalist to work in the gay press. After earning a journalism degree from the University of Missouri in 1947, he edited a weekly and two dailies in Missouri and Colorado before joining the *Kansas City Star* in 1950. Arrested on a homosexual morals charge in 1952, Call was fired from the *Star* and moved to San Francisco, where he wrote for an insurance trade magazine, the job he held when he founded *Mattachine Review*.

The Ladder added two more journalists to the genre. Phyllis Lyon had served as editor of the *Daily Californian*, the student newspaper at the University of California at Berkeley, where she earned her journalism degree in 1946. Lyon then covered police and city hall for the *Chico Enterprise*, a daily in Chico, California. In 1951, she moved to Seattle and edited two trade journals for the building industry. While in Seattle, Lyon met Del Martin, the other driving force behind *The Ladder*. Martin had reported for the *San Francisco Chronicle* while in high school and had studied journalism at San Francisco State College. In her junior year, Martin dropped out of school, married, and gave birth to a daughter. Martin soon divorced and, in 1949, moved to Seattle and began editing a newspaper at the same company as Lyon. Lyon and Martin became lovers and, in 1953, moved to San Francisco. Lyon headed the shipping department of an import-export company, while Martin worked as a bookkeeper. Within a few years, however, publishing *The Ladder* and leading the Daughters of Bilitis became a full-time task that consumed more of their time than did their jobs.

The founding editors of all three magazines used their real names in print. Jennings recalled: "We were young and tired of whispering to each other. We were tired of locking the doors and pulling down the shades whenever we wanted to talk about who we were. So we just decided: 'What the hell?' "[43]

Lyon's route was more circuitous. In the initial three issues of *The Ladder*, the editor was identified as "Ann Ferguson," a combination of Lyon's middle name and her mother's maiden name. The fourth issue carried Ferguson's obituary. "I confess. I killed Ann Ferguson," Lyon wrote. "We ran an article in the November issue of THE LADDER entitled 'Your Name Is Safe.' Ann Ferguson wrote that article. Her words were true, her conclusions logical and documented—yet she was not practicing what she preached. Now there is only Phyllis Lyon."[44]

Most contributors to all three magazines used pseudonyms. In fact, to camouflage the fact that only a handful of people were writing most of the articles, the most frequent contributors wrote under several pseudonyms. Martin said proudly: "That's one of the greatest things about how the early lesbian press was different from the mainstream press. We weren't writing for our egos. We didn't mind giving up our bylines for the good of the publication. That's not something you hear mainstream journalists saying."[45]

Struggling in the Shadow of McCarthyism

It did not take long for gay and lesbian journalism to attract enemies. Some of the nemeses were known to the founders at the time; while others surfaced only recently when the 4,000 pages of material the FBI had collected on the Mattachine Society was examined. Although FBI officials deleted many specific references before releasing the files in response to a Freedom of Information Act request, the material still reflects the scorn federal authorities felt toward the pioneering publications.

Three months after *ONE* was founded, FBI agents in Los Angeles began searching copies of the publication for material that could be classified as obscene or supportive of Communism. In July 1953, the FBI opened a formal investigation of the magazine, which included sending each issue to FBI headquarters in Washington. After *Mattachine Review* and *The Ladder* began appearing, the investigation was broadened to include them as well. The FBI reports were riddled with adjectives describing articles as "subversive," "disgusting," "shocking," and "heinous." Other comments referred to "possible communist infiltration or control" and "the unsavory nature of this entire crowd." One memo stated that at least 60 percent of the persons involved with the publications were members of the Communist party.[46]

"What is so amusing to me today is that very, very few of the people writing for the publications at that time could even be described as politically liberal, much less leftist," Kepner said recently. "They were just gay and wanted to talk to other people about what they were feeling. I was the only one who had ever joined the party. And as soon as the Commies found out I was gay, they threw me out!" Kepner had joined the Communist party and worked as a copy boy and writer for the *Daily Worker* in New York City from 1945 to 1948. When his homosexuality became known, he was ousted from the party. He then moved to California and began writing for *ONE* in 1954.[47]

FBI agents reviewing the magazines checked the names of the editors to determine if any of them—Block, Jennings, Kepner, Legg, and Slater from *ONE;* Call from *Mattachine Review;* and Lyon and Martin from *The Ladder*— had ever been arrested. The only record they uncovered was Jennings's solicitation charge, which had been dropped. Even so, the agents sent the names to local police and conducted personal background investigations that included contacting the various editors' current and former employers. Such contact could be devastating, as employers at that time routinely fired workers rumored to be homosexual. Miraculously, all eight men and women were allowed to keep their jobs. Lyon said: "My boss got more than eight hours of work out of me. He would have been a fool to fire me, though he could have."[48]

In their letters to the editors' employers, the agents routinely described the editors as "queers," "perverts," "deviants," and "security risks." Block said, "None of us can prove it, but obviously those conversations and those letters did severe damage to all of our careers. The authorities did all they could to keep the queers in their place." Legg added, "In the 1950s, for a boss to be told his employee was a faggot most certainly put a stop to career advancement."[49]

The FBI was not the only force trying to shut down the magazines. By August 1953, postal authorities in Los Angeles believed they had enough examples of obscene material to prevent *ONE* from being mailed. So they seized all copies of that month's issue. After officials in Washington scrutinized the content, however, the magazine was allowed to be mailed. The editors wrote defiantly on the cover of the next issue: "*ONE* thanks no one for this reluctant acceptance. As we sit around quietly like nice little ladies and gentlemen gradually educating the public and the courts at our leisure, thousands of homosexuals are being unjustly arrested, blackmailed, fined, jailed, beaten, and murdered."[50]

In early 1954, U.S. Senator Alexander Wiley, a Republican from Wisconsin, became the first member of Congress—many would follow him in future decades—to attack the lesbian and gay press. Wiley, chairman of the Senate Foreign Relations Committee, fired off a letter to Postmaster General Arthur Summerfield, saying: "The purpose of my letter is to convey the most vigorous protest against the use of the United States mails to transmit a so-called 'magazine' devoted to the advancement of sexual perversion. I am sure that, with your keen sense of moral principle, you will give this matter your prompt attention."[51]

Postal officials confiscated the October 1954 issue of ONE, calling the material "obscene, lewd, lascivious and filthy." It may be more than coincidental that the issue seized was the same one that carried the first advertisement featuring a suggestive image—the model in the sheer harem-style pajamas.[52]

With the question of whether the magazine was mailable in the hands of the courts, FBI agents shifted their energy to intimidating the editors. Lyon routinely received telephone death threats from unidentified callers she believes were FBI agents, and agents often arrived unannounced at the editors' homes to interrogate them. "I told them no names and gave them no mailing lists," Call said recently. "I told them everyone knew [FBI Director] J. Edgar Hoover was queer. I told them their whole operation was hypocritical and instead of harassing faggots like me they should find out whose cock their boss was sucking. I told them the same things forty years ago that historians are just publishing today."[53]

The interrogations escalated after ONE published an article titled "How Much Do We Know About the Homosexual Male?" The November 1955 article carried the byline of David L. Freeman and contained the statement: "They work for TIME magazine or the NEW YORKER. They are in the diplomatic service; they occupy key positions with oil companies or the FBI (it's true!)."[54]

When agents sent a copy of the article to Washington, it created a series of comments that, in light of recent revelations about the homosexuality of Hoover and Assistant FBI Director Clyde Tolson, are truly extraordinary. When the report noting the magazine's statement reached Tolson, he wrote on the bottom of the page, "I think we should take this crowd on and make them 'put up or shut up.'" When the report reached Hoover, he scrawled his own endorsement beneath Tolson's, adding simply, "I concur."[55]

For the next several years, agents repeatedly invoked those two comments— writ large—as justification for sustained interrogation of gay journalists. Tolson later reiterated the message when an agent suggested the bureau might want to downgrade the intensity of its investigation because the magazine might "endeavor to embarrass the Bureau." Tolson wrote emphatically on the bottom of the memo, "I don't agree."[56]

Particularly frustrating to the agents was their inability to identify David L. Freeman, the author of the article suggesting gays worked at the highest level of the FBI. Agents continually referred to the author by that name, not knowing it was a pseudonym used by Chuck Rowland, an occasional contributor to *ONE* who has since died. Agents who questioned staff members repeatedly asked them to identify Freeman, suggesting that Hoover and Tolson may have been concerned that the author had proof of their own sexual orientations. The reports give no indication that the agents ever determined Freeman's identity, though their vehement efforts continued for several years.[57]

Legg became the agents' primary interview subject. Although his name has been expunged from the FBI reports and memos, Legg later recognized the descriptions of the interviews as ones he participated in. Legg acknowledged that he curried the attention the FBI agents accorded him. The octogenarian Legg said in 1993: "I find it quite endearing—both then and now—to have handsome, earnest young men eagerly asking me questions. But that doesn't mean I gave them any answers. I admit it: I can be a tease."[58]

The reports indicate the agents found Legg's witty repartee quite exasperating. Several reports characterize Legg as "sarcastic." One states: "He was specifically asked whether he had any information that there was anyone employed by the FBI who was a homosexual. He replied: 'Do you have information that there are none?'" The agents went on to say that Legg "smirked and smiled as if he were thoroughly enjoying the situation"—which the agents clearly were not.[59]

Legg sometimes reversed the roles of intimidator and cowering victim. On one occasion when an agent displayed his credentials, Legg grabbed them and began copying the agent's name and identification number. The agent became flustered and jerked the credentials away from Legg. At the end of the interview, Legg asked, "What would you gentlemen say if this had been taped?" The agents told Legg they had no objection to having their interview tape-recorded, but their report tells a different story. It states defensively: "No recording equipment was observed. It is very doubtful that the interview was recorded."[60]

Legg further aggravated FBI officials when, in spite of the ongoing interrogations, he had the audacity to refer to their boss in his monthly column. Though the statements were merely offhand comments, Legg managed to thumb his nose at the hypersensitive agency. One item read, "FBI boss Hoover recently said cops oughtn't be called cops. Not nice." Another stated, "J. Edgar Hoover sez rise of sex crimes." Despite their brevity and innocuous content, each item produced a flurry of memos between FBI offices in Los Angeles and Washington.[61]

Triumphing in the Courtroom

From the beginning of their venture, *ONE*'s founders recognized that publishing a magazine devoted to homosexuality would make them vulnerable to attack by federal officials. That knowledge led the men to hire a heterosexual attorney who advised them to steer clear of fiction. Fiction could too easily be characterized as entertainment, he said, which could be construed as violating the educational focus defined in the corporate charter for ONE, Inc., as a non-profit organization. It soon became apparent, however, that so little gay and lesbian news was available that fiction had to be published if the magazines were to fill their pages.[62]

After the poem "Lord Samuel and Lord Montague" and the short story "Sappho Remembered" appeared in the October 1954 issue of *ONE*, FBI and postal officials pulled the magazine into court. The satirical poem portrayed homosexuality as being widespread among English lords, stating: "Some peers are seers but some are queers... / And some boys WILL be girls." FBI documents said of the poem, "This is obscene because of the filthy words contained in it." The strongest word in the poem was *damnation*. In a memo to FBI chief Hoover, the Los Angeles Field Office wrote of the short story: "This story is obscene because lustfully stimulating to the average homosexual reader." Although the story described a twenty-year-old woman who left her fiancée for another woman, it contained no sexual language. The most graphic description of the two women's physical contact stated, "She touched the delicate pulse beat beneath the light golden hair on the child-like temple."[63]

ONE's lawyer, Eric Julber, protested to federal district court that the magazine was not obscene. Julber wrote, "It strives to create understanding of an extremely knotty social problem." The judge, however, sustained the postal officials' decision, ruling that the material could not be mailed: "Stories are obviously calculated to stimulate the lust of the homosexual reader."[64]

The editors advanced their case to the federal appeals court, where the judge also ruled against the magazine, saying, "It is dirty, vulgar and offensive to the moral senses." The judge went on to condemn homosexuality in general, stating, "Social standards are fixed by and for the great majority and not by or for a hardened or weakened minority."[65]

Despite legal expenses of more than $2,000, the editors continued their battle, appealing to the highest court in the land. Finally, in January 1958, the editors triumphed when the U.S. Supreme Court unanimously reversed the decision of the lower courts. Although the justices did not issue a written opinion, the landmark decision established that the subject of homosexuality is not, per se, obscene. Gay and lesbian publications had won the right to be distributed through the mail.[66]

In his next issue, editor Don Slater was jubilant: "*ONE Magazine* no longer asks for the right to be heard; it now exercises that right. It further requires that homosexuals be treated as a proper part of society free to discuss and educate and propagandize their beliefs." In fact, Slater's euphoria reached the point of inflating the significance of the court decision: "Never before have homosexuals claimed their rights as citizens. *ONE Magazine* has changed the future of all U.S. homosexuals."[67]

For a fledgling minority group attempting to wrest equal rights from a hostile society, such overstatement can be excused. For the decision was, indeed, a huge boost. In addition, the victory netted the gleeful editors a few lines of positive publicity—for the first time in history—in such leading newspapers as the *New York Times* and the *Washington Post.* For years to come, such comments would be few and far between.[68]

Further, the courtroom triumph helped gay journalists by taking the wind out of the sails of the FBI investigations. Two months after the Supreme Court decision, FBI officials told their agents in Los Angeles to discontinue sending copies of the gay and lesbian magazines to Washington.[69]

Defining the Gay Ideology

The magazines put into print the conversation that had begun behind closed doors in Los Angeles living rooms at the beginning of the decade. Jennings recently recalled: "Before we started *ONE* magazine, we had repeatedly sent statements to newspapers and had doggedly attempted to convince reporters to talk to us. We wanted to express ourselves and discuss the issues that were dominating our lives, but we couldn't get a word in the popular press." Slater said: "There was no doubt as to the message. The magazines were shouting: 'We are! There is a movement!' Homosexuals were no longer whispering among themselves."[70]

ONE's inaugural issue established that the magazines welcomed divergent views. In a statement preceding a piece by a guest writer, the editors admitted they had debated long and hard over the article but finally had decided to print it. "It is exactly this type of strong, personal opinion which *ONE* means to present to its readers," the editors said. "Perhaps you'll even write an answering opinion of your own." The piece tackled the subject of bisexuality, arguing that bisexuals were sitting on a fence. The author spoke directly to readers: "Jump off that rail and cast your lot with either the heterosexuals or the homosexuals. This is one time when being half-and-half doesn't mean you are the cream of the crop. It just means you are confused—let's face it!"[71]

A *ONE* reader from Chicago provoked a fiery debate on another sensitive topic when he criticized the high level of sexual activity among gay men, referring to the "*demimonde* of bar flies and bar-flitting, of promiscuity." He continued: "We must reform the so-called 'gay' life in order to earn respect for ourselves as homosexuals." Liberal activists responded by characterizing sexual promiscuity as an integral part of gay liberation, particularly in a society that did not sanction monogamous relationships between members of the same sex. One man wrote, "Promiscuity is an important and meaningful aspect of homosexuality which should be valued highly." Another put this side of the debate in concise terms by saying he was "appalled" at the suggestion that gay men should stop being promiscuous: "No more sexual abandon? Imagine!"[72]

ONE editors deliberately sparked discord among readers by pursuing controversial subjects. They highlighted the explosive topic of gay marriage, for example, by devoting a cover to it. They also raised the even more incendiary issue of whether gay couples should be allowed to adopt children. Block recalled: "It was a hoot sitting around chatting about what topic we would bring up next. Finally, we could commit to paper the topics that had made gay dinner parties social events *par excellence* for years."[73]

On most issues, the editors allowed readers to speak without editorial comment. Block continued: "There was a lot we wanted to say, but we didn't want to cut off discussion. Gays had been silenced for years. It was high time someone allowed them to speak freely." Only on the topic of effeminacy did the editors fail to restrain themselves. When a writer said that all gay men feel a need to "swish" at times, the editors added: "The editors must challenge this. Take it from us, Buster, it ain't so."[74]

Another provocative piece suggested lesbians might be able to solve the population explosion that was of great concern in the 1950s: "It is time to call for at least half the women of the world to do their duty and NOT have babies, at least not more than the world can support. We can think of no better way to ensure this than by encouraging more women to join in permanent and highly moral partnerships with one another."[75]

The most jaw-dropping article published in early issues of ONE provided a taste of the haughtiness and sense of superiority some gays feel vis-à-vis straights. The article proposed that lesbians and gay men with IQs of 175 or higher create a race of homosexual superwomen and supermen. Under the plan, lesbians would be inseminated with sperm from gay men, and then the girls would be raised by the women, the boys by the men. The article stated: "Heterosexuals have had their procreation of endless numbers of babies of no quality. Homosexuals should now have their own procreation—one of only excellent quality babies." The article then launched into a general indictment of heterosexuals, expressing the pent up anger—with style if not grace—many gays had been feeling for centuries: "Let the heterosexuals kill themselves with over-breeding. Further, homosexuals should stop catering to or serving the heterosexuals. Let the heterosexuals wave their own hair and decorate their own houses. Let their poor taste manifest and demonstrate itself. There is no sense in homosexuals trying to cover up for them. Let the heterosexual go, let them drop to their own level—their natural vulgarity."[76]

Raising a Voice of Accommodation

Mattachine Review offered readers a drastically different perspective, reflecting the Homophile Movement's commitment to accommodating to the norms of heterosexual society. The *Review*'s philosophy was designed to win acceptance on mainstream society's terms, rather than to challenge conventional values. Editor Hal Call said recently: "To get along we had to go along. We had to stay in step with the existing mores of society. We had to because we didn't have the strength of tissue paper to defend ourselves."[77]

An editorial in the *Review*'s first issue insisted that the public attitude toward homosexuality would improve as soon as "sex variants" began behaving in accordance with societal norms. The article urged readers to adopt heterosexual mannerisms, stating: "All must condition themselves to act and react intelligently and with forethought of the consequences so that it becomes a habit. There is a socially desirable standard by which we must act." In another essay, Call distanced himself from any effort to organize homosexuals, stating of the magazine: "It is NOT seeking to become a political pressure group of any sort."[78]

Throughout its history, the *Mattachine Review* routinely denigrated gays, referring to them as "dependent people" who were characterized by "arrested emotional development," "personal selfishness," and a tendency "to avoid individual and group responsibility." Self-loathing was another recurring theme. The second issue carried the pejorative statement "The homosexual adjusts best who can make the greatest compromises with his own social and sexual needs, and the best adjusted individuals are those with the fewest contacts in the homosexual world."[79]

That gay men continued to read such degrading material—although the *Review*'s circulation was one-fifth that of *ONE*—speaks to the lack of self-respect of many in a society whose overriding attitude toward homosexuality was contempt.

On the rare occasion that the *Review* took an editorial stance in defense of homosexual activity, it did so on the grounds of expediency rather than equality.

In opposition to efforts to close gay bars, Call wrote: "To close the places of congregation will mean that homosexuals will flow in greater numbers into the more elite bistros of hotels, supper clubs, and other downtown areas. How much better, it would seem to us, is a situation where homosexuals can be among their own kind, thereby offending the least number of non-homosexuals." In other words, Call was supporting gay bars not because they had a right to exist but because gay men were inherently offensive and, therefore, should be isolated from polite society. Furthermore, Call's commitment to conforming to the dictates of a homophobic society is illustrated by his use of the words *their own kind* and *offending.*[80]

Expanding the Venue to Lesbian Issues

Although *The Ladder*'s editorial stance tended to be in keeping with the *Review*'s philosophy of conforming to heterosexual society, Phyllis Lyon believed her most important goal was to encourage lesbians to speak—even if they disagreed with her. Lyon understood the repression that was part of lesbian consciousness, and she was determined to offer readers a vehicle they could use to articulate their own thoughts while conversing with each other. Her effort was much like Lisa Ben's in *Vice Versa,* but on a larger scale. Lyon recalled: "*The Ladder* broke the silence. Finally. Before it came along, there was absolutely nothing about lesbians in the major press. We sent the papers press releases about our DOB meetings, but they wouldn't even print the times and meeting places—straight facts. We wanted to get the word out about this funny little movement that was just getting started. We saw *The Ladder* as a forum for ideas, even ideas we disagreed with."[81]

One topic that permeated the pages was whether lesbians should dress, groom, and behave according to the feminine standards of the time. It was clear where *The Ladder* stood. A reader wrote, "The kids in fly front pants and with butch haircuts and mannish manner are the worst publicity that we can get." An editorial then stated, simply and unequivocally, "Very true." *The Ladder* continually campaigned for conformity in hopes of breaking the stereotyped image of the masculine lesbian, eventually conducting a survey that showed its readers to be middle-class women who were masculine neither in appearance nor behavior.[82]

Opposing masculine appearance and behavior was a practical decision, as women knew the simple decision to wear trousers could lead to police harassment. In 1957, when three female students at San Francisco State College wore slacks to a bar, they were arrested and charged with the crime of "wearing men's

Through the drawings on its cover, America's first widely distributed lesbian magazine subtly encouraged women to come out. Courtesy of Phyllis Lyon.

clothes." After reporting the arrest, *The Ladder* counseled lesbians not to wear trousers in public. Most readers agreed, saying a feminine appearance improved their social relationships. One wrote, "It pays to make this small concession."[83]

The mainstream media's stereotyping of lesbians as Amazonian creatures surfaced when *Pageant,* a general circulation magazine of the era, mentioned *The Ladder* and described Lyon as "burly." Del Martin checked her dictionary for the definition of the word and then came to her lover's defense—her tongue securely in cheek. Martin wrote: "Those who have made the personal acquaintance of Phyllis Lyon would hardly call her large of body, bulky or stout. She has a trim figure—34 bust, 24 waist (maybe slightly larger after recent Holiday parties) and 36 hips—considered by many as 'very nice'. Is our editor burly? We think not!"[84]

As the decade moved toward its end, however, the occasional voice argued that women who preferred a less feminine appearance should follow their instincts. When a successful businesswoman described how she had hidden her homosexuality from her family and coworkers while having a relationship with another prominent woman who also was "well groomed, fashionably dressed, completely feminine," another reader was not impressed. Saying she had lived with a lesbian lover without negative repercussions for twenty years, the second woman angrily confronted the first: "Would you lose your job, your mother's love or your right to vote Republican if you let slip just a couple of small hairpins, took a flat with your friend, and started to make up for all the time you have lost? See to it that there's only one bedroom with a full size double bed. You won't, either of you, be so well groomed in the future—but it will be worth it."[85]

Such advocates of nonconformity were the exception rather than the rule with regard to the subject of lesbian bars as well. Lyon recently recalled: "The bars were working against the successful integration of lesbians into society. It was not healthy to spend so much time in those places." After establishing the Daughters of Bilitis as a social alternative to the bars, Lyon and Martin used the embryonic power of the lesbian press to try to wean women from the fast lane. In 1956, *The Ladder* reported that San Francisco police had raided a club and arrested three dozen women. In an editorial response to the raid, Martin said of the lesbian: "To seek others like herself is only natural. However, it is often this problem of meeting others that leads the Lesbian into circumstances and places, not particularly of her taste or choice, which may expose her vulnerability to prejudice and suspicion."[86]

The magazine continually reinforced the anti-bar message. One article stated: "The 'better' kids are rarely seen as they keep to themselves and don't frequent the drinking places." The same article characterized *Ladder* readers by saying, "We aren't 'bar-hoppers,' but people with steady jobs"—implying that a person could not possibly go to bars *and* have a steady job. After analyzing the results of its reader survey, the magazine boasted, "The group as a whole does not conform to the stereotype with respect to heavy drinking and continuous attendance at 'gay' bars."[87]

Despite Lyon and Martin's strong stances on appearance and social activities, they did not censor more progressive opinions. Lorraine Hansberry was one of the first writers to speak defiantly through the magazine, connecting antihomosexuality with antifeminism: "It is time that 'half the human race' had something to say about the nature of its existence. Otherwise, without revised basic thinking, the woman intellectual is likely to find herself trying to draw conclusions based on acceptance of a social moral superstructure which has never admitted to the equality of women and is therefore immoral itself. Homosexual persecution and condemnation has at its roots not only social ignorance, but a philosophically active anti-feminist dogma."[88]

Serving Gay and Lesbian Readers

Gay men and lesbians of the 1950s had access to scant information about legal and moral issues that grew out of their homosexuality, even though these subjects produced tremendous anxiety in their lives. To counteract this dearth of information, the pioneering magazines were committed to incorporating reader-service articles into their pages.

ONE introduced this editorial element with a two-part series describing the legal limits of police entrapment. Other articles explained how much information a person was required to give a police officer and summarized relevant bills pending before the California legislature—including a proposal to prohibit homosexuals from driving cars.[89]

Reader-service articles were a staple of *Mattachine Review* as well. A flood of first-person essays focused on whether a person should divulge his sexual orientation to others. In concert with the magazine's conformist philosophy, one author wrote: "Homosexuals should not shout their propensities from rooftops; there are many ways of imparting truth, within the bounds of propriety and good taste." Another went a bit further, urging readers to disclose their sexual orientation to friends—but drawing the line at telling parents. Basing his logic on one of the conventional beliefs regarding the cause of homosexuality at the time, the man wrote: "Parents would realize it was for the most part the imbalanced emotional relationship of one or both of them to us as children which caused many of us to develop with a predominantly homosexual bent." Employment issues were another frequent topic of reader-service material in the *Review*, with the magazine offering strategies that readers could use to avoid—although not fight—job discrimination. One suggested a homosexual should give up his job at the first hint of potential problems: "If he finds himself in an employment situation in which he must rely heavily upon heterosexual social contacts to be successful, the variant would be wise not to continue there."[90]

The Ladder's most frequent reader-service debate focused on whether a homosexual woman should remain in an unfulfilling marriage to a heterosexual man. One reader wrote a poignant piece telling how she had married and borne two children in hopes of squelching her attraction to women. She said her experiment had failed, leaving her torn between remaining with her children or breaking free of a suffocating marriage: "I belong to the twilight world—the world of the 'third sex,' neither normal woman nor normal man— a world unexplored like a little-known, far-off planet hanging in the darkness of space. I have never been able to cure myself of being what I am—a masculine soul, with masculine desires, in a feminine body."[91]

Other readers displayed no ambivalence. One woman saw only one logical course of action: "Rather than destroy everything she has built up through the years, most lesbians with successful heterosexual marriages should keep their fears within themselves, trusting to luck that the tightrope of their lives will remain intact." The comment prompted an opposite view from a Texas woman who argued a wife should divulge her sexuality to her husband, even though such honesty might result in divorce. The woman insisted that it was immoral for a woman to be unfaithful to her husband, and no husband should be expected to tolerate such disreputable behavior in his wife, whether she be straight or gay.[92]

Another form of reader-service material in *The Ladder* evolved as an attempt to counteract the influence of lesbian pulp novels. Since the 1940s, publishers had been churning out hundreds of paperback novels featuring lesbian characters. The pulps, aimed at titillating men, were packaged with lurid covers designed to heighten their pornographic appeal. The preposterous plots characterized lesbians as bitter, sex-hungry, vampirelike monsters who preyed on young girls and inevitably either committed suicide or found "happiness" in the arms of the "right" man. These novels offered lesbians the only images available of women loving women and also gave readers a sense of how to dress and where to meet other women, but they also perpetuated myths about lesbians.[93]

Lyon and Martin were among the millions of American lesbians who struggled to reconcile these debilitating images with their own innermost feelings. So, as a service to their readers, the editors used *The Ladder* to redefine lesbian images. An article in the second issue set the magazine on its course. In "The Positive Approach," Martin wrote: "The Lesbian is a woman endowed with all the attributes of any other woman. As an individual she has her own particular quota of intelligence and physical charm. She has equal opportunity for education, employment, intellectual and cultural pursuits. The salvation of the Lesbian lies in her own acceptance of herself without guilt or anxiety, in her awareness of her capabilities, and in her pursuit of a constructive way of life without misgivings or apology."[94]

Month after month, the editors dotted their pages with depictions of happy, productive gay women—images that had never before appeared in print. Whether describing women involved in loving relationships or women thriving on the independence of single life, these sketches served readers by providing role models and strategies for happiness.

Some articles exposed readers to the range of relationships available to them. A socially prominent woman wrote that she and her lover had met at a society tea fifteen years earlier and had remained true to each other ever since. They did not live under the same roof but were together one day a week, as well as weekends and vacations. She concluded: "There is nothing 'cheap' about the deep love that we have shared. I would not change my way of life, even if I could."[95]

Other reassuring words came from relatives of lesbians. One mother described her daughter as a career woman who was living "a full, rounded-out life of contentment and security." The mother included advice for other people who learn that a loved one is gay: "From the beginning I knew she would need love, appreciation and understanding from me; not censure, shame or withdrawal. As a consequence, I think I have my daughter's love and loyalty—even to a greater degree than most mothers."[96]

The Ladder's most remarkable effort to serve its readers began in 1958 when the magazine created the first comprehensive profile of the American lesbian. After sending a questionnaire to the 500 women then on the subscription list, Lyon and Martin compiled the data to create a composite snapshot that was fascinating as well as flattering. During a time in American history when only 6 percent of American women had graduated from college, 46 percent of the women responding to the survey had college degrees; while only 13 percent of American women worked in a profession, 38 percent of *Ladder* readers did; and while the average woman worker earned $1,310 a year, the average *Ladder* reader earned $4,200—more than triple the average.[97]

Compiling Research about Homosexuality

Mattachine Review led the journalistic trio in summarizing social science studies relevant to gay readers. This was an important contribution because, in the eyes of most of American society, homosexuals were sexual deviants whose lives were defined by perversion and psychoses. The *Review* offered readers a more balanced picture of homosexuality that was beginning to emerge from progressive social scientists.

Research published in the *Review* included groundbreaking revelations. Dr. Evelyn Hooker, the first psychologist to conduct research on gay men who had not been diagnosed as mentally ill nor convicted of crimes, used the pages of the magazine to challenge the theory that all homosexuals were unhappy. It also was in the *Review* that Dr. Alfred Kinsey first objected to homosexuals being classified as the "third sex," and Dr. Havelock Ellis argued that homosexuals could be intelligent and have strong moral fiber.[98]

Sociologist Paul Tappan reported findings *Review* readers greeted even more eagerly. During the 1950s, some officials in the American legal system argued that the only logical response to male homosexuality was castration. Jennings recalled: "When someone was taken to court on a homosexual morals charge, many judges would give you two options. You could be imprisoned for the rest of your life or you could be castrated. Those were your only choices. I hate to think how many men made the bad choice." Tappan studied the subject, including experiments in Europe, and concluded that castration should not be used in the United States. Tappan's report in the *Review* was the first step toward deleting the castration provision from the California penal code.[99]

Research findings summarized in the *Review* were not, however, uniformly positive. Reasoning that homosexuals lacked the credibility to advance their own cause, Call believed they could not speak for themselves but had to depend on heterosexual experts to speak for them. Fear and lack of confidence also played a role in this decision, which ultimately led to a crippling dependency by gay men on such authorities during the Homophile Movement. Call, as well as other gay men committed to the accommodationist view, eagerly embraced authorities who often were part of the problem rather than part of the solution.

Articles routinely labeled gay men "sexual psychopaths," casually grouping them with child molesters and rapists. In addition, studies accepted the conventional classification of homosexuality as a disease and focused attention on possible "cures." Dr. Richard Robertiello, a psychoanalyst, announced that most gay men and lesbians engaged in sadomasochistic activities and that an "unloving mother" would create female homosexuality. He then "reassured" readers that cures were possible. Robertiello said with surety: "It usually takes five years. In general, a very effeminate man or a masculine woman is harder to treat."[100]

Dr. Kenneth Fink, who wrote two books about homosexuality, perpetuated several myths the *Review* further reinforced. Fink insisted that all gay men were depressed and all gay relationships ultimately disintegrated into violence. Although Fink had little hope that homosexuals could be "cured," he added: "Any progress attained is worth the sweating out process in terms of improved adjustment and relationship with society! I would rather see homosexuals at least TRY to get cured."[101]

The most important piece of research summarized in *The Ladder* appeared in 1959. The magazine devoted four pages to the findings of the country's first scientific examination of the personality types dominant among American lesbians. The results, which *The Ladder* published a year before they appeared in a scientific journal, exploded many myths about lesbians. The study found, for example, that they are neither more dependent nor more hostile toward men than straight women are.[102]

Following *Vice Versa*'s lead, *Mattachine Review* and *The Ladder* also published bibliographies of books and articles about homosexuality. These lists— often accompanied by critiques—were invaluable to men and women struggling with their sexual identity. The entries eventually numbered more than a thousand in the *Review* and more than 500 in *The Ladder*.

Politicizing the Lesbian and Gay Press

Although *ONE* and *Mattachine Review* both specifically stated that they refused to become involved in politics, *The Ladder* made no such pledge. Indeed, the lesbian magazine led the publications into the political arena, while simultaneously encouraging creation of a lesbian and gay voting bloc.[103]

From its founding, *The Ladder* encouraged readers to galvanize into a collective unit. In the premier issue, Lyon wrote that she expected her magazine to help unite lesbians. In an editorial three pages later, Martin communicated a similar message: "What will be the lot of the future Lesbian? Fear? Scorn? This need not be—IF lethargy is supplanted by an energized constructive program, if cowardice gives way to the solidarity of a cooperative front." The editors' decision to capitalize the word *Lesbian* was also a political statement suggesting lesbian empowerment.[104]

In 1958, *The Ladder* campaigned for equal rights for lesbians and gay men through a series of articles. The first proposed that gay couples be allowed to file joint tax returns. The next argued that such couples demand joint home insurance policies. The third evolved from the summary of *The Ladder*'s historic survey, with the summary proudly stating of the magazine's readers, "Over 80 percent are registered voters."[105]

The event that propelled *The Ladder* full tilt into politics began in 1959 when Russell Wolden, a candidate for mayor of San Francisco, stated on KNBC radio that Mayor George Christopher had transformed the city into "the national headquarters for sex deviants." Further, Wolden said that the Mattachine Society had passed a resolution praising Christopher for his support. Wolden further pointed out that the Mattachine Society and Daughters of Bilitis, which he called "sort of a woman's auxiliary" of the society, both had their national headquarters in the city because of the climate the mayor had fostered. Wolden also distributed pamphlets warning parents that their daughters were not safe because the city's many lesbians were constantly stalking them.[106]

Lyon and Martin called an emergency meeting of their organization, initially expecting only to discuss the situation. But the editors soon learned that they had underestimated the trust and confidence readers had in *The Ladder*. Martin later recalled: "Those readers insisted that if we published a special edition of *The Ladder* explaining the facts, that would turn the tide. So that's what we did. We went into overdrive and published right away." Even though that remarkable special edition, the first in the history of the lesbian and gay press, was published at the height of the crisis, Lyon wrote in the rational tone of a journalist rather than the hysterical tone of some activists. In a comprehensive article that continued for seven pages, she laid out the facts with no commentary— but with convincing clarity.[107]

With Lyon's guidebook for reference, the city's daily press then began covering the issue as well. The *San Francisco Chronicle* characterized Wolden's accusations as an orchestrated campaign to destroy Christopher. It exposed how a Wolden campaign worker had infiltrated the Mattachine Society in order to propose and shepherd through the resolution supporting Christopher, specifically so the resolution could be used against the mayor. When Wolden's deceit became public knowledge, his scheme backfired. The *Chronicle* not only endorsed Christopher but also called for Wolden to withdraw from the race because of his mendacious tactics.[108]

On election day, voters sided with Christopher. The mayor was reelected with 61 percent of the vote, and Lesbian and Gay America won its first major battle against antihomosexual politicians. Lyon and Martin wrote: "This catapult into the realm of politics keynoted an awakening interest in the homophile community which was to result some years later in a strong voting bloc. It also broke through what the movement had previously termed the [mainstream] media's 'conspiracy of silence' on homosexual issues."[109]

Movement leaders were quoted in several *Chronicle* articles, giving them an opportunity to raise the public profile of lesbians and gay men. The Mattachine Society received further news coverage when it filed a slander suit against Wolden. Although the society did not win its case, the news media's coverage of it communicated to society that homosexuals, when maligned, would fight back.[110]

Riding the momentum of the victory in San Francisco and anticipating the upcoming national political conventions, Martin wrote a powerful editorial in which she asked a point-blank question that would reverberate well into the 1960s and beyond: "Is there, or could there be, a homosexual voting bloc?"[111]

As the new decade began, *The Ladder* could rightly take credit for making homosexuality—for the first time—a political issue. The magazine urged gay people to become a visible and active political force in what was to become one of the most turbulent periods in American history.

"No One Was Going to Shut Us Up"

ONE, Mattachine Review, and *The Ladder* provided a forum in which gay people were able, for the first time, to discuss subjects the mainstream media deemed unspeakable. To construct such an arena demanded that the editors invent a national medium for which there was no model. The venture required commitment, as the founders had to donate not only huge blocks of time and enormous quantities of energy, but also the financial support advertisers refused to provide. Most of all, creating such a public forum required the courage to defy the social order during one of the most repressive eras in American history, a time when to be accused was to be assumed guilty. In the words of Jim Kepner: "None of those early magazines ever sold more than a few thousand copies. But we kept them coming out—come Hell or high water. We had found our voice, and no one was going to shut us up."[112]

It is noteworthy that this voice emerged during an era generally not known for new ground being broken. The 1950s are generally characterized as a period of conformity, a time of mind-numbing acceptance of the most conservative of American values. It is ironic, then, that this was the decade in which the lesbian and gay press not only bobbed to the surface, but also swam against the historical tide. While most of the country was lounging in the status quo, an ongoing gay press began speaking on behalf of a forbidden people.

Although none of the founders of the three magazines had ever seen a copy of *Vice Versa* when they established their publications, their editorial mix was similar to Lisa Ben's. Like her trail-blazing publication, theirs depended heavily on personal essays and fiction. The 1950s magazines also followed *Vice Versa*'s lead in publishing editorials, letters to the editor, book reviews, and lists of recent books and articles relevant to homosexuals. The three new publications made a major addition to this list, however, by adding news content. Their summaries of news events from around the country were extremely important, as they provided the only documentation of the era's shameful record of physical and psychological abuse of gay citizens.[113]

Another characteristic of the 1950s publications that refined an element introduced by their predecessor revolved around design. Ben demonstrated a strong commitment to her magazine's appearance, and the founders of *ONE* and *The Ladder* advanced this commitment by using bold graphics and arresting images to make design one of their publications' most distinctive elements. *ONE* further emphasized visuals by introducing suggestive images of men, destined to become a staple of the gay press.

The publications also advanced lesbian and gay journalism in other important ways. They increased circulation, widened distribution, and established that this new genre could achieve stability. Phyllis Lyon said recently: "We felt a personal commitment to keep going. It really wasn't ego. It was for all those lonely women who wrote us, saying the only bright spot in their whole month was the arrival of our little magazine."[114]

In a larger context, *ONE, Mattachine Review,* and *The Ladder* demonstrated that the lesbian and gay press would exhibit traits and fulfill functions that scholars have identified as also characterizing other social movement presses. First, the three publications were created because the mainstream press had refused to allow gay people to speak. Just as African-American, women's suffrage, and women's liberation journals had been founded to create outlets through which their respective readers could talk to each other, the pioneering gay magazines offered readers the opportunity to express themselves—even when those readers disagreed with the editors. By the 1950s, it was clear that the nascent lesbian and gay press would be committed to maintaining an open forum for the divergent views of its readers. *Vice Versa* had attempted to do this; the 1950s magazines succeeded.[115]

The magazines also were similar to the women's suffrage press in that they spread the concept of homosexual liberation to a much larger and much more diverse audience than the handful of women and men who had founded the earliest lesbian and gay organizations. As shown by the geographic spread of the letters to the editor that the publications received, people in small towns as well as large cities throughout the country were not only reading the articles but were becoming engaged in the debates. Readers were not passively accepting information from the editors but were actively participating in forging the ideology of gay liberation.[116]

Finally, just as the founding of the first African-American newspaper, *Freedom's Journal* in 1827, has been credited with marking the beginning of a national movement to secure black civil rights, by creating a communication medium that allowed women and men all over the country to converse with each other, *ONE, Mattachine Review,* and *The Ladder* likewise began to build a national gay and lesbian community. As readers engaged in an ongoing dialogue with each other, they started to identify their common aspirations. Aided by the discourse in the magazines—such as Dale Jennings saying, "Were all homosexuals and bisexuals to unite militantly, unjust laws and corruption would crumble in short order," and Del Martin asking, "Is there, or could there be, a homosexual voting bloc?"—gay men and lesbians from coast to coast began to consider their potential as a unified political force. In the words of Don Slater: "These early publications were not a *fore*runner of anything. They were the *start* of the homosexual movement in America."[117]

That birth was not made any easier by the specter of a threat that other alternative presses generally did not have to contend with, but one that would continue to plague the lesbian and gay press in the decades ahead: legal disputes. *ONE's* four-year courtroom battle with postal officials was the most dramatic illustration of this theme, which was reinforced when FBI agents repeatedly interrogated the editors and damaged their careers by contacting their employers. Although *ONE* triumphed in its court case and the FBI eventually closed its investigation, the incidents were only the first in what was to be a long list of unpleasant encounters with governmental authorities.

The incident with postal officials introduced another element that would play a major role in the evolution of the gay press. This one would become something of a love-hate relationship, as publications struggled to weigh their need for financial support against the complications involved in opening their pages to advertising. Yes, running that first paid ad helped *ONE's* finances, but publishing the suggestive images simultaneously forced the editors to alter their antieroticism policy while also alienating some readers. As the editors' defense of their decision illustrated, the incident involved moral principle as well. They concluded their statement to readers: "*ONE* is, and must continue to be, dedicated to tolerance." This would not be the last time the gay press would wrestle with the complexities of balancing fiscal stability, advertising policy, and moral principle.

λ 3

Raising a Militant Voice

The election of a vibrant young American president in 1960 signaled the beginning of a tumultuous decade of change. John F. Kennedy was prophetic on Inauguration Day when he said: "Before my term is ended, we shall have to test anew whether a nation organized and governed such as ours can endure. The outcome is by no means certain." African Americans, women, and college students all tested the strength and endurance of a democratic society by marching out of their ghettos, kitchens, and classrooms to take to the streets and demand social justice as never before.

Bolstered by the courage of these other dissident groups, lesbians and gay men also began to paint placards and organize picket lines. The tiny size of those early public demonstrations belie their significance. For the direct-action protests vividly demonstrated that homosexuals would no longer tolerate what author Christopher Isherwood labeled the "heterosexual dictatorship." The new breed of activists rejected the behind-the-scenes approach of the 1950s in favor of the public and confrontational tactics popularized by the other dissident groups. Not only would gay people no longer hide in their closets, but they now *demanded* public attention.[1]

A new generation of publications led the shift toward militancy. Written and edited by the same women and men who organized and marched in the picket lines, the publications of the mid-1960s articulated the political philosophy that fueled the new defiance. Barbara Gittings, the leading editor of the era, recently recalled: "During the 1950s, homosexuals had looked inward, focusing on themselves and their problems, begging society for tolerance. In the 1960s, we looked *outside* ourselves for the roots of the problem. We came to the position that the 'problem' of homosexuality isn't a problem at all. The problem is society. Society had to accommodate us, not try to change us." The publications of the era directed this dramatic change from conforming to the dictates of heterosexual society to building a national gay community with values often in conflict with those of heterosexual America—and proudly so.[2]

African Americans, women, antiwar protesters, and college students all had discovered they could place their issues on the national agenda by focusing public attention through the news media, and the lesbian and gay groups followed their examples. The historic protests of the era were media events as much as political ones. Although the protesters could not realistically expect immediate changes in the laws that bound them to second-class citizenship, they certainly could hope to begin to reeducate the public through the media.

Because gay leaders recognized that effective internal communication is essential for an organization to articulate its ideology, develop a political consciousness among its members, increase its size, and sustain itself, the leaders established that producing publications would be a central element in their strategy for social change. Although *The Ladder* already had moved the lesbian press into the political arena with its special issue on the 1959 San Francisco mayoral race, the 1960s magazines went the next step of institutionalizing politics as an ongoing element in lesbian and gay journalism. What's more, they did not merely use their pages to tell readers when protests would take place and then describe what had been accomplished at them; they quickly advanced to the more sophisticated levels of political journalism. The activists/editors boldly stated whether particular mainstream political candidates were friends or foes, interpreted how complex court decisions represented stigmatizing of gay people, and issued dramatic calls to action to identify specific steps readers could take to help gays cast off their repression—while simultaneously building a visible and assertive national community.

As the magazines led the movement in calling for civil rights for their readers, they simultaneously carried their evolving genre of the movement press across the country. Previous publications had been based solely on the West Coast, but the most progressive new voices emanated from New York, Philadelphia, and Washington. With the lesbian and gay press spreading across the national map, publications and their activist editors were increasingly allowing even women and men living outside urban centers to feel that they, too, could be foot soldiers in the emerging battle for gay civil rights.

The shift to the East was propelled at least in part by gay and lesbian journalism's recognition that a major battlefront had to be the nation's capital. Attempting to end the federal government's ban on employing homosexuals and the law enforcement community's systematic entrapment of gay men became cornerstones of the new militancy, which meant that the White House and other symbols of power became prime targets. Activists in New York and Philadelphia became intimately familiar with the roadways leading to Washington.

To focus attention on public demonstrations, the new publications placed a much greater emphasis on news. For the lesbian and gay press began to expand from a medium consisting primarily of social comment to a medium also containing an abundance of reportage. As the genre's first generation of news magazines, the leading publications of the day gave extensive and animated coverage to activism and militancy, with myriad news reports on public marches and demonstrations, law suits, and tactics being developed to apply political pressure. Consequently, for the first time in American history, gay people were able to read about events of the day from a perspective that was *not* homophobic.

These editorial advancements did not significantly affect the advertising content of the magazines or, consequently, the fiscal status of the magazines. Very few businesses were willing to identify themselves with the lesbian and gay market. Gittings said: "We were still perceived as demons. Advertisers knew we were steady customers, but they wouldn't take the risk of publicly acknowledging us. So the finances of our publications was always tenuous."[3]

Those economic difficulties were the major reason the genre continued to be dominated by magazines aimed toward men. With editors and writers still having to pay many of their expenses out of their own pockets and during an era when men were paid much higher salaries than women, *The Ladder* remained the only magazine aimed toward lesbians.

Many editors and writers also continued to use pseudonyms. Such caution was not paranoia. During the mid-1960s, Jack Nichols, one of the most eloquent and prolific writers in the history of the gay press, was climbing the ladder of success as a salesman for the International Inn in Washington, having been promoted to assistant sales manager. Then, in 1967, he agreed to appear on a CBS television documentary to talk publicly about his homosexuality. Nichols said recently: "My friends all counseled me not to do it, but I knew the only way things were going to change was if we took risks. I thought the world was ready." He was wrong. The day after Nichols appeared on the television show, his boss fired him.[4]

Of the 1950s magazine triumvirate, only *The Ladder,* under a new East Coast editor, kept pace with the march toward militancy. In fact, the venerable voice of Lesbian America led the new wave of the gay press that, by its twentieth birthday, truly had become national in scope. By mid-decade, new publications had eclipsed the moribund *ONE* and *Mattachine Review,* whose circulations dwindled in large part because the editors were unwilling to adapt to the changing times. The most important of the new magazines were the *Homosexual Citizen* in Washington and *Drum* in Philadelphia, which joined forces with *The Ladder* to create a new triumvirate of gay journalism for the new decade. Other new publications did not contribute as significantly toward the trend toward militancy. *Tangents* in Los Angeles adopted an editorial tone similar to *ONE's*; *Vector, Citizens News*, and *Cruise News & World Report* in San Francisco served as precursors for the entertainment-oriented publications that would play a major role in the future of the gay press. Despite the editorial, philosophic, and geographic diversity of the publications, by 1965 their monthly circulation still totaled only 20,000. Numbers aside, the assertiveness reflected in the leading magazines of the era made it clear that lesbian and gay journalism was well on its way to becoming a formidable institution at the forefront of an aggressive social movement.[5]

The Ladder Articulates a New Philosophy

After editing *The Ladder* for six years, Phyllis Lyon and Del Martin passed the responsibilities to a young woman who was to have profound influence on both the emerging Lesbian and Gay Liberation Movement and the press that led that movement. Barbara Gittings enrolled at Northwestern University but became so obsessed with researching homosexuality that she dropped out of school after one year. In 1950, at the age of eighteen, she moved to Philadelphia and began earning her living in a series of low-paying jobs, such as clerking in a music store and operating a mimeograph machine for an architectural firm. In 1958, she founded a chapter of the Daughters of Bilitis in New York City, hitchhiking from Philadelphia to preside at the weekly meetings.

Although Gittings did not have a journalism background, her huge collection of lesbian books and articles demonstrated her commitment to the written word. After Gittings wrote for *The Ladder* for five years, the DOB leadership appointed Gittings editor in 1963. A year later, she quit her job and began editing the magazine full-time—without pay. Like other pioneers in lesbian and gay journalism, Gittings made severe financial sacrifices. She recently recalled: "I survived on a small trust fund and by living very frugally. I was so committed to the movement that I saw no alternative to giving it all of my time. Gaining equal rights for homosexuals was my number one priority. I simply couldn't manage a full-time job in addition. Making a living was entirely secondary."[6]

When Gittings began editing the magazine, her personal philosophy was still developing. As it did, she increasingly rejected the conformist ideology of the 1950s—and of the DOB leadership. Reflecting the new editor's personal evolution, *The Ladder* gradually became the leading mouthpiece for the new militancy. Some of the first changes came through the message readers received regarding their wardrobes and grooming habits. No longer did the magazine urge readers to conform to society's narrow definition of feminine appearance. Sounding like something of a lesbian version of *Vogue, The Ladder* said in 1964: "Pants are proper! This season you can wear pants absolutely anywhere—which means dandy pants for town and fancy pants for evening. Combine with a champion-swimmer hairdo sleeked back behind your ears and a cropped coat."[7]

The new editor next accomplished one of her most daring changes through a mere three words: *A Lesbian Review.* Since its founding in 1956, *The Ladder* had never explicitly stated that it was aimed at lesbians. But in 1964, Gittings changed the cover to read *The Ladder—A Lesbian Review.* Through the subtitle, Gittings was encouraging American lesbians to approach their sexuality with a new level of frankness. She recalled: "Adding those words to the cover helped our readers gain a new sense of identity and strength. That subtitle said, very eloquently I thought, that the word *lesbian* was no longer unspeakable." Gittings gradually altered the designs of the covers so the title shrunk while the subtitle grew increasingly large.[8]

The assertive editor made another bold political statement by replacing the line drawings on the cover with photographs of lesbian "cover girls." Gittings said: "Heterosexuals, as well as many lesbians themselves, had weird ideas of what most lesbians looked like. We wanted to show everyone that lesbians were normal, happy, wholesome women—every mother's 'dream daughter.'" Women initially were reluctant to allow their images on the cover of a magazine that identified itself as being for lesbians. But before long, the politically adept Gittings had convinced enough women of the merits of the new militancy that she had a waiting list of women eager to have their photographs on the cover: "It definitely was a political statement. Every one of those women was saying, 'We're here, we're proud, and we're beautiful!'"[9]

The idea of placing the images on the cover originated with Kay Lahusen, Gittings's lover. Lahusen, who worked as a researcher at the *Christian Science Monitor* during the late 1950s and early 1960s, took many of the photographs and served as *The Ladder's* assistant editor. She and Gittings became lovers in 1961, although their relationship remained a commuter one with Gittings in Philadelphia and Lahusen in New York. During the mid-1960s, Lahusen, like Gittings, worked at a series of short-term jobs. She recently recalled: "The activism was the main thing. Our 'careers' weren't careers at all. They were just dinky little jobs that were totally subsidiary to the movement."

Another element in Gittings's transformation of *The Ladder* into a voice of militancy involved sources of information. During the 1950s, gay publications looked to psychiatrists, psychologists, and ministers—virtually all of them either heterosexuals or closeted homosexuals—as the experts who could properly talk about homosexuality. "We were so grateful to have anyone at all pay attention to us," Gittings recalled, "that we accepted everything they said, regardless of how demeaning it was."[10]

But in the mid-1960s, Gittings revolutionized this concept by arguing that gay people were the true authorities on gayness, even if they did not have "Dr." or "Rev." in front of their names. She said: "The publications of the 1950s gave undue deference to 'authorities' and 'experts.' The true experts on homosexuality— then as well as now—are homosexuals. As editor of *The Ladder,* I set out to show that we could speak perfectly well for ourselves, thank you very much."[11]

The leadership of the Daughters of Bilitis did not agree with Gittings's decision to decrease the presence of heterosexual "experts" in the magazine. In 1965 Gittings published an article suggesting it was time to stop researching and start demanding equal rights. The theme so conflicted with the DOB stance that the organization's research director bitterly attacked the article. Gittings published the attack but insisted that her perspective be the final word, printing a third article pointedly titled "Emphasis on Research Has Had Its Day."[12]

Instead of publishing research by heterosexuals, *The Ladder* showcased lengthy interviews with gay women who were living open and fulfilling lives; through a uniformly positive tone, the interviews carried the thinly veiled message that all lesbians should abandon their closets. Typical was Gittings's eight-page interview with Ernestine Eckstein. A veteran of the Civil Rights Movement, the African-American lesbian expressed strong feelings about the path lesbians and gay men should follow: "The homosexual has to call attention to the fact that he's been unjustly acted upon. This is what the Negro did. I feel homosexuals have to become visible and assert themselves politically. Once homosexuals do this, society will start to give more and more."[13]

Gittings's commitment to providing an arena in which lesbians could speak did not, however, guarantee that the editor allowed her speakers free rein in their discourse. Gittings had a strong personality and her own agenda. Her tendency to influence what interviewees said can be seen in how she phrased her questions. During the Eckstein interview, for example, Gittings either consciously or unconsciously attempted to put words in her subject's mouth, with her own statements often overshadowing Eckstein's responses. Gittings said: "Some homosexuals feel we shouldn't let prominent heterosexuals control or determine the way things go, shouldn't allow them to take over to any degree or gain a superior influence. What do you think?" In response, Eckstein did little more than mimic the editor's words: "There seems to be some sort of premium placed on psychologists."[14]

The strongest influence on Gittings's increasingly militant worldview was Franklin E. Kameny, a man who needed no one to lead him. Born in the Bronx, Kameny earned a doctoral degree in astronomy from Harvard University. He then moved to Washington, teaching on the Georgetown University faculty for one year before taking a job with the United States Army Map Service (now the Defense Mapping Agency). Simultaneously, Kameny became involved in the city's sub-rosa gay network. Material preserved by the FBI indicates that J. Edgar Hoover may have had a direct role in the next major event in Kameny's career—one that changed his destiny. In 1957, when an agent confiscated a newsletter intended only for local gay men, Hoover told his agents to determine whether any of the people involved in the network worked for the federal government, which banned the employment of gays. Kameny was fired later that year.[15]

Denied the security clearance that was a prerequisite for success in his field, the defiant Kameny fought his job discrimination in the courts. Although he was rebuffed at every level, he continued to push the case through the complexities of the court system. Finally, in March 1961, the U.S. Supreme Court refused to reconsider the lower court rulings.

Eight months later, Kameny founded the Mattachine Society of Washington, which adopted the name of the California-based group even though it had a very different agenda. The Washington society became the first organization in the country to take a proactive stance toward securing gay rights. Kameny then earned his livelihood in what he described as "third-rate jobs in fourth-rate companies" that were willing to hire someone without a security clearance. None of the jobs challenged him, allowing Kameny to pour his considerable intellect and energy into mobilizing American homosexuals. He soon became a militant spokesman for the movement, becoming the first openly gay candidate to run for the U.S. Congress and coining the national rallying cry "Gay Is Good!"[16]

Upon meeting Kameny in 1963, Gittings was drawn to his firm resolve that gay people should fight for first-class citizenship. Kameny soon became the first man to secure a prominent voice in *The Ladder*. Gittings said: "It didn't matter to me that Frank was a man. What was important was his message—that mere information and education were not going to get gay people, lesbians as well as gay men, the equality society denied us."[17]

Stirring Up the Nation's Capital

Kameny soon had his own publication. The *Homosexual Citizen* was the first lesbian and gay periodical publicly distributed in the nation's capital. Founded in 1966, the magazine was published by the Mattachine Society of Washington. *THC*, as the volunteer staff called the magazine, continued the tradition of gay publications looking like scholarly journals. The magazine's sober subtitle— *News of Civil Liberties and Social Rights for Homosexuals*—further emphasized its serious tone. Its editorial philosophy, however, illustrated a leap forward from the 1950s magazines. By the time the *Homosexual Citizen* came into being, the Homophile Movement was dying. West Coast organizations and publications had become bland and nonassertive. Their day had passed. Kameny, by contrast, insisted, "It was time to fight for our rights in the rough-and-tumble world of social activism."[18]

Public officials had their first glimpse of Kameny's strategy when they began receiving copies of the *Homosexual Citizen* in the mail. Kameny called mailing the magazine to President Johnson and members of the U.S. Congress and Supreme Court "tweaking the lion's tail." J. Edgar Hoover was one lion who did not care to have his tail tampered with—at least not by Kameny. Soon after the FBI director received his first copy of the magazine, two agents contacted Kameny and told him to remove Hoover from the mailing list. Kameny said he would stop sending Hoover *THC* only if the FBI stopped maintaining files on the Mattachine Society. The FBI did not respond to Kameny's offer; Hoover continued to receive *THC*.[19]

This anecdote illustrates Kameny's personal assertiveness, which paralleled that of the magazine. Speaking with the unwavering self-confidence that has characterized Kameny's contribution to the movement press, he said: "The ideology of the *Homosexual Citizen* can be perfectly summarized in three words: Activist. Militant. Radical. Those were dirty words in 1966, but that's who we were. We were the cutting edge of the movement. The *Homosexual Citizen* reflected our activism—the unifying and protesting mindset on the vanguard of the movement. That sums it up completely."[20]

Another powerful voice in *THC* was Jack Nichols, who helped Kameny place Washington at the forefront of the movement. Nichols, a handsome man who stands six foot three inches tall, became a spokesman for Gay and Lesbian America. He lectured on university campuses and appeared on radio and television programs—often feeling the wrath of a hostile society. "Today we feel insulted if someone calls one of our leaders a 'fag,'" Nichols said recently. "Thirty years ago you felt lucky if you appeared on a TV program and left the studio with your genitals intact." Nichols said people also were far more ignorant about homosexuality at the time. "People asked me, as a public homosexual, if I had the sex organs of both sexes."[21]

Nichols's intense passion and graceful writing style combined to create rousing messages reminiscent of the inspirational words written by Thomas

In June 1965 Lilli Vincenz led a picket line in front of the U.S. Civil Service Commission headquarters in Washington, an event that became the cover image for an issue of The Ladder. *Courtesy of Barbara Gittings. Photo by Eva Freund.*

Paine two centuries ago. Nichols wrote, for example: "When homosexuals stand up in a positive fashion for their rights, when they take their destiny into their own hands to make a world for themselves and for their fellows that is free of fear, confusion, and discrimination, they are casting aside their own fear and confronting the forces of darkness and despair with a healthy vigor. They cannot help but benefit from their assertion of human freedom and dignity."[22]

Although Kameny and Nichols boomed from the pages of the *Homosexual Citizen,* neither committed his energies to the mechanics of editing it. Those tasks were left to the only lesbian in the Washington organization. Lilli Vincenz was born in Hamburg, Germany, in 1937. It was after earning degrees in French and German that Vincenz felt the first sting of discrimination. She joined the U.S. Army, but, after nine months, another woman accused Vincenz of being a lesbian, and she was forcibly discharged. After earning a master's degree in English from Columbia University, Vincenz worked as an editor at Prentice Hall Publishers. A year later she relocated to Washington and, while editing the *Homosexual Citizen,* worked as a technical typist for a printing company and an editorial secretary for a trade association. As editor of the magazine, Vincenz wrote some articles and edited all copy, but her most time-consuming task was painstakingly typing all copy on a typewriter to achieve a uniform typeface. "Jack and I were the loudest voices, but Lilli did all the real editorial work," Kameny admitted. "That's how it happened back then. The women typed. And the publication appeared each month with total regularity—never so much as a day late."[23]

In the first issue, Vincenz discussed the juxtaposition of *homosexual* and *citizen* to create the magazine's title, saying, "These words must seem irreconcilable to the prejudiced. All we can say is that these people will be surprised— for patriotism and responsible participation in our American democracy are certainly not monopolized by white Anglo-Saxon Protestant heterosexuals."[24]

The magazine concentrated on sending its messages to homosexual citizens in the nation's capital. Circulation of the magazine, which sold for fifty cents, never exceeded 400.[25]

Philadelphia Finds a Voice

Drum, a Philadelphia monthly founded in 1964, sounded many of the same themes—but with considerably more style. The magazine was published by the Janus Society, a gay rights organization formed in Philadelphia in 1960, and took its name from a quotation by Henry David Thoreau: "If a man does not keep pace with his companions, perhaps it is because he hears the beat of a different *drum*mer." The first movement publication that proudly announced an intention to amuse as well as inform, *Drum* carried the subtitle *Sex in Perspective*. Editor Clark P. Polak wrote: "I began DRUM Magazine as a consistently articulate, well-edited, amusing and informative publication. I envisioned a sort of sophisticated, but down-to-earth, magazine for people who dug gay life and DRUM's view of the world."[26]

A major feature of gay life, as *Drum* defined it, was sexy men, and the magazine became the first gay publication that combined news content with homoerotica. The cover as well as inside pages of the magazine often showcased men wearing only swimming trunks. Jim Kepner said: "Other publications like *Tomorrow's Man* had a strong gay readership, but they never identified themselves as gay, per se. *Drum* was the first to have the courage to do that."[27]

Polak's formula was a smashing success. After two years, his circulation had reached 10,000—surpassing that of all other lesbian and gay publications combined. *Drum* led the era's publications in size as well; while the other magazines hovered around twenty pages, Polak's swelled to sixty. "Clark was the first editor to put real *punch* in his publication," Kepner said. "*Drum* was factual in its content, but it was never dull. It sparkled with wit and style. People loved it."[28]

Drum's militant view, similar to that of *The Ladder* and *THC*, criticized the antihomosexual disdain that had permeated *Mattachine Review* and *The Ladder* during the 1950s. Polak lambasted those who sought tolerance as "Aunt Marys who have exchanged whatever vigorous defense of homosexual rights there may be for a hyper-conformist we-must-impress-the-straights-that-we-are-as-butch-as-they-are stance. It is a sell-out." Polak also attacked gays who boasted that they had no problems as long as they did not "flaunt" their sexuality, arguing that such people betrayed their sexuality just as light-skinned blacks betrayed their race if they "passed" for white.[29]

Polak argued against accommodation not only on a philosophic level, but also on a practical one. Despite gay people of the 1950s depending on straights to lead the effort to reform antihomosexual laws, he pointed out, no substantive progress had been made. "Enough of this Doctor and Lawyer Window-dressing," he said. "Efforts of the homophile movement and others concerned with sex law reform have been virtually without meaning to Legislatures."[30]

Promoting Public Demonstrations

The most visible expression of the new gay assertiveness was direct-action protesting. Beginning in the spring of 1965, Gittings and Lahusen from *The*

Ladder; Kameny, Nichols, and Vincenz from the *Homosexual Citizen;* and Polak from *Drum* all engaged in a new type of social activism. In addition to crafting militant prose at their typewriters, they began carrying militant slogans in picket lines. They became the first women and men in American history to conduct public demonstrations to protest the unfair treatment of homosexuals. Their protests were very much in keeping with the times, as that same spring 20,000 Americans marched on Washington to protest the Vietnam War.[31]

Nichols organized the first history-making gay march in the nation's capital on May 29, 1965. He recently recalled, "It signaled a new direction in our struggle for equal rights. We were leading the country by, for the first time, actively seeking to secure our civil liberties. We were finished paying lip service to heterosexual America." The broad goal of the first group of marchers—three women and seven men—was to raise the public profile of homosexuality and pressure the federal government into allowing gay people to be employed by the federal government and serve in the armed forces.[32]

Such protests are commonplace today, but the first one was extraordinary. Vincenz said: "People had no idea that homosexuals look just like everyone else. And we went out of our way to dress properly—skirts and stockings for the women, suits and ties for the men—so that no one could say we were disgusting rabble, the way they did about the anti-Vietnam protesters. We were well dressed and well groomed. So we defied all the myths. Pedestrians just stopped and stared at us. They were absolutely awe-struck."[33]

The protest was the first in a series—May at the White House and United Nations Building in New York, June at Civil Service Commission headquarters in Washington, July at Independence Hall in Philadelphia and the Pentagon in Washington, and August at the State Department. Initially they lettered their pickets by hand, but the crude appearance offended Polak's design sense. Lahusen recalled, "Clark was distressed that the signs were too amateurish. So he paid for the next set to be professionally lettered." At the same time that the pickets increased in quality, the picketers increased in quantity. By the time they returned to the White House in October, their numbers had swollen to sixty.[34]

But the activists knew that their much larger audience was available through their printed publications. Although the mainstream press largely ignored the demonstrations and the human rights issues that prompted them, the protests became major news in *The Ladder, THC,* and *Drum.* Gittings gave the protests the most prominent coverage by placing photos of the picket lines on her cover, and all three editors provided in-depth coverage that included laudatory statements by the participants as well as detailed accounts of how the police and public responded.[35]

The biggest cluster of heterosexuals reading about the marches may have been at the FBI. For the public demonstrations caught the attention of agents who, like the lesbian and gay press, dutifully reported the details of each event. Agents also included the names and physical descriptions of demonstrators. A background investigation was then conducted on each protester, similar to the investigations of editors and writers in the previous decade—again including identifying the activists to their employers.[36]

Although many gay people questioned whether it was judicious to conduct public demonstrations, the editors and writers behind the three publications had no doubt such direct action would advance the movement. Polak wrote in 1965, "Picketing is, to date, the most effective method yet found to promote the movement." Gittings still agrees, saying recently: "Those pickets were our earliest form of confrontation. As a lesbian, I felt very proud that I was able to be on the vanguard, both as a participant and as an editor who spread the word to thousands of others who weren't ready—at least not yet—to take to the streets."[37]

To bring their readers as close to the streets as possible, the advocacy journalists expanded far beyond who-what-when-where coverage. They reproduced the messages on the placards—"Employment Based Upon Competence, Ability, Training; NOT Upon Private Life," and "Equal Opportunity for All Means *ALL*." They quoted the supportive comments from passersby—"I give them credit for what they're doing," and "That's a good-looking group. I'm surprised." They also reprinted the leaflets distributed during the marches, highlighting statements of outrage such as "In no walk of life, and in none of his dealings, whether with his fellow citizens or with his government, is the homosexual American citizen treated as equal to others; he is always placed in a status of inferiority."[38]

The editors also wrote eloquent prose designed to inspire their readers to support the new militancy. Lahusen concluded a five-page account of Fourth of July picketing at Independence Hall by stating, "This dignified protest, which startled many a citizen into fresh thought about the meaning of Independence Day, might well have been applauded by our Founding Fathers, who were intent on making America safe for the differences."[39]

The magazines were soon able to report on yet another angle of the public demonstrations: impact. Picketing of the State Department in 1965 resulted in a member of the Washington press corps asking Secretary of State Dean Rusk, during a public press conference, to explain why homosexuals were barred from the department. *The Ladder* turned the question and Rusk's response into a full-page article. Since 1962, Kameny had tried repeatedly to meet with U.S. Civil Service Commission officials to discuss the ban on gays in the federal workforce. Two months after the picketing at commission headquarters, Kameny had his meeting. It would be another decade before the ban was officially lifted, but lesbian and gay journalists could rightfully boast that their public demonstrations had advanced the process.[40]

West Coast Publications

The largest direct-action activities were concentrated in Washington, Philadelphia, and New York, partly because the most powerful citadels of government were centered in those Eastern cities. But California activists also organized picket lines and public demonstrations, while manifesting the new militancy in other forms as well. The most important new publication on the West Coast was *Vector,* a San Francisco monthly founded in 1964 by a gay rights organization called the Society for Individual Rights. *Vector* departed from other gay magazines by adopting an eight-and-a-half-by-eleven-inch format. The change signaled that publications were beginning to look less like scholarly journals and more like newsletters—a shorter distance from news*papers.*[41]

   Vector also departed from other magazines by expanding the definition of gay militancy. An editorial stated, "Not just protests, but *every* group action openly engaged in by the homosexual community is a social action. A dance, a play, going to the theater, bowling, hiking, etc., must take on aspects, for homosexuals, of political ramifications." In other words, *Vector* argued, for a self-identified minority group creating itself from within a homophobic society, every social activity served as a political statement. As San Francisco increasingly became the country's gay Valhalla, it hosted a plethora of social activities. *Vector*'s first editor, Bill May, represented a new generation of gay journalists who were not willing to allow the movement or movement journalism to subsume their social lives. May recently recalled: "I was barely thirty years old when *Vector* started. Getting the word out was important, but I had no intention of devoting every free moment to it. I didn't just write about the life—I lived it."[42]

   Vector dutifully reported on the handful of public protests that occurred on the West Coast. When an Episcopal priest who supported the gay community was relieved of his position, and again when state fair officials rejected a gay organization's request to operate an information booth, *Vector* accorded the picketing front-page coverage. More consistently dominating the magazine, however, were the less visible activities that—according to *Vector*'s definition—were simultaneously articulating the new militancy. By highlighting gay picnics, theater productions, and drag shows, the magazine legitimized those activities while acknowledging their profound importance to the evolving social movement. *Vector* thereby became the first publication to recognize that there would be no revolution until activists coaxed larger numbers of gays to come out of the bars and into the streets.[43]

May's highlighting of social activities extended to the illustrations that became a major element of his magazine. *Vector* contained more photos than any gay publication that had preceded it, and May cites this emphasis as the most important advancement he made to the evolving genre. "It was the first time any publication ever showed gay people having a good time. It was a new era of militancy. The days of hanging our heads were over."[44]

That *Vector*'s front page showcased social activities more often than public marches did not lessen the defiance of its editorial voice. The publication echoed the assertiveness of its brother and sister magazines 2,000 miles to the east. "We demand our rights. First, we shall use the framework of established order. But if existing circumstances do not answer our demands, we shall create new approaches," the magazine declared. "Let society adjust to us. We will not accept compromise any longer."[45]

Two other San Francisco publications directed toward gay men were independent monthlies produced by entrepreneur Guy Strait. He introduced *Citizens News* as a bimonthly in 1961 and then added *Cruise News & World Report* in 1965, with the two magazines then alternating their publication dates so one or the other appeared each month. Founded as business enterprises rather than activist publications, *Citizens News* and *Cruise News* were dominated by advertising and self-promoting articles for Strait's male erotica mail-order business. Mixed in with the ads for his books and photographs of naked men were gay male personal ads, opinion pieces, feature articles, and a few news items. But Strait was more interested in selling his products than creating a high-quality news organ. An article about the picketing on behalf of the Episcopal priest ended up on page 6; coverage of the protests at the White House and United Nations landed on page 16.[46]

San Francisco's oldest gay magazine, *Mattachine Review*, was totally out of step with the militant shift. Sounding like a man from a previous century, Hal Call continued to support a philosophy of accommodation, viewing homosexuality in terms of a problem he begged straight society to tolerate. In 1964 he was still writing, "Foremost in the solution to the problem of homosexuality is the attainment of acceptable standards of public behavior which are not offensive." The concept appealed to fewer and fewer readers, and the *Review* plummeted in circulation. By 1964 the magazine began appearing only sporadically.[47]

Expanding News Content

The articles the militant publications printed to chronicle and promote public demonstrations led editors to commit more of their time, energy, and editorial space to news. Barbara Gittings recalled, "Fiction began to fade from our pages. Finally, we had news to report." Gradually, the columns of news briefs expanded into comprehensive news articles. For the first time in history, Lesbian and Gay America began reading news stories not from the hostile viewpoint of mainstream newspapers, but from the supportive perspective of their very own press.[48]

The gay angle was particularly important when sensational incidents sent the mainstream press into lurid overdrive. In 1964, when White House adviser Walter Jenkins was caught in the bathroom of a Washington YMCA having sex with another man, Jenkins's arrest created a national scandal and forced him to resign from his job. As reporters around the country recited the grisly details of the case, Polak raised a question in *Drum* that had not appeared in the mainstream press, but that was on the minds of millions of gay people. Polak asked, "Will this bring another McCarthy witch-hunt?" Unrestrained by the limitations of objectivity, the advocacy journalist went on to insist that the climate of the times had changed drastically in the ten years since McCarthyism had subsided. Polak's response to his rhetorical question was packed with muscle: "Let those who might attempt such a witch-hunt clearly recognize that homosexuals are NOW prepared to take a stand."[49]

Drum became the first all-news gay publication. Polak, who was from a prominent Philadelphia family, poured his own money into his magazine. In 1965 he used his personal resources to employ a professional clipping service. The service sent him some hundred news articles a month taken from mainstream newspapers across the country. So he no longer had to rely on the hit-or-miss process of readers clipping and sending articles. Instead, the editor could be assured of having a reasonably comprehensive record of what newspapers were saying about homosexuality. Lahusen recalled, "When Clark [Polak] hired the clipping service, he boasted that he was leaving the rest of us editors in the dust. And he was right."[50]

Polak, not particularly concerned about the costs of telephone bills, used many of the clippings merely as story ideas, telephoning sources around the country to gather the additional details necessary to write full-length news stories entirely from a gay perspective. Those stories, which often ran several pages in length, detailed such topics as the American Civil Liberties Union stance on gay issues and the case of a North Carolina transvestite convicted of sodomy.[51]

The *Homosexual Citizen* followed *Drum*'s example and filled its pages entirely with nonfiction material. The magazine's Washington location brought
an abundance of items describing efforts to force the federal government to
change its oppressive policies toward gay people and chronicling the continuing inhospitable attitude toward gays in the nation's capital, seen in events
such as congressmen ridiculing gays during congressional hearings. News accounts described events in other parts of the country as well. Extensive coverage was allotted to gay leaders meeting in New York and Kansas City to set a
national agenda and to Illinois becoming the first state to decriminalize
sodomy.[52]

The Ladder did not become an all-news publication, but Gittings as editor
and Lahusen as ace reporter emerged as a formidable journalistic duo. They
illustrated their professional ability during a 1964 conference of activists in
Washington. As the leaders prepared to begin a panel discussion on gays and
the church, a member of the American Nazi Party entered the conference
room. Relying on the instincts she had developed while at the *Christian
Science Monitor,* Lahusen quickly flipped on her tape recorder. The article she
wrote for *The Ladder* used the telegraphic style of a professional news reporter: "He is blond, good-looking, well-built, quietly dressed. He is self-
confident and smiling. He speaks with a southern accent. He carries a huge
pink gift-wrapped box marked QUEER CONVENTION." *The Ladder* printed
verbatim the transcript of the altercation Lahusen had recorded, complete
with the intruder's references to "kikes" and "queers." The newswoman followed
up on the story by reporting that the young Nazi was charged with disorderly
conduct and fined ten dollars.[53]

Another progressive step in the evolution of news involved the scope of
stories. By the mid-1960s, the publications began synthesizing information
about activities taking place in various cities across the country. So, instead of
writing independent articles about isolated events, *The Ladder, THC,* and
Drum began pulling material together to provide their readers with a broad,
national picture of trends that were developing. Because of the clipping service Polak employed, *Drum* was a leader in this practice. Polak wrote of the
monthly cache of articles sent by the service: "The clippings are first reviewed
as a group to determine what patterns exist. If any such trends are noted, all
clips in those categories are assembled together and a broader story is written."
An example of the kind of final product that emerged from Polak's analysis
was a roundup article summarizing the legislation that had been drafted in
various states around the country in efforts to decriminalize sodomy.[54]

The other two publications with a strong news orientation followed *Drum*'s lead. In June 1966 *The Ladder* published summaries of three separate court cases involving gay rights in California, New Jersey, and Florida, but rather than publishing separate articles, Gittings combined the information into a single article. A month later when gay people joined in the protests when the military draft was reinstated, Vincenz at the *Homosexual Citizen* opted not to run separate articles about demonstrations in five cities but to create a single article synthesizing the protests from New York to San Francisco. The article, which carried the headline "Nationwide Attack on Draft Injustices," not only suggested gay people were of one mind on the issue, but also that they represented a force of considerable political power.[55]

While news items were neither flowery in style nor hysterical in tone, they adhered to the advocacy tradition established by the early-nineteenth-century African-American press and maintained by the twentieth-century feminist press. In short, writers saw news columns as an appropriate arena for interpretation. Rather than simply reporting that residents of Brooklyn Heights, New York, were attempting to force gays out of their neighborhood, *THC*, for example, characterized the residents as "initiating a vendetta" against gay residents. Likewise, in an article about the FBI, Nichols referred to agents as "Federal Bedbugging Investigators." *Citizens News* was particularly prone to editorializing. The final statement in its coverage of White House picketing read "New attacks are planned on the very harsh and unwarranted treatment of the homosexual by the federal government."[56]

On the rare occasions when the new militancy led to immediate judicial victory, the journalists did not refrain from pointing out the progress that could occur when gays asserted their rights. In 1966 New York gay activists made advance reservations at a Washington hotel but then, when they arrived, were refused accommodations. When they filed a discrimination suit and won a $500 out-of-court settlement, Kameny wrote boastfully of the incident: "It demonstrates, clearly, that homosexuals are not going to tolerate abrogation of their rights, or treatment as second-class persons. The Manger-Hamilton [Hotel] apparently felt that a formal contract, entered into with a homophile organization, could be violated with impunity. They have been shown otherwise."[57]

Turning the Tables on the Establishment Media

While such developments were the stuff of headlines in lesbian and gay monthlies, daily newspapers largely ignored them. Neither the *New York Times* nor the *Kansas City Star* covered the national gay planning conferences in their respective cities, even though the events marked the largest meetings of homosexuals

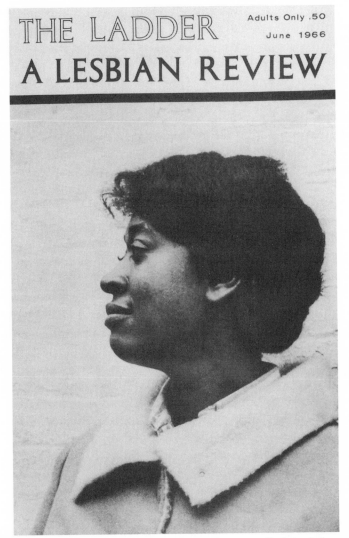

THE LADDER   Adults Only .50
                    June 1966
A LESBIAN REVIEW

The Ladder's *featuring Ernestine Eckstein as a "cover girl" showed the commit-ment the early lesbian press felt toward diversity.* Courtesy of Barbara Gittings. Photo by Kay Tobin Lahusen.

in American history. Neither the *Washington Post* nor the *Washington Evening Star* covered the White House or Pentagon demonstrations in 1965, and the *Los Angeles Times* ignored a massive raid on the city's gay bars on New Year's Eve in 1966.[58]

Gradually, though, what gay journalists of the time called the "conspiracy of silence" began to yield to a curiosity about the mysterious and exotic world of homosexuality. Even the ultraconservative FBI began to acknowledge that if it had any hope of controlling homosexuals, it was going to have to try to understand them. A 1962 report to Hoover included some bizarre information about gay men of the era—information so inaccurate that it must have been as unfamiliar to gay FBI agents as to straight ones. The report stated that every homosexual man wore a diamond ring on the little finger of his right hand and when a homosexual referred to his "mother" he was speaking of his first sex partner. The report ended by defining several words. It stated that a "gay" was a man who "goes only with known homosexuals"; while a "homosexual" was "one who picks up and propositions persons who are not homosexuals."[59]

The smattering of articles that began appearing in the country's leading publications were not as inaccurate as the FBI's information, but they certainly painted an unflattering portrait. On the other hand, the coverage at least acknowledged that homosexuality existed. In 1963, the *New York Times* published an alarmist front-page article titled "Growth of Overt Homosexuality in City Provokes Wide Concern." In 1964 *Life* magazine featured a titillating ten-page glimpse into gay life—including a photograph and quotes from *ONE* editor Don Slater. In 1965 a five-part series on the front page of the *Washington Post* took readers on a voyeuristic tour of the haunts frequented by gay men. In 1966 *Time* magazine vilified homosexuality, writing, "It deserves no encouragement, no glamorization, no rationalization, no fake status as minority martyrdom, no sophistry about simple differences in taste—and, above all, no pretense that it is anything but a pernicious sickness."[60]

As such denigrating articles began to appear in the most widely circulated publications in the country, journalists working in the movement press grew increasingly concerned with the negative tone of mainstream coverage. So lesbian and gay editors began to use their knowledge of journalistic conventions to analyze articles appearing in establishment publications, alerting their readers to the techniques the establishment news media were using to send negative messages about homosexuality.

In response to the *Time* essay, *The Ladder* published a scathing letter to the editor by Kameny—a letter *Time* refused to print. In his haughty style, Kameny wrote: "The entire essay is pervaded by loose, superficial reasoning used to justify pre-determined conclusions, and by a dread of seeing change in an outmoded and gravely harmful status quo." *Life* magazine's biased article prompted Lahusen to write: "Those homosexuals who are quiet-living, constructive people get short shrift in the *Life* article. The most sensationalistic touch was the big chunk of space devoted to depicting police entrapment techniques."[61]

The most remarkable rebuke of establishment press coverage was *The Ladder's* detailed critique of the front-page *New York Times* article. The author walked his readers through the *Times* piece paragraph by paragraph, dissecting each phrase. The analysis read: "From a journalistic viewpoint, this passage is shocking. 'A homosexual who had achieved good progress toward cure through psychoanalysis' (note the plug for analysis, the pat-on-the-back air of 'good progress,' the implication that here is a worthy witness because he's going to the doctor to be cured) 'recently told his analyst' (unnamed even though he is being cited as an authority). This is news reporting?"[62]

Drum, in keeping with its commitment to amusing its readers as well as informing them, employed hyperbole to poke fun at the establishment media's outlandish treatment of gay subjects. After *Life* published its "Homosexuality in America" article, Polak printed an article—under the name "P. Arody"—titled "Heterosexuality in America." He wrote: "Heterosexuality shears across the spectrum of American life—the professions, the arts, business and labor. It always has. But today, especially in big cities, heterosexuals are openly admitting, even flaunting, their deviation."[63]

The entertainment-oriented publications responded to critical articles not with analysis or satire, but with screams. Shortly after the *Life* article appeared, *Citizens News* ran a front-page piece headlined "Life Bigotry" in which it denounced the magazine for attacking homosexuals as a means of maintaining the financial status of its owner, "Saint" Clare Boothe Luce. The publication was not so foolhardy, however, as to think that such attacks would have any real effect. The *Citizens News* ended its article with the colorful metaphor: "The Citizens News commenting on LIFE is as a belch in a cyclone, but at least we got it off our stomach."[64]

Building a Lesbian and Gay Community

The magazines of the 1960s, building on the work of their predecessors of the previous decade, continued to progress toward galvanizing their readers into a unified political body. Gay people vary widely with respect to factors such as age, socioeconomic level, education, and geographic location. And yet, in order for progress to be made, these diverse individuals ultimately must coalesce to form a single community. As one scholar of social movements wrote: "A pressing rhetorical problem for aggregates of individuals moving towards a sense of community is the creation of a common identity. People create a common consciousness by becoming aware that they are involved in an identifiable group and that their group differs in some important respects from other groups. To come to such awareness, the members need to identify their collective self." Scholars have identified the 1960s as the time during which this process advanced markedly among gay people as the movement went from minuscule to mass in a single decade, although lesbians remained largely segregated from gay men. Those same scholars have repeatedly pointed to the era's publications, which also remained largely segregated along the gender fault line, as pivotal in this process.[65]

The most dramatic contribution to building a unified gay community through the press has been credited to *Vector*. Historian John D'Emilio wrote of the magazine, "Its success rested in no small part on its willingness to acknowledge that the bars played a central role in the lives of many urban homosexuals and constituted the one site where large numbers of otherwise scattered, invisible gay men gathered." Rather than denigrate the gay bar culture as *Mattachine Review* and *The Ladder* had done in the 1950s, *Vector* embraced the culture and celebrated its ability to equalize persons of diverse social strata. Indeed, the magazine rightly identified gay bars as central to the growth of the movement.[66]

Vector placed news about the bars on its front page, listed the names and addresses of the dozens of bars in cities around the country, and made sure copies of each issue were available in every bar in San Francisco. The most daring of Bill May's bar-culture innovations was a monthly column summarizing activities in the gay nightspots up and down the West Coast. "From the very first column, the readers loved it," the editor recently recalled. "It was an instant hit, definitely the most popular page in the magazine." Signed by "Tequila Mockingbird," the "Bar Tour" column was written in a lively and colorful style that virtually seduced readers into San Francisco's gay fast lane. A typical item read: "Rarely do we have an establishment of the scale and magnitude of Leonarda's open for our pleasure and entertainment. We first became aware of Leonarda's with their ad in last month's VECTOR. The ad sent us scurrying to our city map to find out just where Leland Avenue is. Leonarda's bar is an intimate, tasteful place."[67]

While journalistic purists would dismiss such writing as blatantly violating the conventional separation between news content and advertising, the column seemed perfectly appropriate in the context of the magazine's commitment to encouraging social activities as political acts. Gay dances, hiking trips, and theater activities dominated the front page; snippets of gossip and entertainment news dotted inside pages. *Vector* reinforced the importance of gay community with monthly editorial statements such as "The individual dedication to oneself must grow into a dedication to our groups; our group dedication to all homo-sexuals' plight." And in 1965 the staff further demonstrated its commitment to building a community by using its pages to promote a campaign that ultimately led to San Francisco establishing the country's first gay community center.[68]

Second only to *Vector* in community building was *Drum*. Polak believed that gays feeling alone and isolated in an unfriendly society magnified the need for gay organizations to create programs similar to those offered by civic and church groups. The editor insisted: "Shortsightedness in not providing such programs and services is generally based on the notion that the achievement of the move-ment's ends rests on homosexuals appearing as heterosexual as possible. Such defensiveness, in itself, both causes and sustains anti-homosexual sentiments."[69]

Drum also supported the bar culture, with Polak praising the gay bar as a social melting pot for Gay America. Himself a frequent patron of bars in Philadelphia and Washington, he knew men of all socioeconomic levels came together in bars because they offered the only public refuge from an unaccept-ing world. Polak wrote, "The gay bar is the only consistently and readily avail-able homosexual gathering place." *Drum* championed the bar scene by running features such as a three-part "Beginner's Guide to Cruising." The series con-tained practical, shoot-from-the-hip advice such as "Stay away from the lad who is always superbly dressed. He is interested in himself and in his impact on other men, not in you."[70]

Cruise News & World Report and *Citizens News* contained copious material to help build a sense of community among their readers. Articles were written in a chatty, informal style that made readers feel as though they were having a casual conversation with the writers. Page 1 of the premier issue of *Cruise News* carried a warning that began: "The matter contained herein is not lewd nor ob-scene but it might have some reference to sex." The item continued for three more sentences before finally letting the reader know it was to be taken with one's tongue firmly in cheek: "This warning is intended to sell more copies of this publication because, frankly, it is rather dull."[71]

San Francisco's fading gay publication, *Mattachine Review,* contributed little to the construction of a gay community in the city. Indeed, editor Hal Call seemed to work *against* building any such network of support. While other les-bian and gay journalists were marching on the country's most powerful institu-tions, Call told the mainstream *San Francisco News-Call,* "Believe me, we aren't trying to build some pressure group." When Call claimed that the Mattachine Society spoke for the country's fifteen million homosexuals, the reporter ques-tioned how that was possible when the society's membership had dwindled to 225. Call's response again demonstrated that he remained firmly planted in the self-denigrating 1950s. Call said: "We must admit we're doing a poor job at reaching our community."[72]

Anyone reading *The Ladder* or *Homosexual Citizen* could not possibly have agreed with Call's assessment. The magazines provided readers with a support system as those individuals struggled to survive in a society that forbade their very existence. This support system is well illustrated by the magazines' sensitive treatment of one of the most traumatic experiences in a gay person's life—coming out. In the 1960s gay people could not turn to the mainstream media for guidance on this anxiety-filled topic, but they could turn to their own magazines, which broached the subject with empathy and diplomacy. In *THC* Vincenz counseled readers about revealing their sexual orientation to parents: "The 'cold turkey' treatment is recommended only for the strong and courageous; it is a blunt delivery of the truth and abruptly divests parents of their comforting illusions about our heterosexuality. Not all parents can withstand this shock. A more gentle approach may be desirable. Preliminary preparation for breaking the news is helpful." Vincenz, who today is a professional psychotherapist, devoted the next three pages to giving her readers examples of "preliminary preparation," much of the material coming from her own trial and error.[73]

Nichols also shared personal experiences from earlier in his life. The son of an FBI agent who could not accept having a gay son, Nichols had felt such shame about the sexual feelings he had toward men that he had, at the age of thirteen, swallowed 100 aspirins in a suicide attempt. Nichols said: "After that, I knew if I was going to develop internal integrity, I had to accept myself as healthy, not sick. The mental attitude of our own people toward ourselves as less than healthy was responsible for untold numbers of personal tragedies. We had to douse the sickness allegation." Insisting that homosexuality was perfectly healthy, therefore, became a consistent theme in Nichols's journalistic work as he dotted *THC*'s pages with straightforward statements such as "Homosexuality is not an illness," and "That is utter nonsense."[74]

The journalists were relentless in urging readers to discard any remnants of passivity. Month after month, they implored readers—usually with a tapping finger, sometimes with a sledge hammer—not to hide in the closet or accept oppression. Vincenz set the standard in her initial editorial: "Negroes are stepping forward to claim their just rights and are showing the way for other invisible men and women to emerge from the shadows to share the rights and responsibilities that are part of the American heritage. The day will come when the homosexual can openly play his role as a first-class citizen free of fear and discrimination. Let us help lead the way!"[75]

Staff members advised readers on such topics as how to deal with threats from blackmailers and how to respond during police interrogations. *Vector* collected donations from bar owners to publish 10,000 copies of "Know Your Rights," writing, "The information contained in this pamphlet can save everyone who uses it hundreds of dollars and a life of misery."[76]

Another device the magazines developed to build a sense of community with their readers also became one of their most popular features—personal advice columns. Typical were the plaintive words in *Drum* written by a lesbian living in Mississippi, one of the few women who wrote to the magazine: "I love sports and I hate high heels. This has created a variety of problems. All thru my life there has been pressure on me to try to disguise my masculinity. Often I feel uncomfortable and, frankly, I'm not sure what to do." Polak's response was at once supportive and constructive: "Each of us must come to terms with herself, finding acceptance within her own mind before thinking of whether she wants others' acceptance. If a woman is more comfortable in dungarees, hammering together a house for her dog, perhaps she should avoid situations which compromise her image of herself."[77]

The Ladder further supported its readers by publishing lengthy testimonials by women who were succeeding both professionally and personally while living openly as lesbians. A standing feature, called "Living Propaganda," subtly communicated that lesbians could prosper and thrive, both individually and as a community, if they accepted their sexuality. The series was written by Barbara Grier, a woman who would have profound impact on the evolution of the lesbian press. Gittings also contributed to the growing sense of a lesbian community by establishing a college scholarship for lesbian students.[78]

Throughout their written work, the activists/journalists used the power of the press not to complain about their minority status, but to celebrate it. In a letter to a contributor, Vincenz wrote: "Glory be to God for dappled things. Let's enjoy our differences and eccentricities instead of suppressing them. By affirming what is our own—our idiosyncrasies, our special way of thinking or feeling—we can reach through to others."[79]

Editorial Disputes

Despite such positive statements, a sea change in editorial philosophy as drastic as the one experienced by the lesbian and gay press between the 1950s and 1960s was neither painless nor without controversy. Several magazines suffered internal disagreements that proved fatal; others survived only by reshaping themselves into less militant forms.

Although *ONE* had been the most progressive magazine of the 1950s, it failed to embrace the new militancy. Therefore its ideological discussions lacked the bite that direct-action protests—and the news and editorial coverage of them—carried. Circulation peaked at 5,000 in 1960 and then dropped to 3,000 by 1965. *ONE* also suffered from severe differences of opinion within its staff. From the founding of ONE, Inc., in 1953, W. Dorr Legg had not only directed the corporation with an iron hand, but also had been its major financial benefactor. Legg's primary interest was not in publishing the magazine, however, but in building the organization's library. The acerbic Legg constantly disagreed with *ONE* editor Don Slater about the allocation of resources and Slater's insistence upon maintaining high quality in the publication. During the early 1960s, Legg increasingly tried to control the editorial content of the magazine, even though his official title was business manager.[80]

By 1965 Slater had had enough. He recently recalled: "I couldn't take anymore of Dorr's autocracy with regard to the magazine. So I heisted the damn thing. One night I just went in and stole everything from the office, including the mailing list." Slater then continued publishing *ONE*—as did Legg. In fact, in one of the more bizarre moments in the history of the gay press, each month from May until October 1965, two entirely different magazines were published under the title *ONE*. Legg went to court and, as director of the corporation, won the exclusive right to the name. Slater, who was allowed to keep the office equipment, then renamed his magazine *Tangents*.[81]

Both magazines continued to be published from Los Angeles during the second half of the decade. *Tangents* ultimately became the superior of the two in substance as well as design, with Legg placing the publication of *ONE* beneath other priorities of the corporation. Kepner recalled: "Dorr had no interest in editorial quality. It would have been fine with him simply to reprint the phone book." Ironically, Legg agreed with that critical assessment—without apology. When told of Kepner's comments, Legg responded: "Jim's right. The *ONE* I edited was of despicably poor quality. I was building the finest library and educational institution for homophile studies the world would ever know. I had no interest in the publication." With neither *ONE* nor *Tangents* at the forefront of the movement, editors of the militant publications made light of the dueling *ONE*s. Polak wrote: "It seems that Don Slater, editor or ex-editor, according to where you stand, made off with the goodies. Now there are two magazines. Round and round the old lady goes, and where she stops, nobody knows—but one thing for sure is that the homophile movement can do without such goings on."[82]

Yet that was only the first of numerous editorial control disputes to plague the 1960s press. The next was at *The Ladder*. As Gittings used the publication to lead the movement toward its assertive stance, her relationship with the Daughters of Bilitis leadership became increasingly acrimonious. One specific disagreement surrounded the words *for adults only,* which had appeared on the cover throughout the magazine's history. As part of her revamping, Gittings wanted to remove the disclaimer. "It was useless," she recently pointed out. "If the post office decided the material was obscene, those words would not have helped one wit. I saw no reason to hide behind words, especially when they had no power. But DOB was still running scared—stuck in the past." At the time, Gittings had the magazine printed on the East Coast and then sent the printed copies to DOB headquarters in San Francisco to be distributed. So in January 1965 she simply removed the disclaimer from the cover, had the copies printed, and sent them west. When the magazines arrived, Phyllis Lyon and Del Martin were outraged. They chastised Gittings for making such a radical change without their approval and stamped *for adults only* on every copy before sending them out. After three years of such disputes, the old guard removed Gittings from the editor's chair and returned the editorial offices to San Francisco where Martin became editor.[83]

The *Homosexual Citizen* also suffered from internal conflicts. Throughout the publication's first seventeen issues, Vincenz had been given free rein to determine the editorial content of the magazine. After the May 1967 issue was published, however, Kameny and other members of the executive board of the Mattachine Society of Washington voted to reject an article Vincenz had already accepted for the next issue. The article involved astrology—a subject most astronomers, including Kameny, denounce. Vincenz thought the article's application of astrological interpretation to gay people would amuse readers; Kameny said the article was irrelevant to the magazine's goals. Kameny, a man who often considers being nice to be a waste of valuable time, refused to discuss the difference of opinion, rejecting the article without allowing Vincenz the opportunity to defend her decision. Kameny's unilateral action prompted Vincenz to resign from her editorship. Without Vincenz to tend to its production, *THC* never published another issue.[84]

Drum's fortunes were more impressive, although it, too, had to overcome severe difficulties. Polak initially established an attractive business relationship with Guild Press, a mail-order company that supplied erotic books and photographs to gay men in small towns all over the country. *Drum* published samples of the company's "tasteful" photographs, along with information about where readers could order additional—presumably *un*-tasteful—photographs. In exchange, Guild printed the magazine on its presses free of charge. The arrangement allowed *Drum* to attain the financial stability that had eluded other publications. In fact, it became the first financial success story in the history of the gay and lesbian press, providing a tidy profit for the Janus Society. But the financial arrangement lost its luster when Polak learned, in 1965, that Guild Press was printing several thousand extra copies of *Drum* each month and selling them on its own, pocketing the profits. Polak then severed his relationship with Guild Press and created Trojan Book Service, his own mail-order company that specialized in homoerotic photographs and books, which he promoted in the magazine.[85]

Homophobia continued to create impediments for the gay press as well. When Polak attempted to hire an editor to help him produce *Drum,* the *New York Times* and *Village Voice* both rejected the paid advertisement he submitted; when Strait tried to broaden the circulation of *Citizens News* by seeking subscribers in other cities, the *Dallas Morning News, New Orleans Times-Picayune,* and *Chicago Tribune* all rejected his ad as well. FBI agents frequently tracked the most militant of the journalists, even to the point of attending a panel discussion at American University in Washington, D.C., because Kameny and Polak were among the speakers. The editors also continued to struggle to market their magazines. Gittings tried to hire a professional magazine distributor, but none would touch a lesbian publication. So each month Gittings and Lahusen had to service the two Philadelphia bookstores and one New York newsstand they had persuaded to carry the magazine. "We had to deliver the copies at the beginning of the month and then go back and collect the unsold copies at the end of the month," Gittings said. "It was an enormous task, but of course we did it. We had no other option."[86]

Despite their daunting commitments of time and energy, none of the journalists received any payment. "It was a matter of budgeting every penny," Lahusen recalled. "Looking back, it's hard to see how we managed. But, still, I have no regrets. It was rewarding in a way that most jobs were not."[87]

"They Created the Mindset"

The period dominated by the new lesbian and gay militancy was brief. It was sandwiched between, on one side, the nonaggressive years that stretched throughout the 1950s and into the early 1960s, and, on the other side, the shift toward the youth counterculture of the late 1960s. A handful of publications defined the militant era, as the same leaders who organized the historic picketings simultaneously edited or wrote for the leading magazines. The beginning of the militant period is best dated to early 1963, when Barbara Gittings assumed the editorship of *The Ladder;* its end coincided with Gittings's removal from her position in the summer of 1966. It was during those three and a half years that the most important public demonstrations occurred—spreading from Washington to New York to Philadelphia, and then to the West Coast.

Other publications joined *The Ladder* at the forefront of the movement. Indeed, the *Homosexual Citizen* and *Drum* walked arm in arm with their assertive sister. While *Vector, Citizens News,* and *Cruise News & World Report* followed several steps behind the East Coast leaders, they too added unique dimensions to the new momentum that encouraged readers to join other oppressed minority groups in defying the American social order. At the same time that the magazines were shaking readers out of a resigned acceptance of the status quo, they also were actively engaged in defining a common ground for Lesbian and Gay America. In short, the handful of publications were coaxing their readers to take the first steps toward social revolution.

Although this brief period of militancy has been largely eclipsed by the dramatic events that erupted in the Stonewall Rebellion at the end of the 1960s, the era and the publications that led it played a crucial role in the evolution of the movement. In the self-assured words of Franklin E. Kameny: "It was very much a continuum. Expressing our outrage in those early publications laid the psychological groundwork for what was to come. *The Ladder,* the *Homosexual Citizen, Drum*—they created the mindset. Everything builds on everything else. If we had not aroused the consciousness of gay people, it is very likely that Stonewall would not have occurred. We simply would not have had the riot at the Stonewall Inn had it not been for the work that was initiated by the militant gay press of the mid-60s."[88]

When the publications are considered in the context of social movement presses, the mid-1960s marked the rise of several important themes. That the publications promoted picketing was reminiscent of nineteenth-century African-American newspapers being a driving force in the rise of protests against racial injustice of the era, and of the women's liberation press consistently taking an activist approach. In addition, the editors of the movement publications also being leaders of the public protests coincided with a similar duality of roles between the editors of the early black press, women's suffrage press, and women's liberation press and the movements they represented. Finally, the lesbian and gay press covering events from a specialized perspective unique to their readers paralleled the same theme prominent among African-American, women's suffrage, and women's liberation publications.[89]

By the mid-1960s, however, even more important than gay magazines imitating other movement presses was that this new genre of alternative media was developing characteristics distinct unto itself. Scholars have not identified these themes as playing significant roles in the printed voices that have served other social movements, but there is no question that they were helping, by this period, to define the lesbian and gay press.

One such theme that surfaced in the mid-1960s was the importance of visual images. When Barbara Gittings and Kay Lahusen boldly placed photographs of beautiful lesbians on the cover of *The Ladder,* they transformed those images into a political statement. Bill May followed their lead in *Vector* when he published photographs of happy, smiling men engaged in such enjoyable social activities as gay dances and drag shows. Both sets of images were breakthroughs for Lesbian and Gay America, as they shattered the stereotypes of lesbians as unattractive and gay men as doomed to lives of loneliness and despair.

Another distinctive theme of the mid-1960s magazines was that of making a determined effort to build a lesbian and gay community. Although both movement and mainstream presses have been credited with reflecting the values of the communities they serve, they have not played the proactive role of actually *constructing* a community. Yet that was exactly what *The Ladder, Homosexual Citizen, Drum, Vector, Citizens News,* and *Cruise News & World Report* did. Gay people are a self-identifying minority group. In other words, a gay person, unlike an African American or a woman, must come to recognize that his or her attraction for the same sex determines that he or she is homosexual and, therefore, a member of a minority group. Particularly during the 1960s when virtually all of American society felt contempt for homosexuality, women and men with same-sex desires turned to movement publications to help them understand both their own feelings and the largely invisible minority group to which they rightly belonged. Editorial elements such as advice columns and articles about coming out provided a vital service to lesbian and gay readers, gently ushering them into the national gay community that was emerging.

Not all of the themes unique to the gay press are positive ones. One such problematic theme is the symbiotic relationship that was developing between gay publications and homoerotic images. *ONE* hinted at the issue during the 1950s when the first paid advertisement it published contained suggestive sexual images, followed a month later by the magazine being hauled into court. In the mid-1960s, the theme was raised again when *Drum* editor Clark P. Polak established what initially was a financially lucrative arrangement with a mail-order company willing to print the magazine in return for free promotional advertisements for its homoerotic photographs. After less than a year, Polak learned the relationship was not the idyllic one he had presumed, however, when he discovered that the company had been exploiting the relationship.

Other editors were to learn the same difficult lesson in the turbulent decades ahead, as they learned time and time again that it was not easy for the gay and lesbian press to earn a financial profit while maintaining moral and professional integrity.

A second problematic theme was illustrated by the editorial disputes that ended Gittings's editorship of *The Ladder*, destroyed the *Homosexual Citizen*, and imperiled the future of *ONE*. These incidents provided early examples of a debilitating force that would continue to disrupt the smooth operation of the genre. Internal staff conflicts, turf battles, and bitter infighting were to become a recurring chapter—often the final one—in the histories of dozens of publications. Like the Lesbian and Gay Liberation Movement itself, the press that served that movement would constantly struggle against internal acrimony. W. Dorr Legg observed: "There's no question about it. Queens are their own worst enemies. Put two of them together and ask them a question. You've got a cat fight. They'll claw each other's eyes out over who has the better quiche recipe."[90]

λ 4

Connecting with the Counterculture

During the late 1960s, two factors created an estranged American youth culture that was unprecedented in size, visibility, and impact. The first was a demographic bulge in the population as the percentage of young adults swelled. This surge in the youth population marked the beginning of the influence that the baby boomers, Americans born during the period of economic vitality following World War II, would have on the political fabric of this country. The second factor was a growing despair among America's young people as their idealistic dreams for change were shattered by an increasingly unpopular war and a series of assassinations that claimed the lives of three of the nation's most gifted and revered heroes—John F. Kennedy, Robert F. Kennedy, and the Reverend Martin Luther King, Jr. Dreams of a better world evaporated as college campuses erupted with discontent and violence, police bashed the heads of political outsiders, and urban centers went up in flames. Disillusioned by these events, throngs of young people followed the lead of the beatniks of the 1950s and "dropped out" of mainstream society to create the largest youth counterculture in American history.

The lesbian and gay press reflected the times. Barbara Grier, who became editor of *The Ladder* in 1968, recently recalled: "The whole world seemed to be spinning out of control. Those of us who remained sure that the pen was the mightiest of human forces sought security in publishing. At *The Ladder,* we were convinced that we were saving the world for the lesbians of the future."[1]

Gay publications adopted many of the same themes that came to define the youth rebellion. In particular, the new sexual freedom that was a hallmark of the Counterculture Movement fit in snugly with gay liberation. The New Left emphasis on "free love" and sexual exploration accepted male-to-male and female-to-female sexual activity as had no social movement before it. In addition, widened dissemination of the birth control pill ended the pretense that heterosexuality was superior to homosexuality because the purpose of straight intercourse was to procreate. Sex became a major element in the gay and, to a lesser extent, lesbian press. With a stylish bravado, gay male journalists seized the moment to escalate their discussion of topics such as promiscuity and anonymous sex, while gay male as well as lesbian journalists broke new boundaries in the publication of homoerotic images.

It was not coincidental that the most salient editorial voices of the era were located in the cities most closely connected with the "youthquake." The most memorable of them was a groundbreaking column written by gay press veterans Jack Nichols and Lige Clarke. Leaving the stuffiness of the nation's capital far behind, the lovers joined the Counterculture Movement and created an innovative new type of gay press outlet. Their "Homosexual Citizen" column in *Screw,* a raunchy sex tabloid, reflected the values of the couple's new environs of New York's bohemian Greenwich Village—a hub of nonconformity that was soon to become the site of an event of seismic proportion in the history of gay liberation.

The second most visible editorial voice was based 2,000 miles away in another of the centers of the counterculture. The *Los Angeles Advocate* became the genre's first true newspaper, destined to evolve into the largest publication in the history of the gay press. Los Angeles also produced gay journalism's first attempt at an erudite publication, *Pursuit & Symposium,* as well as continuing to serve as home to the patriarch of gay publishing, *ONE,* and its offspring, *Tangents.*

San Francisco, the third epicenter of the youth rebellion, remained a focal point of gay journalism, with *The Ladder* reflecting the changing values of Lesbian America, and five publications attempting to do the same for the city's burgeoning population of gay men. *Mattachine Review, Vector, Citizens News,* and *Cruise News & World Report* were joined by *Town Talk,* which focused very specifically on capturing the essence—and the advertising potential—of the bar scene in the country's gay mecca.

Philadelphia's *Drum,* although not located in one of the centers of the counterculture, also continued to push the envelope, as it had in the mid-1960s, by combining militant editorial content with increasingly explicit homoerotic images.

These media outlets set a frenetic pace as Gay and Lesbian America lunged toward the explosive Stonewall Rebellion that was to signal the end of one decade and blast the movement into the next. The youthful population preferred the term *gay* to *homosexual. Gay* came to represent a commitment to personal and social change, as well as a lifestyle—a personality and identity that marked a proud, self-determined social and political territory. *Homosexual,* on the other hand, stood for repression and a lack of gay consciousness. Along with celebrating the sexual revolution in their pages, the publications embraced other prominent themes of the day as well. In keeping with the elevation of nonconformity, they stretched the limits of conventional newspaper design in new directions while also revolutionizing the language of journalism—not only with the liberal use of sexually explicit terms but also with the creation of a unique lexicon shared only with their readers. And, finally, the publications used the social liberalism that defined the era to forge an intriguing blend of personalized journalism and editorial defiance.

These new themes clearly appealed to readers. By tapping into the New York market and making history as the first overtly gay-oriented material featured in a straight-oriented newspaper, the "Homosexual Citizen" column dwarfed the circulation figures of its predecessors. By mid-1969, the column boasted a circulation of 150,000. On the West Coast, the *Los Angeles Advocate* was setting records of its own, doubling the circulation of any gay publication before it. When the figures for the magazines in Los Angeles, San Francisco, and Philadelphia were added to that of the *Advocate,* in mid-1969—on the eve of the Stonewall Rebellion—the circulation of the gay and lesbian press surpassed 55,000. If the circulation of the "Homosexual Citizen" column in *Screw* were added, the figure jumped to 200,000. In less than half a decade, from 1965 to mid-1969, the circulation of this emerging form of alternative journalism had increased a staggering tenfold. The gay press most assuredly had taken a huge leap forward.[2]

It was also during this era that Gay and Lesbian America broke into the electronic media. In April 1969 "New Symposium" debuted on WBAI, the New York station in the nonprofit Pacifica radio network. Barbara Gittings was a driving force behind the radio program on which host Baird Searles declared his love for men and then invited listeners to call in to talk about issues such as gay sex and gay relations—two months *before* Stonewall.[3]

The "Homosexual Citizen" Hits the Sidewalks of New York

Jack Nichols and Lige Clarke met and became lovers in Washington, D.C., in 1964. A year later, Nichols organized the first gay picket line at the White House, and Clarke lettered signs for the marchers. The couple entered journalism the next year, writing for the *Homosexual Citizen.* But in 1967, Nichols and Clarke, like the gay press as a whole, were transformed. After Clarke completed his military service, he moved to the Lower East Side of Manhattan and worked as a model and yoga instructor. Clarke was a blond, lithe, twenty-five-year-old who was so handsome that he turned heads even at the trendiest of bars—gay or straight. Nichols joined Clarke in the Village, the very eye of the counterculture. They revamped their wardrobes, let their hair grow to their shoulders, and experimented with new types of sexual activity as well as with numerous forms of drugs.

Nichols and Clarke's new journalistic outlet was fully in sync with their rebellion against the dominant culture. Shortly after Nichols began editing true-confession magazines for a publishing company, a coworker named Al Goldstein asked Nichols and Clarke if they would like to write a gay column for a sex-oriented tabloid he was in the process of creating. They agreed, but they objected to Goldstein's proposed title for the column: "Cornhole Corner." Recalling the name of the magazine that had launched their journalistic work in Washington, they opted for the more dignified "Homosexual Citizen." Their byline read "Lige and Jack," with no surnames.

Screw, arguably the most vulgar and sexually explicit newspaper in the history of publishing, hit the streets of Manhattan in November 1968. Editorial content included reviews of X-rated films, a personal ads section called "Cocks & Cunts," and a two-page center spread featuring full-frontal nudity of half a dozen men and women frolicking in Central Park. Goldstein began his publication as a biweekly with a press run of 7,000. But the racy tabloid took fire and, after only six months, soared to its 150,000-circulation figure.[4]

The "Homosexual Citizen" was simultaneously making its own history—and a much more savory one, at that. Never before had openly gay men written about gay lifestyles for a publication aimed primarily toward straights. Nichols recently recalled: "Al got high on being 'the first' of anything. He would have been happier if we had written more lurid stuff, but we insisted on substance."[5] The premier edition of the column, which filled the back cover of the twelve-page tabloid, endorsed Hubert H. Humphrey in the upcoming presidential election. Later columns documented contributions gay people had made to world history, took readers into the exotic life of gay hustlers, and criticized the film industry's degrading portrayals of gays. News items appeared only occasionally, as brief items tacked onto the end of a column and labeled "Gay News Flash." One item announced that New York college students, for the first time in American history, were planning a dance exclusively for gay students; another promoted a local art gallery that sold homoerotica.[6]

Nichols and Clarke devoted an entire column to another daring business venture that made more history for Gay America. The Oscar Wilde Memorial Bookshop in the heart of Greenwich Village stocked a full range of lesbian and gay publications, making it the first such operation in the country. Previously, people had defined gay bookstores as "porn shops." After Craig Rodwell invested $1,000 of his personal savings to open his business in 1967, that definition no longer applied. Instead, the bookstore became an unofficial gay community center, though that status also meant that its windows were smashed and Rodwell received numerous bomb threats. In their column, Nichols and Clarke pulled out all the stops to praise Rodwell, who also advertised in *Screw:* "It takes guts to open a business and base one's cash and credit on books to be sold for public enlightenment about our 'shadowy,' 'furtive,' and 'much-feared' group. And yet that is precisely what Craig Rodwell, an enterprising and idealistic young man, has done." Nichols and Clarke went on to catalog the types of books Rodwell stocked, list the address and telephone number for the shop, and even describe the front window: "A bright little sign announces unashamedly that 'Gay Is Good.'"[7]

Nichols and Clarke's consistent portrayal of homosexuality in a positive light gave their readers a welcome escape from the negative view dominating most public discourse on the topic. In one column, they recalled their animated response when asked if they regretted not being straight. "The only answer we've got to this question is based on our present life together," they wrote. "We're having a ball!" Even when writing on the most serious of topics, the gregarious couple maintained an upbeat tone while simultaneously expressing a defiant pride in being gay. After expressing incredulity that people merely accused of committing homosexual acts were barred from jobs with the federal government, the columnists wrote: "We who differ from the majority in our sexual preferences are judged as a group or class rather than on our own individual merits. This is contrary to the principle on which our nation is founded." Because most of *Screw*'s readers were heterosexual, such statements allowed Nichols and Clarke to expose many of their readers to the oppression gay people felt.[8]

At the same time, the youthful lovers believed the gay press sometimes took itself too seriously. So the columnists mixed their substantive comments with humor and wit, always making sure their prose was a pleasure to read—and filled with surprises. In a column characterizing the Bible as sexually repressive, they wrote: "The *Bible* is anti-sexual from start to finish. Its first curse is a sexual one, leveled at poor Eve for the 'crime' of curiosity (Can you hear us, Eve? We'd have tasted the apple, too!)"[9]

Goldstein initially paid Nichols and Clarke five dollars a week to write their column, but, as *Screw* became a publishing sensation, they asked for more money. Nichols recalled: "The trouble is, we could never really *document* how many gay people were buying the paper strictly because of our column. We knew a lot were because they told us, but we couldn't prove it." Goldstein eventually relented and raised their salary to fifteen dollars.[10]

The *Los Angeles Advocate* Becomes America's First Gay Newspaper

The second major addition to the gay press during the era was the *Los Angeles Advocate,* founded in September 1967. The *Advocate* became the country's first true gay newspaper. Like *Drum* and the *Homosexual Citizen* before it, the *Advocate* published only nonfiction. The Los Angeles monthly shifted into a newspaper format, however, by abandoning the scholarly journal style and publishing first on eight-and-a-half-by-eleven-inch paper and then as a tabloid on newsprint. The *Advocate* also was the first publication to operate as a commercial business that paid staff members and was financed entirely by advertising and circulation revenue, completely independent of any membership organization. Renamed *The Advocate* in May 1970, it was transformed into a gay lifestyles magazine in 1975 and today is a slick biweekly magazine.[11]

The *Los Angeles Advocate* evolved from *PRIDE Newsletter,* which had been published by Personal Rights in Defense and Education, a gay organization that orchestrated rallies and protests against police brutality in Los Angeles. When Richard T. Mitch, a member of PRIDE, was appointed editor, he renamed the newsletter. And as the organization began to disband in early 1968, Mitch persuaded his lover, Bill Rau, and another friend, Sam Winston, to continue publishing the *Advocate* as a commercial newspaper. They paid PRIDE one dollar for the paper. Throughout his quarter century at the forefront of gay journalism, Mitch was known by the pseudonym Dick Michaels. Born in Rochester, New York, in 1926, Michaels worked on his high school and college newspapers. He earned a doctoral degree in chemistry from the University of Notre Dame and worked as a scientific researcher, first for the U.S. Army and later for a private firm in Los Angeles. When he founded the *Advocate,* he was working as a technical writer for a chemistry magazine.[12]

The catalyst for Michaels's gay activism was his arrest in a Los Angeles bar in 1966. Because of that raid, the bar was forced to close and several patrons were fired from their jobs. Michaels paid $600 in legal fees before being found not guilty. He later recounted the details of his arrest: "Vice cops came in and arrested twelve people. I was one of those tapped on the back. I was charged with a misdemeanor, lewd conduct—and I hadn't done a damned thing! Up to that time, I'd always said to friends, 'If you're not doing anything wrong, nothing's going to happen to you.' But after my arrest, I knew there was something radically rotten going on. There probably wouldn't be any *Advocate* if it were not for that one tap on the back." After the incident, Michaels committed his energies to fighting gay oppression. "One of the principal things any movement needs is a press of its own, a newspaper," he said before he died in 1991. "Without that, you can't inform people of what's going on. You can't tie together widespread elements."[13]

News stories dominated the twelve-page monthly. Michaels said, "All of our resources were directed toward what the straight press wouldn't print, and what gay people needed to know about what was happening in the world." Although the *Advocate*'s forte was hard news, it also contained personal columns, editorials, book and film reviews, and an activities calendar. Nichols and Clarke began writing a "New York Notes" column for the *Advocate* in early 1969.[14]

Michaels invested several thousand dollars of his savings in the offset newspaper. He kept expenses low because Rau worked in the mailroom at the Los Angeles offices of the ABC Television Network and surreptitiously printed the first several issues on the printing press there. Michaels initially took copies to the city's gay bars, but when newsstand operators saw there was a demand for the paper, they agreed to begin stocking it.[15]

And demand there was. By the *Los Angeles Advocate*'s first birthday, the original press run of 500 had jumped to 5,500, and Michaels had moved the operation out of his apartment and into its own office. In June 1969 Michaels resigned from his magazine job to work full-time on the *Advocate*. By the paper's second birthday that September, circulation had risen to 23,000, and copies were being distributed in Chicago, New York, Boston, Washington, and Miami.[16]

Advertising soared as well. The first issue carried twenty-seven-dollars' worth of ads, only twelve dollars of which was ever collected. But by the end of the first year, ads were bringing in several hundred dollars an issue. The largest were from mail-order companies specializing in homoerotic books and films. Smaller ads promoted local bars and restaurants catering to gay patrons. Bar ads gradually became a major presence in the pages, and by mid-1968 advertising revenue rose to the point that Michaels hired a part-time ad salesman.[17]

Some authors who have made passing reference to the gay press have characterized the *Advocate* as being interested in making a financial profit rather than in supporting the movement. There is no evidence, however, that such was the case during the newspaper's early years. Jim Kepner, who reported for the *Advocate* during that time, insists that Michaels's profit-making interests were secondary: "Dick definitely started the newspaper as a movement effort. He was angry at how we were being treated. He was determined to improve the gay man's status in society."[18]

Reflecting Counterculture Values

The youth rebellion played a central role in the evolution of lesbian and gay liberation. "Development of the counterculture on America's streets and campuses was an essential condition of the gay revolution," Laud Humphreys said in his book *Out of the Closets!* "It supplied special skills, an ideology, and the necessary reinforcement to increase autonomy for the youthful gays." The Counterculture Movement was particularly important because its members tended to be in their teens or early twenties, while lesbian and gay leaders of the 1950s and early 1960s had been in their late twenties or thirties. Connecting with the counterculture added a youthful vibrancy to the movement.[19]

The "Homosexual Citizen" column provided gay journalism's strongest reflection of the social liberalism that defined Greenwich Village during the period, mirroring the life experiences of its authors. Clarke led the couple's personal transformation by incorporating health foods, yoga, and Eastern philosophy into their lives. Nichols was older and the changes were somewhat harder for him, but he followed his lover's lead. How Clarke and Nichols were transformed between the mid- and late 1960s was dramatically shown in how they dressed. During the public protests at mid-decade, the dogmatic Franklin E. Kameny had insisted on a strict dress code—which meant suits and ties for the men. But after moving to New York, Nichols followed Clarke's example and slid into bell-bottom jeans and tossed a peace-symbol medallion around his neck. Those outward signs were symbolic of the couple's participation in one of the most powerful cultural shifts in American history.

That same shift was reflected in their journalism as well. Nichols recalled: "The 'Homosexual Citizen' column was very much part of the Counterculture Movement. It broke societal barriers just as the Gay Liberation Movement did. The counterculture provided the climate needed for massive change to occur. The great advances that took place not only stood on the shoulders of the early gay press, but also on those of the counterculture."[20]

One theme central to the libertine attitude driving the counterculture was adding new terms to the language. The mercurial "Homosexual Citizen" was in step with this shift. Every column was peppered with words that had not yet found their way into dictionaries—*hip, turned on, swinging, a drag*—as well as new ways of putting words together—"a group of groovy gals" and "a guy who knows where his head is at."[21]

The column also embraced the counterculture's celebration of nontraditional social behavior, best captured in the motto *Do your own thing*. The outer boundaries of dress, grooming, drug use, and sexual activity all evaporated as part of the new social liberalism. Nichols recalled: "Lige and I were consciously part of the Counterculture Movement. We rubbed elbows with Timothy Leary and Allen Ginsberg, we smoked pot, and we took our share of LSD. Gays were fully embraced into that scene, and bisexuality was absolutely rampant."[22]

The column overflowed with references to the new culture. Some endorsed drug use: "LSD has immense therapeutic potentials." Others encouraged free love: "Everyone should make love to everyone else: male and male, male and female, female and female." Still others espoused a live-and-let-live philosophy: "We dig people as people. A person's sexual preferences are about as important to us as what color toilet paper he uses."[23]

Nichols and Clarke were not, however, easygoing about the war in Southeast Asia. They announced in the lead of one column: "We are staunch foes of the Vietnamese conflict." In sync with a growing tide of Americans, Nichols and Clarke adamantly opposed the war not merely because their countrymen were being killed, but also because they were among the sea of young people opposed to U.S. imperialism and all human conflict. Nichols and Clarke referred to the leaders of the American armed forces by such derogatory epithets as "psychotic warmongers," "military maniacs," and "pathological-bomb-happy nitwits." The column containing their strongest antiwar rhetoric carried the bold headline "Four Star Fuck-up." In addition to the serious indictments of the war, the column also was dotted with playful antiwar slogans such as "Bring the beautiful boys home," "Make each other, not war," and "Stop beating off and start beating the draft: suck cock."[24]

The columnists obviously felt no qualms about using explicit language that most news media eschew—in the late 1960s as well as today. *Damn, shit, pissed off,* and *fuck* appeared routinely in the "Homosexual Citizen," as they did throughout the pages of *Screw.* Nichols and Clarke introduced sexual innuendo in their first column about the 1968 presidential race, referring to "Purity Pricks" and "Rigid Dick" Nixon, while also encouraging readers to vote for Hubert Humphrey if they hoped to "Lick Dick."[25]

Nichols and Clarke's use of coarse terms knew no bounds. In a column saying that they did not distinguish between genders when selecting friends, they anticipated the reaction of their readers and added the aside: "You're screaming, 'Don't you assholes know the difference between cocks and cunts, tits and chests?'" The men began another column about lesbians with the statement: "Lesbians. What sorts of images does this word bring to your mind? Do you think of two beautiful women spread-eagled on a bed engaged in marvelously perverse acts: kissing, caressing, fondling, and stimulating each other's clits with hungry tongues?"[26]

Although the *Los Angeles Advocate* used ribald language less frequently than the "Homosexual Citizen" did, it also embraced the values of the counterculture. A year-long correspondence with a gay soldier in Vietnam gave readers a firsthand account of the savagery of war. The *Advocate* also published an occasional *damn, bitch, bullshit,* and *blow job,* usually in personal columns. And a first-person account of prison rape stated: "In jail a 'punk' is a kid who likes to be fucked," and "At the moment that conditions are right, time is far too short for anything but action. It's kiss-kiss-wham-bam, get your rocks off, and pull your pants up."[27]

Drum celebrated the increased freedom as well. Because editor Clark P. Polak was a strong advocate of decriminalizing marijuana, for example, drug use maintained a high profile in the magazine. One six-page article detailed the history of various hallucinogens and praised the sensations they caused. The article included quotations from gay men about their experiences with drugs—all positive. The final paragraph, which was tantamount to an endorsement of marijuana use, synthesized the beliefs of the dozen men interviewed for the article: "Marijuana for them is simply another valuable human experience."[28]

The Ladder was more restrained in how it reflected the shifting values, although, by 1968, the mouthpiece of the Daughters of Bilitis had another new editor who, like Barbara Gittings before her, was eager to lead the magazine in new directions. Barbara Grier recently recalled, "I wanted to take the magazine to a level of quality no one had ever hoped it could reach." Grier's ability to improve the magazine was aided by lesbian journalism's first "angel," an anonymous donor who gave *The Ladder* $1,000 a month. Although Grier never knew the identity of the benefactor, she had learned a great deal about the woman. Grier said, "She was an old-line butch—the 'Honey-bring-me-a-beer' type—who, but for the absence of a penis, looked and behaved exactly like a man." The only two women who had contact with the angel are no longer living. Grier's vision was to reshape *The Ladder* into a high-quality literary journal to create a lesbian *Atlantic Monthly*. The essay format enabled the magazine to stay in step with the country's new cultural milieu.[29]

Some of the most compelling essays came from the typewriter of Martha Shelley, an aggressive New Yorker who had particularly strong feelings about the Vietnam War. Shelley, who began writing for *The Ladder* in 1968, said recently: "The war was the fault line. The oldtimers in DOB and Mattachine were very assimilationist. They bowed to the government. But we young people had no taste for assimilation and even less taste for war. And besides, the war was the doing of the government. That was the whole focus of the youth rebellion. We wanted no part of the government's war."[30]

One signal that times were changing, both in Lesbian America and *The Ladder*, was a cover drawing that showed two women dressed in the modish fashions of the day and holding two objects that aptly symbolized the Counter-culture Movement. One woman sniffed a flower, while the other took a drag off a marijuana cigarette. The magazine's editorial content further promoted liberal attitudes. In one essay, Grier said of the new sense of freedom: "Above all, it demands that we do not force our personal point of view on our neigh-bor. Love and let love." The magazine's range of subject areas included drugs and the generation gap, approached in the language of the counterculture—*turned-on, dropped-out.*[31]

Celebrating Gay and Lesbian Sex

The counterculture made its most significant contribution to gay liberation by defying the conventional definition of acceptable sexual behavior. For in the context of the sexual revolution that had erupted as part of the Counterculture Movement, homosexuality was no longer being considered—at least by some segments of American society—a drastic departure from sexual normality.[32]

Nichols and Clarke applauded this shift in sexual mores. They thumbed their noses at the concept of sexual fidelity and lauded the joys of sex, including in groups and at the Mafia-owned gay bars and bathhouses that proliferated in Manhattan as the size of the gay community made such operations increasingly profitable. "Society is being opened by new psychedelic keys," the columnists wrote. "Younger people are not as uptight about homosexuals as in previous years. Many, in fact, openly admit to bi-sexual leanings. Things have moved comfortably away from the 1957–1960 syndrome." At the same time, the liber-ated columnists insisted that gay people had to establish their own moral val-ues. "We need a sexual culture of our own," they argued. "Homosexuals need to develop public forums where such questions as 'What makes a happier gay marriage?' can be discussed. Right now, there are millions of gay people who are stumbling around in the dark."[33]

The columnists' most controversial stand on sexual ethics was fast becoming a hallmark of gay liberation: supporting recreational sex. Gay activists argued that monogamy was a draconian concept that, because it was preached by a society that refused to recognize same-sex relationships, should have no influence on gay people. Nichols and Clarke firmly believed that having sex outside of a commit-ted relationship did no harm whatsoever to that union. In fact, they argued that such sexual infidelity could strengthen a relationship because it demonstrated the trust the couple shared. The sexually liberated couple wrote: "There's nothing shameful or impure about love-making, whether it lasts for a lifetime or only for a few minutes. If two people bring pleasure and excitement into each other's lives, refreshing one another with healthy bodily contact, it's a million times preferable to retreating from touch and depriving oneself and others of pleasure." Nichols and Clarke did not stop at merely validating sex outside a relationship as acceptable behavior, but they went on to promote such activity. They wrote, "A one-night stand can be a glorious, beautiful, fulfilling experience."[34]

Although the popular journalists took the lead in integrating frank discussions of sexual behavior and promiscuity into the gay and lesbian press, others also used their editorial positions to advance the theme. Indeed, it may have demanded more courage for writers outside of the insulated environment of Greenwich Village to make statements on the subject. Polak actively participated in the gay fast lane and then translated his experience into editorial statements in his Philadelphia-based magazine. *Drum*, with its subtitle *Sex in Perspective,* devoted considerable space to examining and promoting gay male sex with a frankness earlier publications had assiduously avoided. The "Beginner's Guide to Cruising" series boasted that it was easy to identify men who would be willing sex partners, simply by the clothes they wore. The fastest route to the bedroom, the series advised, was by looking for young men wearing "electric blue slacks with a tight crotch and rear." The series said of such men: "They are up for grabs. Such can be taken home and so to bed with little bother."[35]

Like Nichols and Clarke, Polak praised recreational sex as fundamental to the gay subculture, saying "Homosexual behavior almost *by definition* includes promiscuity." The editor went on to say that the key factor was the male sex drive. Because men place a higher priority on sexual activity than women do, he contended, it is only logical that when two gay men engage in sexual activity with each other, they will produce more sexual energy. "The number of sexual partners is, of course, higher," Polak concluded.[36]

Drum's descriptions of sexual activity became graphic in a two-part series describing homosexual activity in prisons. The articles, which reported that 60 percent of male prisoners participated in sexual acts with other men, discussed details such as prisoners trading cigarettes for sexual favors and using axle grease as a lubricant during anal intercourse. Even more graphic was an article describing how using drugs enhanced sexual pleasure. One man said that smoking marijuana made every part of his body, but especially the head of his penis, more sensitive. Another offered a stream-of-consciousness manifesto for gay anonymous sex: "When I'm high on pot, it's not that I don't care who I'm in

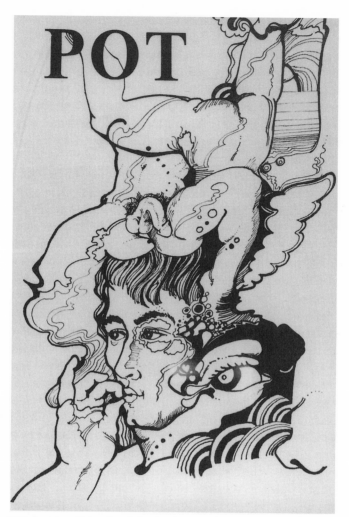

Psychedelic drawings featuring drugs and sex, such as this one appearing in Drum *magazine, were common in the lesbian and gay press during the Counterculture Movement.*

bed with, but he and I become almost like mechanisms for sexual satisfaction. His cock is important to me as 'a cock,' if you know what I mean. It's my moment alone, and it often comes to a point that it really doesn't matter who he is as long as he has the right equipment."[37]

Vector's approach to sexual activity was not as explicit. Representative was the magazine's in-depth look at the mix of people living in San Francisco's tenderloin district. The reporter incorporated interviews with a variety of people—from hustlers to men living totally in the closet—into his piece, treating each person with respect and no trace of ridicule. He quoted a male-to-female transvestite as saying that she was ecstatic because she had found a sexual identity. "I made a complete switchover," the woman said. "When I did it, I knew it was the best thing. I was a psychological morphodyte. All I can think about is that I'm really me now, and I like it."[38]

Jim Kepner adopted a more literary approach to the topic of sex as part of his effort to create a gay magazine similar in sophistication to *The New Yorker.* In his premier issue of *Pursuit & Symposium,* Kepner used the first-person *us/we* point of view as he recounted his first gay sexual experience: "He kissed us then, wetter than we ever imagined a kiss would be, and longer, first inserting his tongue, then drawing ours deeply into his mouth, till we were desperate for breath. His fingers gently explored, and his other hand, warm, soft, moist, found our hand and guided it south. We'd never felt one, besides our own, before, and this was more impressive than our own."[39]

Two other new West Coast publications, both based in San Francisco, also approached sex head-on. "*Town Talk* was an early version of the bar rags," Kepner said. "The writing was just gossip created solely for the purpose of filling the space between the ads, and that goal called for straight talk about gay sex." Hal Call started *Town Talk* when he finally began to acknowledge that *Mattachine Review*'s day had passed. His decision to fill the four-page *Town Talk* with ads for bars and erotic publications reflected the values coming to dominate gay San Francisco. Among those values, Call knew, was an emphasis on sexual activity.[40]

Although the voice of Lesbian America did not engage in such graphic sexual discussions, it was moving in that direction. By mid-1969, *The Ladder* was acknowledging that the youth rebellion had implications for lesbians: "It applies to youth, to race, to politics—to sex," and was speaking in sexual terms and raising sexual concepts missing from contemporary publications for straight women. One essay argued that no one can "measure" love, and then continued: "But we can measure behavior. We can count orgasms, and what else is 'love' but orgasms? It's orgasms that make the world go round." In fact, *The Ladder* was challenging the very foundations of heterosexuality. In one essay, Martha Shelley, on her way to becoming one of the most radical theorists in the history of the lesbian and gay press, questioned whether heterosexual sex was even natural. Citing numerous studies showing that straight women rarely achieved orgasm, she asked point-blank, "If heterosexual coitus is so 'natural,' why do women, who are biologically capable of orgasm, have to learn how to achieve it?" Another article in the same issue chastised lesbians for being sexually repressed but rejoiced that sex between siblings appeared to be on the rise. The author finished the article by raising an explosive issue: "Why not sex with animals? Why should cat lovers and dog lovers remain so inhibited?"[41]

Legitimizing Homoerotic Images

Historians who have mentioned the rise of the gay press have attributed the emergence of male beefcake to the spate of tabloids that burst forth in the wake of the Stonewall Rebellion in the summer of 1969, but the rise of those images is rightly credited to the publications that came *before* Stonewall. The historians are certainly right, however, in that such images were profoundly important in the gay world. In concert with this value system, the bare skin of handsome young men has come to dominate more pages of the gay press than have gray columns of type.[42]

The widespread use of such images was very much in keeping with the Counterculture Movement as well, as one dimension of the palpable sense of liberation was that people had no reason to feel ashamed of displaying their bodies. This also was the era, beginning in 1965, when the U.S. Supreme Court handed down rulings establishing that nudity is not, per se, obscene. Even mainstream publications such as *Playboy,* which had existed for more than a decade, were gradually expanding the limits of their images, although they did not show genitalia.[43]

Kepner recently articulated why homoerotic images are fundamental to the evolution of the gay press: "Validating erotic images was extremely important to our liberation. As the gay press came into its own, the publications began to extol the many virtues of the beautiful male physique. They screamed: 'Yes, gay men are sexual. And, yes, we are proud of our desires. Yes! Yes! Yes!' "[44]

Homoerotic images grew increasingly prominent and explicit, in both news and feature material and advertisements, in the *Los Angeles Advocate.* Initial artwork was mild and playful. One in-house ad consisted of a drawing of two men in bed, reading the *Advocate* as a puppy slept at their feet. During 1968 the images shifted from drawings to photographs. When the newspaper's first promotional campaign centered on a "Groovy Guy" beauty pageant with hand-some young men baring their chests to win cash prizes, the *Advocate* featured the winner—wearing nothing but blue jeans and a boyish smile—on its front page.[45]

The increased degree of explicitness reflected Michaels's growing under-

No Groovy Guy..But 20th Century Adonis?

HOW TIMES CHANGE. This was Governor Ronnie back in 1940 when he played George Gipp in the movie *The Life of Knute Rockne.* Chosen by the division of fine arts of the University of California as a "Twentieth Century Adonis" possessing the most nearly perfect male figure, Reagan poses for professor Merrel Gage's sculpturing class. His measurements—at that time, anyway—were: waist, 32 inches; chest, 41 inches; height, six feet one inch; and weight, 180 pounds.

"Governor Ronnie's" youthful physique appeared in the Los Angeles Advocate, *the country's first true gay newspaper, in 1969, courtesy of a publicity photo MGM Studios had distributed to promote Reagan's 1940 film,* The Life of Knute Rockne.

standing of his market. Kepner said, "Dick learned that pretty pictures on the cover would sell the papers, would get them off the racks and into people's hands so they would read what was inside." Beginning in July 1968 every issue of the *Advocate* featured a front-page photo of a man with either his chest or buttocks exposed. It was more than coincidence that during the second half of 1968 the newspaper also tripled in size, jumping from sixteen pages in June to forty-eight by December.[46]

One particularly noteworthy photograph showed the man the University of California's division of fine arts had, according to the caption beneath the photo, labeled a "Twentieth Century Adonis." The image was of a handsome young man wearing only undershorts while posing for a class of sculpture students. It was taken during the filming of the 1940 motion picture *The Life of Knute Rockne.* By the time the *Advocate* ran the photo, the young actor had become politician Ronald Reagan, the state's conservative governor.[47]

The *Advocate's* most shocking images were in its ads, with many of them carrying sadomasochistic messages. Ads for the *Dungeon* book series featured a photo of a naked young man (from the rear) chained to a torture device, and another of a naked man tied spread-eagled on a pool table (again from the rear) as five other men, all wearing boots and leather jackets, approached him menacingly. Even in these ominous images, however, Michaels refrained from showing full-frontal nudity, fearing he would lose the ads for straight-owned restaurants and shops he was beginning to attract.[48]

East Coast publications were breaking taboos more quickly. *Drum* led the pack, with Polak defining homoerotic images as a political statement. In 1966 he wrote, "I have attempted to produce a magazine that illustrates—rather than pontificates on—the philosophy that, to use a cliche, it's OK to be gay." His depictions of handsome young men in suggestive poses began in the first issue. The cover showed a man dressed in swimming trunks and poised to dive into a pool. The last page of the issue showed the same man lying on a chaise lounge and gazing across the pool, as if waiting for someone—such as the reader—to rise suddenly from the water to join him.[49]

During his second year of publishing, Polak developed two entirely separate types of homoerotic images. The copies of the magazine he sold at newsstands continued to carry suggestive depictions of partially nude men, although these still did not expose any genitalia. But for readers who subscribed to the magazine and, therefore, received their copies in the mail, Polak added a supplement of eight full-page photographs of naked men with their genitals fully exposed. The insert was stapled into the center of the magazine. Readers loved the nude photos. A Los Angeles man gushed, "You are the best combination of knowledge, humor and a healthy-minded approach to sex around." Polak did not include the photos in the copies of *Drum* he sold in newsstands because the owners refused to stock magazines featuring full-frontal nudity. Despite his caution, Polak failed to escape the eye of the censor. Federal postal authorities seized the March 1966 issue and sent a sample copy to Washington for review. After a three-week delay, the officials allowed the magazine to be mailed.[50]

Drum also advanced the use of visual elements by creating the first comic strip in the gay and lesbian press. Harry Chess was a tall, dark, and handsome cartoon character with a square jaw, bulging muscles, and a bumper crop of curly black chest hair—though he lacked intellectual timber. Other characters included lesbian bartender Big Bennie. Chess's "sexploits" involved adventures crafted both to amuse readers and to affirm gay values. When Chess was being tortured, his call for help read, "If there was only someone to save us...like Superman or Batman or Sean Connery...sigh!!" Seeing such statements in black-and-white validated the readers' sexual desires. The comic strip carried political messages as well. By depicting life in the gay fast lane, it reinforced another of *Drum*'s major themes—the Gay and Lesbian Liberation Movement should embrace, rather than oppose, the gay social life.[51]

While the *Advocate* and *Drum* were gradually breaking visual taboos, the "Homosexual Citizen" column was advancing at a supersonic pace. Since the founding of *Screw*, explicit photos had been a staple of the racy tabloid. The cover of the first issue displayed a woman dressed in a string bikini and holding a huge salami; inside photos included full-frontal nudity of men as well as women. Nichols and Clarke were influenced by *Screw*'s sexual content as well as by the unrestrained sexual activity central to the counterculture. Male genitalia first appeared on the "Homosexual Citizen" page in April 1969. The photo, which had no relation to the content of the column, was a frontal nude shot of a teenage boy sitting on a rocky cliff. After that breakthrough, penises and testicles routinely accompanied the column—regardless of the subject. Goldstein selected the photos, with Nichols and Clarke tacitly giving their approval by continuing to write their column for him.[52]

Nichols and Clarke became intimately involved in homoerotic images when Goldstein approached them about posing for nude photos. The columnists agreed. Goldstein took the photos and published a two-page photo essay of the two men titled "A Man Loves a Man." The photos showed Nichols and Clarke engaging in oral and anal sex, although shadows and camera angles obscured their genitalia as well as their faces.[53]

Early in 1969, *Vector* also began publishing erotic images when a new editor quickly connected the magazine to the counterculture. Leo Laurence, a reporter for KGO radio station in San Francisco, had witnessed the bloody confrontations between police and antiwar demonstrators at the 1968 Democratic National Convention in Chicago. Laurence was, therefore, primed to rebel against the social and political order. *Vector*'s April cover showed Gale Whittington, Laurence's twenty-year-old lover, wearing nothing but low-slung cutoffs as he smiled and motioned the reader toward a bed in the background of the photo. The coverline: "An Invitation." When the reader opened the magazine, he faced a full-length photo of a handsome young man standing naked in the shower, with his genitalia facing the camera. The caption: "It feels so good!"[54]

Laurence soon learned that his embrace of counterculture values did not coincide with the philosophy of the leadership of the Society for Individual Rights, the organization that continued to publish *Vector*. Nor did the organization's leaders take kindly to Laurence's public criticism of them. In the April issue he wrote: "Timid leaders with enormous ego-trips, middle class bigotry and racism, and too many middle-aged up-tight conservatives are hurting almost every major homosexual organization." The final paragraph of Laurence's article read: "I fully expect the up-tight officers and members of SIR to try to stop me as Editor. But, I promised *Vector* is going to be honest in its reporting, even if it makes our middle class homosexual community mad." A month later Laurence had been evicted from the editor's chair.[55]

No such controversy exploded when *The Ladder* published its first homoerotic image, although the photo was not nearly as explicit. The image on the cover of the April 1968 issue was of two beautiful young women locked in a passionate embrace, with their eyes closed and a sense of ecstasy enveloping them as one woman kissed the cheek of the other. The photo was of actresses Anne Heywood and Sandy Dennis, both fully clothed, in a scene from the film *The Fox*. Inside the same issue, Barbara Grier argued that lesbians should not be embarrassed to use homoerotic images to become sexually aroused. She wrote, "There is no reason why the sensual pleasures of the body should not be stimulated by works of art—be they words or pictures."[56]

The themes of the counterculture were at odds, however, with some of the publications that had their roots in less liberal times. *ONE* and *Tangents* both continued to reflect the values of more establishment-oriented segments of the gay community. The dichotomy created a huge gulf between the numerous magazines on the cutting edge of the youth rebellion and the two that remained grounded in the 1950s. As the new magazines championed the rapid realignment of values fundamental to American society, *Tangents*, for example, questioned the grammatical correctness of transforming the adjective *gay* into a noun. As late as 1970, the magazine stated, "The current misuse of the word 'gays' as a synonym for homosexuals is born of ignorance."[57]

Redesigning the Gay and Lesbian Press

Publications at the vanguard in the late 1960s made several major design modifications. These changes transformed stodgy-looking publications into much more modern ones. Most dramatic was discarding the scholarly journal format. The five-and-a-half-by-eight-and-a-half-inch size had defined gay and lesbian journalism since the founding of *ONE* in 1953. After a decade and a half, in an era of rapid change, it was time for a makeover. In addition, the widespread availability of offset printing beginning in the mid-1960s made such a new look possible—financially as well as technologically. Finally, the new emphasis on homoerotic images led publications to seek formats conducive to displaying those images more invitingly.[58]

Vector made the first major change. When it was founded, the San Francisco publication broke from the format established by its predecessors and printed on eight-and-a-half-by-eleven-inch paper, similar to a newsletter. In March 1966 *Vector* added a glossy cover and a second color of ink on inside pages. With its new look, the magazine became the first gay publication that actually *looked* like a magazine.

Kepner's *Pursuit & Symposium* added a touch of class to gay press design a month later when its premier issue appeared. In keeping with its goal of becoming the genre's first upscale publication, it featured a photograph of a Greek statue on its glossy cover and tasteful etchings on inside pages. To the casual reader thumbing through the magazine, the design appeared comparable to that of *The New Yorker* or *Esquire.*

Lesbians too were being offered a more upscale look in their reading matter. Thanks to its angel's financial support, *The Ladder* celebrated its twelfth birthday in October 1968 by adding a glossy cover. Grier also gave her literary-oriented magazine a more substantial look by shifting from a monthly to a bimonthly publication schedule, thereby replacing a rather flimsy twenty-four-page magazine with a hefty forty-eight-page one.

The "Homosexual Citizen" moved the gay press a giant step toward the tabloid format. Goldstein filled *Screw* with huge photos that helped him titillate readers with large expanses of bare skin and body parts. The format also served Nichols and Clarke well, as the "Homosexual Citizen" column secured its own full page in the newspaper. When Goldstein wrapped artwork and a headline around the columnists' words, the package became relatively easy for gay readers to locate within the sea of heterosexual vulgarity.

The next step in the evolution of the gay tabloid occurred on the West Coast. After Michaels experimented with front-page male images for six months and found they boosted circulation, in January 1969 he transformed the *Los Angeles Advocate* into a tabloid. To take full advantage of the visual appeal of the large images he then was able to showcase on his front page, he simultaneously hired a distributor to place the papers in vending machines throughout Los Angeles.

The switch to a tabloid format was part of the larger trend among alternative publications of the time, such as the *Berkeley Barb* and the *East Village Other,* which soared in readership as the size of the country's army of rebelling youths swelled. Adopting the tabloid format was a natural step for the gay press, fully consistent with the counterculture's insistence on being different. All the major social movements of the 1960s—women's liberationists, antiwar advocates, Black Panthers—expressed their dissatisfaction in the pages of tabloid newspapers, rather than full-sized ones, as a tangible statement of the distance they wanted to create between themselves and the establishment. In the world of journalism, to be outside the mainstream of society meant to jettison the broadsheet newspaper format.[59]

The second major design element originating in the late 1960s gay press involved headlines. Pioneer editors had limited their headlines to little more than labels, but the new breed of editors became much more creative in their efforts to appeal to readers. They often used shocking words and expletives never before seen in American newspapers.

The weekly column about the mysterious world of gay men provided *Screw*'s Goldstein with ample opportunity to demonstrate his no-holds-barred brand of journalistic sensationalism. Goldstein printed the title "Homosexual Citizen" in eighteen-point type, dwarfing it with the outrageous headlines he dreamed up for each edition—in forty-eight-point type. "Al took pride in crafting headlines that were patently crude and offensive," Nichols recalled. "He whiled away hours and hours thinking of new ways to shock his readers."[60]

The tasteless words often were at odds with the content of the column, as the headline usually had little relevance to Nichols and Clarke's chosen topic. In one column, the writers attempted to destroy the myth that all aging gay men are lonely, bitter, and miserable. They described the various older men they knew as "magnificent" and "inspiring," leading into their advice on how to enjoy old age. With sincerity and sensitivity, the columnists wrote, "The truly happy older homosexual has cultivated a circle of dear friends and a wealth of experience and knowledge." Despite the positive portrayal, Goldstein ran the story under the demeaning headline "Old Boys: They Just Blow Away." Headlines over columns about other serious topics were equally crude. He labeled a column about men agonizing over their sexual identity "Undecided Dicks," and when Nichols and Clarke endorsed Hubert Humphrey for president, Goldstein played on the candidate's last name to create the headline "Humping a Winner?" The inch-high headlines routinely included sexually explicit language. A column on an anti-homosexual hate group was labeled "Do Homosexual Citizens Suck?" and one about lesbians asked "Are Creamy Cunts Kosher?"[61]

Despite the inappropriateness of the headlines, Nichols and Clarke never complained. Because they had total control of the body of the column, they were reassured that serious readers would look beyond Goldstein's sensationalized headlines to find the substance in the editorial content. Nichols recalled: "Al could have fun playing with the headlines, but we had the last word on the real content. He never changed a word we wrote."[62]

Although the other leading publications of the era did not ride the craft of headline writing to the depth of crudity the "Homosexual Citizen" did, sexual innuendo and double entendre became firmly established as a staple of the gay press. Typical were *Vector* headlines for a feature on San Francisco's venereal disease center: "Applause for Clap Clinic," and its headline over a fashion photo essay complete with a model dressed in skin-tight trousers: "The Male Emergence."[63]

Introducing the Gay Lexicon

The milieu created by the Counterculture Movement encouraged the various movement presses to begin to speak in the language used within their particular community. Publications written by and for women's liberationists read very differently from those aimed at members of the Black Panther party, with neither limiting its vocabulary to the standard dictionaries written by the white patriarchy. Movement presses used new words partly because the existing vocabulary could not adequately describe the experiences and concepts of the era, and partly to distance themselves from the establishment.

For the gay press, just as celebrating homoerotic images was a political statement of extraordinary importance to the emerging culture, so was speaking in the gay lexicon. Both acts served to legitimize and affirm gay values.

Historians of the modern Lesbian and Gay Liberation Movement who have mentioned the gay press of the 1970s have cited its graphic language as one of the elements distinguishing it from the mainstream press. Those scholars have ignored the fact, however, that in the late 1960s, publications such as the *Los Angeles Advocate, Drum, Vector,* and the "Homosexual Citizen" column already had shattered the conventions of journalistic language, introducing a plethora of terms and phrases never before published in American newspapers. The vocabulary the publications adopted would have been unintelligible to many readers, as gay men had developed an idiosyncratic code to allow them, as members of a repressed minority, to identify and communicate with each other.[64]

Many of the words originated in the 1940s and 1950s with the growth of a sub-rosa gay and lesbian network of bars and secret meetings. Some were crude and vulgar terms the ostracized men and women used—indeed, flaunted—to strike back at the society that repressed them. But other entries in the unwritten lexicon were clever and witty, demonstrating the style and flair that have always been synonymous with the community.

Terms unique to the language of gay men proliferated in the *Los Angeles Advocate.* Kepner recalled that gay self-respect was a primary concern when Dick Michaels founded the newspaper. "He knew gays were guilt-ridden and we had to get rid of that. He knew gay men had to get comfortable with themselves and their community, and that included validating the language we used.

We knew what our words meant. Why not print them? The *Advocate* was aggressively being who we are."[65]

A first-person article about police entrapment contained the statement "A gorgeous vice officer in white levis and showing quite a basket came through and broke the tension"; readers knew a *basket* refers to the bulge created by a man's genitalia. An article about a gay rights demonstration stated that protesters would be directed to the staging area by signs reading "THIS WAY, GIRLS"; readers knew that many gay men refer to each other in feminine terms, a practice designed partly to break down traditional gender roles. An editorial cartoon depicted a police officer preparing to draw his gun against a muscular cowboy whose holster held a copy of the Bill of Rights and whose back pocket had a tube of K-Y jelly protruding from it; readers knew that gay men use the jelly as a lubricant to facilitate anal intercourse.[66]

Another venue for the gay lexicon was the popular classified ad section—titled "Trader Dick"—that ran on the *Advocate*'s back page. By the late 1960s, personal ads were supplying a huge chunk of the newspaper's revenue, as they provided a convenient way for gay men to make contact with sexual partners. Hundreds of personal ads filled more than a dozen pages in the newspaper as gay men tried to outdo each other in a race of wit, whimsy, and pure lust. Readers knew that an ad beginning, "Are you getting your share?" was not talking about a guy's share of financial profits, and one offering "MEXICAN HOUSEBOYS. Live-in type" was suggesting the men would do more than wash windows. Likewise, savvy *Advocate* readers knew that when an ad stated, "Turn On, Tune In, Turn Over," the last reference was to a man readying himself to be the receiving partner in anal intercourse.[67]

Drum also was filled with terms that would have caused straight readers to stumble. The series of articles about sexual activity among prison inmates referred to *trade*, a term for straight men who participate in homosexual acts if they are paid, and an article about drug use contained the term *trick*, a term gay men use for sex partners of limited duration. *Drum*'s Harry Chess comic strip overflowed with words and phrases from the gay lexicon as well, most of them carrying sexual messages. When the gay version of 1960s secret agent James Bond was described as a "rugged, virile, sensuous, clever, top agent," gay readers knew a *top agent* was the active participant in anal intercourse. They also recognized references to Chess as *Popperman* as allusions to the chemical substance many gay men inhale during sex to enhance physical pleasure.[68]

Vector dipped liberally into the gay dictionary. An in-depth discussion of the pros and cons of having sex in public places included references to *tea-rooms* and *glory-holes,* words readers understood to be public bathrooms where some gay men have sex and the holes those men sometimes chisel into the partitions between bathroom stalls to facilitate having anonymous oral or anal sex.[69]

As gay journalism's first effort aimed at the high-brow segment of the community, *Pursuit & Symposium* traveled a higher road than its counterparts, attempting to trace the derivation and purpose of the gay lexicon. Kepner credited Christopher Isherwood, for example, with popularizing *gay camping.* Kepner wrote of the novelist: "According to his perhaps camping definition, 'camp' was a sensibility, a quality, that emphasized style, texture, decorativeness, putting form before content, always laying it on a bit thick, elegantly, humorously, or with a purple display of sentimentality. And ostrich feathers."[70]

Lesbians did not write so colorfully about their culture. They had developed a language all their own, but it, like explicit lesbian images, would not be committed to print for another decade. In the American culture, women—straight or gay—simply had not been conditioned to be as outspoken as men, and such cultural traditions would not be overturned quickly.

Indeed, a *Ladder* article introducing the terms *butch* and *femme* into print was written by a man rather than a woman. In 1967 Kepner took a stab at describing lesbian role playing, writing: "Lesbians generally expect one another to be either soft, weak, sweet and dressed accordingly or rough, hard and heavy, with mannish clothes and no feminine frills, and to play that one role without compromise." Kepner criticized the bar culture as perpetuating the butch/femme roles as a crude imitation of straight society. He lamented, "A great many girls are badly hung up on this question of how to identify themselves."[71]

Personalizing the Lesbian and Gay Press

In a style reminiscent of *Vice Versa* some twenty years earlier, late 1960s publications emphasized a personal form of journalism crafted to help them connect with their readers. Grier recalled: "Our most needful readers were the isolated lesbians who, for one reason or another, lived in areas where they had no personal contact with anyone else like themselves. Through our writing, we strived to become a lifeline for those women. We were a loyal friend who arrived every month for a chatty visit."[72]

Many *Ladder* authors sought to engage in conversation with their readers by writing from a first-person perspective. Anita Cornwell used such an approach when she shared her experiences as a black woman in the predominantly white Lesbian and Gay Liberation Movement. "The moment I or any other black forgets we *are* black, it may be our last," she wrote. "For when the shooting starts *any* black is fair game. The bullets don't give a damn whether I sleep with woman or man, their only aim is to put me to sleep forever."[73]

Of all the writers of the era, Nichols and Clarke most epitomized personal journalism. They often spoke from the "we" point of view, and the italicized editor's note preceding each column summarized the peripatetic couple's personal philosophy. The note, written in the language of the 1960s, read: "*Lige and Jack are male lovers who dig life together and think it's a groove. They find fault with silly laws and prejudices that discriminate against love.*" The city's burgeoning gay community affectionately wrapped its arms around Nichols and Clarke. In *The Gay Insider: USA,* the first anthology of American gay life, author John Paul Hudson recalled his personal reaction to the column: "Lige and Jack wrote an upbeat, no-nonsense, unapologetic, vibrant, sexy, and liberated weekly message that was gobbled up by thousands like me, rendering the authors the most celebrated and recognizable homosexuals in America. They were witty, wise, straightforward, and *pretty.*" Just as Nichols had become a public spokesman for the gay community of Washington in the mid-1960s, he and Clarke gave speeches and appeared on radio and television talk shows in New York City in the final years of the decade.[74]

The men adopted a chatty style, calling sources by their first names and often patting friends on the back. In their column about the Oscar Wilde Memorial Bookstore, they recounted how founder Craig Rodwell had joined the various picket lines they had organized earlier in the decade. They also shamelessly promoted their friend's business: "Whatever book you are looking for about homosexuality, call Craig's store." Their relaxed, personal tone allowed them to slip in a little self-promotion now and again as well: "Craig himself may welcome you into his shop. If so, try to muster the courage to tell him that SCREW sent you."[75]

Personalizing messages was a popular activity in *Town Talk,* too. The bar-oriented publication desperately wanted to gain reader loyalty, and that meant writing in a chatty style. Call filled his pages with puffery such as "The best buys in town are the dinners in the bars and restaurants," and "Catch the show at the Hula Shack. Real great." Even when he wrote about the San Francisco City Health Clinic, his tone was anything but clinical. The article focused on the scourge of gay men: venereal disease. Sounding like a concerned buddy, Call wrote, "This reporter sincerely hopes no one is so stupid and naive as to think he can treat VD himself."[76]

Raising a Defiant Editorial Voice

That gay publications connected with the youth rebellion did not mean they stopped demanding that mainstream society grant equal rights to all gay Americans—young as well as elderly, hip as well as square. Like the militant publications earlier in the decade, the leading publications of the late 1960s insisted their readers should receive the rights promised by the Constitution.

An editorial in the *Los Angeles Advocate*'s first issue articulated the newspaper's mission: "Homosexuals, more than ever before, are out to win their legal rights, to end the injustices against them, to experience their share of happiness in their own way. If the ADVOCATE can help in achieving these goals, all the time, sweat, and money that goes into it will be well spent."[77]

Some authors who have written about the movement have criticized the *Advocate* for accommodating to the standards of the larger society. One writer described the early *Advocate* as "totally unlike gay liberation papers" of the 1970s because it adopted "a guarded position" on gay rights. Such statements are inaccurate. From its earliest issue and throughout the period, the *Advocate* was unrelenting in its support of gay rights, consistently speaking with defiance—and volume.[78]

Its most vigorous editorial crusade was against the Los Angeles Police Department, which was averaging 3,000 gay arrests a year. Although Dick Michaels did not specifically mention his own arrest, he spoke from experience when his editorial in the second issue accused vice squad officers of inflating their arrest records by unjustly arresting innocent patrons of gay bars. He protested: "Is there police harassment? Hell, no! This is *persecution*." The editorial ended with a sense of strength and power: "We do not ask for our rights on bended knee. We demand them, standing tall, as dignified beings." The newspaper's aggressive attitude sometimes resulted in police harassment. Kepner said, "Police cars would park in front of the office and flash their lights at everybody who came in, determined to intimidate us."[79]

Michaels was undeterred. His campaign against the police reached a crescendo during the 1969 Los Angeles City Council campaign that pitted incumbent Paul Lamport, who supported the police department's harsh treatment of gays, against Jack Norman, a police critic. After two gay bars were raided within a week, the editor's page-one editorial made a startling accusation: "Two sets of arrests in a week lead inevitably to the question: Is the LAPD working for Councilman Lamport? If not, it is an amazing coincidence because both of the bars have been very active in the campaign of Jack Norman." The *Advocate*'s charge resonated through the community, and Lamport was defeated. The day after the election, Lamport attributed the loss to gay opposition. In its next issue, the *Advocate* cheered, "Gay power DOES work!"[80]

The movement's first newspaper was eager to play a leading role in galvanizing the gay community's political power. Before the 1969 election, Michaels sent questionnaires to candidates for mayor and city council. He then compiled the responses, wrote news stories about them, and endorsed the pro-gay candidates on the editorial page. The two-fisted newspaper also encouraged gays to defy authority. In the summer of 1968 a Los Angeles bar raid foreshadowed the Stonewall Rebellion. When police entered the Patch and arrested two men, the 250 customers did not cower or flee from the bar. Instead, they stood their ground and mocked the police. Recognizing the significance of the event, Michaels labeled it "historic" and said it signaled "a new era of determined resistance" among the Los Angeles gay community. He wrote: "The ADVOCATE salutes the customers of the Patch for their courage, individually and collectively. It was a positive act. And only by a series of such positive acts will the LAPD learn once and for all that it cannot use its power to persecute people."[81]

The newspaper's most proactive effort to mobilize readers came in an editorial encouraging them to organize a fund-raising event to establish a gay legal defense fund. After three months passed with no response, Michaels scolded his readers for ignoring him and repeated the proposal. This time it caught fire. Plans for a dance were made, and three months later the Homophile Effort for Legal Protection (HELP) was founded.[82]

The *Advocate* helped unify its community in less direct ways as well. Almost two years before the movement exploded into history with the famous raid in New York City, the West Coast newspaper was writing as if a revolution were already in full swing. News stories routinely used terms such as *the movement, the Cause,* and *Gay Power.* The banner headline across the top of the *Advocate*'s first front page read, "U.S. Capital Turns on to Gay Power."[83]

In fact, the hard-hitting newspaper spoke with defiance throughout its pages. Although the editorial in the premier issue boasted that all opinion expressed in the newspaper would be confined to editorials, in reality the *Advocate* was, as its name implied, a gay rights advocate that blended interpretation into its news stories. A page-one article about the California Supreme Court upholding the legality of drag shows, for example, contained the editorial statement, "The new changes in the regulations are a welcome step in the right direction—one that is long overdue." A front-page article reporting that two PRIDE members had been acquitted on moral charges carried the forty-two-point headline "PRIDE WINS!!"[84]

That lesbians were doubly discriminated against, both as homosexuals and as women, did not preclude lesbian journalists from speaking with any less defiance than their gay brothers. Indeed, as had been the case from the founding of the lesbian and gay press, some of the most powerful voices of the late 1960s were women. One of the strongest was also one of the most veteran. Del Martin, who helped her lover Phyllis Lyon found *The Ladder* in 1956, had been largely eclipsed by Barbara Gittings during the mid-1960s, but, as the decade neared its end, Martin's verbal assaults on homophobia again rose to prominence.

Martin's *Ladder* editorials were based on hard facts and presented in a no-nonsense fashion. She observed, for example, that the fight for gay rights was shifting to the battleground of economics: "There has been a growing emphasis upon homosexuals as consumers and a drive to support homosexual merchants and boycott those businesses which discriminate against homosexuals." In another straightforward editorial, Martin argued that the new generation of gays, as a product of the youth rebellion, simply would not be bullied by the old techniques of police raiding the bars. Martin wrote of the new power generated by gay youths: "The pressure is on. It is an unrelenting pressure on the collective conscience of society."[85]

Martin did not confine her attacks to antihomosexual forces. As the winds of liberation increasingly empowered American women, lesbian journalists expressed a rising frustration with gay men. And Martin led the chorus. In 1967 she commended the newly formed National Organization for Women as a possible alternative to the gay organizations that had long relegated lesbians to second-class citizenship. She said that lesbians were not really considered members of the homosexual community: "In reality and certainly for all practical purposes, this is a myth, a delusion, a bill of goods sold to us by male homosexual organizations which pretend to be co-educational."[86]

Barbara Grier was even more controversial, as her opinions often conflicted with those of her gay brothers *and* her lesbian sisters. Grier was committed to sexual monogamy, for example, and insisted on referring to the two lengthy romantic relationships in her own life by the politically incorrect term *marriages*. She also insisted that there are no valid excuses for gay people hiding their sexual orientation. She said recently: "Long before phrases like 'out of the closet' came into vogue, I argued that we had to acknowledge our sexuality. I wasn't saying we had to yell it from the rooftop. I was saying—and I still say—that if you travel through life being honest, that honesty ultimately will pay off."[87]

Among the new generation of lesbian journalists, the strongest words boomed from Martha Shelley. A brilliant theorist as well as a graceful writer, Shelley was a leading force in creating a revolutionary ideology as the foundation for the modern Lesbian and Gay Liberation Movement. Her initial editorials in *The Ladder* were aimed at the researchers who studied gay people. Not in the least bit intimidated by the stature and prestige of the leading anti-homosexual scientists, Shelley boldly criticized their conclusions as well as their methods. She said, "To suggest that homosexuality is a disease because it involves guilt feelings, confusion about one's sexuality, and other psychological problems is a sophistry." For the scientific studies to have any value, Shelley argued, they had to be reconceptualized to acknowledge that most of the problems gay people face are not caused by homosexuality, but by society's *response* to homosexuality.[88]

Nichols and Clarke's column, like Shelley's articles, lambasted straight psychiatrists and psychologists who claimed to be experts on homosexuality. The message echoed Nichols's assaults in the *Homosexual Citizen* earlier in the decade, but those attacks now were festooned in the colorful language of the counterculture. The columnists routinely referred to psychiatrists as "loony dogmatists" and "witchdoctors." Nichols and Clarke also were among the first activists opposed to expending time and energy to determine the cause of homosexuality. Like the generations that followed them, the columnists argued that the concept of "cause" is dangerously close to the concept of "blame."[89]

Drum also was unequivocal in demanding an end to gay oppression, arguing that change would come only through open rebellion. "Homosexuality is speaking its name—more boldly, more intelligently than ever before," editor Clark P. Polak wrote. "And if this is a sign of a revolution, it's a revolution which has not been 'made,' rather it has 'come.'"[90]

Leo Laurence, during his brief time as *Vector* editor, was even more enthusiastic about the prospect of a gay revolution. Bearing in mind that the Stonewall Rebellion in June 1969 was led by a group of women and men in their early twenties, Laurence's statement in April 1969 is prophetic: "Only about one percent of the homosexual leaders I've interviewed are willing to publicly say: 'I'm gay and I'm proud!' About the only people with that kind of courage are the new breed of young gay kids. The old-timers are scared that these kids will come in and really create a gay revolution."[91]

Setting the Course for Future Generations

During the late 1960s, an increasing number of homosexuals shed their cocoon of fear and self-loathing as Lesbian and Gay America continued its gradual transformation from crawling caterpillar to soaring butterfly. Fueling that metamorphosis was the Counterculture Movement that emerged in the second half of the decade to create a youth rebellion of unprecedented size and impact. The gay and lesbian press reflected the values of the rebellion by, for example, expanding the linguistic boundaries of American journalism to include words and phrases establishment newspapers eschewed as patently offensive. Again, as in its earlier stages, this profoundly creative genre of the alternative press demonstrated a unique ability to speak the unspeakable.

Beyond gay journalism reflecting the counterculture, it simultaneously was shaped by it. The editorial content of the leaders of the genre in the late 1960s—the "Homosexual Citizen," the *Los Angeles Advocate*, and *Drum*—were strongly influenced by the sexual revolution. This liberated attitude ushered in the frank sexual discussions and homoerotic images that earlier publications had steered clear of. By the end of the 1960s, sexual content had mushroomed into a dominant element of the gay press. The social liberalism of the era shaped gay journalism in other ways as well. The rebellious atmosphere tacitly gave publications permission to redesign themselves into the tabloid format that had come to define alternative media and to speak in the lexicon that had developed in sub-rosa gay networks.

The era did not, however, avoid a long list of casualties. *Mattachine Review,* the strongest proponent of homosexuals accommodating to heterosexual society, had appeared only sporadically since 1964 as Hal Call gradually shifted his energies to publishing his "bar rag" and operating a gay bookstore and X-rated movie theater. Call published the final issue of *Town Talk* in 1966 and the *Review* in 1967. Although Call had been the first professional journalist to work in the gay press and had devoted twelve years to the genre, he never returned to journalism. He said recently: "It's not an easy field to work in. I ran out of steam." The next publication to expire was the much younger *Pursuit & Symposium.* That demise, in addition to indicating that Gay America had not yet evolved to the point where it could support an erudite magazine, spoke to the increasing financial challenges inherent in gay journalism. Printing costs for the first issue pushed the magazine $4,000 into the red, and, despite contributions from an outside investor and Kepner mortgaging his home, the magazine was forced to cease publication after only two issues.[92]

The problems encountered by Guy Strait, one of gay journalism's early purveyors of erotica, proved fatal to his two publications as well. The conservative mainstream news magazine *U.S. News & World Report* was not pleased with the similarity between its name and that of Strait's *Cruise News & World Report.* Kepner said, "*U.S. News* was not interested in sharing its name with some faggot publication." *San Francisco Chronicle* columnist Herb Caen featured the controversy in his popular column in 1966. Caen quoted *U.S. News*'s attorney as telling Strait: "I've read your publication quite carefully, and I don't understand why you're using that title in the first place. There's nothing in it about cruises." Caen also published Strait's witty response: "You're using the King's English. I use the Queen's!" Strait's humor did not impress *U.S. News*, which sued him for copyright infringement. Strait then ceased publishing *Cruise News*, as well as *Citizens News*, in 1967, and focused his entrepreneurial energies on his mail-order erotica business.[93]

The saddest fatality of the period was of the venerable *ONE*. The first national voice for gay men had failed to adapt either to the militancy of the mid-1960s or the counterculture values of the late 1960s. After sixteen years, *ONE* died in December 1969. *Tangents*, *ONE*'s imitator, followed a few months later. The era witnessed the end of an important East Coast magazine as well. In 1967 Clark P. Polak, whose *Drum* was the first gay publication to print full-frontal nudity, was charged with publishing and distributing obscene material, leading to an eighteen-count indictment by a federal grand jury. To avoid a prison sentence, Polak agreed to cease publishing his magazine and move from Philadelphia to Los Angeles.[94]

More important than the specific themes of the late 1960s press or the passing of individual magazines was an overarching concept. By this period, it had become clear the lesbian and gay press had evolved into a distinct form of journalism—exhibiting themes and characteristics unique from those of either the mainstream press or other alternative presses. Some themes had been established some twenty years earlier in *Vice Versa* or had been introduced in the publications of the 1950s and mid-1960s; others had surfaced with the rise of the counterculture. Regardless of exactly when they originated, these themes were of profound significance. Most important, they were distinct. Historians studying other forms of the alternative press—African-American, women's suffrage, and women's liberation publications—have not identified these themes as significant factors in the development of those media. In addition, these themes have continued to define the several generations of gay publications that were to evolve in the 1970s and 1980s. Indeed, these same themes inform the lesbian and gay press today.[95]

Among the themes is an emphasis on design. Lisa Ben introduced this concept in 1947 when she painstakingly typed and retyped each word in *Vice Versa* not only to strive for typographical perfection, but to attain it. Ben established that the lesbian and gay press being nonconformist did not dictate that it would be ragtag in appearance. The founders of *ONE* reinforced this theme during the

1950s, insisting that their magazine be professionally printed and using bold graphics to make design one of its trademarks. The publications of the late 1960s reinforced the central role of design, with *The Ladder* dressing itself up in a slick cover and the *Los Angeles Advocate* pioneering the tabloid format that would soon become synonymous with gay journalism.

Closely related to design is a strong emphasis on visual images. *ONE* deserves credit for introducing this contribution, courageously publishing sexually suggestive advertisements in 1954—and suffering the consequences by being hauled into court the next month. *The Ladder* solidified the theme through its cover images, first with striking line drawings in the 1950s and then with demythologizing photographs of beautiful lesbians in the 1960s. *Drum,* the "Homosexual Citizen," *Vector,* and *The Ladder* carried the theme dramatically forward in the late 1960s as they broke new ground by publishing the first erotic images, which quickly grew to dominate the genre.

The editors of the 1950s magazines deserve both credit and blame for introducing a high level of discord as a third prominent theme. In the 1950s, the major enemies were the Post Office and the FBI, as federal authorities attempted to censor gay magazines. But in the 1960s staff members became the enemies within as personal and ideological disputes destroyed some publications, such as the *Homosexual Citizen,* and severely damaged others, including *ONE* and *The Ladder.* In the late 1960s, internal as well as external confrontations held sway. A *Vector* editor's embracing of counterculture values resulted in his being expelled from the editor's chair; the sexual content of the gay press renewed the specter of the censor and exposed the collision of homoerotic images and straight advertisers as a continuing trouble spot. Fractious relationships, both external and internal, were firmly established as a recurring plotline in the genre's unfolding story.

A fourth theme is the blurring of the "church/state" line. One of the principles of journalistic professionalism is that a news organization should not favor, in its news and editorial content, businesses that buy advertising space in it. If an advertiser demands favorable news coverage, the editorial staff is expected to reject—with considerable indignation—such an outlandish proposal. With the lesbian and gay press, however, the issue is not so black-and-white, as the march toward gay civil rights and the rise of gay businesses often intersect. In the 1950s and 1960s, for example, the bars emerged as a major battleground for gay rights, as they were where gay people wanted to meet, dance, and show affection for each other just as straight people did, without being arrested. In addition, the bars functioned as unofficial gay community centers, as demonstrated by *Vice Versa, ONE,* and the *Los Angeles Advocate* all initially being distributed in the bars of Los Angeles because newsstands and bookstores refused to touch such publications. It was only logical, then, for the gay press to promote the growth of the bars, as well as the development of other businesses geared toward responding to the needs and desires of a gay clientele. *ONE* in the 1950s and *Drum* in the 1960s began to blur the "church/state" line as they struggled to achieve financial stability. Nichols and Clarke obliterated that line when they shamelessly promoted the founding of the Oscar Wilde Memorial Bookshop as an event of historic proportions. It was clear by the late 1960s that the economic vitality of Gay America would cause its press to evolve very differently from that of other repressed minorities.[96]

It was during the mid-1960s that gay journalism firmly established it would be a specialized genre of the media dedicated not merely to informing its readers, but also to amusing them. Lisa Ben introduced this theme by founding *Vice Versa* as a gimmick to improve her social life and punctuating "America's Gayest Magazine" with phrases such as her Valentine's Day message "Heart-y Greetings!" *Drum* reinforced amusement as a major theme by welcoming the virile Harry Chess as a flavorful addition; while *Vector* followed with popular features, such as its "Bar Tour" column written by "Tequila Mockingbird," that redefined the parameters of American journalism. The "Homosexual Citizen" column in *Screw* stretched those limits even further with its highly personalized approach to journalism.

A sixth distinctive characteristic of the gay press did not surface until the youth rebellion of the late 1960s invited the realignment of so many aspects of American culture. It was in that milieu of social upheaval that gay publications began conversing in a unique lexicon largely unintelligible to heterosexual society. It was not coincidental that the *Los Angeles Advocate*, the first publication to look and read like a newspaper, pioneered many of these words and phrases. Speaking in its own language was a political statement of enormous significance to the gay press, serving at once to affirm and to validate the gay community.

These half dozen characteristics are crucial, both individually and in aggregate, to understanding the history and evolution of the lesbian and gay press. Further enhancing their significance is the timing of their emergence. All six of these distinct characteristics came into existence *before* the Stonewall Rebellion. Establishing that these elements were firmly in place before the explosive events that began the night of June 27, 1969, is significant because it is in concert with other recent scholarship about the Lesbian and Gay Liberation Movement. Early chroniclers of the movement ignored efforts that occurred before Stonewall, crediting that single event for beginning—or even creating—the momentum for combatting gay oppression. More recent scholarship, however, has documented that the movement began much earlier than 1969.[97]

The same early chroniclers of gay history, in passing references to the gay press, denigrated pre-Stonewall publications as retarding the struggle for liberation. So, just as recent scholarship has illuminated the importance of activities preceding the rebellion at the Stonewall Inn, close examination of the lesbian and gay press of the 1940s through 1960s shows that it laid the groundwork and established the dominant themes that have continued to define the genre throughout the second half of the twentieth century. In addition, the publications born on the eve of Stonewall also recorded the most spectacular growth in the history of lesbian and gay journalism; never before and never since has the circulation of the gay press surged tenfold in half a decade.

λ 5

After Stonewall:
Transforming a "Moment" into a Movement

The Stonewall Rebellion was the point of departure for Lesbian and Gay America. As the explosive event that thrust an oppressed minority full force into social upheaval, it marked the birth of gay and lesbian pride on a massive scale. The courage and defiance that patrons of the Stonewall Inn displayed served to announce to the nation that gay people would no longer tolerate second-class citizenship. It was a psychological milestone of great importance.

Despite the significance of the event, however, a single moment of rebellion cannot create a revolution—it can only ignite a revolution. After that rebellious act, it was left to the lesbian and gay press to debate the myriad issues facing the revolutionaries, thereby fanning the spark of defiance into a raging forest fire that ultimately would engulf all gay people and, indeed, all Americans. *Gay Sunshine,* one of the radical new voices, acknowledged the leaders of the Homophile Movement but then continued, "It is time to move on, and the ground rules and basic assumptions of that movement are no longer acceptable." The Stonewall impulse served as a call to action, and gay journalism responded with a level of energy not witnessed before or since. The handful of publications existing in June 1969 recorded the details and speculated on the significance of the rebellion. Then those journalistic veterans scurried to keep up with the surge of in-your-face newspapers that burst into print in the wake of Stonewall—voicing outrage, demanding justice, and shrieking at the top of their lungs. The old and new voices ultimately coalesced to create a seminal generation of the gay and lesbian press that provided a forum for the fiery debates that followed. By airing these dialogues, the publications set the course for the ongoing revolution.[1]

As with many agents of change that explode into action, the first wave of post-Stonewall journalism was defined by its excesses. While the pre-Stonewall *Ladder, Vector,* and *Los Angeles Advocate* had already introduced the elements that became staples of the gay tabloids, none produced those elements with the abandon or in the abundance as the "wild and woolly" papers born in the heady days after the rebellion. Those elements took on a life of their own as the upstart tabloids fed on each other, pushing the envelope of good taste further and further, and then further still. Screaming headlines, titillating images, anarchistic concepts, and language designed more to shock than to illuminate—all contributed to the fervor of sensationalism that informed this new chapter.

Merely listing the names of the newspapers that burst onto the streets of New York City communicates a palpable sense of what they stood for: *GAY, Come Out!, Gay Times, Gay Flames.* The shock waves reached the West Coast as well, producing such radical voices as *Gay Sunshine* and the *San Francisco Gay Free Press.* Between the two coasts, the tremors created *Lavender Vision* in Boston, *Gay Liberator* in Detroit, and *Killer Dyke* in Chicago. Although many of the publications were short-lived, they left an indelible mark that—for good or bad—the genre would never again equal.

After the apocalyptic Stonewall impulse, the press erupted in so many directions that it is impossible to document when each publication was founded, how long it existed, or who edited it. Much like the American patriots of two centuries earlier, some editors merely posted their revolutionary rhetoric on a tree or door perhaps only once or perhaps in the same spot for several weeks or months, without ever including the date of publication or name of its creator. When names did appear, they often were only first names or *noms de guerre* such as "Gay Commandoes." The catalyst was neither public recognition nor personal profit, but the spreading of impassioned prose and revolutionary ideas. Those ideas often called for breaking the law, so their authors opted for anonymity.

From this era through the present, the total circulation of this form of alternative press can only be estimated. *Our Own Voices: A Directory of Lesbian and Gay Periodicals* lists 150 publications being produced in 1972. Many were internal newsletters of the professional organizations gay people created after Stonewall. The aggregate circulation figure surpassed 100,000. If the circulation of *Screw*, which continued to publish the "Homosexual Citizen" column, were added, the total was upward of 250,000.[2]

Regardless of their circulations, the publications created an arena in which lesbian and gay leaders waged their battles over what their social movement would be and where it was headed. Editors and writers stood at the front lines of the ideological warfare, defining the themes debated in New York City and across the country well into the next decade.

Gay journalists stood on other front lines as well. For after the Stonewall riots, the FBI began investigating movement leaders. John O'Brien, who participated in the riots and then founded the street newspaper *Gay Times,* was a favorite. The agents believed O'Brien had to be a straight revolutionary who had infiltrated the Gay Liberation Movement—which they called the "Fag" Liberation Movement—because the twenty-year-old young man's husky and rugged-looking appearance did not jibe with their image of a gay activist. In their reports, agents routinely referred to gay men as "sissies" and "pansies." Therefore the agents assumed that O'Brien was merely agitating the gay men, whom they assumed were easily influenced by such a virile young man. After observing O'Brien distributing his newspaper and leading political discussions, the agents were shocked at the amount of information he had about President Nixon's travel plans. Concerned that O'Brien was planning to assassinate the president, the agents conducted an intense investigation into O'Brien's personal life, which became part of the 2,800 pages of material the FBI collected on the immediate post-Stonewall leaders.[3]

Martha Shelley, who also participated in the riots, became one of the most powerful journalists of the era. After having written for *The Ladder* in the mid-1960s, Shelley shifted to the radical *Come Out!* She recently recalled: "It was that marvelous moment at the very beginning of a new adventure when everything—absolutely *every*thing—seems possible. Every topic was on the table. We didn't agree a lot, but we always gave each other respect. We'd all been involved in other movements where gay people were second class. No more. Now we had our own movement, and we were primed to debate just where that movement would take us." The debates embodied key issues that would not be easy to resolve. Indeed, some remain central to the gay rights struggle today.[4]

It was during the period immediately after Stonewall, however, that the debates rose to their highest decibel level, trumpeted through the shrillness of a sensationalistic press: Should gays unite with African Americans in a unified struggle for civil rights? Is a persecuted minority group justified in using violence to end its oppression? Is anarchy the only route to gay and lesbian liberation? Should gays create a society totally separate from straights? Are the issues, values, and cultural differences between gay men and lesbians so great that they require two separate movements? Should the core of the movement distance itself from fringe groups such as drag queens and "dykes on bikes"? Should the gay and lesbian culture adopt sexual mores different from those of the heterosexual community? What should be the primary target for reform—fighting police harassment? breaking into mainstream politics? improving media coverage? ferreting the Mafia out of gay businesses?

Stonewall Rebellion

The straight media covered the police raid in Greenwich Village much as they had covered previous events involving gay people—as criminal acts to be treated with scorn and ridicule. By using the adjective *hostile* in its headline, the *New York Times* sent out the message that gays were enemies of civilized society: "Hostile Crowd Dispersed Near Sheridan Square"; the *New York Daily News* portrayed the activists as laughable: "Homo Nest Raided; Queen Bees Are Stinging Mad." The *Village Voice* joined the mockery with the headline: "Full Moon over the Stonewall." The disdainful tone permeating the *Voice* was particularly disheartening because the tabloid was *supposedly* an alternative to the establishment press. Yet the *Voice* blithely filled its story with taunting words and phrases—"prancing," "forces of faggotry," "fag follies," "wrists were limp, hair was primped." *Time* and *Newsweek* chose to ignore the event, not even mentioning it until four months after it had occurred.[5]

In addition to being biased, mainstream coverage lacked the background information that could have provided perspective on the Stonewall Inn. After failing as a straight restaurant and nightclub, the bar had reopened in 1966 as the epitome of the grim realities of the New York gay bar scene. It was operated by three Mafia figures—Mario, Zucchi, and Fat Tony—who routinely referred to their clientele as "faggot scumbags." Paying only $300 a month rent and raking in $5,000 every weekend, the trio turned a tidy profit, even after paying off the officers from the Sixth Precinct and the local Mafia don—Matty "the Horse" Iannello. Police raids were routine. Indeed, the bar had been raided in mid-June, only to reopen the next night.[6]

The Stonewall Inn lacked many amenities. Because there was no running water behind the bar, after a customer used a glass, the bartender merely dipped it into a vat of stale water and then filled it again for the next customer. Despite the health hazards and overpriced drinks, gay men flocked to the bar. Because the Stonewall Inn had the only gay dance floor in the city and bartender Maggie Jiggs dealt acid and uppers with aplomb, it attracted a lively clientele. Most noticeable were the drag queens and throngs of chino-clad young men in their late teens or early twenties who were pursued by a sprinkling of older men—known in gay parlance as *chicken hawks*—who lusted after underage boys, with a handful of lesbians thrown in for good measure.[7]

June 27, 1969, was the day New York buried music legend Judy Garland, a favorite of many gay men. Some 20,000 people had waited up to four hours in the blistering heat to view Garland's body, with many of the gay admirers hitting the bars that night to unwind. Except for that event, the Friday at the Stonewall

Inn seemed like most every other one. Then, at 1:20 A.M., eight police officers stormed through the front door. And all hell broke loose.

The *Los Angeles Advocate*'s story began with a lead that was straightforward but also communicated the importance of the event: "The first gay riots in history took place during the pre-dawn hours of Saturday and Sunday, June 28–29, in New York's Greenwich Village. The demonstrations were touched off by a police raid." The *Advocate* reported that after patrons were removed from the bar, they gathered in the street and began jeering at police. If a single individual fueled the crowd's resistance, it was a lesbian who, when an officer shoved her into the street, pushed back. Emotions flared as the angry gays turned steely and began tossing beer cans, rocks, and even a parking meter or two. When police retreated inside the bar, the defiant gays set the building ablaze. The police somehow found a fire hose and escaped from the bar that night. But the exhilarated gays rioted again and again throughout the week, with their pent-up energy escalating into a full-scale rebellion involving 2,000 gay men and lesbians, 300 police officers, thirteen arrests, and four injured police officers.[8]

The *Advocate* article was not dominated by statistics; reporter Dick Leitsch also included anecdotes to capture the flavor of the historic moment. He described a senior police officer being chauffeured through the streets: "The fat cop looked for all the world like a slave-owner surveying the plantation, and someone tossed a sack of wet garbage through the car window and right on his face. The bag broke and soggy coffee grounds dripped down the lined face." Leitsch also praised the courage and creativity his gay brothers displayed. One anecdote read: "A cop grabbed a wild Puerto Rican queen and lifted his arm to bring a club down on 'her.' In his best Maria Montez voice, the queen challenged, 'How'd you like a big Spanish dick up your little Irish ass?' The cop was so shocked he hesitated in his swing, and the queen escaped." The most vivid vignette described police officers stopped in their tracks when they came face to face with a chorus line of drag queens who kicked their legs in the air like the Rockettes and sang at the top of their sardonic lungs:

We are the Stonewall girls
We wear our hair in curls
We wear no underwear
We show our pubic hair
We wear our dungarees
Above our nelly knees![9]

The most insightful comments about the uprising came from gay press veterans Jack Nichols and Lige Clarke, who covered Stonewall in their "Homo-

sexual Citizen" column. Nichols and Clarke's coverage of the rebellion en-
sconced them as journalistic prophets of the post-Stonewall era. After the
decades of abuse gay people had suffered, their enthusiasm for the new era
throbbed with their every word. They wrote that they were "thrilled by the violent uprising" and then placed the pivotal event in historical context: "A new
generation is angered by raids and harassment of gay bars, and last week's riots
in Greenwich Village have set standards for the rest of the nation's homosexuals
to follow. The Sheridan Square Riot showed the world that homosexuals will
no longer take a beating without a good fight. The police were scared shitless
and the massive crowds of angry protesters chased them for blocks screaming,
'Catch them! Fuck them!' There was a shrill, righteous indignation in the air.
Homosexuals had endured such raids and harassment long enough. It was time
to take a stand."[10]

Nichols and Clarke did not rely only on their own analysis but also reported
the uprising through the eyes of a leading guru of the Beat generation. A few
days after the riots, the columnists walked through the riot-torn area with poet
Allen Ginsberg. Not only did they document his announcement of his own
homosexuality, but they also recorded what became the most poignant description of the change the rebellion created. They wrote: "Ginsberg said, 'Gay
power! Isn't that great! It's about time we did something to assert ourselves.' He
walked in the Stonewall, dancing and bouncing to the music. He said, 'The guys
are so beautiful. They've lost that wounded look that fags had 10 years ago.'"[11]

GAY Sets the Pace

After writing for the *Homosexual Citizen* magazine in Washington and creating
the "Homosexual Citizen" column in *Screw*, Nichols and Clarke finally began
editing their own newspaper in December 1969. And what a newspaper it was.
GAY became the newspaper of record for Gay America. In the words of the first
anthology of gay nonfiction, *The Gay Insider: USA,* written in 1972, "The spirit
of Lige and Jack is that of the Gay Press." Lilli Vincenz, who wrote a lesbian-
oriented column for *GAY,* said, "It was the newspaper of the day. If you were gay
and you wanted to find out what was going on in the world, you turned to
GAY." Although the tabloid summarized gay and lesbian news from across the
country, its most memorable elements were those of personalized journalism—lively columns, editorials, and graphics. In their first issue, the editors
promised: "*GAY* is pleased to welcome you to a new experience in the field of
publishing: a newspaper which is interesting, entertaining and informative.
GAY realizes that homosexuals are sexual beings, but many other things in

addition! It will bring to its readers the full range of human interests as viewed by people who are attracted to their own sex."[12]

The editors applauded the prominent role sex and fantasy play in the gay male culture and used that concept to connect with their readers. Each issue featured a full-page photo of a handsome man on the cover and a plethora of homoerotic images and references inside. Photos of genitalia were commonplace. To illustrate a three-inch article about arrests at a pornographic bookstore, for example, the editors used a five-by-twelve-inch photo of a man wearing nothing but a come-hither glance. The caption identified the man as Studio Bookshop employee Rick Nielsen.[13]

Reader-service material had a strong presence. Vincenz, former editor of the *Homosexual Citizen,* advised readers on how to talk to parents about their sexual orientation and how to meet potential life partners. Other items provided information on health-related issues that were vital to sexually active gay men—such as how to avoid gonorrhea and anal warts—but were not discussed in other publications available to a lay audience. Such articles were written not in medical jargon but in the idiomatic language of the streets. A column on proper hygiene urged readers to be careful when "rimming," the sexual activity that brings a person's mouth into contact with a lover's anus: "Rimming snowmen may be the only surefire way to avoid Hepatitis. Otherwise, and for good measure, douche. With whatever you please: salty water, soapy water, a mild vinegar solution, or some mad scented preparation reputedly for ladies only. It's a nice thing to do. Considerate. It's so sweet to meet someone who has gone to the trouble of readying himself for you."[14]

Such language reflected the eagerness of the gay press to flaunt its new freedom, but it also attested to the fact that *GAY* needed to attract a large audience. Unlike most gay and lesbian publications, *GAY* was not affiliated with an activist organization and therefore could not depend on membership dues to pay the bills. It was a business—the East Coast equivalent of the *Los Angeles Advocate*—that relied on advertising and circulation revenue. In announcing the debut of the newspaper, *The Ladder* characterized *GAY* as a "middle-of-the-road commercial" publication that carried "only sufficient sensationalism to provide the revenue to keep it in print." *The Ladder* went on to praise *GAY*'s editorial stance as "politically conservative." Conservative perhaps, but never dull. The paper's horoscope was labeled "Hornyscope" and its crossword puzzle the "Peter Puzzle"... a review of *Everything You Always Wanted to Know About Sex* was titled "Is There an Onion Up Your Ass?"... and when closeted FBI Director J. Edgar Hoover died, *GAY* celebrated with the headline: "Ding! Dong! The Wicked Witch Is Dead!"[15]

GAY was financed by Al Goldstein. Having established *Screw* as a successful enterprise a year earlier, Goldstein invested $25,000 in *GAY* in hopes of earning a hefty profit. Goldstein distributed the newspaper and found advertising to support it; Nichols and Clarke supplied the editorial content.[16]

The new sense of gay liberation that soared in Greenwich Village after Stonewall gave *GAY* a ready audience. Some 20,000 people plunked down forty cents to buy the first issue, and within a month circulation reached 25,000—surpassing the figure it had taken the *Advocate* two years to build. So, by the end of 1969, *GAY* boasted the largest circulation in the history of the lesbian and gay press. Within six months, the twenty-page biweekly had grown to a twenty-four-page weekly, making it the first gay publication to appear with that frequency.[17]

The winds of liberation also helped *GAY* attract advertising. In the tradition of *Screw*, *GAY* was eager to accommodate advertisers by publishing display ads that contained erotic images. As the number of Mafia-owned gay bars and bath houses exploded in the largest urban center in the country, an increasing proportion of *GAY*'s pages were filled with graphic ads that gloried in full-frontal nudity.

Come Out! Raises a Radical Voice

The archetype of the revolutionary journals that erupted after Stonewall shrieked onto the streets of Greenwich Village in November 1969. In that inaugural issue, the bimonthly *Come Out!* dramatically demonstrated both the diversity and continuing acrimony among the citizenry of the gay press by calling for an economic boycott of *GAY* because it was owned by a straight businessman.[18]

Come Out! did not aspire to journalistic fairness. Instead, it rejected the conventions of the established social and political order, including those of the Fourth Estate. The first issue called readers to action: "Come out for freedom! Come out now! Power to the people! Gay power to gay people! Come out of the closet before the door is nailed shut! *Come Out!* has COME OUT to fight for the freedom of the homosexual; to give voice to the rapidly growing militancy within our community; to provide a public forum for the discussion and clarification of methods and actions nexessary to end our oppression."[19]

Come Out! was the printed voice of the Gay Liberation Front, born in New York City in July 1969 but quickly spreading across the country. The front was composed of young gay men and lesbians whose revolutionary fervor had been inflamed by U.S. military involvement in Vietnam and the academic establishment's refusal to allow students to play a role in university governance. The Gay Liberation Front became to the Gay and Lesbian Liberation Movement what the Black Panthers had become to the Civil Rights Movement. The leftists demanded not only gay rights, but the overthrow of American society. By September, members were producing angry leaflets to spread their revolutionary ideas to a larger audience. By November the leaflets evolved into *Come Out!*[20]

Headlines were used, and copy was typeset in two- and three-column formats, but journalistic conventions ended there. Many pages carried no numbers, and articles were riddled with typos and grammatical errors. Language was far more colorful and explicit than in most newspapers. Police were referred to as *pigs, fascists,* and *swine. America* became *Amerika. Fuck* and *cunt* appeared with regularity. Staff member Martha Shelley recently spoke for all the writers: "We had no respect whatsoever for either the uniformed police or the thought police. Both were front-line goons of the government, and the government was our enemy."[21]

The editorial mix in *Come Out!* was dominated by essays and commentary pieces written by an equal number of lesbians and gay men. Less prominent elements included poems, letters from readers, and reviews of books and films. Illustrations consisted mostly of homoerotic drawings and photographs that depicted women as well as men. News articles were sprinkled throughout the twenty pages. One reported that members of the front had disrupted a political forum for New York City mayoral candidates. Another item said the *Village Voice* had censored a classified ad *Come Out!* had placed to solicit articles; the *Voice,* which heralded itself as publishing ideas the mainstream press would not accept, had deleted "Gay Power to Gay People" from the copy for the paid ad, stating that the word *gay* was obscene. Although most news articles focused on events in New York City, some reported embryonic gay liberation efforts in such cities as Provincetown, Massachusetts, and Tallahassee, Florida.[22]

Editorial content reflected the new sexual freedom. A two-page spread titled "Cocksucking Seminar" discussed how to increase the pleasure of oral sex. It was illustrated with photographs of male genitalia and men engaging in sexual activity. Although such material pushed journalistic reader-service articles to new limits, it provided information gay men needed and were eager to read.[23]

In keeping with their nonconformist leanings, staff members rejected hierarchical structure. Instead, *Come Out!* was published collectively by members of the front. Names of contributors were listed, but no one carried the title of editor. The masthead stated "The basic Staff—editors, layout, co-ordinators, etc.—is drawn by lots and changes with each issue." During a gay press panel discussion covered in *GAY,* staff member Lois Hart explained the philosophy behind the lack of structure: "We have a definite view that the society is what's fucking us up. That a male-dominated, capitalistic, heterosexual society is the root of all our problems. We think competition and producing to earn money is the root of a lot of our problems."[24]

The newspaper contained no advertising, and staff members received no salaries. Indeed, paying writers conflicted with the newspaper's anticapitalism philosophy. In a letter to potential contributors, the staff wrote: "*COME OUT* will not insult you by offering you payment." *Come Out!* had a press run of 6,000. Most copies were sold on the streets of Manhattan, while a few hundred were mailed to other Gay Liberation Front chapters in Chicago, San Francisco, and Los Angeles.[25]

Uniting with Other Oppressed Minorities?

One of the first issues post-Stonewall publications tackled was whether gay revolutionaries should unite with other oppressed groups to form an omnibus social movement. In particular, they debated whether to form a coalition with the Black Panthers. The logic behind the proposal centered on the power of numbers. Rebelling gays and rebelling blacks both aspired to the basic goal of social change. Society had ignored the cries for justice from both groups, but if they banded together to become one united force with a larger membership, society might no longer be able to discount them. The relatively inexperienced gay and lesbian radicals—most of them middle-class whites—were further attracted to the Panthers because the inner-city guerrillas had built, since forming in 1966, a reputation as fearless revolutionaries who willingly put their lives on the line. And, finally, that the Panthers were led by Huey P. Newton added to their appeal. Newton's elegant mulatto face and trim, muscular body caused many gay men to line up behind him, especially when he put on a leather jacket and sporty beret to become a fearless warrior against the establishment.

Radical publications lauded the idea of uniting with black revolutionaries. A Gay Liberation Front leaflet distributed in August, labeled "A Radical Manifesto," stated: "We see the persecution of homosexuality as part of a general attempt to oppress all minorities and keep them powerless. Our fate is linked with these minorities; if the detention camps are filled tomorrow with blacks, hippies and other radicals, we will not long escape that fate."[26]

When the leaflets evolved into *Come Out!,* the premier issue endorsed the coalition concept: "Come Out hopes to unify the homosexual community and other oppressed groups into a cohesive body." Later issues were dotted with items about activities of the Black Panthers, as well as those of Puerto Rican and Latin American revolutionaries, and included several articles written in Spanish.[27]

Strong support for a revolutionary coalition also came from *Gay Sunshine*, a tabloid founded in August 1970 by gay men living in a Berkeley, California, collective. In its first editorial, *Gay Sunshine* vowed to unite all people who were oppressed by the white, straight, middle-class establishment. The newspaper, determined that gays should join African-American revolutionaries, vowed to "call together all those who see themselves as oppressed" and "harken to the cause of human liberation, of which homosexual liberation is just one aspect."[28]

Pat Brown, one of the eight men who created the newspaper, dressed in "hippie" garb and allowed his blond hair to extend far below his shoulders. He recently recalled: "We were all determined to be radicals, and that meant that we were totally committed to the working class, even though every single one of us was born and reared middle class. We absolutely supported Huey Newton and the Black Panther Party—body and soul." *Gay Sunshine*'s debut issue in August showcased an interview with Newton, characterizing him as having a vision of uniting all oppressed people, including gays. The newspaper commended Newton effusively, gushing: "We all warmly acknowledge his support for Homosexual liberation. The oppressor of Homosexual women and men is also the oppressor of Black people everywhere, the racist, sexist, capitalist U.S. empire." In its second issue, *Gay Sunshine* reprinted a manifesto Newton had written to his followers, in which he said of homosexuals, "We should try to unite with them," and "When we have revolutionary conferences, rallies and demonstrations there should be full participation of the gay liberation movement."[29]

Newton's statements were indeed remarkable. For they marked the first time the leader of an African-American organization had acknowledged the oppression of gay people, much less made an effort to connect with them. The National Association for the Advancement of Colored People had consistently distanced its civil rights efforts from those of gay men and lesbians—and, in fact, would continue to do so until well into the 1990s. In addition, Newton's fellow Black Panthers Eldridge Cleaver and Bobby Seale had freely expressed their homophobia.[30]

Spurred on by the charismatic Newton's supportive words, *Gay Flames* added its name to the radical publications calling to unite with the Panthers. The newspaper was founded in September 1970 by men in the Gay Liberation Front who lived in the Chelsea section of Manhattan. In endorsing a coalition in its inaugural issue, the paper reasoned that such a united front would serve gays well because they were not yet experienced in the workings of a "people's revolution." *Gay Flames* praised the Panthers for their experience and clarity of purpose: "The party is the clearest of all us radical groups in its understanding of the nature of the fight."[31]

The strongest endorsement of all came from *Gay Times*, a short-lived street newspaper that preached socialism. The *Times* advocated a broad coalition of African Americans, Chicanos, gay men, lesbians, and straight women. John O'Brien, who single-handedly created the mimeographed newspaper, began pasting copies of his radical prose on the utility poles of Greenwich Village in October 1970. He used Carnation evaporated milk as an adhesive: "Once that milk dries, nobody can get it off. Your words are there to stay." O'Brien had worked in the Civil Rights Movement, and was fully committed to uniting black and gay revolutionaries. He recently recalled: "I was—and still am—a dogmatic Marxist. There was no doubt in my mind that the only valid approach was for all working class people to unite."[32]

Moderate publications, on the other hand, resolutely opposed uniting with the Black Panthers. Nichols and Clarke raised the possibility of a revolutionary gay-black alliance in their news coverage of Stonewall: "There have been some who are worried about outside groups who are offering to help the gay community and to channel its energies toward causes which have nothing to do with homosexuals. Extremists of various sorts have been trying to capitalize on their own causes by leading the new revolutionaries down their own paths." The terms *worried, outside groups,* and *extremists,* along with the phrase "causes which have nothing to do with homosexuals," clearly showed the authors' opposition to such a coalition.[33]

The *Advocate* also argued against any movement toward a gay-black coalition. Editor Dick Michaels wrote: "If you make every organization into a broad-spectrum organization dealing with all of the world's problems—about Vietnam and the Panthers and the blacks and the Chicanos and everything else, then who is going to do *our* work? Certainly not SDS!" News editor Rob Cole echoed the negative sentiments, decrying a gay-black alliance as nothing but "a strange marriage of convenience." Cole continued: "The Panthers use the word 'faggot' as an insult almost on a par with 'pig.' Malcolm X was quoted as saying that to him, 'all white men are blond, blue-eyed faggots.' Why, in the face of such expression from their chosen bedfellows, do so many of the more militant young Gays continue their affectionate attentions?"[34]

By the early fall of 1970, radical publications began to question the values of the black revolutionaries as well. Gay writers expressed concern about the Black Panthers murdering their own comrades and using racketeer-style methods to shake down struggling African-American businesses. Even the gay men who were bedazzled by the handsome and virile Newton became concerned that his cocaine habit was raging out of control. But the most vocal critics were lesbians writing for *Come Out!* They led the shift in attitude by vehemently attacking the Panthers's sexist attitude toward women. Lois Hart wrote of revolutionary black men: "No matter how great a person he might be, the straight man glorified is my oppression. Do I relate to the Black movement at this time in history and say fuck it to my struggle? Or do I say fuck it to anything that oppresses me—even revolutionary sisters and brothers?" Another lesbian writing in *Come Out!* insisted: "Speaking from our guts, from the depth of our oppression, we say that the Black Panthers are sexist. We will take no one's shit."[35]

These comments in the leading radical publication opened the floodgates for critics to question whether the other repressed groups were reciprocating the support given by gays and lesbians. In November Martha Shelley wrote in *Gay Sunshine* that the Panthers were patronizing toward gays and their reciprocal support was lukewarm at best. She accused gay activists of being so desperate for affirmation that they had embraced Newton too hastily. Expressing anger along with biting sarcasm, she asked: "Why was Huey Newton's patronizing statement on Women's Liberation and Gay Liberation received with such touching gratitude? Why did some gay people walk so tall after receiving Good Huey's seal of approval, as if their needs could not be considered valid, nor they revolutionary, unless the Black Panther Party approved of them?"[36]

By early 1971, *Gay Flames* had joined the radical publications that had shifted from support to opposition, arguing in favor of a one-issue approach to gay liberation without entangling alliances. *Gay Flames* pronounced the Black Panther party's unwavering support of the nuclear family to be counterrevolutionary as well as antihomosexual. By the winter of 1972, *Come Out!* had become so disenchanted with the Panthers that it referred to them as "pigs" and to their rhetoric as "vile."[37]

Embracing Violence?

Another issue dividing the gay press into two distinct camps was whether to use violence as part of their strategy for achieving equality. The Black Panthers not only advocated violence, but incorporated it into their revolutionary strategy. So militant gay men and lesbians debated whether they, too, should support the exertion of physical force. *GAY* and other moderate publications opposed violence; *Come Out!* and its imitators, reflecting the views of many young Americans whose worldview had been profoundly influenced by the murders of King and the Kennedys, fully endorsed violence. Pro-violence publications generally

In the last several weeks, the Lesbian-Gay-Transvestite community has come to an awareness concerning the conditions of lesbians and gay males and transvestites being held in the prisons, hospitals and juvenile centers of New York City. This new consciousness began when Street Transvestites Action Revolutionaries (STAR) brought the pleas of a transvestite being held at Bellevue Hospital to public attention, and it increased greatly when Raymond Lavon Moore, a black gay male, was murdered by guards in The Tombs (for details, see Gay Flames nos. 7-8). The exposure of the Lavon Moore atrocity by the Young Lords (who ignored the gay aspects) and the Vandenheuvel Commission (which whitewashed the brutality in general) made people active in the community groups, from Mattachine to GLF, take note of our incarcerated sisters and brothers and we have all begun to act.

The Gay Community Prisoner Defense Committee was formed to coordinate activities. Plans are being made to provide bail for jailed lesbians, gay males and transvestites who have not been convicted of anything except poverty. That is, because they can't afford bail, they rot in jail. The Defense Committee is also planning a demonstration for Feb. 27, at 2 p.m., at The Tombs, 100 Centre St. (corner of White, near City Hall), to bring to public attention the conditions of lesbian, gay male and transvestite inmates.

Gay Flames believes that the most important thing which can be done at this point is to push the city to prosecute whoever was responsible for Moore's death. We feel that the case reflects the concept of blame established at Nuremberg and relevant to the My Lai massacre -- that is, it is ultimately the city officials the ruling class who are responsible. Although the guards must be tried, and really their trial should be by black gay

- Contd. on page 6

Images of hand grenades, machine guns, and clenched fists dotted the pages of the militant gay and lesbian tabloids that erupted in the wake of 1969's Stonewall Rebellion.

saw destroying property as a sufficient demonstration of gay power, although some advocated the taking of human life as well.

Nichols and Clarke had become convinced that the major force impeding gay advancement was a lack of understanding on the part of the larger society. That society would begin to change, they believed, as soon as straights became aware of what gays were like and what they wanted. The editors supported acts of civil disobedience such as demonstrations and marches—after all, Nichols had organized the first public protest in Washington in 1965—to raise the gay and lesbian profile. *GAY* endorsed "kiss-ins" and "dance-ins," during which gay people engaged in public displays of affection, by devoting front-page news stories and editorials to such nonviolent events. It also gave extensive coverage to the first Gay Pride parade up New York's Sixth Avenue in 1970, commemorating the anniversary of Stonewall. The parade attracted 10,000 participants and ended with a Central Park "gay-in," where same-sex couples held hands and kissed while smoking pot. But *GAY* drew the line at confrontations that resulted in physical harm or property damage. Nichols and Clarke wrote unequivocally: "We abhor violence in any form."[38]

GAY supported the tactics of the Gay Activists Alliance, a nonradical offshoot of the Gay Liberation Front. The alliance staged many of the acts of civil disobedience *GAY* spotlighted. Those actions included "zaps," surprise kamikaze-like raids. Two notorious zaps—both endorsed by *GAY*—occurred when protesters publicly confronted New York Mayor John Lindsay to demand that he halt police harassment of gay men, and when gays invaded the offices of *Harper's* after an essay in the magazine labeled homosexuality "permanent niggerdom." *GAY* condemned, on the other hand, violent activities of the Gay Liberation Front. When radicals disrupted a peaceful gay march down Seventh Avenue by setting fires in trashcans and breaking store windows, Nichols and Clarke wrote: "Violence is not a wise tactic." And when youthful members of the Los Angeles front threw beer in the face of the group's middle-aged founder, Morris Kight, *GAY* again denounced violence.[39]

Dick Michaels of the *Los Angeles Advocate* also opposed using physical force, writing, "The answer is not in violence and destruction." One reason for Michaels's nonradical approach was his increasing emphasis on making his newspaper a profit-making enterprise. In early 1970 he shifted from monthly to biweekly publication and dropped "Los Angeles" from the flag to become *The Advocate*. He then began to transform his local newspaper into a national one by hiring a professional clipping service to gather news from across the country.[40]

The Ladder adamantly opposed violence as well as the other revolutionary initiatives that exploded after Stonewall. In fact, most of *The Ladder*'s articles seemed like quaint tracts from another century compared to the no-holds-barred content of the new tabloids. Some articles even questioned whether carrying banners and marching in parades were judicious actions. The magazine's most fundamental commitment, however, was to providing a public forum. Editor Barbara Grier said, "Our unwritten contract with our readers was to allow them to speak." So, when angry women wanted to argue in favor of violence as a means of fighting back against the patriarchy, *The Ladder* gave them an arena.[41]

One *Ladder* writer who passionately supported violence was Rita Mae Brown. In 1970 she wrote: "Our struggle is against the male power system which is a system of war and death. If in the process of that struggle we are forced to mutilate, murder and massacre those men, then so it must be." Brown's subsequent contributions to *The Ladder* were built on this foundation, and those writings included a concept that would become the authoritative definition of political lesbianism, shaping the lesbian ideology of the 1970s. At the heart of Brown's thinking was a statement that would shape the consciousness of millions of American women: "A lesbian is the rage of all women condensed to the point of explosion." Brown said that men opposed any woman who attempted to break out of rigid sex roles and gain a degree of independence. To defuse the strength and credibility of such a woman, Brown argued, men branded her a lesbian. "Lesbian is a label invented by the Man to throw at any woman who dares to be his equal," Brown wrote. The term was chosen, she continued, because of its pejorative connotation in a society that had an irrational fear of homosexuality. "In this sexist society," she concluded, "for a woman to be independent means she *can't* be a woman—she must be a *dyke*." According to Brown, any woman who became enraged by the limitations of the patriarchy, therefore, had to become a lesbian—at least politically—and fight for equality.[42]

Although support for violence arose only occasionally in moderate publications, it was a consistent theme in radical ones. Pat Brown of *Gay Sunshine* recalled: "When you've been pushing for a very long time and you don't see any progress, you do what you need to do to raise the visibility of your plight. We were not opposed to violence as a means of underscoring our frustration. We were willing to smash a few windows here and there. Cadillacs make wonderful barricades, and those big, huge gas tanks burn for a very, very long time."[43]

This philosophy translated into pro-violence rhetoric, such as *Gay Sunshine* insisting: "We as homosexuals must learn to be 'Violent Fairies' and shake off the silly passiveness idea that straights have handed us. We are Revolutionaries and not 'Passive Pansies.'" *Gay Sunshine* pulled no punches in identifying who should be the object of gay violence: "The enemy is straight society."[44]

The most dramatic way the radical voices demonstrated their support of violence was through visual images. The publications were strewn with graphic symbols of armed revolution. Drawings of hand grenades, bombs, machine guns, rifles, and clenched fists jumped off the pages. Huge photographs showed crowds of angry gays marauding through the streets, vehicles overturned by gangs of gay revolutionaries, and the incendiary words carried on signs in gay demonstrations: "Seize Your Community" and "We Will Smash Your Hetero-Sexist Culture."

Some of the era's radical publications endorsed violence at the top of the front page of each issue. *Gay Times* communicated its stand with a logo depicting a hand grasping a rifle, encircled with the words "To Love We Must Fight." The newspaper reflected the value John O'Brien placed on violence. He participated in the Stonewall riots, and today he speaks with pride of burning a Greenwich Village record shop to the ground because it discriminated against gays. Further, he boasts that destroying the shop led to the owner's heart attack and death. "I'm very proud of that," O'Brien said. "He was a total bastard. Some people deserve to die."[45]

Gay Times was not the only thing well-informed FBI agents were reading. They also collected *Come Out!* and *Gay Flames,* sending the copies directly to J. Edgar Hoover in Washington. O'Brien quipped, "J. Edgar jacked off while reading our papers. I just know it."[46]

Killer Dyke, a radical tabloid founded in September 1971, lived up to its name by cramming its pages with pro-violence rhetoric and artwork. To create one drawing, the editors reproduced Whistler's mother sitting sedately in her rocking chair—and then modified the photo by placing a machine gun in her hand. In its first issue, the Chicago newspaper warned: "Sexist pig oppressors... beware! Those motorcycles roaring in the night... is that the Killer Dykes foaming at the mouth? zooming to get you?!"[47]

Gay Flames, which carried the subtitle *A Bulletin of the Homofire Movement,* named itself for the bundles of sticks used during medieval times to burn homosexuals at the stake. In its first issue, the paper stated: "We are faggots and we are flaming with rage. Rage at those who tied us together like a bundle of sticks and set us afire. Rage at those who still put us down and try to make us hide." *Gay Flames* continued to endorse violence in later issues, publishing such inflammatory headlines as "We're Fighting Back!" and "OFF THE PIGS!! POWER TO THE PEOPLE!!!" The newspaper did not limit its threats to police, but warned the entire population to be concerned for its safety: "Not a single straight person in this city will feel secure in his home or school or business until every gay sister and brother is FREE. GAY POWER TO THE GAY COMMUNITY!!! TO LOVE WE MUST FIGHT!!!" *Gay Flames* also went beyond mere rhetoric, publishing an editorial that advocated burning the Women's House of Detention to the ground because its staff abused inmates.[48]

Come Out! initiated violent rhetoric in its first issue: "We're involved in a war—a people's war against those who oppress the people. POWER TO THE PEOPLE!" A year later, when gays rioted after a police raid on a Village bar, the newspaper covered every nuance of the mayhem, relishing its description of the angry crowd throwing bottles at the police, overturning cars, and looting stores. *Come Out!* promoted further violence by echoing the chant the demonstrators shouted at the police: "You better start shakin'—today's pig is tomorrow's bacon!" *Come Out!* also urged members of the Gay Liberation Front to join the organization's rifle club to prepare for the armed combat that it predicted was on the horizon. *Come Out!* took its most pro-violent stand when it proposed burning the City College of New York because it encouraged establishment thinking.[49]

The *San Francisco Gay Free Press,* founded in December 1970, was another radical tabloid that insisted Lesbian and Gay America would achieve equality only by wrenching it forceably from straight society. The tabloid peppered its pages with terms such as *gay genocide* and drawings of bullets exploding in the faces of police officers. Editor Charles Thorp promoted violence, he told readers, because he had repeatedly been attacked while distributing gay newspapers. On one occasion Thorp's face had been slashed and on another he had been struck in the head with a baseball bat. A *Gay Free Press* open letter to straight men stated: "I'll not wait in line or be your slave. *I* demand of *you* my complete freedom and if that displeases you, I'll take *what is* mine, by any and all means necessary." The venomous article, which was illustrated with a drawing of a man raising a clenched fist, left no doubt what means might be necessary. "I've got my gun loaded," the angry author continued. "You shall burn amid the ill-life you created, while I build over you a future for my well-being. *I'm rising up gay to smash your cock-power,* understand?"[50]

The *Gay Free Press* went beyond rhetoric by reporting the violent action already being taken by gay revolutionaries. "Guns are being loaded," it warned. "Knives are being sharpened. Bombs are being made. We declare war on our oppressors." The tabloid reported that large numbers of gays already had been trained for guerrilla warfare: "All are committed to violent Gay revolution."[51]

Supporting Anarchy?

Some of the most radical editorial voices—like those of the Black Panther Party—insisted that even violence would not be sufficient to end oppression. The Gay Liberation Front leaflets distributed immediately after the Stonewall Rebellion, *Come Out!,* and *Gay Liberator* all endorsed anarchy, saying that homophobia was so ingrained in the American culture that gay and lesbian liberation could not be achieved by merely reforming society, but only by eliminating all social and political authority. For these radical tabloids, the enemy was implacable and the only antidote to gay oppression was a revolution that would obliterate the heterosexual dictatorship once and for all.

The moderate publications did not agree. The *Los Angeles Advocate,* speaking against revolution, challenged gay radicals to consider what would be left if all societal institutions were destroyed. Dick Michaels wrote: "The overwhelming majority of Gays, we believe, do not want to destroy this nation and replace it with—well, what are you going to replace it with? We see virtue in evolution. We think it is possible to change the 'system'—to make it what it is supposed to be."52

Vector was another moderate publication that found anarchy far too radical. Arguing that it spoke for the majority of Lesbian and Gay America, the San Francisco magazine believed abolishing all institutions was anathema to older gay people who had for decades struggled to assimilate into heterosexual society. *Vector* columnist Dennis Altman said: "The language of the gay liberation press ensures that it is likely to be more acceptable to the straight underground than to the square gayworld."53

Even before the radicals had time to publish their first newspapers, they were advocating a very different strategy. The leaflets that sprang up in July 1969 as a form of rapid, grassroots communication had little interest in *evolution* but demanded all-out *revolution.* One that was widely distributed in Greenwich Village two weeks after Stonewall stated: "Do you think homosexuals are revolting? You bet your sweet ass we are. We're going to make a place for ourselves in the revolutionary movement. We challenge the myths that are screwing up this society." Another leaflet reiterated the radicals' support of anarchy: "Sexual liberation for all people cannot come about unless existing social institutions are abolished."54

When the leaflets evolved into *Come Out!* four months later, the tabloid took its place in history as the first lesbian and gay publication to advocate anarchy. In its premier issue, the voice of the Gay Liberation Front argued that gay people would achieve equality only by abolishing all political authority: "We must overthrow any system that breeds slavery and oppression." *Come Out!* insisted that the American government was allowing power and control to rest in the hands of a ruling class that exploited the good intentions of voters. People think politics can bring about change, the staff wrote, but corporate America maintains overall control. The gay revolutionaries said that real change could not occur until all established institutions were destroyed: "'Reforms' amount to nothing but pacifiers, tokenisms, and crumbs of our real needs and wants. By totally rejecting these false gods we will believe in ourselves and therefore develop the power to control our own destinies. Power to the People!" *Come Out!* continued its strident calls for anarchy in later issues as well. In 1970 it screamed, "Destroy the Empire!" and "Babylon has forced us to commit ourselves to one thing—revolution!"[55]

Gay Liberator picked up the anarchistic cry when it was founded by the Gay Liberation Front of Detroit in April 1970. The newspaper blared: "Until the birth of gay liberation movements we were stupid and afraid. If we continue in this manner we deserve to be oppressed. Do something more than flap your lip. Get up and fight to remove the legal capabilities of taking your livelihood and happiness away from you." Not content merely to rouse anarchy-inclined readers to action, *Gay Liberator* also assailed readers who preferred a more moderate approach. It wrote: "To those of you who sit back and continue to say 'so what'. . . I sincerely hope the ring in your nose is a very good fit."[56]

Come Out! and *Gay Liberator* both increased their repertoire of anarchistic discourse by joining the Liberation News Service, an underground press syndicate tied to Students for a Democratic Society. The service increased the amount of material in the newspapers that spoke not only about homosexuality but also about undermining establishment institutions. Typical of the items from the news service was a statement that *Come Out!* reprinted: "The no. 14 brass washer ($2.60/lb.) with tape over the center hole works in all 3-slot telephones. They also work in all parking meters, cigarette machines, juke boxes, stamp machines, etc."[57]

Forming a Separate Gay Nation?

Many radical activists came to believe that the only logical approach to achieving justice was through gay nationalism. The concept was a strident version of the separatist point of view Lisa Ben had espoused some twenty years earlier in *Vice Versa*. Although Ben merely preferred to distance herself from heterosexuals, however, post-Stonewall radicals insisted that gay people would not gain equal rights unless they built a society totally separate from that of straight America. This issue created another fault line between radical and moderate publications.

Among the most ardent champions of gay nationalism were the lesbians and gay men who created *Lavender Vision*, a radical Boston tabloid, in November 1970. The editors believed that straight society was consciously working to destroy all gays: "We have to divorce ourselves from straight society." Personal essays reinforced the separatist theme. One woman described a series of disappointing personal experiences with straight women before concluding: "I'll stick with my own people. And my people are lesbians. With those women I'll protect myself against anyone who tries to mess with our community, whether they're pig men or fucked-up straight women."[58]

Another strong endorsement for a gay nation came from the West Coast. "We tried to isolate ourselves totally from straight society," Pat Brown of *Gay Sunshine* recalled. "All of us wanted to eat, drink, and sleep—especially sleep—gay. So separatism definitely was injected into our editorial content." The Berkeley tabloid gave gay nationalism its editorial blessing, saying: "It's time for us to take full charge of our lives, to seize control of our own world and make it fit to live in. In the short run, homosexual majority districts are necessary to consolidate our strength and articulate our interests vis-a-vis heterosexuals. In the long run, homosexual separatism is essential."[59]

The radical tabloids insisted that social, political, and economic injustice would not end unless gay people created their own police forces, judicial systems, schools, and community infrastructure. "The only way we can become liberated is through revolution," *Gay Flames* wrote in its first issue. "The revolution we seek is not to replace one bureaucratic monster with another, but to give all power to the people and gay power to the gay people." *Gay Flames* envisioned a gay nation to be a utopian society that would offer free education, housing, and medical care, as well as one in which psychedelic drugs would be legal and all resources would be distributed equally. In 1971 *Gay Flames* published "A Gay Manifesto," applauding San Francisco for becoming a gay mecca—but arguing that there was a huge distance yet to travel because straight businesses still robbed gays of their resources and the tax system forced gays to pay for schools operated for the children of the straight majority.[60]

The first concrete proposal to create a gay nation emerged six months after the Stonewall Rebellion. In December 1969 members of the Gay Liberation Front in Los Angeles announced a proposal to take over rural Alpine County in Southern California, centering their plan on the irresistibly named town of Paradise. They proposed to turn the tiny resort community—population 367—into the first all-gay city in the world, complete with a gay civil service system and a museum of gay arts, sciences, and history. Under California law, new residents of a county were required to wait only ninety days before becoming eligible to vote and recall current county officials. Activists, therefore, proposed replacing all Alpine County officials with gays. Not surprisingly, county residents did not roll out the red carpet. One tavern posted a sign reading: "Homo Hunting Licenses Sold Here."[61]

The *San Francisco Gay Free Press*, however, reported the results of a survey that found 83 percent of gay San Franciscans supported the gay nation proposal. "Gay people have given the Alpine Liberation Front a mandate to go on," the newspaper wrote. The *Gay Free Press* further suggested that Alpine County be renamed "Stonewall Nation" and encouraged gay people to buy the nine major businesses in the county. The coverage was written by Don Jackson, one of the drafters of the proposal, who planned to attract enough gay welfare recipients to the county to have it classified as impoverished, leading to millions of dollars in public assistance being used to erect public housing and other free services. When the Bank of America, the only lending institution in the county, refused to lend money to gay entrepreneurs, Jackson threatened to lead California's two million gays in a boycott of the bank.[62]

Other newspapers, both radical and nonradical, were less enthusiastic about creating Stonewall Nation. Even though *Gay Sunshine* supported gay separatism, it opposed the Alpine County project. "We saw it as bourgeois gay opportunism," Pat Brown said recently. "It was clearly an attempt by the propertied class to exploit the gay working class. We opposed anything that smelled of bourgeois." *Gay Sunshine* wrote: "It is surely not Gay Liberation for queens to become kings."[63]

The Advocate was lukewarm. Although not denouncing the project, the Los Angeles newspaper wanted the organizers to move at a slower pace: "They are too much in a rush—too impetuous in their actions." Speaking from its familiar stance of moderation, the newspaper urged activists to proceed gradually, moving to the county slowly and buying businesses a few at a time.[64]

Other newspapers opposed the project, regardless of how quickly or slowly it was to take shape. *Gay Flames* accused the organizers of exploiting the gay community for their own profit. *Gay Liberator* wrote, "It is a thoroughly reactionary idea and deserves condemnation." In addition to questioning the viability of a gay nation, the Detroit tabloid accused the gay separatists of being racists. It pointed out that half the residents of Alpine County were Native Americans, and yet the organizers of the Stonewall Nation proposal were plotting to give that long-oppressed group no representation in the new county government.[65]

The strongest voices on *Come Out!* joined the opposition. Martha Shelley recalled: "A lot of us said, 'OK. Let's get real.' I mean, blacks outnumbered us ten times over, and they made no headway at getting their own separate piece of land. It made no sense for us to waste our energy on gay nationalism. You have to pick your battles. Most of us never really paid much mind to the Stonewall Nation idea."[66]

By early 1971, when a Christian Right organization threatened to respond to the gay initiative by moving its own members into Alpine County, it was clear

that the proposal would not evolve into reality. The gay and lesbian community ultimately came to think of Stonewall Nation as a joke.[67]

Lesbians and Gay Men: One Revolution or Two?

Another separatist debate focused on whether the issues and values defining
lesbian oppression were so distinct from those of gay men that the two groups
should create two independent movements. Throughout the 1950s, organizations and publications had struggled to maintain a balance of women and men,
but that effort had largely failed. The early 1960s had seen some progress toward co-gender activities, but by the end of the decade that success had faded as
well. Most gay men assumed that lesbian concerns could simply be folded into
a movement led by gay men. Most lesbians disagreed. In fact, lesbian activists
pointed out that gay men were undeniably part of the biggest problem lesbians
faced: men. *Come Out!* staff member Lois Hart spoke for thousands of gay people when she wrote: "We are in a really tough situation. We want to be able to
call each other brother and sister, yet we are still in some ways in the roles of oppressor and oppressed."[68]

   The Ladder saw the gender gulf as so imposing that it refused to refer to the
two groups in the same terms—gay men were *homosexuals;* gay women were
lesbians. Typical was the statement "Most women are not aware of their status
as slaves, so some Lesbians do not understand the subtle ways in which homosexuals attempt to undermine Lesbians." The venerable voice of Lesbian America further challenged readers who continued to support the Gay Liberation
Movement to rethink their allegiances, writing: "Most authentic and concerned
Lesbians have left Gay Lib for women's and Lesbian liberation groups." *The
Ladder* urged readers to rank their gender ahead of their sexuality, stating, "We
are women first, and Lesbians second," and campaigning for an entirely independent Lesbian Liberation Movement. "What we need is a Lesbian Movement
where we come FIRST!" Although the proposal never advanced into concrete
action, concerns about the status of women in the Gay Liberation Movement
led to the movement and the movement press losing some of their most talented and dedicated leaders.[69]

   One enormous loss was Del Martin. She abandoned gay rights in 1970 with
a devastating denunciation of male chauvinism that echoed through the movement for the next two decades. As founders of both the Daughters of Bilitis and
The Ladder, Martin and Phyllis Lyon had been the country's most visible lesbians since the 1950s. So it was a major setback when Martin committed her
massive energies to women's liberation. She wrote in *The Advocate* that neither

the programs nor the publications gay men had developed were relevant to lesbians: "So I have come to the conclusion that I must say, 'Goodbye to All That.' Goodbye to the wasteful, meaningless verbiage of empty resolutions made by hollow men of self-proclaimed privilege. They neither speak for us nor to us. I will not be your 'nigger' anymore."[70]

Ironically, at the same time Martin was giving up on the Gay Liberation Movement, *The Ladder* was giving up on her—along with other members of the Daughters of Bilitis. *The Ladder* had moved further and further from gay liberation, limiting its coverage of the Stonewall Rebellion to a three-paragraph brief. Barbara Grier and many of her readers believed that Martin and Lyon's approach to lesbian rights was outdated, stalled in the 1950s. Grier said recently: "Whenever we appeared in public, we were to wear skirts and behave like school marms. We were to dress alike, walk alike, talk alike—always in couples, paired up like the animals marching two-by-two off Noah's Ark. Del and Phyl acted like the King and Queen of Lesbian America. They ran DOB like a church—a cult, really."[71]

After editing *The Ladder* for two years, Grier decided that the magazine could better serve its readers by breaking all ties to the DOB to become an independent lesbian journal with a strong feminist philosophy. So in early 1970 Grier separated the magazine from the organization that had founded it fourteen years earlier. "We stole it," Grier said. "We went into the office and took the mailing list and all the editorial submissions that were on hand." The renegades did not take the money from the magazine's account, however, and suffered no retribution from Martin and Lyon. "No one at DOB gave a God damn about *The Ladder*," Grier said. "I saw the magazine as the tail wagging the dog. They saw the opposite."[72]

After what Grier called "the divorce," she moved the magazine from San Francisco to Reno, Nevada, where subscriptions were processed. Articles by and about lesbians continued to be part of the editorial mix, but the word *lesbian* was removed from the cover, and content was broadened to include topics of concern primarily to straight women, such as birth control. Grier titled the first editorial in the independent journal "Women's Liberation Catches Up to *The Ladder*." The expanded scope widened the magazine's appeal. In two years, subscriptions more than tripled, jumping from 1,200 to 3,800.[73]

Lesbians who produced radical post-Stonewall tabloids viewed the lesbians-versus-gay-men debate from a dramatically different perspective. They saw homophobia as a powerful force that bonded lesbians and gay men to each other, superseding gender differences. They insisted that society's greatest injustice was its treatment of homosexuality and that this shared injustice created a bond between lesbians and gay men. Placing their revolutionary goals ahead of both their gender and their sexuality, radical lesbians argued that to square gay men off against gay women would weaken both groups.[74]

Killer Dyke raged, "It is counterrevolutionary to try to rank oppressed peoples or to claim that one liberation movement is more important than another." One insightful essay advanced the argument to a more theoretical plane, drawing a curious parallel between bigotry aimed at lesbians and bigotry aimed at gay men: "'Dyke' is a different kind of put-down from 'faggot,' although both imply you are not playing your socially assigned sex role, are not therefore a 'real woman' or a 'real man.' The grudging admiration felt for the tomboy, and the queasiness felt around a sissy boy point to the same thing: the contempt in which both women and those who play a female role are held."[75]

Even the radical lesbians who placed their sexuality ahead of their gender admitted, however, that lesbians faced a pernicious form of discrimination that gay men did not: economic oppression. Just as African Americans saw economic deprivation as a reality separating them from gay men, lesbians recognized that society valued and rewarded *man*power, whether gay or straight, far more than *woman*power. They knew that winning gay rights would improve the status of lesbians, but they still would face job discrimination. In other words, if gays and lesbians were guaranteed equal employment rights, lesbians would not have to fear being fired—from the boring, poorly paid jobs women were allowed to have.[76]

Lesbians pinpointed male dominance in business and politics as the culprit, observing that this dominance transcended the gay/straight line to give all men an advantage. A defiant Boston woman wrote in *Lavender Vision:* "We can't pretend that those few flaps of skin that make up the masculine apparatus are just a few ectodermal gatherings. That stuff is the proof of a right to have access to privilege. Some men reject that privilege, but they always have the possibility of whipping it out in an emergency."[77]

Another obstacle to gay men and lesbians remaining united was the dramatic difference between their perspectives on sexual activity. While gay and lesbian activists both saw sexual freedom as central to liberation, their specific goals seemed profoundly different. Many men wanted the movement to endorse orgies and promiscuity; many women preferred only that the movement sanction same-sex relationships. *Come Out!* summarized the difference: "Gay men are obsessed with sex. Lesbians are obsessed with love."[78]

Although radical lesbians were separated from their gay male counterparts by gender, they were separated from their straight sisters as well. When feminists demonstrated at the 1968 Miss America pageant, straight women dispersed when hecklers yelled: "You're all a bunch of dykes!" And, in the late 1960s and early 1970s, National Organization for Women founder Betty Friedan and some other leading feminists opted to exclude lesbians from their efforts. They purged the movement of open lesbians—known as the "lavender menace"—for fear that the presence of gay women would make it more difficult for straight women to secure equal rights. Friedan publicly accused "man-hating lesbians" of trying to dominate NOW, prompting some lesbians to dub her "the Joe McCarthy of the women's movement."[79]

Lavender Vision illustrated the valiant effort some lesbian and gay journalists made to try to bridge the gender gap. An editorial in the first issue described how women and men in Boston had begun to discuss their common issues but soon discovered huge differences. So the editors opted for a creative approach. The cover of the first issue read "For the Gay Women's Community"; page nine carried a separate cover labeled "For the Gay Male Community." The first eight pages were written by and for lesbians; the last four, by and for gay men. "For now, the back-to-back format expresses the degree of togetherness that is comfortable to us," an editor wrote. "Maybe sometime in the future after we work together the differences may cease to exist." That time never came. The second issue carried a cover labeled "For the Lesbian Community," with no articles written by or for gay men. That issue was the last ever published.[80]

Drag Queens and "Dykes on Bikes": Celebrated or Shunned?

Another issue that has continued to polarize Lesbian and Gay America is the role fringe groups should play in the movement. Many gay people are uncomfortable with gay men who drape themselves in feather boas and "swish" their hips, or lesbians who dress in leather jackets and race Harley-Davidsons. More socially liberal gays argue that this rich cultural diversity should be celebrated by inviting drag queens and "dykes on bikes" to lead the colorful parade toward full liberation. The issue of drag queens was particularly volatile in the wake of the Stonewall Rebellion because they had played a prominent role in the uprising.

GAY stepped boldly into the fray. In June 1970 it began a full-page feature with the cut-to-the-chase statement: "The drag queen is doing for homosexuality what the Boston Strangler did for door-to-door salesmen. Neither transvestites nor transsexuals serve any useful function for themselves or anyone else." Despite a flurry of scolding phone calls and letters after the inflammatory article was published, Nichols and Clarke stood firm: "The *visibility* of the drag queen has given society an erroneous impression of the nature of homosexuality: namely that we are men *trying* to be women and women *trying* to be men.

We do not believe that drags, transvestites, and transsexuals have any inherent connection with homosexuality."[81]

The Advocate also crusaded against drag queens, although it took a different tack. Rather than categorizing them as a minority group separate from gay men, *The Advocate* attempted to distance drag queens from the movement by depicting them as misfits who deserved pity. Its definitive editorial on the subject stated, "The most flamboyant, nelliest 'queen,' if one takes the time to try to know him, is revealed as a very unhappy individual."[82]

Virtually all the radical papers took the opposite view, welcoming drag queens into the movement—and urging them to participate fully in the lesbian and gay press. In fact, *Gay Sunshine* argued that men who dressed in drag epitomized not only gay liberation, but also the liberation of women: "When a man in our society grows his hair long, puts on a dress, and walks among us, she is in effect giving up his male privilege. When every man is able to cross the sex role boundary, then and only then will women cease to be sex objects. Queens are in the vanguard of the sexual revolution."[83]

Come Out! publicized meetings and social activities for transsexuals and transvestites and gave them a venue in which to speak freely about the movement, with news articles as well as commentary pieces. "We were always comfortable with drag queens," Martha Shelley said of the *Come Out!* staff. "I remember after Stonewall that the feeling of liberation was so euphoric that I knew I would never go back to a job where I had to wear skirts. So I gave all my old skirts to the drag queens. They loved them!"[84]

Angela Douglas, a male-to-female transsexual, became a strong editorial presence in the *San Francisco Gay Free Press*. When she was arrested for cross-dressing, the tabloid blanketed the story across its front page, complete with a two-inch-high headline: "Free Angela Douglas!" Coverage included a news article, photo, Douglas's first-person account, and an appeal for funds to support her court battle. The appeal concluded: "Right on, Baby!"[85]

Gay Flames also campaigned on behalf of transvestites and transsexuals, saying, "The pigs use half-sisters to take out their hatred for those of us they can't reach so easily." When the street paper got wind of a drag queen being mistreated in the psychiatric ward of Bellevue Hospital, two reporters went to the hospital and interviewed the man. He told them, "I'm treated much more worse because of my femme tendencies and I'm always criticized about my hair or I'm always criticized about my face or something like that." *Gay Flames* again protested when a gay man working at New York University was fired because he wore a dress to work; the paper demanded that transvestites receive proper treatment in New York City prisons, hospitals, and juvenile centers.[86]

Radical publications insisted that straight society's tolerance merely of ordinary-looking gay people was not enough. In an article in *Killer Dyke,* Shelley combined her intellectual insight with her ability to write graceful prose to demand that all of society embrace the full, glorious dimensions of Gay and Lesbian America: "We are the extrusions of your unconscious mind—your worst fears made flesh. From the beautiful boys at Cherry Grove to the aging queens in the uptown bars, the taxi-driving dykes to the lesbian fashion models, the hookers (male and female) on 42nd Street, the leather lovers. We are the sort of people everyone was taught to despise—and now we are shaking off the chains of self-hatred and marching on your citadels of repression."[87]

Some of gay journalism's more moderate voices also veered from the middle of the road to support transvestites and transsexuals. *Vector,* for example, paid little attention to the Stonewall Rebellion, stating begrudgingly: "Revolution is, like it or not, now upon our American society." In keeping with its emphasis on the gay social life, however, the magazine dotted its pages with photos and articles about the drag queens whose stage performances had become a staple of San Francisco's gay bars. George Mendenhall, editor of *Vector* in the early 1970s, recalled, "My readers enjoyed reading about them and seeing their pictures." *Gay Liberator* also supported drag queens. One article began, "If the homosexual is the 'nigger' of the first half of this decade, transvestites and transsexuals may be those of the second half." The Detroit monthly campaigned to prevent social service authorities from denying welfare benefits to transvestites.[88]

Radical lesbian publications focused their attention on women who wore masculine clothing and displayed masculine behavior. Their discourse included a theoretical base to support such choices. That theory began with the argument that liberation meant lesbians should reject the guilt a homophobic society attempted to make them feel merely because they dressed and behaved in ways society defined as unnatural. Wearing nontraditional masculine clothing, the theory continued, would help lesbians overcome the passivity they were socialized to feel. *Lavender Vision* said, "If we in the women's movement reject as 'male' every characteristic assigned to men by pig society, then we're accepting their sexist categories and I don't understand how we intend to win our war."[89]

Although Nichols and Clarke opposed having drag queens be part of the movement, *GAY*'s lesbian columnist supported lesbians who opted to dress in masculine clothing. Lilli Vincenz showcased a lesbian couple—a femme named Laura and a butch named Bobbie—who had been legally married in a Baptist church. Vincenz's article betrayed no pejorative attitude whatsoever as she objectively described the bride's wedding gown as well as the groom's suit.

Vincenz recorded all the details without judgment, even when Bobbie admitted that she had worn a false moustache and lied about her gender to secure the marriage license.[90]

In the afterglow of the liberating feelings prompted by Stonewall, even *The Ladder,* which in the 1950s had opposed women wearing trousers and short hair, encouraged masculine-inclined lesbians to dress as they chose in order to expand society's limited definition of the woman's sphere. Barbara Grier said recently: "I personally am no more a butch than I am a tree toad. But, as a feminist, I support women being and doing anything they choose." The magazine therefore adopted a liberal view committed to expanding the role of all women, particularly of lesbians. One *Ladder* article asked rhetorically, "Want to wear pants?" And then answered, "They're *your* pants, so they are women's wear."[91]

Sexual Mores

One element of the evolving ideology that virtually all moderate as well as radical journalists agreed on was that gay people should discard the moral dictates established by straight society. They insisted that exclusive sexual relationships denied free will. Reflecting this philosophy, many male-oriented tabloids filled their pages with homoerotic images and graphic discussions of homosexual acts, while lesbian publications occasionally did the same with homoerotic images of women.

Even before Stonewall, devotees of Jack Nichols and Lige Clarke's "Homosexual Citizen" column knew the columnists were champions of open sexual relationships. The lovers promoted their philosophy in *GAY* as well. They described orgies they had participated in and repeatedly expressed their opposition to monogamy: "Only first-class morons think they should have exclusive rights to their lover's body. Sensible people don't go around asking, 'Has anybody besides me been seeing, touching, or making use of your genitals?' The term 'unfaithful' has nothing to do with the use of the sexual organs."[92]

The publications argued that traditional relationships should be redefined into two categories. Physical relationships consisted exclusively of sexual activity, with no mental or emotional element involved; such activity was labeled recreational sex. Emotional relationships, on the other hand, included sexual activity as well as emotional commitment; these relationships were similar to the traditional marriage pursued by most of society.

Lesbian and gay journalists considered adopting such new social mores to be fundamental to their liberation. *Gay Flames* said, "We want the right of self-determination over the use of our bodies: the right to be gay, anytime, anyplace." *Come Out!* added: "No one has the right to tell another what to do with his or her own body. We must be free." Editorial content contained strong sexual themes—a *Come Out!* article on how to get the most out of oral sex, a *Gay Flames* essay labeled "What's Wrong with Sucking?," and a *Gay Sunshine* piece titled "How to Get Fucked (and like it)."[93]

Publications also gave their editorial blessing to promiscuity and anonymous sex. "We gave each other a lot of space on sexual freedom," Martha Shelley said. "Who the hell cared how many people you slept with?" Typical was a *Come Out!* article celebrating the proliferation of gay "fuck bars" throughout the Village. The first-person article stated: "The Fuck Room was exactly that! No games, no bullshit, no hassles—just simple, direct, down-to-the-nitty, old-fashioned sex! No little blue pill could come close to relieving the nervous tension that my two hours in that room did. I touched, I communicated, I related and I loved."[94]

Gay Flames glorified anonymous sex by publishing a comic strip featuring the heroic deeds of the Lavender Kid, a gay superman who rescued victims from homophobia. One cartoon focused on Kentucky Fried Chicken refusing service to a gay man named Butch, with Colonel Sanders saying, "I don't sell fried chicken to cock-suckers!" After the handsome and physically well endowed Lavender Kid rescued Butch, he swept the young man back to his apartment for an afternoon of recreational sex.[95]

The *San Francisco Gay Free Press* was so determined to expand homosexual lifestyles that it coined a series of terms to replace monogamy. *Diasporady* described a person who engaged in numerous sexual relationships—illustrated by a smiley face with arrows connecting him with three other equally exuberant smiley faces. *Syzygoty* described two people who limited their sexual activity to each other—illustrated by two figures whose smiles had been turned into frowns.[96]

Radical lesbian newspapers joined in redefining sexual mores. *Killer Dyke* followed the *Gay Free Press* in creating a new sexual lexicon, calling for the terms *heterosexuality, homosexuality,* and *bisexuality* to be replaced with the single term *pansexuality*. *Lavender Vision* campaigned against monogamy by arguing that such behavior is unnatural for lesbians because women tend not to limit themselves to one exclusive relationship but to build communities. "Sexuality with women is a collective experience growing out of our struggle," the Boston tabloid argued. "I might cuddle with one sister tonite because we were together and felt close and I might crash on some mattress with a bunch of women tomorrow because we all danced together half the nite."[97]

Although seeking to break the chains of monogamy, lesbian tabloids did not necessarily embrace the sexual goals of their gay male counterparts. *Lavender Vision,* for example, attacked the traditional male approach to sex. In the oppressive American society, the tabloid insisted, sex reflects the same ideology as other establishment institutions: "It is goal-oriented, profit & productivity oriented. It is a prescribed system, with a series of correct & building activities aimed toward the production of a single goal: climax."[98]

Despite such denunciations by lesbians, publications aimed toward gay men filled their pages with erect penises, along with frank discussions of oral and anal sex. This editorial content served two purposes—sending the message that homosexual sex is perfectly acceptable behavior, while also attracting readers. *Vector* editor George Mendenhall conducted a poll to determine what readers wanted in the magazine. When the 300 responses were counted, number one on the list was nudity. Mendenhall later said: "So *Vector* became the first to put a nude man on the cover of a gay magazine. Making those photographs attractive was what drove us to using a slick cover, too—to make the men's equipment come to life, so to speak. That kind of photo was shocking at the time, but it was what our readers wanted. We were not the least bit embarrassed to reflect gay values." *Gay Sunshine*'s effort to affirm homoeroticism included a cover drawing of a man with an erect penis flying through the sky.[99]

While both the moderate and radical wings of the press joined forces to broaden the sexual mores of the evolving culture, *The Ladder* remained a lone voice in the wilderness. "I'm an old-fashioned person, a believer in strict monogamy," Barbara Grier said. "I think all women are exciting and beautiful, but I'm personally monogamous." So, just as the editor allowed other lesbians to have their say—even when their opinions differed from her own—she also found room for an occasional swipe at the movement's march toward nonmonogamy. In one article discussing lesbians in committed relationships, Grier slipped in a plug for what she referred to as lesbian marriages: "There are far more of these than any statistical survey is likely to uncover."[100]

Defining a Reform Strategy

The post-Stonewall press was fully committed to attacking human injustice. American society manifested its homophobia in so many forms, however, that publications differed on exactly where to focus their efforts. What's more, the status of the publications divided them into two distinct groups. Most received their financial support from political organizations, allowing them broad latitude regarding the targets of their editorial attacks. But the largest newspapers— *GAY* and *The Advocate*—would continue to publish only as long as they attracted

The radical agenda of the late 1960s and early 1970s included encouraging anarchy, creating a separate gay and lesbian nation, and supporting violent confrontations with police.

advertising, and the fact that gay bars and bathhouses had emerged as major ad-vertisers clearly compromised the two newspapers' choice of reform efforts.

The Advocate maintained a tight focus, with Dick Michaels continuing to expose and deride the bigotry of the Los Angeles Police Department. Fueled by the bar incident that had thrust him into activism, Michaels targeted police ha-rassment as his editorial raison d'être. When police broke into a private home in the middle of the night to arrest two men on charges of lewd conduct, *The*

Advocate's coverage filled page one, and an editorial scolded apathetic readers: "We are bleeding now, and L.A. Gays sit in their big homes and fancy apartments planning their next garden party. Wake up! It isn't just the bar queen and the street walker who is in danger. Our fancy homes and apartments are no longer all that safe. Our lives and our freedom are on the line."[101]

GAY adopted a broader strategy. One battlefront was the unjust legal system. When the newspaper's own columnist, Dick Leitsch, and his lover filed a joint income tax return, *GAY* showcased the act of defiance in an article and two photos on its first news page, opposite an editorial congratulating the couple. The newspaper also gave expansive treatment to two men who applied for a marriage license, fifty lesbians and gay men who staged a sit-in at a New York bar that refused to serve gay customers, and a gay couple from Denver who joined the bridal registry at a downtown department store.[102]

GAY also fought to elect mainstream politicians who were committed to gay rights. The newspaper reasoned that the winds of liberation had shifted the political tide in New York City to the point where it was time for candidates to court gay voters. Leitsch wrote that the secret ballot enhanced the political power of what was fast becoming one of the country's largest voting blocs. He pointed out, "Not every homosexual can commit himself in public, but the voting booth is a very private place." When Bella Abzug became the first mainstream candidate in New York history to woo lesbians and gay men, *GAY* gave her exuberant editorial support—and she won her seat in Congress.[103]

Trying to improve mainstream media coverage formed another prong of *GAY*'s reform strategy. Rather than following the techniques of radical publications—*Come Out!* screamed about the media's "slanderous journalistic techniques" and "the twisted shit they print"—Nichols and Clarke monitored news coverage and, when newsworthy events were ignored, initiated mass letter-writing campaigns. When the *New York Times* failed to report that thirty members of the Gay Activists Alliance had surrounded gubernatorial candidate Arthur Goldberg's limousine, *GAY* told its readers to write to the *Times* and threaten to cancel their subscriptions. The editors ended the editorial directive with a suggestion that succinctly characterized their approach to reform: "Be polite."[104]

Neither *The Advocate* nor *GAY*, however, marshaled its journalistic power to confront Gay America's most insidious enemy: the Mafia. Gays knew the Mafia controlled the bars they frequented, as only the Mafia was powerful and wealthy enough to pay off the police and keep the business establishments open and producing revenue. On the one hand, gays wanted to sever their ties with the Mafia, but, on the other, bars remained the only public place they could come together to relax, enjoy each other's company, and, ultimately, strengthen their sense of community. But *The Advocate* and *GAY* faced the additional complication that Mafia-controlled bars and bath houses represented their most lucrative sources of advertising revenue. "It was hard to get advertising," Nichols said. "All we could get was the erotic stuff—bath houses, bars, X-rated movie houses. In the early seventies, it was still very, very tough to get any other ads for a gay newspaper."[105]

Rather than railing against the Mafia, the two largest gay newspapers in the country wrote laudatory articles about Mafia-run businesses. Typical was the lead of a full-page story in *GAY* that read more like an ad than a news story: "The Beacon Baths at 227 East 45th Street in Manhattan is well worth a visit." The tone of the coverage was further enhanced by two photos of employees of the baths, including a nude shot of the manager. In keeping with the editors' personalized style, the appeals to readers often were blatant. An editorial headlined "Support *GAY*'s Advertisers" went on to plead: "*GAY*'s growth in great part depends on its readers' support of advertisers."[106]

By contrast, New York's noncommercial gay press vehemently attacked the Mafia's stranglehold on its community. *Come Out!* led the way, launching the campaign on page one of its premier issue: "Our friendly neighborhood tavern is a Mafioso-on-the-job training school for dum-dum hoods." The same issue described the Mafia bar owners as "money-hungry opportunists." The tabloid was relentless in its criticism, accusing the Mafia and police of marching arm in arm against gays: "All of New York's gay bars are Mafia-run. When the Mafia bar-owners fail to pay off sufficiently, the pigs get unhappy and move in."[107]

When *Gay Flames* began appearing a year after Stonewall, it joined the anti-Mafia campaign. The first issue referred to "the exploiting bars," and another early issue stated, "We're victims of criminal profit-hungry syndicates." *Gay Flames* maintained the pressure throughout its lifespan, charging, "Mafia control of bars and baths in NYC is only one example of outside money controlling our institutions for their profit."[108]

Gay Times told readers to stop patronizing bars that prevented gays from being affectionate with each other. O'Brien's opposition to the Mafia-controlled bars was partly in response to their refusal to allow him to distribute his newspaper to their patrons: "The bars were hostile to the gay press. The concept of liberation was very threatening to them. They wanted us to remain frightened and in the closet. As long as we were scared, they had a lock on us and our money. They knew that if gays became stronger, that lock would end. We would start operating our own bars, and they'd be out of business. They thwarted our every effort." When the bars refused to allow O'Brien to distribute *Gay Times,* he took copies to the cruising areas in and around Central Park, while continuing to lambaste the Mafia in print.[109]

The radical New York newspapers did not rely solely on the impact of verbal assaults but also worked with their parent organization, the Gay Liberation Front, to create an alternative to Mafia-owned bars. In the spring of 1970, the front sponsored dances at Alternate University, a radical institution on Sixth Avenue. *Come Out!* promoted and covered the dances, stating, "The purposes which we set out for the dances are to provide an alternate to the exploititive [*sic*] gay bars in the city." *Gay Flames* publicized the dances and their goal, personalizing the message: "We'll rap and be real and learn to come together!"[110]

Only on the issue of the Mafia-controlled bars, however, did the radical newspapers offer practical reform measures. On other issues, they merely listed the problems of society without suggesting realistic solutions. When combined into a single list, the specific elements the publications wanted to purge from society provide a sense of the extreme editorial stances the newspapers adopted. *Come Out!* urged annihilation of the nuclear family. *Gay Flames* advocated an end to capital punishment, law enforcement, prisons, religion, and the judicial system. *Killer Dyke* called for eliminating mental institutions, marriage, private property, and the state. *Gay Sunshine* added schools and businesses to the enemies list. The only specifics given regarding how such elements could be abolished or what could replace them was an equally outrageous list of demands. *Killer Dyke* called for all Americans to be given free food, free housing, free clothing, free education, and free marijuana. *Gay Flames* topped off the list by demanding that the government supply drag queens with free sex changes and free jewelry on demand.[111]

O'Brien, though radical in many of his editorial stances, drew the line at the final two items on the list. Although he was eager to form a coalition with the Black Panthers and fully supported violence as part of gay and lesbian revolution, the editor of *Gay Times* could not endorse the entire grab bag of proposals advanced in the gay press. On gays being given free sex changes, he spoke with outrage: "We see this demand as advocating the mutilation of the human body." On gays being given free jewelry, he said bluntly, "This demand is frivolous."[112]

The Revolution Subsides

By the end of 1972, lesbian and gay radicalism had faded from the political landscape. The demise was due to a resounding lack of tangible progress in securing equal rights. Although the 1969 Stonewall Rebellion marked the beginning of the modern phase of the movement, the intoxicating fumes of liberation had failed to produce any substantive change in the status of the American homosexual. Only the state of Connecticut had joined Illinois in legalizing sex between consenting adults of the same gender. In early 1972, the New York City Council—at the very center of the revolution—vetoed a proposal to ban discrimination against gay people in employment, housing, and public accommodation. Later that year, Democratic presidential candidate George McGovern ran ads in *The Advocate* promising reform in federal employment and military policies—before being trounced by Richard Nixon.

In the light of such distressing developments, the Gay Liberation Front, home to the most radical and visible activists, disintegrated into chaos. The front fell victim, in part, to internal unraveling because of grievances and subgrievances and sub-sub-grievances, many of them regarding the front's structure, that have often been a paralyzing element of gay politics. The most disruptive ideological issues of the Gay Liberation Front revolved around the role of violence and the leaders' insistence that the organization should fight other forms of oppression beyond that faced by gay men and lesbians. As the front's violent confrontations ended, activists began to explore more sophisticated ways of combatting discrimination, thereby moving Lesbian and Gay America into a new phase of its evolution.

Surprisingly, this was one of the few chapters of lesbian and gay press history when editorial discord was *not* a major theme among the publications. Even though many issues created huge fault lines between radical voices and moderate ones, the newspapers rarely attacked each other. "It is curious," Martha Shelley said recently. "But that's always been the case with our press. When we have an enemy, we put all our energy into fighting it. Otherwise, we're at each others' throats. After Stonewall, our enemy was all of America—with a 'K.'"[113]

From the historical distance of two decades, journalism clearly played a central role in the three-year period during which the revolutionary impulse held sway. For it was in the pages of the lesbian and gay press that activists debated the ideological issues fundamental to the movement. The publications succeeded in moving some issues to resolution. With regard to the possibility of forging a coalition with African-American revolutionaries, the debate concluded that such an alliance was untenable. On another issue, the content of the publications—both editorial and graphic—resolved that this most certainly would be a social movement that redefined sexual mores.

Other questions were asked but not answered. Differences of opinion would continue to boil in the next generation of gay and lesbian journalism, and the next, and the next. Indeed, many of the issues are still very much alive a quarter of a century later. The relationship between gay liberation and women's liberation, for instance, would remain murky; because of the commonality of lesbians, the two movements were destined to remain married, but that marriage would be a rocky one. Likewise, the role fringe groups, particularly drag queens, would play in the movement would continue to baffle the community. Finally, it remained unclear which of the many reform efforts would be primary, or whether the battle would be fought simultaneously on many fronts— to end police harassment, increase political clout, gain fair coverage in the mainstream media, and break the Mafia stranglehold on the bars.

Some issues were resolved by default because of the demise of the radical publications that supported certain positions on them. Violence as a central tactic along with anarchy and gay nationalism evaporated as major topics of debate when the publications that supported them were extinguished in the early 1970s. Some of the radical publications were buried in the same coffins as the organizations they spoke for. *Come Out!* and *Gay Flames* died with New York's Gay Liberation Front; *Gay Liberator* died with the Detroit branch. Others that were produced by individuals or collectives—*Gay Times, Gay Sunshine, Killer Dyke,* the *San Francisco Gay Free Press,* and *Lavender Vision*—did not have a sufficient financial base or workforce to sustain them.[114]

One of the saddest losses occurred in the fall of 1972, when financial difficulties forced *The Ladder* to close up shop, bringing an end to one of the most salient publications in the history of the lesbian press. The magazine's economic position had begun to falter soon after it separated from the Daughters of Bilitis because the angel who had been donating $12,000 a year was not happy with its feminist philosophy. Barbara Grier recalled, "She was an old-line butch who was so male-identified that she didn't want to see anything feminine in the magazine." After the woman withdrew her support, Grier tried to stay afloat through advertising, but very few businesses were willing to advertise in a lesbian publication. "All we could attract were ads from pornographers," Grier said. "Their adults-only material would have horrified the women who read my magazine." In a final editorial, Grier lashed out at readers for not supporting *The Ladder*: "For those of you who have casually read us through the years, indeed sometimes intending to subscribe, but not ever quite getting around to it, we wish you whatever you deserve and leave it to your own consciences to decide just what that might be."[115]

As time passed, Grier shifted from criticizing readers to praising contributors. In the introduction to a 1976 anthology of essays originally published in *The Ladder,* she wrote of the women who produced the magazine for sixteen

years: "No woman ever made a dime for her work, and some worked themselves into a state of mental and physical decline on behalf of the magazine. I
believe that most of them believed that they were moving the world with their
labors, and I believe that they were right."[116]

The publications that survived the aftershocks of Stonewall were those with
a combination of calm voices and stable finances. Foremost were *GAY* in New
York and *The Advocate* in Los Angeles. The editorial stances of these moderate
publications generally carried the day in the debates, and it was these commercial enterprises that possessed the financial stamina that would allow them to
influence the next phase of gay and lesbian liberation. Also joining their ranks
would be reincarnations of some of the radical publications. Financial problems and splintering of energy among members of the *Gay Sunshine* collective
led to the end of the Berkeley-based tabloid in early 1971, but it reappeared a few
months later as a journal that communicated its message through literary
works. Detroit's *Gay Liberator* traveled a similar route, suspending publication
in 1971 but resurfacing six months later as an independent newspaper.

Pat Brown of the original *Gay Sunshine* collective recalled: "The gay press
had been born and, like the movement, wasn't going to die. Not ever. Those
were heady days when we liked to allude to mythology. I'm sure we saw *Gay
Sunshine* rising from its ashes like the phoenix. Well, actually, I'm not sure we
said it that way then. But if we didn't—what the Hell?—we should have."[117]

λ 6

Defining Lesbian Culture

After the revolutionary fervor detonated at the Stonewall Inn had run its meteoric course, lesbians and gay men embarked, during the mid-1970s, on a new stage of their history. Although this phase may not have had the dramatic impact of Stonewall, it was profoundly important. After the winds of liberation had swept women and men out of the closet in unprecedented numbers, that newly empowered generation set out to define exactly what being gay meant. The first critical mass of openly gay people marched boldly forward to explore the many facets of a culture they were, at once, both discovering and defining.

Gay journalism played a singular role in leading the movement in this exhilarating new direction. In the mid-1970s, the spate of sensationalistic tabloids that had burned themselves into oblivion were replaced by a wide pastiche of publications—newspapers, magazines, journals—that probed the breadth and depth of the burgeoning lesbian and gay culture. Never before had the gay press felt such freedom to delve below the surface of its readers' lives. And so the publications of this era—from roughly 1973 to 1977— ultimately created a tangible record of the activities, fantasies, and ideologies gay people valued and cherished as their very own.

It was also during this era that the lesbian and gay press received a morsel of recognition by the larger world of publishing. Toward the end of the decade, the media criticism journal *Alternative Media* printed a lengthy critique of the genre, titled "Fag Mags," that began, "There hasn't been a more exciting or un- expected success story in the Seventies." In addition to describing and cri- tiquing gay and lesbian publications, the article lauded the "array of magazines that no one who wishes to be really and truly well up on what's actually going on can afford to ignore."[1]

One fundamental theme of the era was that the press was not, in reality, a single entity. More than at any other time in the history of the genre, this cultural period witnessed a split into two distinct presses—one for lesbians, one for gay men. Since the days of *Vice Versa,* most publications had been directed primarily at one gender or the other. But in the 1970s the two groups divorced. Dramatic evidence of the split came with a survey of who read *The Advocate;* though the largest gay publication in the country claimed to appeal to women as well as men, the survey found that an astonishing 97 percent of the readers were men.

The most prominent themes in the journalism of the era, therefore, are rightly ascribed to either the lesbian press or the gay male press. Only a few themes overlapped and, when they did, they were expressed in very different terms. In keeping with this separatist approach, many lesbian magazines refused to accept submissions from men, and some explicitly stated on their covers that they were absolutely *off limits* to all men, regardless of sexual orientation. This stridency affected the overall tone of the lesbian press as well; throughout the period, women's publications were far more serious than men's, which often were much more playful and irreverent in their approach. Because of the dichotomy in the mid-1970s, this chapter focuses only on the lesbian press of the era; the next looks exclusively at the gay male press.[2]

The lesbian press was led by two profoundly different flagship publications. *The Furies* exploded with the radical theories of a dozen lesbians living in a Washington, D.C., collective. Although the newspaper survived barely a year, it published such a treasure trove of political and personal essays that its title is rarely spoken without an adjective between the two words—*The* "legendary" *Furies.* The other salient publication of the era was a Los Angeles magazine that won its place in history as Lesbian America's first all-news publication. *Lesbian Tide*'s news stories and editorials combined to set a journalistic standard that to this day remains unparalleled in the annals of the lesbian press.

By no means, though, did *The Furies* and *Lesbian Tide* monopolize the era. Literally dozens of players crowded onto the stage, their number and variety soaring as never before. Nor were those voices confined to urban centers. Publications popped up seemingly wherever a group of high-energy women clustered, with Oakland, Milwaukee, and suburban New Jersey all becoming publishing centers. What's more, the new generation spoke with a sense of power unknown to its predecessors. *Lesbian Tide* editor Jeanne Córdova recently recalled, "Lesbian publications had an 'umph' because they were influenced very much by the Feminist Movement—the 'I am woman, hear me roar' syndrome."[3]

This increased sense of power and pride was communicated through the publications' brash titles: *Amazon, Amazon Quarterly, Dyke, Lesbian Feminist, So's Your Old Lady.* Others were less bold in their names, but no less assertive in content: *Albatross, Azalea, Lavender Woman, Sisters, Tribad.* The publications expressed the new lesbian strength in their language as well. Publications routinely used terms most of society considered unspeakable, except perhaps in men's locker rooms—terms such as *lezzie, dyke, fuck, cunt,* and *clit.* Turning

"Peace on Earth, Goodwill Toward Women" is an example of how lesbian publications emphasized the rise of all women—but particularly lesbians—during the 1970s.

these derisive epithets into terms of common usage was a conscious act of rebellion against the social order. The publications also created, as did feminist journals of the era, substitutes for the term *women*. Demonstrating their desire to distance themselves from the patriarchy, they developed alternative spellings ranging from "wimmin" to "wymon" to "wymyn"—any phonetic combination that did *not* contain *m-e-n*.

Whether the lesbian press was articulating why many women had replaced tight skirts with loose-fitting trousers, discussing lesbian sex, or chronicling—with unabashed hubris—the contributions lesbians were making to music and literature, delving into the lesbian culture was the ultimate mission. For the journalists knew such exploration increased the self-esteem of individual women while also strengthening the community as a whole. "Those were important years of building and maturing," said Córdova. "We were getting to know each other, as well as ourselves. We were defining who we were—what we valued." In 1973 *Sisters* framed the message in slightly different language, observing that culture had become the keystone of Lesbian America: "The CULTURE that is developing is similar throughout the country. COMMUNICATIONS is the next crucial step in our movement. We must develop a highly effective media to unify. Unity equals strength."[4]

The radicalism of the immediate post-Stonewall press did not, however, totally disappear. In fact, several new lesbian publications were as politically strident as *Come Out!* or *Killer Dyke,* insisting that violent overthrow of the system offered lesbians their only hope of survival. This thinking reached a crescendo in 1976 when *Dyke* magazine published the CLIT Papers. The revolutionary documents were written by radical lesbians who called themselves Collective Lesbian International Terrors—or CLIT—and attacked the establishment on every front. They denounced the International Year of the Woman, for example, as a PR sham designed to placate feminists. But CLIT did not buy it: "We will always remember 1975 as the year AmeriKKKa stretched its deceitful mindfucking liberal smile to the limits of its plastic face." Even publications that tried to distance themselves from politics found the task impossible. Gina Covina, coeditor of *Amazon Quarterly,* recently recalled: "We tried to stay focused on the arts rather than politics. But it seemed like every cultural topic had a political dimension, too."[5]

One of the era's most significant contributions was raising the concept of cooperative journalistic activities. *Lavender Woman* proposed the idea in 1972. The Chicago newspaper asked, on the same page as it ran ads for lesbian publications from Los Angeles and Washington: "Anyone for a national lesbian news service? Lesbians across the country are writing about what they are doing. We would hope to gather this data and get an overall picture of the lesbian movement." Although the concept did not take fire immediately, a year later lesbian editors organized the first workshops to discuss their common problems—a major step toward cooperative ventures that would continue to tantalize the genre in future decades.[6]

According to *Our Own Voices,* some fifty lesbian publications existed in 1975. *Amazon Quarterly* was the largest, with a national distribution of 9,000. Total circulation of the lesbian press hovered around 50,000—less than that of *The Advocate* alone. But Joan Nestle, cofounder of the Lesbian Herstory Archives in New York City, insisted that numbers do not accurately gauge impact: "A woman would read just one article that touched a certain sensibility in her—and suddenly her life was turned upside down. She embraced the lesbian culture as the center of her very existence. When that process is repeated for women in tiny, isolated communities from coast to coast—women who previously trembled in fear but then began asserting their own self-worth—the impact cannot be measured in mere numbers."[7]

The Furies: A Legend in Lesbian Culture

The confluence of forces that gave birth to *The Furies* in 1972 was duplicated in communities across the country. Radical women were tired of serving as minions for the men who dominated leftist organizations, lesbians were tired of being ignored by the male leaders of the Gay Liberation Movement, and lesbians involved in the Women's Liberation Movement were tired of straight feminists considering lesbianism a bedroom issue too hot to handle.

The twelve lesbians who came together to form a collective in Washington had been involved in various social movements, but each woman was still looking for a home, a crusade that captured her passion while also stretching out its arms to her. Rita Mae Brown's experience with a gay group while she was a student at Columbia University was typical. She had been one of only 2 women among 100 men. "We were just ignored and rolled over," Brown said. "It took me six months to figure out these guys didn't give a shit whether I lived or died. So I left and went to the women's movement. Which was *worse*. I got beaten up. I got harassed. I got bomb threats. I got thrown out of NOW because I was lesbian."[8]

Women in the Washington collective ranged in age from twenty-eight-year-old Brown, whose essays in *The Ladder* had already identified her as a cogent and fiery theorist, to a pair of fresh-faced eighteen-year-olds. All were white, but their backgrounds ranged from working to upper class—a butcher's daughter to a Vassar coed. They moved into three houses in southeast Washington and developed an income-sharing plan, with the most highly educated women securing good jobs to supplement the incomes of their less privileged sisters.

Consciousness-raising sessions quickly illuminated what the women embraced as their common mission: to create a lesbian-feminist ideology. To share their anticipated insights with a larger audience of lesbians and would-be lesbians, they decided to publish a newspaper. To avoid hierarchical structure, no woman would wear the mantle of "editor," but all would contribute in whatever form they chose. *The Furies* was founded in January 1972. Though called a newspaper, it consisted mainly of personal essays and contained only an occasional news item.

Essentially, the women believed that even if capitalism, racism, and imperialism were eradicated, lesbians would still be oppressed because the root of their persecution was sexism, which they believed included homophobia. Restating the argument Brown had made in *The Ladder* early in the decade, *The Furies* argued that becoming a lesbian was not a matter of sexual orientation but a political choice every thinking woman had to make if she hoped to end male supremacy. Ginny Z. Berson's lead article in the first issue stated, "Lesbians must get out of the straight women's movement and form their own movement in order to be taken seriously, to stop straight women from oppressing us." Charlotte Bunch, another collective member, reinforced the message in her first essay. In "Lesbians in Revolt: Male Supremacy Quakes and Quivers," Bunch argued that lesbians had to form their own political movement because only by rejecting male domination in politics as well as sex would lesbians threaten male supremacy.[9]

The Furies turned Lesbian America upside down. When the members of the collective sent the 3,000 copies of their newspaper to friends in cities across the country, their words and concepts spread like wildfire, exposing thousands of women to an evolving ideology unlike anything they had ever heard before.

Members of the collective paid printing and distribution costs from the money they amassed from their pooled paychecks. They also sold ads to a few women-owned businesses, but at ten dollars an ad those revenues did not add up to much. Printers repeatedly refused to print more than one issue, saying they were afraid of being sued or picketed. Ultimately, the only print shop that would continue to publish the newspaper was a pornographic press on Long Island.

After three months of exhaustive effort, the collective changed its publishing schedule from monthly to bimonthly. After seven months, half the founders had left the collective. The tabloid also began to shrink, dropping from twenty-four to sixteen to eight pages. It ceased publication after its tenth issue, in June

1973. Only two of the founders—the eighteen-year-olds—were involved in publishing that final issue.

When *The Furies* died, the women did not mourn the passing of their venture. Berson said recently, "We had said what we wanted to say, and it was time to move on." And move on they did. Members of the collective went on to help found Diana Press, which became one of the country's major lesbian publishers, and Olivia Records, the highly successful all-woman record company.[10]

Lesbian Tide: Setting a New Standard for Lesbian Journalism

Jeanne Córdova was the driving force behind *Lesbian Tide*. A former nun, Córdova founded the publication in August 1971 as a newsletter for the Los Angeles chapter of Daughters of Bilitis. Five months later, the *Tide* became an independent news magazine. Córdova recalled: "Bigger things were happening than DOB. I was 23 years old and wanted to cover them my way." The conservative leaders of the organization equated feminists such as Córdova with Communists. So they gladly bid her farewell.[11]

The *Tide* then became the second leading voice for lesbian feminism—a West Coast equivalent of *The Furies*. Like its East Coast sister, *Lesbian Tide* defined lesbianism as the capacity of every woman to make a conscious decision to reject heterosexuality and devote all her energies to women. The magazine defined lesbian feminists as women who committed themselves exclusively to women for social, emotional, physical, and economic support. The *Tide* saw lesbian feminism as a logical step in the evolution of every liberated woman, a political imperative for any woman committed to the advancement of her gender. Córdova recalled: "Before that time, a lesbian was a woman who liked to fuck women. But with feminism, the very definition of 'lesbian' went up for grabs. I adopted the definition that all women had the potential to be lesbians, even if they never actually slept with women. *Lesbian Tide* became the bible of lesbian feminism."[12]

On a journalistic level, Córdova broke new ground by transforming the *Tide* into an all-news publication. Building on Barbara Gittings's precedent of beefing up the news content of *The Ladder* in the mid-1960s, Córdova took the next step and eliminated all fiction from her magazine. News items came from readers in cities as distant as Minneapolis and Baltimore. Among the top stories in 1974, for example, were items reporting the election of the country's first two openly lesbian officials; Kathy Kozachenko won a spot on the Ann Arbor, Michigan, city council, and Elaine Noble secured a seat in the Massachusetts state legislature. Córdova also published interviews with women on the cutting edge of lesbian feminism, including writer Kate Millett and Carter White House aide Midge Costanza.[13]

Lesbian Tide became the first news outlet in history to adopt an editorial policy of lesbian primacy. For, regardless of the topic covered, the *Tide* not only focused on the lesbian angle but also limited its sources to lesbians, rejecting any information that had come from either straight people or gay men. Córdova stated at the time, "We feel our readers learn best from reading about each other."[14]

Finances were a problem. Circulation revenue and private donations paid about half the expenses, leaving the other half to come from advertising. Finding 100 percent of its ad revenue in the embryonic lesbian business community proved to be a formidable task. Córdova said: "I knew women made less than men, but I always thought that maybe that figure of fifty-nine cents to men's one dollar was an exaggeration. But I found that figure was a dramatic *over-statement.*" The bimonthly *Tide* had to depend on ads from fledgling lesbian-owned bookstores and other businesses, with ads rarely measuring more than an eighth of a page. Córdova periodically pleaded with her readers for support. A typical headline read: "WE ARE FLAT BROKE! PLEASE SEND MONEY!"[15]

The *Tide* started as an eighteen-page mimeographed newsletter. Within a year, Córdova began having copy typeset. After two years, she expanded to forty-four pages, and by mid-decade circulation had jumped from an initial 100 copies to a whopping 3,000. By 1977 the *Tide* was being sold in eighty bookstores nationwide.[16]

Córdova refused to exploit women, insisting on paying for every article and photo in the *Tide*, although payment was often only five dollars. She was the only full-time staff member, and her salary as publisher did not cover her expenses. "I was a full-time political activist," she recalled. "So I'd get on food stamps and welfare and anything I could think of—billing the government for my services." By the time the *Tide* ceased publication in 1980, Córdova was making only $7,500 a year. In 1981 she founded the *Gay Yellow Pages*, which listed gay-owned businesses, and her annual salary jumped to $75,000.[17]

Politicizing Personal Appearance

The boldness driving the new era of lesbian journalism was illustrated by how it covered physical appearance as a form of oppression. Adopting an opposite stance from the one espoused by *The Ladder* in the 1950s and 1960s, the 1970s press characterized conventional definitions of female beauty as unacceptable values because they had been imposed on women by men. Publications insisted that lesbians should develop their own. "Lesbian feminist ideology said no lipstick, no earrings, no cute hair," Córdova said. "Those decisions were political statements of the first order."[18]

Lesbian Tide set the pace. In an article and accompanying before-and-after photographs, the magazine urged women to replace the expensive and sometimes painful items in their wardrobes with clothes that were cheap and comfortable. High heels were out. Bras were out. Nylon stockings were out. The *Tide* also advised lesbian feminists to discard low-cut blouses and tight skirts, quoting one woman as saying, "I now wear an army surplus jacket, which not only keeps me warm, but reminds me that my struggle is with that of all courageous sisters fighting imperialism in Southeast Asia, Palestine, Ireland, Africa and South America." The *Tide* attacked another front of the appearance war in "The Politics of Fat," an article that castigated the diet industry for transforming being overweight into a crime against humanity.[19]

Dyke, a magazine produced by a New York collective, joined the campaign against makeup, long hair, dresses, stockings, and high heels. "I refuse to wear feminine clothes," editor Liza Cowan said in her first issue. "I would just as soon wear a ball and chain." Cowan described how she had hired a lesbian designer to create an outfit uniquely suited to her tastes and needs. Made of smokey green velour with trousers cut like sweat pants and a jacket similar to a bathrobe, the outfit came complete with a flying horse appliqué on the back. Cowan was pleased: "It was a knockout! It looked like a combination costume of a magician, mandarin, karate fighter and outer space woman."[20]

Visual images reinforced the message that women should refuse to conform to societal standards of feminine beauty. Cowan's article was illustrated with a dozen headshots showing how she had transformed her appearance during the previous eight years. Early photos showed her with makeup and long, curled hair; later ones showed her with no makeup and a shaved head. *Dyke*'s standard house ad carried images of a high heel (labeled *A*) and hiking boot (labeled *B*) alongside the question "Which shoe fits you?" Below the images ran the punch line: "If you chose 'B,' DYKE magazine is for you. *DYKE!* A new magazine of Lesbian culture and politics."[21]

Albatross, founded in 1975 by an East Orange, New Jersey, collective, combined photography and the written word to create a striking feature titled "On Body Hair." The author explained why she refused to shave: "I will not denigrate myself by removing my normal hair to conform to this rigid and unnatural notion of feminine beauty." The piece was illustrated by an image that would have shocked women reading traditional women's magazines of the day, such as

Redbook or *Ladies' Home Journal:* a quarter-page closeup photo of a woman's unshaved arm pit.[22]

Not all lesbian feminists rejected traditional standards of feminine beauty. One strong voice on this issue—as on many others—was Rita Mae Brown. Orphaned at an early age and having grown up in a working-class family, Brown contended that, for her, assigning a politically correct dress code was oppressive. She wrote: "If I see one more woman in a work shirt, I may puke. I really may! I just loathe that whole downward-mobility, make-yourself-ugly trip. If one comes from a world of pretty clothes, it may be liberating to take them off. However, for those of us who come from rags, you give them to me!" Brown argued that choice was fundamental to liberation and that lesbians, therefore, should be allowed to dress any way they chose. When the women's festivals of the 1970s became a sea of baggy dungarees and drab-colored work shirts, Brown continued to express her individuality. She was easy to spot in makeup, jewelry, and a tight-fitting blouse.[23]

Celebrating Physical Prowess

Publications combined words and photographs to document lesbians expressing their physical strength and athletic ability. Gay women always had tended to be interested in strenuous physical activity, but it was not until the 1970s that the lesbian press consistently chronicled this aspect of the culture.

Each Sunday, members of the *Furies* collective organized softball games in Washington's city parks. So, in their premier issue, one player began a series on how to keep physically fit. Initial pieces focused on karate and calisthenics; while later ones told readers how to defend themselves against physical attacks. "If a man attacks you," the author wrote, "first knee him in the balls, punch to the stomach, elbow to the head or karate chop his neck." Each article was illustrated by drawings.[24]

The bulk of the editorial material devoted to physical culture reported on the organized athletic events that, by the 1970s, had evolved into a major element of life in Lesbian America. While mainstream newspapers were only beginning to acknowledge women's sports, lesbian publications filled their pages with features and news reports on a wide range of athletic activities. Multipage photo essays in *So's Your Old Lady,* published in Minneapolis, celebrated both the success of lesbian volleyball players and the joy the women received from interacting with each other.[25]

Some publications included sports sections in every issue. *Amazon,* a Milwaukee newspaper, promoted softball with photos as well as supportive comments that portrayed the popular sport as a lesbian melting pot. One article read, "Women of all socio-economic backgrounds and ages play." The laudatory article then reported that 2,000 women participated in the local league. Other publications covered athletics sporadically through occasional features. *Lesbian Tide,* whose staff members formed their own football and softball teams, published features focusing on basketball, weightlifting, backpacking, and motorcycle racing—which the magazine unabashedly headlined "Dykes on Bikes."[26]

Lesbian Feminist, a New York City newspaper, covered a variety of athletic events when it reported on the first-of-its-kind Women's Olympics. Sponsored by the local lesbian feminist community, events ranged from volleyball and softball to a number of individual track and field activities. One runner relived the day in a first-person account: "I felt positively matriarchal, supreme. I was unbeatable."[27]

Other articles also went far beyond sterile box scores. A *Tide* feature on lesbian softball captured the mood at the ballpark with a detailed description: "Women swagger around the field braless, chomping gum, decked out in an odd assortment of hats and T-shirts embellished with double women's symbols. Many more women are in the stands, some wearing lavender cheerleading outfits, complete with pom-poms."[28]

Promoting Women's Music as a Political Venue

Another social activity of far-reaching importance to 1970s lesbians was playing and listening to women's music. It was a decade in which millions of Americans found that music succeeded better than any other medium in enabling them to communicate their feelings. Women's music reinforced the feminist consciousness, and lesbian feminists participated fully in that experience. In addition to the multitude of opinion pieces focusing on the role of women's music, reviews of albums and concerts featuring lesbian musicians filled an enormous number of pages in the lesbian press.

Members of the Daughters of Bilitis in San Francisco initiated the coverage of lesbian music in 1973 when their publication, *Sisters,* reported that women musicians in Chicago had become the first in the country to insist upon being identified as lesbian feminists, even though many people warned them that the label would alienate potential audience members. The defiant women responded: "To be a closet band is invalidating to all lesbians. We are not entertainers! We are political musicians." The group performed only music written by women, hired only female sound technicians, and performed only at all-women concerts.[29]

The philosophy supporting lesbian music was so central to the culture that it became the subject of an in-depth roundtable series in *Lesbian Tide*. "Musicians Look at Culture" provided a forum for leading performers to share their ideas about why music was so valuable to lesbians. Casse Culver contributed some of the most perceptive observations. She argued that straight women musicians had received at least some recognition because their work was designed to please men, but lesbian musicians had been denied even that affirmation. The singer also theorized that lesbians make the best musicians: "Their persecution gives them a greater depth of soul." The *Tide*'s commitment to providing a forum for lesbian musicians to discuss their motivations and philosophies did not end with the series. The list of women interviewed by the magazine reads like a who's who of lesbian musicians, including Margie Adam, Meg Christian, Holly Near, and Cris Williamson.[30]

Lesbian Tide further emphasized music's importance by devoting large quantities of editorial space to features and photo essays about women-only music festivals. The Michigan Womyn's Music Festival, founded in 1976, became an annual event drawing thousands of lesbians and spawning similar gatherings around the country. As many as 10,000 women would transform hundreds of acres of pasture into "womyn's space" that showcased music, dance, theater, poetry, political lectures, and workshops on any number of subjects. "Women's music festivals became the political conventions of the seventies," Córdova said. "I didn't dare miss one—either in my editorial coverage in the *Tide* or in my personal schedule." Coverage routinely included photos of bare-breasted or naked women watching and participating in performances.[31]

Lesbian stand-up comics often provided humorous interludes between the musical sets. Robin Tyler, one of the most prominent of the humorists, spiced up her jokes with a healthy dose of politics. Among her most crowd-pleasing lines were "Anti-feminist Phyllis Schlafly is to women what the Hindenburg was to flying," "I always believed 'monogamy' was a kind of dark wood you polish," and "I happen to agree with the right-to-lifers, 'cause if you don't agree with them, they'll kill you!"[32]

A much less pleasant by-product of the music festivals was the issue of women bringing their male children to the events. The organizers of some women's music festivals barred even male infants, and *Lavender Woman* went the radical step of suggesting that if a lesbian gave birth to a male child, she should take drastic measures. "The male child of a lesbian feminist will become a man with the same male privilege as a boy raised to be a sexist," the newspaper argued. "Therefore, lesbians should give up their male children."[33]

The music festivals provided a venue for lesbians to express their spirituality through devotion not to the male-oriented God who had dominated religion for 2,000 years, but to the Goddess Movement that captured the allegiance of many women of the 1970s. *Lesbian Tide* published dozens of articles about the movement and its leaders such as Z Budapest and Live Oak Womon. One full-page article described trysting, an ancient ritual that formalized relationships in which women were equal. Many lesbians adopted the ritual as their own and conducted bonding ceremonies for couples during music festivals. The *Tide* wrote: "By reclaiming the trysting ceremony, women may construct rituals of life to replace the death rituals of patriarchy. Celebrating love and trust is not the same as being locked into wedlock. Instead, as Z Budapest put it, 'Women making ceremonies of commitment to each other is the beginnings of women's tribes.'"[34]

One of the biggest lesbian success stories of the decade was the rise of Olivia Records. Ten women—including Ginny Z. Berson, who had been a dynamic force in *The Furies*—borrowed $4,000 to create their own record company composed exclusively of women musicians, engineers, producers, and distributors. With hit albums such as Cris Williamson's "The Changer and the Changed" and Meg Christian's "Scrapbook," the label took off. Publications touted Olivia Records for providing the inspirational soundtrack for a generation of American lesbians.[35]

Reviews of musical performances provided an opportunity to publish political rhetoric, as they communicated messages far more profound than mere assessment of the quality of the sound. A review titled "Maxine Feldman: Keep That Dyke on Stage" read: "Her voice is strong and clear and her energy high; when she sings, it is with conviction and impact. Feldman performs openly as a lesbian/feminist and has had her share of 'Get that dyke off stage' scenes. It was a pleasure to see her well received."[36]

Printing the lyrics to songs alongside articles about musicians further spread the politics of music. *Lesbian Tide* reproduced the words to Feldman's "Angry at This," the first song recorded by an openly gay American woman:

> I hate not being able to hold my lover's hand
> Except under some dimly lit table,
> Afraid of being who I am.
> I hate to tell lies, live in the shadow of fear
> We run half our lives,
> From that damn word "queer."[37]

Embracing "Dyke Separatism"

The lodestar of Lesbian America in the 1970s was lesbian separatism, a concept that was a natural corollary to lesbian feminism. As lesbians became disenchanted with both the Gay Liberation and Women's Liberation Movements, many became convinced they would triumph over oppression only by uniting against their common enemies and creating a Lesbian Nation. Living in a civilization created and sustained exclusively by lesbians also would prove—once and for all—their contention that women could survive and thrive without men.

The women whose voices bellowed from the pages of *The Furies* were the first to identify heterosexuality as an underpinning of male supremacy. A lesbian had no choice but to sever all contacts with straight America, the newspaper argued, because valuing men more than women was fundamental to that society. So *The Furies* advocated totally restructuring the social order. "Heterosexuality separates women from each other," Charlotte Bunch said in its first issue. "It makes women define themselves through men; it forces women to compete against each other for men." *The Furies* maintained this perspective throughout its life, with the final issue restating the same message: "Women must stop nurturing men and feeding the institution of heterosexuality. That energy must be given to other women."[38]

Lavender Woman echoed the antimale message, scolding lesbians for foolishly thinking that any other segment of society would advance their cause: "It's time we stop kidding ourselves. Separation is the only answer." In spite of *Lavender Woman*'s commitment to lesbian separatism, it refrained from attacking lesbians who advocated the opposite position. In a story about Barbara Gittings, the former *Ladder* editor who in the 1970s was committing her energy to the National Gay Task Force, *Lavender Woman* gave Gittings the chance to explain her position. It quoted her as saying: "The people who need to be reached are the straight public who hate our guts. I make no apology for working with gay men to educate the straight public." The newspaper simply reported Gittings's views without further editorial comment.[39]

The publications advocated lesbian separatism through the eye-popping parade of antimale comments that marched through their pages. *Dyke* blithely proposed that rapists be castrated and male corporate bosses be punished by being forced to endure anal intercourse with horses, while men in general should have their penises "merrily mutilated." *Lesbian Tide* asserted, "Man-hating is an honorable and viable political act." *Lavender Woman* routinely replaced the word *men* with the word *pricks*. Straight men were not the only targets of the venom. *Tribad* referred to gay men in such denigrating epithets as "shit pack-ers," and *Dyke* said matter of factly, "Cocksucking can cause cancer."[40]

Lesbian Tide advocated separatism through its selection and presentation of news. One article lauded an all-woman collective in New Mexico where the women grew crops and raised animals while avoiding all contact with men. An-other article supported local lesbians who attempted to transform a section of Venice Beach into an area exclusively for lesbians to swim and sunbathe topless. When police arrested the women, the *Tide* protested the "sick culture" that pro-pelled police to arrest topless lesbians on the beach but allowed topless dancers to be exploited in city bars catering to horny men.[41]

Amazon Quarterly advocated constructing the beginnings of a Lesbian Na-tion when it encouraged readers to band together to purchase property and create communal retreats. *Lavender Woman* echoed the sentiment with glowing feature articles such as one titled "Amazon Nation" that described an Oklahoma town peopled entirely by lesbians.[42]

The epitome of separatism in the lesbian press surfaced in 1977 with the founding of a New York City publication entirely dedicated to the concept. *Tribad*, subtitled *A Lesbian Separatist Newsjournal*, carried another defining statement on its cover as well: "TO BE SOLD TO AND SHARED BY LESBIANS ONLY." It reinforced its strident message with a cover drawing of a naked woman kicking Santa Claus in the groin and yelling: "I don't want a doll, you deity non-woman!!! I want the WORLD!!!"[43]

Tribad's editorial content proposed specific ways lesbians could destroy the patriarchy. Editor Susan Cavin advocated, for example, lesbians organizing an international strike during which they would refuse to do any work involving straights. Such a bold action would strengthen lesbians' bargaining position to help them rise above second-class citizenship, Cavin argued. An even more rad-ical proposal exploding from *Tribad*'s pages was that lesbian mothers put their male children up for adoption or otherwise refuse to raise them. Cavin recog-nized the controversial nature of the proposal but said it was merited in light of the practice in many countries of killing female infants: "It is a fair proposition for women to finally make after 2000 years of father-son rule as well as 2000 years of women *pleading* futilely with men to cool it; women will take matters into their own hands and collectively cut patriarchy off at its source: no more sons, no more patriarchy."[44]

Tribad supported the formation of a Lesbian Nation. Similar to the plat-form of the Stonewall Nation movement of the early 1970s, the proposal urged creating small communities inhabited exclusively by lesbians. "Beginning with Amazon villages of say 500 lesbians," Cavin wrote, "we could begin the great exodus of women from patriarchy." The concept included rural lesbians growing food for their urban sisters, as well as providing safe havens for lesbians to flee from abusive men. *Tribad* insisted that if the president and Congress did not set aside federal land to create Lesbian Nation, women should seize the property in a military coup: "WE DEMAND THE FEMALE'S RIGHT TO LANDED SOVEREIGNTY FREE FROM ALL MALE INTERVENTION. WE WANT THE FIRST FEMALE CUNT-RY NOW."[45]

Demystifying Lesbian Sex

Throughout the first two centuries of American history, society had viewed women's sexuality primarily in the context of bringing pleasure to men. The taboo on public discussion of homosexual activity began to be lifted with the sexual revolution of the 1960s, which ushered in frank discussion of sex between men. But it took another decade—and the rise of an assertive lesbian press—before the conversation expanded to sexual activity between women. Córdova recalled: "Sex was the fault line between straight and gay. The Stonewall Rebellion meant freedom of many kinds, but most of us saw it primarily in terms of sex—multiple sex partners, an end to monogamy, S&M if you wanted."[46]

Tribad's title made it clear that lesbian sex would have a high profile in the newsjournal's editorial mix. Each issue contained the statement explaining that *tribad* was derived from the Greek term *tribein:* "It means the apposition and friction of external female to female genitals with or without orgasm; commonly known as bumping and grinding."[47]

Lesbian publications denounced monogamy. Dismissing institutions such as the church and marriage as anachronistic, *Sisters* placed monogamy in the same category as myths such as every woman feeling fulfilled by washing her husband's dirty underwear. "To me, a non-monogamous lifestyle implies touching many people at once, literally as well as figuratively," one author concluded. "There is a great feeling of freedom." The newspaper argued that a woman loving only one woman was, on the other hand, unnatural.[48]

The *Tide* also eschewed the sexual values of straight society, asking the rhetorical question "Isn't it time we started re-defining our own lives and relationships?" Another *Tide* piece relayed the message even more emphatically: "Since heterosexuals have traditionally lived in couples, such a lifestyle must be pronounced 'perverse,' and we must live in threesomes, foursomes, collectives." Córdova spoke for the entire lesbian press when she said recently: "We saw the ethic around monogamy as a patriarchal construct. So we rejected it.

We thought having non-monogamous relationships involving many partners to be very much in keeping with our ideal of the sisterhood and community of women."[49]

Córdova broached an even more explosive topic by becoming the first lesbian journalist to discuss sadomasochism between women, a controversial topic that would continue to divide Lesbian America in the decades to come. The first article quoted a dozen lesbians who engaged in various methods of inflicting and receiving pain. One said, "Taking or having complete control, or having another woman give me that much control—total control—to me is one of the most beautiful experiences I've ever had." Although the *Tide* did not specifically endorse sadomasochism, its mere discussion of the topic detonated strong reader response. Córdova recently recalled: "Feminists were obsessed with politically incorrect sex. We had more letters on our S & M coverage than on any other subject in our nine years of publishing." Most critics objected to the article because, they said, it perpetuated the degrading of women as a sexually stimulating activity.[50]

The most adamant sexual stand *The Furies* adopted was opposing bisexuality, a by-product of its opposition to heterosexuality. Even though huge numbers of lesbian feminists had been involved in physical relationships with men, the separatist newspaper denounced lesbians who continued to engage in heterosexual sex, arguing that such behavior was harmful to the lesbian cause. One article insisted, "Women who practice bisexuality undermine the feminist struggle." Other publications adopted the opposite attitude. *Lavender Woman* campaigned against lesbians excluding bisexual women from their lives. "Women have enough problems without our not supporting each other," the newspaper argued.[51]

Masturbation was a less divisive topic, as the publications encouraged readers to adopt a positive attitude toward self-induced orgasm. Articles supporting sex with oneself frequently included personalized denunciations of the author's previous sexual activities with men. "Men didn't make love to me. They used my body to make love to themselves," a woman wrote in *Amazon*. "I treat my body much more lovingly than any man ever did."[52]

At the same time that publications were plowing new ground in sexual discourse, some were also publishing sexual images. *Sisters* featured nude women on its cover, *Lesbian Tide* illustrated its discussions of sado-masochism with images of nude women pirouetting across the page, and *Tribad* routinely communicated its stridency with etchings of nude women embracing and dancing together. One charmingly memorable image of the era was a photograph the editors of *Amazon Quarterly*, Gina Covina and Laurel Galana, ran with their announcement that they had moved from Oakland, California, to West Somerville, Massachusetts. The whimsical photograph showed two nude women, from the rear, holding each other arm in arm as they entered the back seat of a handsome black touring car. The caption: "The editors take leave."[53]

Amazon Quarterly became a forum for sexual discussions. The magazine specifically opposed lesbians using penis substitutes to enhance sexual pleasure, maintaining that dildos suggested that women could not be fulfilled without men. In another graphic article in *Amazon Quarterly,* a woman explored the meaning of menstrual blood. The writer said that she previously had thought of the blood as a sign of weakness and a source of shame. But her feelings changed one night when her lover suggested that the author drink the blood the lover released. The author continued: "Blood as strength, not weakness; blood the sign of wholeness, not mutilation. Beautiful blood. Woman blood. This blood is part of us, it is real and strong and good—like us. And then I did drink. I drank until there was no more. And I cried. And we laughed. And by then there was more, so I drank again."[54]

Most publications steered clear of bestiality. Not so *Dyke.* The magazine devoted an entire issue to lesbians and their animals, including half a dozen first-person articles about pets as lovers. One woman talked about how her sexual relationship with her dog Brico began in the bathtub but moved to the

THE EDITORS TAKE LEAVE

The editors of Amazon Quarterly *used this whimsical image to announce their move from California to Massachusetts in the summer of 1973.*

bedroom. The woman described the Great Dane learning to help her mistress reach sexual climax: "She participated more and more, and eventually her tongue touched me and brought me to orgasm." But after their sexual relationship developed, the woman worried that the dog might pursue her in public, not knowing sexual activity was a private affair. But the woman worried for naught, saying of Brico: "She was as intelligent and discreet as any woman. She wasn't even jealous when I had a human lover. Yeah, non-monogamy!" *Dyke*'s editors quickly discovered, however, that bestiality was going beyond the limits of most readers. In the words of editor Penny House, the magazine's sexually explicit issue on the topic was "a bomb." In fact, the issue was the last *Dyke* ever published. "The animals issue seemed to just dumbfound readers," House said.[55]

Reclaiming Lesbian "Herstory"

Documenting the heritage of the American lesbian was a more benign topic. Lesbians had been doubly excluded from most historical research, an undertaking dominated by straight men. So, for lesbians, exploring their culture in the 1970s included reclaiming their history. The *herstory*—the term substituted for *history* to emphasize the feminist preference for female pronouns—of lesbians evolved into a mainstay of the publications. Lesbian journalists did not possess the power to give their readers first-class citizenship, but they could document and transmit a heritage readers could be proud of and inspired by.

Merely in selecting the name of their newspaper, the dozen women who created *The Furies* demonstrated their commitment to recovering lesbian history. The Furies were three mythological Greek goddesses described as having wings and hair made out of snakes. "Like Lesbians today, they were cursed and feared," according to the newspaper. "They were born when Heaven (the male symbol) was castrated by his son at the urging of Earth (the female symbol). The blood from the wound fell on Earth and fertilized her, and the Furies were born."[56]

Profiles of famous lesbians thereafter became a standing feature in the newspaper. Berson recalled: "Part of our obsession with history was genuine curiosity about the women. But part of it was a tribute to the serious role we believed we were taking on. We were going to create a revolution like nothing anyone had ever seen before. We had to know how other revolutionaries did it—to emulate what we could, and to avoid what we should." Subjects of *Furies* features ranged from eighteenth-century pirates Anne Bonny and Mary Read to twentieth-century literati Gertrude Stein and Alice B. Toklas.[57]

Details of these women's personal lives were not widely known, as most scholarly biographers had sidestepped the issue of whether a subject had been lesbian. When *The Furies* published a feature on nineteenth-century poet Emily Dickinson, the author stated: "The terrible biographies I consulted for this article are not worth mentioning. The heterosexual bias is stifling and verges on the absurd in its crazy quest for Emily's male lover." To fill the gaps, lesbian journalists had to undertake original research. A feature about Susan B. Anthony quoted from her correspondence with Anna Dickinson, a noted orator of the day, to suggest that the women had a physically intimate relationship. The article quoted Anna Dickinson writing to Anthony: "I want to see you very much, indeed to hold your hand in mine, to hear your voice, in a word, I want you." The article reported that the women remained in close contact for several decades, concluding with the observation that Anthony's friendship and love were devoted exclusively to women.[58]

Other publications followed *The Furies*'s lead and also committed space to herstory. *Amazon* illuminated the lives of aviator Amelia Earhart and birth-control pioneer Margaret Sanger. *Lavender Woman* placed its historical pieces under the heading "Amazons." One item described Bast, an ancient Egyptian goddess associated with joy, music, and dancing; the article was accompanied by an image of Bast, who had the head of a cat and the body of a woman, dancing amid flames.[59]

Lesbian Feminist approached reclaiming lesbian history more directly. Distressed by the invisibility of women at the Museum of Natural History in New York, the newspaper demanded that the female profile at the museum be raised, both in exhibits and on the staff. When Lesbian Feminist Liberation, the group that sponsored the newspaper, organized a public demonstration at the museum, *Lesbian Feminist* committed prominent news space to the criticisms. The newspaper promoted the group's demands, which included rewording museum labels to replace *men* with *people,* and hiring a female anthropologist to research women's history. The protest included 200 picketers, music by an all-woman marching band, and the appearance of a "dykosaur" named Dinah—a 250-pound plaster dinosaur painted lavender. *Lesbian Feminist* publicized the event with a news article and half-page photo on its cover, as well as two feature articles, two photos, and an editorial cartoon inside. The demonstration and publicity had impact, as the museum subsequently hired a female anthropologist and agreed to work with leaders of the protest to resolve their concerns.[60]

Celebrating Diversity in the Lesbian Community

The publications demonstrated a strong commitment to Third World lesbians, a broadly defined category including members of racial and ethnic minority groups in the United States as well as abroad. Although most editors and writers were white and middle class, the oppression they had experienced because of their sexual orientation increased their affinity with lesbians whose backgrounds had pushed them outside of mainstream society. Many women who created lesbian publications also had activist backgrounds that had raised their consciousness about oppression beyond that based on sexual orientation. "A lot of us came out of the anti-war and black civil rights movements," Córdova said. "We saw the connection right away." So journalists felt responsible for providing an arena in which disadvantaged women could express themselves.[61]

Tribad was particularly eager to reach out to racial and ethnic minorities. The newsjournal repeatedly criticized the Women's Liberation Movement's attitude toward minority women. It accused movement leaders of being racist and having usurped the power that should have belonged to minority women, saying, "True revolution should always rise up from the ranks of the most oppressed and not come down on them from an intellectualized political ideology." *Tribad*'s editors vowed they would be more responsive to disadvantaged women than straight women were: "We want to call our sisters, listen to their rage, see how it evokes the pain and rage in our own guts, and figure out how together we can soothe each other and take our revenge."[62]

Part of *Tribad*'s strategy to secure justice for minority lesbians was to call for armed combat to overthrow the white male establishment that they saw as a dictatorship. Women in the collective articulated their plan in an article titled "What This CUNT-ry Needs Is A Dirty Lesbian Army!!" As the core of the womanpower needed for such an army, the women hoped to benefit from the experience of another group of women pushed outside the mainstream of society: lesbians in prison. The publications consistently included lesbians behind bars as part of the diverse community they tried to serve. The staffs of *Lesbian Tide* and *Dyke* organized fund-raising events for lesbian prisoners and sent copies of their magazines to any lesbian inmate who requested them. They also campaigned against physical abuse of lesbian inmates. Córdova went inside a women's penitentiary to interview a prisoner about her treatment, and *Dyke* provided extensive coverage of how a black lesbian being denied medical treatment escalated into the first women's riot in the history of the New York state prison system.[63]

When *Amazon Quarterly* published a series of twenty lengthy interviews with lesbians living in various parts of the country, the editors paid attention to diversity. The series evolved in 1973 when editors Gina Covina and Laurel Galana spent three months traveling across the United States conducting taped interviews with readers. They featured the material in a special double issue containing a remarkable collection of interviews that cut across both the geographic and socioeconomic landscape of Lesbian America as no work had before it. "Because one of the major purposes of our journal was to encourage inclusiveness, we were real conscious of the range of ages and political viewpoints of our subjects," Covina said. "Our readers wanted diversity—it was a major theme of the decade."[64]

In 1977 a new publication specifically by and for lesbians of color was founded. Published by a New York City collective, *Azalea* carried the subtitle *A Magazine by Third World Lesbians*. The founders were so determined not to perpetuate oppression that they refused to assess the quality of contributions sent to them, publishing all material without any editing. Much of that material expressed the rage that erupted within writers who suffered the pain of discrimination. In the words of one African-American woman, "In addition to all the frustrations that plague any aspiring writer, the Third World Lesbian has to cope with the added stumbling block dumped in her path by a white racist homophobic patriarchal society." Although the magazine circulated almost exclusively in the United States, it attracted writers from an impressive range of cultural backgrounds—including women from Asia, Africa, and South America—who took advantage of *Azalea*'s eagerness to publish their words.[65]

Because *The Furies* was published by a collective of women from a range of socioeconomic backgrounds, the women struggled with class issues in their day-to-day lives as well as in the pages of their newspaper. Looking back at all issues of *The Furies,* Berson recently recalled: "I cannot find a single article that did not mention class—even if class was not the point of the article. All of us were in different stages of class awareness, but we all understood that, to succeed, our revolution had to be for all women, not just the privileged."[66]

Creating Ideology Through Literature

Since 1947 when Lisa Ben created *Vice Versa,* literary works had been a staple in the lesbian press. In the 1960s and 1970s, the pioneering efforts of such news-oriented publications as *The Ladder* and *Lesbian Tide* reduced the proportion of fiction. Nevertheless, creative writing remained a staple in many publications because many lesbians found fiction a more effective means of communicating than news or commentary.

Amazon Quarterly became the leading literary outlet of the era, consciously maintaining the open forum that had always been a hallmark of the lesbian press. Covina and Galana founded the Oakland-based journal specifically to fill the void created by *The Ladder*'s demise in 1972. Covina said recently, "When it ended, there was nothing—no national lesbian publication." Covina and Galana sent an appeal for financial support to all former *Ladder* subscribers. When that effort brought in several hundred dollars, *Amazon Quarterly* was born. "Our link to *The Ladder* was more than intellectual," Covina said. "It was also very tangible."[67]

In a deliberate effort to steer clear of the fractious political debates that had destroyed *The Ladder, Amazon Quarterly* adopted a broad purpose. In their first issue, the editors said: "We want to explore through *Amazon Quarterly* just what might be the female sensibility in the arts. This is also a place for lesbians to explore whatever else is on their minds." That invitation drew a strong response, as women from around the country were soon submitting some five hundred works each month.[68]

Amazon Quarterly quickly became the most widely distributed lesbian publication of the era, with a circulation of 9,000. But, unlike gay male editors, Covina and Galana did not put the circulation revenue in their pockets. Instead, they used the money to join *Lesbian Tide* in paying all contributors. The revenue also allowed *Amazon Quarterly* to publish seventy-two pages of material in each issue, making it the largest publication of the era.[69]

Despite the attempt of *Amazon Quarterly* and other publications to focus on cultural topics, the literary component of the 1970s lesbian press was more political than that of previous generations. While earlier short stories and poems often carried veiled messages suggesting themes such as the effects of discrimination or dreams of a utopian future, the new works spoke boldly and directly.

Rita Mae Brown emerged as the literary prophet of lesbian feminism. In addition to helping found *The* "legendary" *Furies*, Brown wrote for *Amazon Quarterly, Lesbian Feminist, Lesbian Tide, Sisters,* and *So's Your Old Lady.* Not only did she find her voice in the lesbian press and speak with a combination of grace, wit, and power, but she also used the publications as a springboard to national prominence and financial success. Her 1977 semiautobiographical novel, *Rubyfruit Jungle,* sold a million copies, and she has published a dozen more books since then. Brown, who also has succeeded as a screenwriter, used her writing talent to attack homophobia by creating lesbian characters who are intelligent, beautiful, and successful.

Brown's earliest literary work was as a poet, and many of the poems published in her first book, *The Hand that Cradles the Rock,* first appeared in *The Furies.* One of the earliest major lesbian literary figures to write unashamedly and with a sense of defiance, she also experimented with innovative techniques. Indeed, Brown was creating her own poetic medium. One poem in *The Furies,* "The New Lost Feminist," took the form of a triptych. The first panel expressed

Nationally known author Rita Mae Brown, featured on this Lesbian Tide *cover, was one of several gay people who used the lesbian and gay press to launch successful literary careers.* Courtesy of Jeanne Córdova.

women's frustration at being powerless. The center panel represented the view of American society as uninterested in women's plight, including references to the "wrinkled robes" of the Supreme Court. The final panel described how centuries of oppression had beaten women down, but ended with the poet's climactic message: "It's time to break and run."[70]

Brown's next experiment was with the personal essay, channeling her literary talent into helping create an ideology to guide lesbian feminists into the future. In one essay, Brown lambasted feminist leaders Betty Friedan and Gloria Steinem as merely celebrities created by the male-dominated media. In the acerbic style Brown can wield with aplomb, she denounced such women as promoting themselves at the expense of other women. "Beguiled by the star," she wrote, "women pin their hopes on the flickering TV images rather than looking for the answer among themselves."[71]

As Brown evolved as a political theorist, her outspoken nature brought her into conflict with many lesbians. Particularly controversial was her opposition to creating a Lesbian Nation. In a *Lesbian Tide* essay, she argued that lesbians should not create an independent society but should overthrow the one that existed. She then used her talent as a wordsmith to create a rallying cry to summarize her point: "We can't run off into the moonlight and think a kiss is a revolution."[72]

Another notable literary figure who published in the lesbian press was Audre Lorde, who carved from the complexities of her race and sexual orientation a series of poems challenging female stereotypes. Lorde's poems in *Amazon Quarterly* and *Azalea* lifted verse to one of the highest points in the history of the lesbian and gay press. Like most of the literary works in the alternative press, Lorde's were political statements. Lorde, an African American, encouraged women to declare their love for other women rather than suffer the psychological damage of "energy-eating secrets" and "worms of sorrow and loss." In contrast, she provided strong, powerful images of lesbians through such terms as *warrior sisters* and *the queendom*.[73]

A third important citizen of the lesbian literary community was Adrienne Rich, the doyenne of feminist literature. Although Rich's poetry was published most often in *Amazon Quarterly*, her most powerful statement appeared in the separatist newsjournal *Tribad*. In an open letter, she explained why she had refused the Gay Academic Union's award for achievement in literature, citing the continued failure of gay male leaders to represent lesbians. The substance of the letter was little different from that of Del Martin's denunciation of the Gay Liberation Movement a decade earlier, but Rich's criticism was articulated in the eloquent prose of a gifted woman of letters. Rich argued that lesbians were duty-bound to distance themselves from gay men—"from whom we have learned so much self-destructiveness." As a lesbian feminist, Rich refused to allow her work to benefit the gay movement that, she said, had so utterly failed to reform its own misogyny. "I cannot make common cause with a male 'gay' movement. And such a movement—even when it 'includes' lesbians—cannot honor me."[74]

Although the literary success of this trio of gifted writers has been well documented, it is impossible to gauge the role that the publications played in the lives of thousands of other contributing writers. Although these writers may not have achieved public recognition, the lesbian press gave them, many for the

first time, a venue in which to raise their voices. A Latina woman writing in
Azalea spoke for many when she praised the lesbian press: "It is a herstorical
record of our existence. Proof that we breathe and we share our thinking—and
we have visions. A dialogue is just what I needed, a space, a forum—a recognition of the need for communication and feedback between us."[75]

Golden Years of the Lesbian Press

Six months after founding *The Furies,* collective members began identifying the
problems that undermined lesbian collectives. "The living part worked to some
degree," Ginny Z. Berson said, "but the working part never quite got together."
The impediments were legion. Confrontations between members about individual character flaws were emotionally draining. Middle-class women carrying the financial load went against the social and ethical values that had been
instilled into their very beings. Most women who belonged to racial minorities
ultimately allied more closely with their race than their sexual orientation.
When such pressures piled one on top of the other, their combined weight
crushed many lesbian collectives.[76]

Publishing created additional strains. When lesbian editors gathered for
workshops to discuss their common problems, dealing with splits in collectives
was high on the agenda. A woman from *Lavender Woman* said: "Half our group
thinks advertising stinks. The other half thinks advertising is a source of much
needed $$$. Some of us think men's letters should not be printed. Others think
men's letters should be. We haven't found our compromises yet." That *The
Furies* was published by a collective enhanced the richness of the ideology it
produced, but also contributed to its early death. At various times in its history,
Lesbian Tide experimented with a collective approach, but each time returned
to traditional structure. "A publication involves tremendous pressure," Jeanne
Córdova said. "If you're going to survive, you have to make decisions, right or
wrong, and get on with it. You don't always have time to sit down with a dozen
other women and talk it out. You have to do it."[77]

As the decade of the 1970s advanced, the collective lifestyle faded and took
much of the lesbian press with it. *The Furies* ceased publication when the col-
lective disbanded in 1973, followed by *Amazon Quarterly* and *Sisters* in 1975,
Lavender Woman in 1976, *So's Your Old Lady* in 1978, *Dyke, Lesbian Feminist,*
and *Tribad* in 1979, and *Albatross, Amazon,* and *Lesbian Tide* in 1980.

And yet lesbian editors of the era did not hang their heads in shame that
they had failed their readers or the movement. Gina Covina recently recalled:

"When we started *Amazon Quarterly* in 1972, there was no national magazine or journal or any publication at all geared to lesbians. So we felt that we had to fill that void. But when we quit to pursue other interests, we didn't feel guilty because we weren't, by any means, leaving a vacuum. By that time, 1975, there were lots of other voices. We weren't needed in the same way that we had been only three years earlier."[78]

Lesbian Tide, as a commercial venture, had more staying power than most of its sisters. In fact, the Los Angeles news magazine, like *Amazon Quarterly*, was financially solvent, though by no means wealthy, in 1980 when Córdova called it quits. Her primary reason for discontinuing the publication was a common one among advocacy journalists: "New vistas were opening up, and, as a radical, I wanted to explore them. I had brought the *Tide* from a low-quality newsletter to the first financially viable news outlet in the history of Lesbian America. It was time to move on."[79]

As the lights of the *Tide* and other lesbian publications of the mid-1970s dimmed, three major accomplishments lived on. First, they had created the halcyon days of lesbian journalism. The quantity and quality of material had lifted the genre to a pinnacle that had never been approached before, and remains the stuff of legend today. Joan Nestle said: "The splendid material on music, the quality fiction, the depth of theoretical discussion . . . When lesbians think of the 'Golden Years' of the lesbian press, they think of the seventies. Perhaps they always will."[80]

Second, the breadth of publications and points of view successfully illuminated the many dimensions of lesbian culture. By exploring subjects such as appearance and sex as political issues, by celebrating lesbian "herstory" and physical activity, by debating such difficult issues as monogamy, sado-masochism, and separatism, the 1970s lesbian press had delved into the culture to unprecedented depths. Discussing the merits and philosophical underpinnings of these topics simultaneously boosted the self-esteem and sense of self-worth of millions of women. What's more, raising the group lesbian consciousness about these subjects helped build a stronger and more cohesive Lesbian America. In the words of *Lavender Woman*, "When oppressed groups realize they are beautiful, they take one gigantic step forward. Acknowledging your beauty is a revolutionary act."[81]

Finally, mid-1970s publications reinforced the idea that lesbian issues were not so very different from feminist issues. A straight woman seeking to feed her hunger for liberation from male dominance would have found sustenance in the lesbian press. For despite "dyke separatism" rising to its zenith, a remarkable number of the topics covered in lesbian newspapers and magazines were bedrock issues of the women's liberation press as well. Considering the political dimensions of personal appearance and sexual activity, finding a voice through music and literature, redefining the past in "herstorical" terms—these were all gender issues that did not limit themselves to women of any particular sexual orientation.

Because this chapter has dealt exclusively with publications produced by lesbians, it is relevant to note three further items. They are themes that scholars have identified as distinctive to women's media throughout American history. Some themes common to publications produced by women—such as providing an open forum and reporting from a unique perspective—surfaced in earlier generations of the lesbian and gay press, but the following three themes appeared only in the mid-1970s in lesbian publications.

First, scholars of women's media have noted that a publication produced entirely by women is more likely to be created by a collective than by a group of people organized in a hierarchical structure. This certainly was the case with the publications created by gay women. Eight of the twelve newspapers and magazines described in this chapter were formed by collectives. Opposition to hierarchy also shaped individual publications—an example is *Azalea*'s refusing to judge or edit submissions.[82]

Second, scholars have found that women's media have embraced the concept of sharing rather than the journalistic convention of competing. Again, the publications highlighted in this chapter reflected this tendency. Rita Mae Brown is the strongest example; her byline appeared in half a dozen different newspapers and magazines, often above identical or very similar articles. Audre Lorde, Adrienne Rich, and Martha Shelley wrote for multiple publications as well, and Jeanne Córdova sent articles to *Sisters* for free at the same time as she was trying to scrape together a livelihood from publishing *Lesbian Tide*. On a broader scale, creating group workshops, *Lavender Woman* calling for a lesbian news service, and *Lesbian Tide* and *Amazon Quarterly* insisting on paying all contributors further speak to the concept of "sharing with" rather than "competing against."

Third, scholars studying women's media have observed that when writers who have different opinions on a subject disagree, they are likely to adopt a non-attack approach that allows opinion to be expressed without name-calling or personal animosity. Again, evidence of this characteristic can be found in the mid-1970s lesbian press. *Lavender Woman* printed Barbara Gittings's explanation for why she worked with gay men, though the newspaper opposed such co-gender activities; *Lesbian Tide* printed Brown's essay opposing a Lesbian Nation, despite the concept being a key one in the magazine's editorial philosophy. Even on such explosive topics as bisexuality and sadomasochism, writers offered their views without criticizing the lesbians who disagreed with them, creating a healthy and enriching dialogue rarely replicated by either gay or straight male journalists of this or any era—as the next chapter dramatically testifies.

λ 7

Defining Gay Male Culture

Among mid-1970s publications aimed at gay men, the decade witnessed one of the most controversial phenomena in the history of the gay press. In 1974 people gasped in disbelief when David B. Goodstein, a Wall Street investment banker, paid Dick Michaels the astonishing sum of $1 million for *The Advocate*. Their shock continued as the multimillionaire poured his massive wealth into reshaping the country's largest gay publication, which dominated the era as no single publication has done since.[1]

An astute businessman, Goodstein recognized that affluent gay men of the 1970s were eager to explore the gay culture. So he revamped *The Advocate* to reflect that emphasis. Goodstein transformed the hard-hitting newspaper into a cultural magazine living up to his new subtitle *Touching Your Lifestyle*. In the words of Mark Thompson, who became Goodstein's lieutenant in charge of cultural reporting, "Constructing our culture was Gay America's most significant accomplishment during the 1970s, and *The Advocate* led the way. Gay people self-defining ourselves—stepping out, forming clusters around our shared interests—is one of the most fascinating stories, journalistically speaking, of the latter part of the twentieth century."[2]

Redesigned with a bold, modern look, *The Advocate* stood on the cutting edge of American magazine publishing. With Goodstein's generous support, it probed the myriad dimensions of an emerging gay middle class. Of course Goodstein used *The Advocate* as his bully pulpit as well. In the new publisher's first issue, he drew a clear profile of the reader he was targeting: "You are employed and a useful, responsible citizen. You have an attractive body, nice clothes and an inviting home." The "Advocate man" lived the good life—working out, spending several nights a week at the bars, enriching his gay sensibility by reading literature and enjoying art. *The Advocate* published forty pages of cultural coverage and twenty pages of advertising—much of it in the form of sexually oriented classifieds—in each biweekly issue. The country's largest gay publication also was inching into mainstream society. Jimmy Carter's 1976 presidential campaign bought full-page ads in the magazine; after Carter won, Goodstein joined Carter for dinner at the White House, and Carter accepted the free subscription Goodstein sent him.[3]

Other publications reinforced the shift to cultural reporting. Jack Nichols and Lige Clarke's *GAY* remained the newspaper of record in New York City, while their "Homosexual Citizen" column in *Screw* continued to give them a second outlet. In San Francisco, *Vector* mirrored the values of that gay mecca by adding the subtitle *Celebrating the Gay Experience.*

There were alternatives to these established—and, in many ways, establish-*ment*—publications. The reborn *Gay Liberator* in Detroit and *Gay Sunshine* in San Francisco spoke with a sense of militancy, providing radical perspectives on a range of cultural topics. They were joined by an even more radical paper from the East Coast. *Fag Rag,* produced by a Boston collective, was dynamic in its graphics and daunting in its jaw-dropping approach to sex. Sounding like some of the radical lesbian publications of the era, the brash tabloid boomed: "We vigorously oppose integration into the existing patriarchal and capitalist institutions. We do not want a slice of the pie; the pie is rotten." *Fag Rag* did, however, agree with the other publications in stressing cultural coverage, stating: "Like the fabulous phoenix, we are arising out of the ashes of a dying civilization. We are creating a gay culture."[4]

Publications demonstrated that gay journalism was becoming increasingly specialized. *Gay Sunshine* emerged as the genre's first literary journal, and *Christopher Street* sought to become a gay *New Yorker.* Three others—*Drummer* in San Francisco, *Gaytimes* in Los Angeles, and *Queen's Quarterly* in New York—traveled a very different route by adopting homoerotica as the element dominating their editorial mix. The decade also witnessed the birth of many news-oriented publications, such as the *Blade* in Washington and *Bay Area Reporter* in San Francisco. News and cultural reporting both held sway in these nascent newspapers that, in future decades, would become major players in the continuing rise of the gay press.

Gay journalism did not differ from its lesbian counterpart merely in editorial content. As gay publications set out to capture the essence of the culture, they also captured quite a lot of advertising. The display and classified ads that peppered their pages built them into hefty publications with growing circulations. In its 1978 critique of the gay press, *Alternative Media* said that the genre was "in the fortunate position to cash in on one of America's most affluent market sectors, the gay man." The media journal went on to say, prophetically: "It's only a matter of time—possibly years, but eventually—before the fag mags

are billing ad pages in the millions from all the major leisure accounts—airlines, tobacco, liquor, clothing, audio and video equipment, possibly even Disney World."[5]

The Advocate led the pack, as Goodstein crammed his magazine with full-
page ads featuring a plethora of skin and bulging body parts. By 1976 *The Advocate* had a circulation of 60,000 and was being recognized by the publishing industry as one of the dozen fastest-growing magazines in the country, gay or
straight. *Our Own Voices* listed some three hundred gay publications existing in
1975, and their aggregate circulation had reached 200,000. Adding the "Homosexual Citizen" column in *Screw* upped the figure to 350,000. These figures were
at least six times those of lesbian publications. By the mid-1970s, the gay male
press was becoming a financially lucrative institution; while the lesbian press
remained a labor of love—and impoverishment.[6]

David B. Goodstein Makes His Mark—Writ Large

David B. Goodstein was the scion of a wealthy Denver family. After earning a
bachelor's degree in economics from Cornell University and a law degree from
Columbia, he practiced law in New York and became a member of Mayor John
Lindsay's Democratic "brain trust." During the 1960s, Goodstein shifted to Wall
Street and founded Compufund, a mutual fund that introduced the investment
world to computerized stock analysis. When Wells Fargo Bank heard Goodstein
had parlayed his business acumen into several million dollars of profits, it set
out to recruit him to the West Coast. After two years of wooing, Goodstein finally moved to San Francisco to develop a computerized investment system for
Wells Fargo.[7]

Goodstein's destiny changed, however, when he casually mentioned his
homosexuality to his boss's wife, who passed the information on to bank officials. They fired him.[8]

Goodstein, a child of advantage who was accustomed to having his own
way, was first shattered by the act of bigotry. Then he was enraged. He asked, "If
they could do this to me, what could they do to some poor devil without any
clout?" Goodstein then committed his massive talent and resources to fighting
for gay civil rights. His initial venue was the Whitman-Radclyffe Foundation,
which he created to educate the public about gay issues. Discouraged by the
media's lack of cooperation, he decided to create a national publication to
speak for the Gay Rights Movement. He wanted to buy *After Dark*, a New York
entertainment magazine that had a strong gay readership but refused to define

itself as a gay magazine. When the owners rejected Goodstein's offer, he began negotiating with Michaels. He purchased *The Advocate* in late 1974.[9]

The magnitude of Goodstein's changes at *The Advocate* was outweighed only by the level of controversy the changes spawned. Because his plan was to emphasize culture rather than news, he changed the concept of the publication. Before his death in 1985, Goodstein said: "The first thing I wanted to do was to make it lively and change over from the newspaper concept to a magazine concept. In the age of television, the old news concept doesn't work, journalistically."[10]

Needing feature writers and designers rather than news reporters and editors, Goodstein immediately fired the entire editorial staff. He also tripled the cover price (to seventy-five cents) and confined news to a single section that was overwhelmed by three others—one for lifestyle features, another for leisure features, and a final huge one for sex-oriented advertising. In another monumental change, Goodstein moved the publication from Los Angeles to San Mateo, which was closer to his home in Atherton; the move was controversial in the gay world because San Mateo is near San Francisco, arch rival of Los Angeles.

Movement leaders steamed even more when Goodstein revealed his penchant for the popular gay sport of personal ax-grinding, using the editorial power of his magazine either to attack or ignore his political adversaries while inflating the accomplishments of his cronies. What's more, movement leaders soon learned Goodstein was a political moderate. He sought gay rights, but, as a successful capitalist and member of the Democratic party establishment, he worked within the system rather than against it. His efforts to reform society through legislative and political means were totally at odds with the Marxist leanings of gay radicals. In short: the man in the gray flannel suit did not fit in a social movement led by men and women in jeans and T-shirts.

The diminished status of news in the country's largest gay publication was another issue, as *The Advocate*'s cover showcased cultural images rather than expressing outrage at the latest affront to gay liberation. *Gay Sunshine* screamed: "News coverage was slashed from the 50 columns in the old Advocate to 14 in the new." Critics saw *The Advocate*'s transformation from a two-fisted newspaper to a lifestyles magazine as nothing but a device to pull in advertisers. *Lesbian Tide* grumbled, "He is a dedicated right winger who has some enormous misconceptions that could be harmful to the gay movement." *Fag Rag* blasted *The Advocate* as undermining the entire movement: "Such a newspaper is destructive of a national gay community." *Gay Liberator* screamed: "News coverage now consists of articles about how gays are trying to get in touch with the status-quo and nothing on what activist groups are doing. At one point we

During the mid-1970s The Advocate *transformed itself from a hard-hitting newspaper into an upscale lifestyles magazine directed at affluent gay men.* Reprinted by permission of *The Advocate.*

could think of two opposing groups, gay and anti-gay, but no longer; the enemy is among us."[11]

Goodstein's personal style irritated movement leaders as well, feeding into the personality disputes that have continually plagued the movement as well as the movement press. Mark Thompson recalled: "David was an overweight, slightly hunchback, neurotic Jewish man—not the handsome and stylish youth that Gay America prefers to canonize. When he blew in from New York and began to turn California on its head, the West Coast queens with their little fiefdoms resented him. They fought him."[12]

One critic was Dick Michaels. *The Advocate* founder had turned down offers from other people to buy his paper; Goodstein was the first to convince Michaels he would not turn the newspaper into a pornographic rag. When Michaels saw what Goodstein actually had in mind, he was outraged. Michaels's anger increased when Goodstein publicly denigrated *The Advocate* as it had existed before he bought it. Goodstein told the *Los Angeles Times*: "Up to 1974, *The Advocate* was pretty much a bulletin board. It was dull." After reading such comments, Michaels considered founding another paper with a strong news orientation, but Goodstein had insisted Michaels sign an agreement, as part of the terms of sale, not to start a competing paper. Michaels could only join the chorus of critics.[13]

Opposition be damned, Goodstein was committed to his vision for *The Advocate*. And he put his money where his mouth was. The 5,000 square feet of plush offices he created rivaled anything in the New York magazine world, and his three dozen full-time staff members and network of part-time correspondents across the country succeeded in gauging the pulse of Gay America as none of their journalistic predecessors had dared imagine. The cost of operating the newspaper soared to more than $500,000 a year, with Goodstein supplementing the revenue side from his personal fortune. By the time the revamped magazine finally began making a profit in 1979, Goodstein's total personal investment had surpassed $3 million.[14]

Among the most sweeping changes was the publication's design. Goodstein hired Dennis Forbes, who previously had worked at *Better Homes and Gardens*, as art director. Forbes recently recalled: "David's chief concern was to communicate that we were the most significant gay publication in the country—by far. Not even our harshest critics could deny that we accomplished that goal." Indeed, *The Advocate*'s dramatic layouts, large-format photos, and daring experiments with other graphic elements propelled the magazine into the ranks of the most stylish in the country.[15]

Goodstein's efforts did not, however, garner the immediate results he had hoped. The publisher's strategy was to create an upscale magazine aimed at affluent gay men living in big cities, expecting circulation to surpass 1 million within two years. The magazine grew, but glacially rather than supersonically. Forbes acknowledged: "It took us awhile to connect with the audience we were aiming at. That's to be expected when a publication changes its entire concept." But by late 1976 *The Advocate* was named one of the twelve fastest-growing magazines in the country, reaching a circulation of 60,000. That figure was still far below Goodstein's goal, as the magazine's focus was proving too narrow to capture the interest of the gay working class or radical element. Indeed, Gay America was far too diverse to be represented by any single voice.[16]

Gay Bars and Baths Dominate the Fast Lane

When the lesbian and gay press was born in 1947, gay bars were dimly lit and generally in unsafe sections of the city. Twenty-five years later, the lights were turned up full beam as gay bars and bathhouses became the twin Goliaths in the gay world, economically as well as culturally. Thick carpets, posh decors, and state-of-the-art sound equipment beckoned the gay dollar. By the mid-1970s, 2,500 bars and 150 bath houses were operating in the United States, with annual receipts of $120 million.[17]

More important, gay liberation ushered an increasing number of men and women out of the closet to become visible players in politics as well as business. In the political arena, this resulted in more states decriminalizing sodomy and the first cities and states beginning to enact gay rights ordinances. What's more, elected officials could no longer blithely sanction bar raids or police entrapment campaigns. With gay-rights organizations and the gay press maintaining a watchful eye, wayward politicians knew they would feel the impact of gay political clout on election day.

In the business community, the critical mass of visible gays meant that the bars finally escaped from the Mafia's stranglehold and into the hands of gay entrepreneurs. Creative gay businessmen also built bathhouses into an institution of enormous magnitude for Gay America. The steam rooms, group showers, and swimming pools with colored lights streaming through the water created an erotic atmosphere where customers quenched their thirst for rampant oral and anal sex with multiple partners.

The growth of bars and baths fit snugly into *The Advocate*'s new emphasis on cultural reporting. Mark Thompson, a San Francisco State University journalism graduate, joined the staff as a feature writer in 1976. "The bath houses were the gay feature writer's dream," he recalled. "They were fantasies literally *oozing* with color and flavor." The large houses transformed individual rooms into exotic settings. One room might simulate a bunk house out of the Old West, the next an army barracks or locker room, the next a rain forest or dungeon or prison cell or fraternity house. A customer paid a single admission fee, placed his clothes in a locker, and entered the world of fantasy. For hours on end, he could wander from room to room wearing nothing but a towel that slipped gently to the floor when he found an appealing partner or partners. The baths contained dozens of small cubicles equipped with beds, as well as larger areas to accommodate nonstop orgies. Thompson recalled, "Sexual pleasure, fantasy, indulgence—it reached an extraordinary level of hedonism."[18]

Because no sex acts were off limits, patrons did not have to sneak into a dark corner to avoid being arrested. The clandestine tenor of previous decades was a dim memory as men, either after or between sex acts, casually played pool, watched television, or grazed the midnight buffet, all of which were part of the bath house experience. *The Advocate* gushed: "It is not uncommon to find students sitting in the lounge area doing homework or groups of friends taking a few hours off just to relax."[19]

The most notorious operation was the Continental Baths in New York. Besides providing sex and entertainment facilities, the Continental featured a live stage where performers played to huge crowds of men wearing nothing but towels. Dozens of nightclub entertainers mounted the stage, most combining their music with humor. The list of headliners included names still familiar to audiences today, along with others that shone brightly but briefly—Barry Manilow, Tiny Tim, Tally Brown, Michael Greer, Liz Torres.

The most famous of the stars was a petite redhead. Bette Midler, before she recorded her first album, earned fifty bucks a night singing at the Continental, tossing bottles of poppers—the volatile liquid that, when inhaled, causes the user's heart rate and blood pressure to increase—to her appreciative audience. She told *GAY:* "As an audience, gay men are spectacular. They're the most marvelous audience I've ever had because they're not ashamed to show how they feel about you." In 1975 she became the first woman to grace the cover of *The Advocate.* Vito Russo, who went on to become a leading film historian, wrote in *The Advocate* that Midler's work at the baths was the turning point in her career, garnering her press attention and a spot on *The Tonight Show.* She received early publicity, Russo wrote, because she dared to sing to gays: "Critics waxed ecstatic about the darling of the decadent New York bathhouse."[20]

Once word of Midler's talent drifted out of the baths, celebrities such as singer Mick Jagger and pop culture icon Andy Warhol started frequenting the sex emporium. The mix became even more interesting when a creative sightseeing company added the Continental Baths as a surprise stop on its tour of the city by night. The newcomers wearing street clothes and the gay men in towels turned gay bathhouses into the place to be in New York in the 1970s. Before long, 1,000 people were cramming into a space meant for 500, and Midler went on to Broadway. During her *Advocate* interview, Midler credited the baths with boosting her career: "They gave me a big push, and that'll always be part of me."[21]

While documenting the glory days of the baths, *The Advocate* paid scant attention to the high prices the owners charged or the drugs that flowed as freely as the semen. "Drugs were out of control," Thompson later said. "Looking back, the gay press should have exposed that part of the story. But at the time, we chose not to write about the downside. I suppose that, on some level, we knew such behavior was going too far, but it was a big part of the life. We didn't judge."[22]

Instead, gay journalists portrayed the bath house phenomenon as a gay political success story of the first order. *The Advocate* boasted: "More people are getting their heads together about being gay and getting more positive images of themselves. They're taking part in the lifestyle as a whole and not just keeping their homosexuality hidden in the bedroom."[23]

The country's leading gay publication also covered the rise of the baths as an economic breakthrough. In 1976 it published a comprehensive business article about the baths. Among the sources was Jack Campbell, who had parlayed a $15,000 investment in a Cleveland steamroom into forty gay bathhouses from coast to coast. Campbell credited the rapid growth of his Club Bath chain to Ohio and other states legalizing sodomy. *The Advocate* article read more like an ad than a news story: "Most cities offer a cornucopia of bars. With each passing year, the fantasies get more elaborate."[24]

Accompanying photos also looked like they had spilled over from the dozens of full-page bar and bath ads that filled *The Advocate.* Art director Dennis Forbes recalled, "Every graphic artist knows images draw readers into editorial content, and we knew exactly the kinds of images our readers were looking for." *The Advocate* business article was packaged with photos featuring half a dozen naked men, several with their genitals fully exposed; a *GAY* feature on the baths included a photo of a naked man playing pool.[25]

Vector also crammed its pages full of ads for bars and bathhouses, surrounded by articles promoting them. One article praised the baths as an oasis from the banalities of life. "The baths are even *spiritual,*" *Vector* wrote, "because raw, glorious sex can be so enlivening, so ego-restoring. Since there's no heaven, the baths will have to do." Publications with strong news orientations acted as cheerleaders for the businesses as well. The *Blade* in Washington recommended the baths as a good place to begin committed relationships. The *Bay Area Reporter,* a San Francisco tabloid, placed full-page ads for bars on its front cover and carried a column of bar-related news items inside. Many such items could easily have run as paid ads. A typical one read: "Cloud 7 has been thoroughly remodeled, brought in professional entertainment and will be offering $2.69 suppers."[26]

Celebrating the Physical Culture

Since *ONE* published its first sexually suggestive ad in 1954, the gay press and its visual elements had continued to reflect the value gay men place on physical beauty. Not until the 1970s, though, did that value become a mainstay in editorial content.

The Advocate introduced the theme in an innovative column, "Body Buddy," with columnist Rod Fuller offering advice tailored to individual readers. One letter began, "I'm in 'fucked up' shape." The writer proceeded to describe how he had been rejected in the bars because his chest was flat. Fuller responded: "Do some chair dips. All you need is any chair in your pad, and you can build your chest fairly well. Place your hands on the outer edges of the seat of a chair. With feet on the floor, extend . . ." The how-to advice was accompanied by a photo of the physically well-developed Fuller, dressed in briefs, demonstrating the exercise.[27]

Other publications followed *The Advocate*'s lead. *Drummer* in San Francisco published features on how to swim, illustrated with a half dozen photo of a model in swimming trunks, and *Queen's Quarterly* in New York prescribed an exercise program for men who wanted to get in shape for summer, accompanied by whimsical drawings of a happy hunk whose penis bounced along while he demonstrated the exercises.[28]

As the decade progressed, sports coverage emerged as a staple, with game coverage of the growing number of basketball and softball leagues in cities such as San Francisco, New York, and Washington. In its effort to become the bible of Gay America, *The Advocate* also committed its formidable resources to reporting on such small-scale activities as gay tennis in Denver, gay football in Wichita, gay sailing in Seattle, and gay volleyball in Houston and Honolulu.[29]

Gay sports received a big boost in 1976 when football star Dave Kopay came out and stated that homosexuality was rampant in professional sports. The rugged six-foot, 200-pound star, who had played for the Washington Redskins and Green Bay Packers, told *The Advocate:* "There are other people like me, younger people, who need to know there are successful gay people in every walk of life, including the life of the pro athlete." *The Advocate* followed up the Kopay interview with news features identifying 1968 Olympic decathlon winner Tom Waddell and 1930s tennis star Bill Tilden as gay. When Kopay published his life story, *Christopher Street*, the attempt at an upscale gay magazine that debuted in 1976, carried a lengthy review along with excerpts.[30]

In 1977 gay sports erupted into a national phenomenon—with *The Advocate*'s help. When the top team from New York's gay softball league challenged its San Francisco counterpart, the magazine dubbed the match "A Gay World Series." In addition to covering the two games (New York won 18–3 and 14–3), an industrious *Advocate* reporter uncovered controversy when members of the New York squad told him they suspected several San Francisco players of being straight men masquerading as gay. In 1977 the National Gay Rodeo also took off as a major event. The first competition a year earlier had attracted only 150 people, but the second drew 1,000. The bronco busting and calf roping events both included gay professional rodeo riders.[31]

As had been the case since the late 1960s, the line between editorial content and advertising was almost indistinguishable, and nowhere was this blurring more apparent than in material related to the role physical pleasure played in gay culture. Again *The Advocate* led the way. Huge quantities of feature articles appeared about the same activities and products that were being promoted in the advertising section. Beyond the dozens of ads for bars and bathhouses, display ads touted guest ranches in the desert, underwear from the depths of fantasy, and a staggering variety of liquids, lotions, creams, unguents, and emollients to enhance sexual pleasure. The ads invariably showcased handsome young men showing lots of skin. In its critique of the gay press, *Alternative Media* rightly called the "page after page of hunks" the "real selling point of gay magazines."[32]

Then there were the *Advocate* classifieds. By mid-decade, the "Trader Dick" section had mushroomed into forty pages per issue. Most prolific were the thousands of ads placed by hustlers, masseurs, male models, and just regular guys looking for a good time. Many of the men were masters of the double entendre, creating an endless string of clever and provocative lines—"Hot muscular whaler with big harpoon seeks big white whales"..."Hung versatile stud seeks young blond live-in slave over 18. Only sincere slaves need apply"... "Skinheads: Shaved heads turn me on. No balds, please"..."Bass Weejuns: W/M preppy 34 digs Ivy types into penny and tassel loafers with sweat sox; love to have your old worn loafers. Larger sizes preferred."[33]

Exploring the Dimensions of Sex

Although sex had been a bedrock element in the visual and editorial content of gay publications of the 1960s, the increasing specialization during the 1970s expanded coverage to discussing sexual activities as political statements. The publications accompanied their coverage with images that were uncompromisingly graphic. Jim Kepner, who continued to write for various gay newspapers in the 1970s, later recalled the prominence that sex played in the decade's gay culture: "Sex was the oxygen of our lives. Stonewall had bestowed upon gay men a visceral sense of freedom, and we defined that, quite literally, as giving us the license to indulge in multiple sex partners and play out an infinite variety of sexual fantasies. If you were not fully prepared to have sex anytime, anyplace— you were betraying Stonewall and everything gay liberation stood for."[34]

The most memorable sex-related articles appeared in *Fag Rag,* a Boston tabloid founded in 1971 with the statement "We're proud to take the straight man's term of contempt, i.e., fag, and throw it back in his face; proud to admit, flagrantly, that we don't fit and don't want to fit in Straight Amerika's definition of manhood." The premier issue set the tabloid's sexual tone by challenging gay men not to hang their heads in shame when called "cocksuckers," but to wear the label proudly. The article continued: "Why not teach first graders, not only about cocksucking, but about how to do it? Why should they have to wait to be twenty-one and become a 'consenting adult' before they can love? SUCK TO BE FREE!!!"[35]

Sex remained a salient theme as editor Charles Shively introduced one of the most provocative series of essays in the history of gay journalism. "Cocksucking as an Act of Revolution" analyzed sex acts in the context of the Gay Liberation Movement, seeking to construct an ideological foundation for gay rights. The premise of Shively's two-year series was that sex is fundamental to being gay, and gay men should celebrate, rather than be embarrassed by, the sexual acts they enjoy. But Shively chastised Gay America, arguing that most men are uncomfortable talking about those acts that, in the eyes of most people, define them. "In a faggot bar," he observed, "a cocksucker is considered less honorable than a cocksuckee." Shively further supported his argument by pointing out that gay men had not even created a word to describe the man who is the passive participant in anal intercourse, or, as Shively put it, "a male who takes it up the ass."[36]

In another essay, Shively threw a hand grenade at Gay America by challenging the premium the community placed on physical beauty. For Shively praised random promiscuity, arguing that to choose a sexual partner based on his physical attributes is to commit an act of discrimination. Shively wrote, "No one should be denied love because they are old, ugly, fat, crippled, bruised, of the wrong race, color, creed, sex or country of national origin." For a man to demonstrate equal respect toward all men, Shively reasoned, he should have sex with any man who wants it. To do otherwise, Shively said, was to be a bigot. This broad net encompassed young men as well, with *Fag Rag* further solidifying its radical position through an article titled "Molestation of the Young Is the Start of Politics."[37]

Shively applauded group sex. Specifically, he said orgies helped build a sense of community among gay men. One essay began: "Each faggot has a mouth, anus, and penis which can all be used at once." Because all of these parts of the male anatomy can be used for homosexual activity, Shively suggested that gay men were intended not to make love only to one man at a time but to many. He further theorized that, just as sex with a partner is better than masturbation, sex among three men is better than sex between two. He ended the essay more concretely with a personal endorsement of group sex: "I know of no sensation so pleasant as having someone fuck me while I'm sixty-nineing with another person."[38]

One of the most intriguing of Shively's essays focused on rimming. He saw rimming as fundamental to revolutionizing society's approach to gayness. "We are taught to fear and hide our 'backsides,'" he said. "This shows up particularly in the language. An 'asshole' is someone mean, malicious, stubborn, impolite, debased; a 'piece of shit' is anything inferior, ugly, cheap or disgusting. And phrases like 'brown nose,' 'ass licker' or 'ass kisser' mean an act of ultimate humiliation. In rimming we fly in the face of the existing sexual mores. Rimming becomes an act of revolution—strategy against the ruling classes."[39]

Shively illustrated his series with striking drawings comparable in graphic impact to the radical nature of his words. Drawn in a style reminiscent of traditional erotica from the Far East, the images showed men freely engaging in every conceivable sex act. Another series of drawings illustrated "the four steps to successful oral sex."[40]

Because *Christopher Street* was aimed at sophisticated readers, it sought to distance itself from graphic sexual discussions or images. Publisher Charles Ortleb said, "No one will ever masturbate over this magazine." Ortleb fully understood the centrality of sex to gay men, however, so he found an alternative approach to the topic. That tack was through the wry humor of cartoons similar to those that had become a trademark of *The New Yorker*. The *Christopher Street* versions were often mildly chastising of the gay fast lane, with some cartoons shaking their fingers at promiscuity and the brief duration of many gay relationships. One showed two men beginning to undress as one said to the other: "I hope this relationship doesn't take too long. I left the motor running." Another relayed a similar message by showing a gay man wearing a T-shirt that read "Looks: 6; Dance: 10; Lovers: 153."[41]

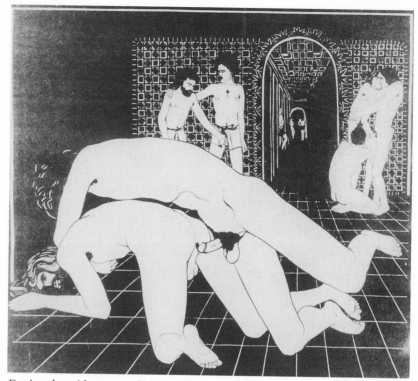

During the mid-1970s explicit sexual images such as this Eastern artwork in Fag Rag *glorified promiscuity and group sex.*

Less refined publications pproached sex very differently. *Gaytimes,* a Los Angeles tabloid, was a gay version of *Screw;* rare was the page that did not showcase a close-up photo of at least one erect penis. But *Gaytimes* also contained some editorial content, including essays on such controversial topics as drag queens and gay men having sex in public places. Although not written with the intellectual depth of *Fag Rag,* the newspaper's straightforward approach communicated similar messages to validate homosexuality and boost reader self-esteem. "If you feel like running over to the local park for a trick," one article began, "you shouldn't have to feel guilty about it." The point was vividly reinforced by a full-page photograph of two young men embracing in a wooded setting—nude, with genitalia in full view. Another *Gaytimes* article took consumer reporting to new depths by comparing the prices of various dildos on the market, illustrated with photos of the "porcupine" and "domed Christmas tree" models.[42]

Even newspapers with a strong news orientation wrote about sex. The *Bay Area Reporter* documented gay men's fascination with "fistfucking," the sexual act during which one man places his fist into the rectum of another. And in response to the mushrooming number of "call boy" ads appearing in the gay press, the *Blade* interviewed the founder of a gay prostitution service operating in the nation's capital. The entrepreneur said that his customers, who paid $40 to $150 for sex partners, liked a variety of body types but he had learned to avoid body builders: "They just stand there and look pretty."[43]

Spanning the Spectrum—From Leather Jockstraps to Feather Boas

The gay press covered the breadth of the culture it sought to reflect and serve, from swaggering leather men to swishing drag queens. *Gaytimes* made the point quite colorfully in 1973: "Whether you're a tow-headed surfer with golden skin and a rippled stomach or a drag queen wearing cheap jewelry, false eyelashes and a spangled gown, if you take it up the ass or down the throat, you are still queer."[44]

With eighty leather bars popping up around the country by the mid-1970s, this segment of the population was no minute minority. *Queen's Quarterly* published lengthy features on Folsom Street, the center of the San Francisco leather district. And the *Blade* conducted a series of interviews to educate readers about this titillating aspect of the culture. Although the series emphasized that wearing leather and enjoying sadomasochistic sex are not synonymous, the *Blade* used the opportunity to discuss the attraction for sexual activity that included physical pain. One man said the essential element was trust: "If you are S, then you'll just have to trust that your partner will let you know if you're going too far. The vibes have to be good. If the vibes are bad and the trust isn't there, you might as well go to sleep."[45]

The Advocate did not merely tell its readers about the leather world, but provided first-person accounts of bars in which chains and leather slings were standard equipment. *The Advocate,* like the *Blade,* paid particular attention to why sadomasochism is attractive. One man explained, "I'm into being used and abused with imagination and wit." Another added: "It is the ultimate statement of love. I want to feel certain stimuli, and my M loves me so much that he will help me to fulfill my desire."[46]

Drummer went even further toward reflecting the growing importance of the leather world by transforming itself, by mid-decade, into a publication targeted specifically toward leather men. The magazine adopted a glossy cover and filled its pages with images of masculine men dressed—or, more often, *un*dressed but accessorized—in leather. Erotic fiction and first-person accounts of sexual exploits dominated each issue, along with the names and addresses of leather bars around the country, from the one in Dotham, Alabama, to the three in Billings, Montana. Features highlighted specific bars, consistently casting them in a glow. "The people are hot, the drinks are good, the food is great," *Drummer* said of the Eagle in Washington. "And if you mention DRUMMER to Bill, the manager, he'll make sure you get the red carpet treatment." Photos accompanying the article showed a dozen motorcycles parked in front of the bar.[47]

Vector also covered the leather world. To create one eye-catching image, it placed a hairy-chested man on its cover, dressing him in nothing but leather briefs and a thick strap extending to a collar around his neck, all adorned with metal studs. The model smiled with pleasure. Five full-page photos inside showed the man in five different leather outfits. The article began, "Whether you're into the ouch (!) end of love or just fancy slipping a little erotica on your ego, you can get yourself hidebound in one of San Francisco's leather liveries." Each photo was accompanied by a block of copy detailing the price tag and name of the local store where items in the photos could be purchased.[48]

Vector was a leader in covering men on the other end of the cultural continuum as well. Indeed, the bare-chested leather man in the fashion spread was accompanied in each photo by Lorelei, one of San Francisco's fun-loving drag queens. The photos showed him wearing a variety of women's wigs and costumes as he playfully ogled the leather man.

Other publications documented the increasing number of drag beauty contests around the country. In a report on the Miss Drag Ohio pageant, *The Advocate* described the winner's "floor-length evening gown and coat of a 'wet-look' silver material with black lace and sequin trim." The *Blade* devoted several stories to the annual Miss Gay America pageant that had, by mid-decade, evolved into an extravaganza with contestants from thirty states competing in talent, evening gown, and swimsuit categories—with the winner taking $1,000 home in his handbag.[49]

Fag Rag published a lengthy interview with Sylvia Sydney, Boston's most famous drag queen, who had begun performing in 1948. The three-page question-and-answer piece took the reader into the drag world as no journalistic work before it. Sydney said, quite confidently, "You know, we're the normal ones, and those straights are the queer ones."[50]

Despite their emphasis on cultural reporting, publications did not shy away from the continuing controversy about what role leather men and drag queens should play in the struggle for equality. Radical publications campaigned for a pluralistic movement. *Gay Liberator* wrote, "More oppressive sexual repression in a society that too often transfers sex desires into power is not needed." Moderate publications, on the other hand, continued to advocate a less visible role. Although *Vector* filled many of its pages with stories and images of men who dressed as women, it opposed them having a prominent role in the movement to secure gay rights. In 1974 *Vector* opined: "It is time to retire the image of gay-person-as-drag-queen in favor of an image of the homosexual as 'an ordinary guy.' It would make good sense if drags stayed out of the spotlight."[51]

Reflecting the Refinements of Gay Taste and Style

Another stereotype growing to prominence during the 1970s was less controversial. As gay men became increasingly visible, their tendency to exhibit an unusually strong sense of taste and style became visible as well. This tendency is enhanced by the fact that most gay men do not have children or dependent spouses, and, therefore, have a disproportionately large disposable income to spend on looking good and living well. In response to the value many gay men place on expressing their personal aesthetic, publications committed abundant space to reflecting the upscale gay lifestyle.

Goodstein, the dominant figure in the decade's gay press, personally epitomized this segment of the population. The well-educated, wealthy, cosmopolitan publisher purchased dozens of Old Masters paintings, building one of the country's finest collections of Italian Baroque art. He was also an accomplished horseman and American Saddle Horse exhibitor who owned riding stables and showed his thoroughbreds at the country's top shows.[52]

In 1970s publications, fashion emerged as a popular venue for expressing the gay aesthetic. Fashion design is a popular vocation among gay men; dressing well is an avocation for millions more. *The Advocate* stayed on top of the latest trends in male fashion through multipage photo layouts. Typical was a six-page feature built on the premise that the heart of the fashion world had shifted from the Champs Elysées to Christopher Street, the New York gay community's Main Street. The article said that the impetus for most cutting-edge fashion statements could be traced to gay men: "Everything from hooded sweaters to updated army fatigues were born on gay thoroughfares."[53]

Cuisine is another medium in which gay men express their personal style—with style. Publications responded to this interest by adding food columns to their editorial mix. Opposite images of hard-core leather men in chains and motorcycle helmets, *Drummer*'s food column, "The Gentleman Entertains," offered readers a recipe for red clam sauce. *The Advocate* labeled its chatty food column "Auntie Lou Cooks," and, in its on-going effort to speak as the nation's gay voice, undertook a survey of gay restaurants around the country. "Where Can You Get a Good Gay Meal in This Town?" critiqued the culinary offerings in eight major cities.[54]

Other publications occasionally published restaurant reviews or feature stories, often in such laudatory hues that they sounded like ads. A *Blade* story read, "We can recommend a great palace for all readers traveling to the Mardi Gras festivities in New Orleans!" The article praised everything from the decor to the vegetables, ending with a final hosanna for the French Quarter eatery: "It is the only restaurant in the Quarter where you can always feel free to hold the hand of, or otherwise display affection toward, that favorite one sharing dinner with you."[55]

Travel stories abounded as well, responding to gay men who turn vacationing into a way of life. *The Advocate* published dozens of domestic and international travel features. Financial limitations forced other publications to limit travel coverage to an occasional feature based on a writer's personal vacation. After Jack Nichols and Lige Clarke returned from Miami and Cleveland, their trips became fodder for "Homosexual Citizen" columns about the growth of gay-oriented businesses—complete with addresses, phone numbers, and superlatives. The content of travel material leaned heavily toward night life, and the tone toward boosterism. A *Gaytimes* article about San Diego included a description of the city's three bath houses. Dave's received the nod as the most comfortable and best decorated, but the Atlas Club was the author's favorite because it had "more visible action" than the other two.[56]

Many gay men funnel their creativity into their homes. During the 1970s, inner-city neighborhoods across America were returned to their former glory as millions of young adults rehabilitated Victorian houses. Some observers estimate that as many as 90 percent of the projects were spearheaded by imaginative gay men who recognized the potential in the decaying buildings. *The Advocate* paid particular attention to the gentrification of San Francisco, a city which by mid-decade was 20 percent gay, and also documenting similar revitalizations in the Back Bay section of Boston and Capitol Hill in Washington.[57]

Radical publications found fault with the various ways gay men express their high levels of taste and style. *Gay Sunshine*, for instance, bitterly attacked men who spent time and energy decorating their apartments rather than fighting their oppression. The newspaper wrote with disdain, "Those aging princesses will simply linger on unto death as past relics of a bygone era in their fantasy world of poodle dogs and Wedgewood teacups."[58]

Decoding the Gay Sensibility in Literary Works

Gays had been writing throughout history, but it had not always been judicious for authors to publicize their sexual orientation. In the 1860s accusations that Walt Whitman was gay cost him his job with the federal government, and, in the 1890s, revelations that Oscar Wilde was gay led to two years in a prison cell. Likewise, homophobia prevented E. M. Forster from publishing his homosexual-themed masterpiece, *Maurice,* during his lifetime. By the 1970s, however, the winds of liberation had provided literary figures with a modest degree of latitude to discuss their homosexuality. The gay press was eager to trumpet their reflections.

The most remarkable contribution to gay literati coming out in print was a series of in-depth interviews in *Gay Sunshine* that ultimately came to define gay literature and the gay sensibility more profoundly than any works that have followed it. The legendary interviews, some as long as 25,000 words, in the country's first gay literary journal began in 1973 and continued through the decade, documenting the connections between the lives and works of some two dozen poets, novelists, and playwrights. The series was shaped by Winston Leyland, editor of *Gay Sunshine,* who also conducted many of the interviews. "I emphasized the cultural *and* the personal," Leyland recently recalled, "engendering from the artists reflections and insights into the connections between sexuality and creativity." Although all of the subjects had discussed their work before, this was the first time many of them had done so in the context of their homosexuality.[59]

One of the most intriguing exchanges was with Tennessee Williams. As the creator of such theatrical masterpieces as *A Streetcar Named Desire* and *Cat on a Hot Tin Roof,* the Pulitzer Prize–winning author is one of the most acclaimed American dramatists. In his interview, Williams was blunt in saying how gay men are different from straight men: "Gay men have more sensibility and they are more inclined to be good artists." Why? "Because they have been rejected." Williams continued with a description of the sensibility of gay writers that was at once eloquent and graphic: "They look deeper into themselves, are deeper into the human heart. Men—straight men, I mean—are all caught up in the competitive rat race. They lose all sensibility and become like so many big, overgrown pigs rushing for first place at the trough."[60]

In Christopher Isherwood's interview, the novelist said he grew ill at ease when not surrounded by gay people: "It's a feeling almost like a lack of oxygen." He concluded his interview by stating that, despite the humiliations that accompany living under a "heterosexual dictatorship," he did not regret being gay, as being straight would have "fatally cramped" his literary style.[61]

The authors also were asked their views on the Gay and Lesbian Liberation Movement. Williams, known for depicting society as disturbed, was critical of drag queens. "I wish the gays would get away from riding around in Cadillac convertibles, especially the fat ones that look like travesties of Mae West," Williams said. "They make the whole homosexual thing seem ridiculous. Homosexuals are not like that."[62]

Sex was a topic of discussion in some interviews. John Rechy, the author of several novels about the underbelly of gay life, described the pleasure he received from sadistic sexual acts: "I want to assert my sexual power over someone else, to humiliate that person. I am excited by it." But Rechy rejected the idea that sadomasochism involved love. "I am not going to say I love the guy who is groveling and doing everything that I want. It is not love," he said. "It has to do with humiliating the other person. Pain and humiliation have nothing to do with love and respect."[63]

By 1978 *Gay Sunshine* had published interviews with the most important gay literary figures of the era, including poets Allen Ginsberg, John Giorno, Edouard Roditi, and Mutsuo Takahashi; novelists William S. Burroughs and Gore Vidal; and playwright Jean Genet.[64]

While *Gay Sunshine*'s role in defining the gay sensibility in literature was unparalleled, other publications contributed to that effort on smaller scales. *Fag Rag* conducted in-depth interviews with literary giants Isherwood and Vidal. *Christopher Street* published a series of articles by journalist Edmund White, who crisscrossed America documenting the varieties of gay experience. *Christopher Street* also printed provocative reviews and features about gay writers, consistently praising their literary contributions: "Gays are outsiders: the dispossessed, the outlawed, the denied. Gays can often make use of their vantage point."[65]

Expressing the Gay Sensibility Through the Arts

Gay sensibility—which had created such masterpieces as David and the Sistine Chapel—was not confined to literature, but exploded in a wide variety of artistic media. *Fag Rag* argued that it was imperative for gays to experiment with new forms of expression: "We have to create our own media. Creating a faggot community means finding new ways to think and love outside straight society." To varying degrees, every publication of the era devoted space to exploring the motivations of artists and the meanings of their work, always in the context of gay liberation. The artists varied widely, from the world's most revered masters to amateurs who quickly returned to their day jobs.[66]

Articles about gay musicians illustrated the diversity. In Ned Rorem's *Gay Sunshine* interview, the Pulitzer Prize–winning composer of five operas had no hesitation about discussing his sexual orientation, but he was at a loss for words when asked how his sexuality informed his work. In Chris Robison's *Fag Rag* interview, on the other hand, the rock star recounted how he had stopped playing with John Lennon's band, Elephant's Memory, in 1971 to record the country's first gay rock album. After recording "Looking for a Boy Tonight," he tried to persuade major record companies to use it as the centerpiece of an album. "No one was ready for it; they were just scared," Robison recalled. "So we said, 'Fuck it,' went down to City Hall and started our own record company." The album was released the next year.[67]

Later in the decade, an *Advocate* article took on yet another tone as Mark Thompson described a dramatically different musical experience: "The Gay Men's Chorus in San Francisco is one of the most inspired examples of a brotherhood transformed from a legacy of bitterness, self-reproach and distrust into a powerful statement of unity, compassion and community service." The *Bay Area Reporter* also devoted considerable space to documenting the rise of the hometown group, the first of dozens of gay choruses to emerge during the decade.[68]

Dance features also ran the gamut. In 1976 *Christopher Street* documented how a strange little troupe of drag ballet dancers doing midnight performances on East Fourth Street in the early 1970s had evolved into the Trockadero de Monte Carlo, by then in demand all over the world. *The Advocate* concentrated on keeping up with a major dance and entertainment phenomenon the newspaper credited to the gay underground: disco. Of particular interest was the Village People, an intriguingly costumed group—Cowboy, Sailor, and Leatherman, among others—formed in 1977 by openly gay record producer Jacques Morali after he watched gay men dancing at a Greenwich Village disco. Other articles acclaimed the success of Michael Bennett, the Tony Award–winning director and choreographer whose *Chorus Line* set records as the longest-running musical in Broadway history.[69]

Publications reported the burgeoning of drama during the decade, as playwrights and actors held the mirror of the theater up to their lives. *The Advocate* cited the Other Side of Silence, founded in 1972 in SoHo, as the country's first gay theater company. The *Blade* and other news-oriented publications helped local theater groups by publishing the reviews and features that the straight press would not. *Fag Rag* received headlines in the mainstream press in 1973 when editor Charles Shively tried to sell copies of his publication at a University of New Hampshire production of Jonathan Ned Katz's play *Come Out!*. Governor

Meldrim Thompson was in the audience, saw a copy of *Fag Rag*, and dubbed it "the most loathsome publication in the English language"—a description Shively later proudly adopted as a red badge of courage.[70]

By the end of the decade, a new breed of defiant playwrights had emerged to affirm gay lifestyles. The bomb thrower among them was the outspoken Harvey Fierstein, who during the 1980s would win Tonys for his theatrical works in which homosexuality was the norm and heterosexuality the oddity. In 1978 the author of *Torch Song Trilogy* told *Christopher Street* why he confined straights to minor roles: "I don't know many straights. It's not that I dislike them as a group. It's just that I've no time for what is basically an ungrateful mass of human leeches. We give them their music, the clothes they wear, the art they buy—in short, their lifestyle. What do they give in return?"[71]

An even more controversial artist surfaced a year later as his photographs began to gain public attention. But this time, *Christopher Street* was not impressed, beginning its article with a bitter denunciation: "Robert Mapplethorpe strikes me as a streetwise kid who figures he can make a lot of money by packaging his slick portraits and S&M photographs as art." A decade before conservative members of Congress would use the same photographs as ammunition to censor the National Endowment for the Arts, the magazine wrote of Mapplethorpe's images of men urinating in each others' mouths: "He titillates the art world with pornography." *Christopher Street*'s concern was not the explicitness of Mapplethorpe's work, however, but his exploitation of the gay world for personal gain: "He knows where the money is and he knows how to get it." The article was illustrated with some of the photos that became the subject of national controversy in the 1990s.[72]

The most comprehensive coverage of the visual arts was an *Advocate* series Goodstein introduced, saying: "We have never found a clearer example of gay liberation being human liberation than looking at homosexuality in the context of the most liberating art of the century." The series traced the gay sensibility from Paul Cadmus expressing his social realism in muscular male physiques to David Hockney depicting the isolationism of the late twentieth century.[73]

Film was yet another medium through which the publications traced gay artistry. Interview subjects ranged from gay porn stars such as Jack Wrangler to actors who starred in major motion pictures, such as Taylor Mead. In 1973 *Gaytimes* quoted porn film director Warren Stephens on his contribution to the culture: "What I'm doing has a very strong sociological value and can fill a very great need in society. We've got to get away from the puritan ethic and come up with a sexual ethic that is more commensurate with man's needs and man's problems. This is part of that movement." *The Advocate* played its familiar role of booster of gay-owned businesses by providing favorable coverage of film-makers such as Fred Halsted. Publications also lauded the proliferation of gay movie theaters. A *Blade* feature said of the Metropole Theater, "Considerable refurbishing has made it roomy and quite respectable looking."[74]

Reclaiming Gay History

Just as lesbian publications of the mid-1970s introduced their readers to impor-tant women whose sexual identity previously had been unknown, gay male publications traveled a similar route with articles about such momentous fig-ures as Michelangelo and Walt Whitman. The men's publications also moved beyond individual biographies to larger histories.

Gay Liberator traced the beginnings of the gay rights movement to Germany in 1864 when Karl Heinrich Ulrichs, known as the grandfather of gay liberation, introduced the notion that homosexuals were a "third sex." The tabloid also de-tailed the work of Magnus Hirschfeld, a late-nineteenth-century German physician who made public speeches about homosexuality and lobbied politi-cians to eliminate antihomosexual laws.[75]

Queen's Quarterly developed an unorthodox approach that emphasized the male anatomy. The magazine juxtaposed articles about gay lovers from history, such as Julius Caesar and King Nicodemus, with photographs of modern-day men engaging in sex acts. Other features accompanied by photos of naked men told of gay life during World War II and the evolution of jockstraps. Although the articles certainly did not coincide with contemporary trends in historical scholarship, they sometimes produced impressive original research. One article pointed out that the glory hole was not a recent invention, but dates back to the sixteenth century when Italian architect Andrea Palladio designed ornate "peep-throughs" for gay nobility. The article continued, "Baroque swirls and whorls were adroitly arranged—'*ben trovato*,' as Palladio said ('well invented')—around the marble urinals so the host could weed out the small from the stupendous without being seen."[76]

Publications also reported that historians were beginning to publish works about the history of Gay and Lesbian America. The "Homosexual Citizen" col-umn in *Screw* defended Donn Teal's book about Stonewall-era activists, *The Gay Militants,* after it had been panned by other reviewers. *The Advocate* inter-viewed Jonathan Katz about his monumental work, *Gay American History. Gay Sunshine* included historian Martin Duberman among the literary figures in-terviewed in its ground-breaking series.[77]

The most compelling of the historical features were those recounting the mass murder of a quarter million gays during the Holocaust. An article in *Queen's Quarterly,* illustrated with a photograph of a young man wearing only a swastika arm band and wielding a huge whip, stated: "*Fags* simply did not fit the Nazis' Wagnerian notion of what Teutonic Supermen of the Super Race ought to be. The Fuhrer liked his men tall, blond, trim, sleekly muscled, and, yes, good-looking—but, no, definitely not *queer.*" *Christopher Street* explained that the pink triangle now celebrated as a symbol of gay liberation originated in Nazi death camps where it labeled gay prisoners. A major source was a German gay man who had survived the Holocaust by agreeing to work in a factory operated by the Nazis—and agreeing to be castrated.[78]

Tracking the Rise of Gay Spirituality

For decades, gay men and lesbians who built their lives on a spiritual foundation had attempted to persuade church leaders to allow them their place at God's table, but mainstream congregations had largely turned their backs. So, as the euphoria that comes with a sense of freedom and strength filled gay people in the 1970s, men and women began to create their own spiritual communities. Like gay politics and the gay press before it, organized gay spirituality initially was dominated by men, with women in a decidedly secondary role.

The Advocate began its support of this phenomenon *before* the first service was held. In the fall of 1968 the newspaper published a small item announcing that the Reverend Troy Perry, a Pentecostal minister, planned to hold a gay church service in his Los Angeles home. When a dozen gay Christians arrived for the service, the Metropolitan Community Church was born. "If it hadn't been for *The Advocate,*" Perry later said, "there would have been no MCC." When *The Advocate* became a cultural magazine, it concentrated much of its coverage of spirituality on Perry, dubbing him the Reverend Martin Luther King of gay liberation. The epitome of tall, dark, and handsome, twenty-eight-year-old Perry and his smoldering brown eyes attracted a huge following.[79]

Perry's pews bulged. By the mid-1970s, 100 MCC congregations were operating around the country, and the denomination's national convention was drawing 1,500 participants a year. Activities were not confined to the sanctuary, as the church also served as a gay civil rights organization. Perry led a crowd of 250 down Hollywood Boulevard in 1970 to demand police reform, the first of many public demonstrations taking gay spirituality into the streets. In 1976, for example, the *Blade* reported on a major rally the denomination organized across from the White House. Perry led followers at sad moments as well, such as when he organized public protests after homophobes burned MCC churches to the ground in San Francisco and Los Angeles.[80]

The gay press tracked the rise of other gay spiritual organizations, such as Dignity for Roman Catholics and Integrity for Episcopalians, as they mushroomed into huge organizations with dozens of local chapters and large national conventions. Gay newspapers provided enormous assistance to these groups merely by announcing their meeting dates and locations, services the mainstream media refused to provide.

The pages of *Christopher Street* served as another arena in which gay Christians and Jews were encouraged to express their spiritual beliefs and ideologies. One blockbuster occurred when the Reverend John J. McNeill, a Jesuit and founder of the New York chapter of Dignity, discussed his book *The Church and the Homosexual.* In the interview, McNeill accused the Catholic Church's unrelenting opposition to homosexuality of driving millions of gay parishioners first to self-loathing and then to alcoholism. Further, he argued that the church's rejection of gay relationships promoted promiscuity.[81]

More than Ogling Groins and Waving Flags

Just as the issues being covered in gay male publications of the mid-1970s differed from those in lesbian publications, so did their overall experiences. As the end of the decade approached, the gay press could not boast that it had created an ideology comparable to the lesbian-feminist ideology cogently articulated in *The Furies* and *Lesbian Tide.* But it could still boast. For while lesbian publications were dying, the gay press was becoming a stable—and, in some instances, a financially lucrative—institution. Most of the newspapers and magazines discussed in this chapter, unlike their lesbian counterparts, were still being published by the end of the decade. In fact, a critical mass of those publications created two decades ago are still publishing today—*The Advocate, Bay Area Reporter, Washington Blade, Christopher Street,* and *Drummer.*

This is not to suggest that men's publications were without their challenges. Gay journalism's persistently troubling theme of editorial discord reached its zenith in the mid-1970s. The conflict ignited by David B. Goodstein's transforming Gay America's largest media outlet from a bare-knuckled newspaper to a trendy lifestyle magazine took the quarreling beyond internal staff disputes and into the public arena. Along with *The Advocate*'s founder and fired staff members, gay and lesbian newspapers publicly attacked Goodstein. *Lesbian Tide, Fag Rag,* and *Gay Sunshine* joined the chorus led by *Gay Liberator,* which denounced Goodstein not only as antigay but as the community's fiercest impediment to securing gay rights.

Despite the criticism, Goodstein and his checkbook clearly advanced the gay press in some significant ways. His vision, coupled with his willingness to share his personal resources, lifted the gay press to the point that it was, for the first time, a player at the highest levels of the American publishing industry, recognized as one of the fastest-growing magazines in the country. Also because of Goodstein and his success with *The Advocate,* mainstream news media began to acknowledge the significance of the genre. The *Wall Street Journal* documented the rise of the magazine with a front-page article in 1975; the *Los Angeles Times* followed with a similar story a year later.[82]

The gay press theme that monopolized the era was the penchant for blurring the line between news and advertising. *The Advocate* was a master of the technique, willingly accommodating the desires of the burgeoning gay business community through uncompromisingly positive features about the bar and bath culture. Other publications were not far behind. The *Blade* recommended the baths as a good place to begin long-term relationships, and *Vector* described the baths as heaven on earth; such articles showed that even moderate voices were eager to portray the gay businesses favorably. More boosterism came with *Bay Area Reporter*'s decision to place bar ads on its front page and *Drummer*'s expansion of editorial content to include lists of the country's leather bars. The most damning example of gay journalism's eagerness to boost bars and baths was its decision not to examine the negative aspects of the freewheeling use of drugs that was a central element in that experience.

Nor did promoting gay-owned businesses stop at the bathhouse door. *Vector* accompanied its photos of leather men with information about prices and the stores where readers could buy the items pictured; *Gaytimes* gave the directors of all-male films free space to describe their latest works.

As in previous generations of the gay press, what initially appears to be blatant pandering to advertisers can be defended. Creating their own businesses continued to be one of the prime ways gay people were advancing toward liberation. When the *Blade* drooled over how well a New Orleans restaurant prepared its vegetables, the praise seemed to be justified in the context of the restaurant being the only one in the French Quarter where same-sex couples could hold hands. The symbiotic relationship between gay liberation and gay business was even more dramatically illustrated by the *Advocate* article lauding the rise of bars and baths into the realms of big business. Not only was this ascendancy a sign of Gay America's progress, but it was no coincidence that the largest bath chain in the country exploded out of a single Cleveland steamroom immediately after the state of Ohio decriminalized sodomy.

In spite of the growth in gay business and, therefore, ad revenue, several publications that helped define gay culture ceased publication before the decade ended. Gay America lost two voices simultaneously in 1973 when Jack Nichols and Lige Clarke severed their relationship with *Screw* owner Al Goldstein over a financial dispute, ending four years as authors of the "Homosexual Citizen" column and three as editors of *GAY*. Although Nichols and Clarke had become part owners of *GAY*, Goldstein refused to show them the books, making the couple wonder if the gay portions of Goldstein's business were more lucrative than he admitted. "The winds of liberation had blown the concept of second-class citizenship clear out of our systems," Nichols said. "If we weren't allowed to be full partners, we weren't willing to be partners at all."[83]

Vector was the next fatality. The editorially moderate magazine that had published regularly for twelve years died in 1976, the same year Goodstein moved *The Advocate* into the San Francisco market *Vector* previously had dominated. *Gay Liberator* died the same year when the collective that produced it ran out of energy. Two publications that depended largely on flesh for their popularity both disappeared in 1978. The demise of *Queen's Quarterly* and *Gay-times* did not, however, leave New York without gay voices, as *Christopher Street* and two new publications not dependent on homoerotic images continued.[84]

To speak to gay New York was, however, no easy task. The highbrow *Christopher Street*, like Jim Kepner's attempt to create an erudite gay publication with his short-lived *Pursuit & Symposium* in the 1960s, struggled financially. Although *Alternative Media*'s 1978 critique of the gay press was positive about the future of the genre, it was not optimistic about *Christopher Street*: "Would any *New Yorker* reader willingly give up Pauline Kael, Charles Addams, John Updike and 'The Talk of The Town' for respectable but slightly less proficient gay versions?" By the end of the decade, *Christopher Street* was not, in fact, turning a profit, and it was becoming increasingly clear that the voice of gay sophistication could continue only if publisher Charles Ortleb could find a new source of funds.[85]

Despite these casualties, mid-1970s publications succeeded in achieving their fundamental goal. Pulitzer Prize–winning composer Ned Rorem put it succinctly in his *Gay Sunshine* interview with editor Winston Leyland: "I like your magazine because of your concern with the whole person, and not just the groin nor just flag-waving." Rorem could have been speaking of the entire gay press. For the remarkably diverse array of publications—from the handsome *Advocate* bulging with ads to the scruffy *Fag Rag* adamantly refusing to be tainted by the tentacles of capitalism—had indeed plumbed the depths of gay culture. Although the discordant voices would have bristled at the suggestion that they composed a united force, together they documented that Gay America had evolved into an extraordinarily rich and talented community that, regardless of the venomous attacks that soon were to bludgeon it, was far too valuable and far too strong to be sacrificed on the altar of bigotry.[86]

λ 8

Fighting Back Against the New Right

Between 1977 and 1982, lesbians and gay men were bloodied on a multitude of fronts. The first assault caught them completely off guard when a fading beauty queen shrieked, "We've put on the armor of God!" Anita Bryant, a born-again Christian and spokeswoman for the citrus industry, persuaded Miami voters to repeal the gay rights ordinance they had enacted only five months before, paving the way for numerous antigay initiatives across the country. The Reverend Jerry Falwell told a Miami crowd on the eve of the repeal vote, "So-called gay folks just as soon kill you as look at you." Such venom began Falwell's attacks as his conservative Moral Majority mushroomed to a membership of 4 million and undertook a full-court antigay media campaign, including an effort to have the death penalty instituted as the standard punishment for being homosexual.[1]

Some observers said the vengeful actions were a backlash to the gradual progress gay people had been making since Stonewall, as twenty states had legalized sodomy and forty cities had passed gay rights legislation. The antigay actions were also part of a larger wave of conservatism that spread across the political landscape when many people interpreted the failed Jimmy Carter presidency as proof that liberalism no longer offered viable solutions to the country's foreign and domestic problems.[2]

Whatever the catalyst, Ronald Reagan's election in 1980 intensified the dramatic shift to the right—and the difficulties for Lesbian and Gay America. On Capitol Hill, Senator Roger Jepsen introduced the "Family Protection Act" to prevent gays from receiving Social Security, welfare, or veterans' benefits; the House of Representatives prohibited the Legal Services Corporation from accepting discrimination cases filed by gays.

The number of "fag bashings" soared. The first killings were in San Francisco, but they quickly spread. Oklahoma teenagers created a Ku Klux Klan chapter to assault gays, and University of Oklahoma students donned T-shirts reading "Bury a Fairy" and "Do the World a Favor—Shoot a Faggot." New York

City was especially hard hit. Two men were killed and six wounded when a former policeman loosed machine-gun fire inside a gay bar in the city. According to crime statistics, one New Yorker a day was physically attacked because of his sexual orientation. Gay America was further beleaguered by a series of tragic fires—many attributed to arson—that destroyed bath houses and theaters in New Orleans, New York, Washington, and San Francisco, killing dozens of gay men and injuring hundreds more.

Antigay violence peaked in 1978 when Dan White, the only member of the San Francisco Board of Supervisors to vote against the city's gay rights law, strapped a 38-caliber Smith and Wesson revolver to his shoulder and climbed through a side window of city hall to reach the office of Harvey Milk, the openly gay member of the board. White pumped five bullets into Milk and four into Mayor George Moscone, killing both men. During the trial, White mounted a bizarre "Twinkie defense," arguing that junk food had diminished his capacity to act rationally the day of the killings. The jury bought it. White was found guilty of voluntary manslaughter—*not* first-degree murder. Gay San Francisco exploded. The violence that followed the verdict created a watershed reminiscent of the Stonewall uprising. Rioters ravaged city hall, burned a dozen police cars, and destroyed $1 million in property.

The tide began to turn as Gay and Lesbian America notched a series of political and civil rights victories into its belt. The most dramatic victory came in California. Barely six months after the Miami gay rights ordinance had been repealed, California State Senator John Briggs spearheaded a ballot proposition to bar gay people from teaching in public schools. Gays raised money and grassroots support to create a superbly orchestrated campaign to defeat the initiative. And defeat it they did. Voters rejected the Briggs Initiative 59 to 41 percent.

Progress came on the national level as well. The first Gay and Lesbian Civil Rights March on Washington drew more than 100,000 participants to Washington for the movement's first large-scale demonstration. The Democratic party adopted a gay rights plank, and at the 1980 Democratic National Convention, Mel Boozer's name was placed in nomination for vice president, marking the first time an openly gay person was nominated for national office. In a passionate address, Boozer, an African American, said: "I know what it means to be called a 'nigger' and I know what it means to be called a 'faggot,' and I understand the differences in the marrow of my bones. I can sum up that difference in one word: *none*."[3]

In other landmark events in the gay resurgence, the state of Wisconsin and city of Philadelphia enacted gay rights ordinances, the "Family Protection Act" was prevented from passing into law, and gay people were not altogether saddened when the citrus industry failed to renew Anita Bryant's contract or when her marriage disintegrated.

Lesbian and gay journalism was not a passive bystander during the community's transformation from victim to victor. Such a sea change does not occur without leadership, and the press used its position as one of the community's most veteran institutions to lead this critical era of fighting back against the forces of bigotry and hatred. The assaults propelled the press to develop a degree of professionalism previously unknown during its thirty-year history. The cultural focus faded as news rose to new heights, with many publications adopting the techniques conventional journalism had long employed to fight the wrongs of society. George Mendenhall, former *Vector* editor who served as news editor of the *Bay Area Reporter* in the late 1970s, recalled: "The gay press had matured. We took gay journalism a lot more serious than in the beginning of the decade. We had to. Marching in the streets wasn't going to get us liberated. The battlefront was the ballot box—and that called for a new kind of gay journalism."[4]

The period of mobilizing for gay civil rights was led by publications located in urban centers with large gay concentrations. *Gay Community News* in Boston emerged as an influential national voice that consistently offered thoughtful political analysis. *GCN* also became one of the first publications in which lesbians maintained a presence fully equal to that of gay men. "Feminism and gay liberation are closely connected," *GCN* cooperative spokesman Richard Burns said in 1979. "So it is natural for men and women to share media which cover that connection." *The Body Politic* became the other salient voice speaking for women as well as men. It was also during this period that *TBP*, based in Toronto but with much of its circulation in the United States, fought the most strenuous censorship battle in the history of the gay press. Meanwhile, two San Francisco biweeklies exhibited an unprecedented level of cooperation by functioning as a single newspaper; the *Bay Area Reporter* and the *San Francisco Sentinel* published on alternating Thursdays to provide timely coverage for the city that had come to represent Gay Nirvana. *Gaysweek* began a brief but important reign in New York, the *Washington Blade* grew increasingly strong as the nation's capital became a major gay rights battlefront, and the *Philadelphia Gay News* and *Seattle Gay News* spoke with strength and power for their activist communities. While *The Advocate* continued to emphasize culture and entertainment, news also increased its presence through the genre's first investigative pieces. In 1980 *The Advocate* replaced its *Touching Your Lifestyle* subtitle with the somewhat misleading, but mercifully more palatable, *America's Leading Gay Newsmagazine.*[5]

Changes were not confined to gay journalism. Lesbian publications, though smaller in circulation, also helped show society that gay people were not willing to roll over and play dead. Los Angeles was home to a pair of powerful voices, *Lesbian News* and *Lesbian Tide*. New York lesbians spoke through the pages of the brashly titled *Big Apple Dyke News*. Other publications of the period consisted of only a few mimeographed pages stapled together, much as *Vice Versa* had three decades earlier. *Leaping Lesbian* in Ann Arbor, Michigan, reached only a few hundred readers and survived only three years, but it also raised the consciousness of untold numbers of lesbians to the reality that the New Right was not, in fact, right.

As this list of publications attests, a by-product of the lesbian and gay press fighting back against religious and political reactionaries was that the press was, indeed, once again a combined lesbian and gay press. When conservative forces attacked the community, they unwittingly helped unite the publications once more. Even while many papers were aimed at either female readers or male readers, they covered the same issues. Jeanne Córdova of *Lesbian Tide* said that it became possible for one publication to provide political news for both sexes: "Lesbian politics and gay politics came together. We were outnumbered and outflanked by a very wealthy, very powerful, and very mean-spirited group of bigots who would not be satisfied until every one of us was dead. We weren't real sure we would survive at all, but we were *damned* sure we wouldn't survive if our ranks were divided."[6]

Even gay male publications that previously had excluded lesbians from their staffs and editorial content allowed women to climb to positions of responsibility. Sasha Gregory-Lewis, who served as senior editor of *The Advocate*, recently recalled: "At straight publications, women had to write fluff. At *The Advocate*, I could write about anything I wanted."[7]

The number of publications continued to grow, with *Our Own Voices* listing 600 publications existing in 1980. A large number of them were the internal newsletters of the local social clubs and political associations gay people organized. *The Advocate* remained the giant, with a biweekly circulation of 80,000. And total circulation of the lesbian and gay press surpassed 500,000—two and a half times that of a mere decade earlier.[8]

Adopting the Standards of Professional Journalism

Lesbian and gay journalists had worked assiduously, throughout the early history of their genre, to distinguish their publications from those of the mainstream press. With the assaults from the New Right, however, they increasingly imitated the establishment press. It was a logical step. With the battlefront of the movement shifting to the voting booth, the astute journalists recognized that the movement had to win the support of mainstream society. One way they could hasten that goal was to create publications that looked and read like the ones straight society was familiar with.

The shift to conventional journalistic standards manifested itself in a variety of changes—some subtle, some bold. *Lesbian News* edited news stories more tightly to make room for more of them. The *Philadelphia Gay News* began listing how Pennsylvania state legislators had voted on issues of particular concern to gay voters. *Leaping Lesbian* sent subscribers "extras" describing Michigan ballot proposals of particular concern to them, and *Gaysweek* published extras when major stories broke. *The Body Politic* secured $5,000 in grants from the Ontario Arts Council and published a community calendar highlighting political events. *The Advocate* compiled news developments from across the country and opened a New York office to keep abreast of events on the East Coast—and to have closer contact with ad agencies on Madison Avenue. *Lesbian Tide* abandoned its policy of using only lesbians as sources, telling its readers: "In the interest of presenting the civil rights news that is so deeply affecting lesbians today, and in the interest of journalistic accuracy, we will print the names of gay men responsible for making news." The unified San Francisco gay paper began publishing corrections and accommodating to the journalistic dictates of good taste—"fucking" became "f——g."[9]

Adopting the conventions of mainstream journalism did not mean that a publication spoke with timidity. Boston's *Gay Community News* followed the style rules of the *Associated Press Stylebook* and used the modular layout popular in American journalism at the time, but the tabloid was committed to social change, and its editorial page spoke unremittingly from the Left. The newspaper, for example, labeled any gay person who remained in the closet "a traitor."[10]

Big Apple Dyke News became another paper that was antiestablishment in its editorial philosophy but strident in its adherence to the rules of professional journalism. The New York tabloid insisted that submissions follow precise guidelines, with no articles accepted if they were longer than four pages—and typed, double-spaced. It further demanded: "All material MUST be signed and include a phone number to contact regarding revisions."[11]

B.A.D. News, as the newspaper called itself, was one of the first lesbian or gay publications to run Associated Press articles. Determined to provide comprehensive coverage of news crucial to its readers, the tabloid recognized that its all-volunteer staff could not keep on top of all the breaking news, particularly when much of the activity was on the West Coast. The wire service also was able to obtain information from fundamentalist leaders who were not willing to talk to gay reporters. One Associated Press story in *B.A.D. News* quoted a Moral Majority spokesman as saying, "I agree with capital punishment, and I believe homosexuality should be coupled with murder and other sins."[12]

Not everyone in Gay America supported movement newspapers using wire services. George Mendenhall said: "A lot of my cranky comrades pointed out that a gay paper using AP or UPI stories meant denying a gay journalist the financial remuneration that would come from paying him to cover that same story. That started as an issue in the early eighties, when papers first started to become more professional, and has remained an issue ever since."[13]

Many publications were willing to pay the expenses necessary to stay abreast of the news. When the repeal vote in Miami evolved into a major story, the *Bay Area Reporter* dispatched Mendenhall to Florida to report on events from a gay perspective. Mendenhall later recalled that antigay forces greeted him with closed fists. He said: "One night all I was doing was trying to get some basic information at one of their rallies, and they started pushing me around. I told them I was just a reporter doing my job, but they weren't impressed. First they just elbowed me a little, but then they got rough. Four or five of those fuckers surrounded me and started throwing punches. One of them kicked me in the balls and then laughed, 'How's that? You got your "information" now?'"[14]

Journalists who were also front-line activists sometimes found it challenging to wear both hats. Jeanne Córdova helped organize the first national lesbian conference. Not only was the event a disaster, she recalled, but she also faced the question of how to portray the conference in *Lesbian Tide*. When she decided to report honestly on the problems, many readers disagreed with her decision. "People gave me a lot of flak, said I was hurting the movement. I was a journalist first and activist second, but it was hard."[15]

The *Washington Blade* was often criticized for giving movement activities a mixture of orchids and onions. Publisher Don Michaels said at the time, "We have to treat the gay movement as journalists would any movement: ask hard questions, probe the institutions and leaders." When the newspaper reported controversies involving plans for the March on Washington, it was deluged with letters and phone calls from irate readers. The *Blade* stood firm. "Many Gays no longer see the world only in black and white, 'us vs. them,' terms," the editor wrote. "A good publication should strive to illuminate the gray."[16]

A new generation of journalists also contributed to the shift toward professionalism. For as the gay press matured and began to gain financial viability, it attracted more young people trained in the craft. Randy Shilts, destined to become the most famous gay reporter in history, earned his journalism degree from the University of Oregon in 1975 and then joined the staff of *The Advocate*. He later said: "My professors all told me I was a fool for identifying myself as gay. They said it would destroy my career because the institution of journalism wasn't ready for that. I worked my ass off to prove them wrong. I was determined to make gay journalism something to be proud of."[17]

Gay publications adopted so many conventions of mainstream journalism that they attracted straight readers—and were not always happy about it. In 1981 the *Philadelphia Gay News* boasted about its high profile in the city: "The people of Philadelphia know our community is here. They can't go very far without seeing our lavender coin-boxes or our newspaper on a newsstand proudly proclaiming that there is *Gay News,* and a substantial community to back it up." But the newspaper also complained about how much time the editors had to devote to helping mainstream reporters who relied on the *Gay News* for story ideas and sources.[18]

Dramatic testimony of how professional the gay press had become unfolded when CBS television aired "Gay Power, Gay Politics." When the documentary focused primarily on sadomasochists, the *San Francisco Sentinel* did not shriek from its editorial page but calmly filed a complaint with the National News Council, the advisory board monitoring mainstream news coverage. The council agreed with the *Sentinel,* saying, "justification cannot be found for the degree of attention CBS gave to sado-masochism." Randy Alfred, the reporter whose critique was the basis of the complaint, said after the decision: "Fifty years ago, journalists didn't have to tell the truth about blacks. Now gay people must be treated with the same respect."[19]

"Nationalizing" Lesbian and Gay News

The various antigay assaults translated into huge quantities of coverage in mainstream media. Bryant's crusade and Falwell's media campaign, in particular, became staples of network nightly news broadcasts and the front pages of the country's leading newspapers. The issues were brimming with conflict, so the titans of American journalism were eager to provide voluminous coverage.

Seeing that the major events were being covered by the establishment media, lesbian and gay journalists adopted a new tack: they transformed local events into national ones—at least in their publications. By the conventional definition of news, the vote on a city gay rights ordinance was of local interest only; by the revised gay press definition, such a vote was fodder for the front page of gay newspapers everywhere. In short, the newspapers "nationalized" gay news.

Gay Community News set the pace. When Arkansas reinstated its law banning homosexual acts between consenting adults, *GCN* reported the vote in a twelve-inch story on page one, even though Arkansas is 1,200 miles from the newspaper's home base in Boston, and the *Boston Globe* ignored the vote entirely. *Gay Community News* readers also were told, in an eighteen-inch lead story on page one, when voters 2,600 miles away in Palo Alto, California, rejected a proposal to ban discrimination on the basis of sexual orientation; *Globe* readers were told nothing of the vote. *GCN* readers were given another eighteen-inch story on page one when Wisconsin enacted the first statewide law banning discrimination based on sexual orientation; again, the *Globe* ignored the event.[20]

Gaysweek also was committed to nationalizing gay news. It showcased voters in Wichita, Kansas, and Eugene, Oregon, repealing their gay rights ordinances. The New York weekly devoted front-page attention to both stories, each exceeding twenty column inches, while the *New York Times* ignored the Kansas vote and gave only one paragraph on an inside page to the Oregon one.[21]

West Coast publications redefined national news as well. *Lesbian Tide* created a "Rights & Referendums" column to track developments occurring around the country. *Seattle Gay News* documented the rise of gay hate crimes in San Francisco. When St. Paul, Minnesota, repealed its gay rights ordinance, the *Bay Area Reporter* led its news coverage with a thirty-inch story about it.[22]

The newspapers reported the activities of gay rights organizations the mainstream media ignored. The National Gay Task Force, founded in 1973, mushroomed in size and importance along with the vitriolic assaults from the New Right. Later renamed the National Gay and Lesbian Task Force, it tried to attract the attention of mainstream media, but the country's leading news outlets rarely responded. Not so the gay press. In 1977, the task force held a press conference to announce a nationwide educational project called "We Are Your Children," along with a pledge to raise $1 million to finance the project. The press conference was held in New York, but at the other end of the continent *Lesbian Tide* gave the story twenty column inches. The *Los Angeles Times,* by contrast, condensed coverage into a single paragraph.[23]

In keeping with the propensity of the gay press for amusing readers as well as informing them, newspapers took great pleasure in documenting Bryant's downfall. The acidic tone of that coverage represented sweet revenge for gay journalism after Bryant proposed, in 1978, that all gay publications should be shut down. The two San Francisco newspapers led the Bryant attack, participating in one of journalism history's more bizarre newspaper wars. The *Bay Area Reporter* took the lead by reporting that death threats and protests by gay

activists had forced Bryant to cancel several concerts. The *Sentinel* jumped into
the game by reporting that a *Ladies' Home Journal* poll had identified Bryant
and Adolph Hitler as the two people who had most damaged the world. *BAR*
regained the lead with a roundup of items listed under the heading "Anita—
problems, problems, problems"; items reported that lesbian activists had disrupted Bryant's appearance in Chicago, NBC had replaced her as announcer for
the New Year's Eve parade in Miami, and sales of her book *The Anita Bryant
Story: The Survival of Our Nation's Families and the Threat of Militant Homosexuality* were sluggish. But the *Sentinel* pulled from behind to win the race when it
broke the story—above the fold on page one—that Bryant was divorcing her
husband of twenty years.[24]

Promoting National Unity

Lesbian and gay publications had always served as a tool for uniting gay people,
but this function increased markedly with the assaults from the right as the
press galvanized geographically separated lesbian and gay communities as never
before. By reading *Gay Community News* articles describing what was happening to gay people in Arkansas and California, readers in Boston were repeatedly
reminded of how their lives and destinies intertwined with those of women and
men living hundreds of miles to the west. A *GCN* spokesman crowed in 1979,
"The greatest success of the gay press has been to foster community."[25]

Reporters recognized that numbers meant strength, and their coverage
promoted the rapid growth of a politically active Lesbian and Gay America.
Journalists reported the huge numbers of people participating in demonstrations, thereby encouraging more people to join the throngs. After the repeal of
the Miami ordinance, the *San Francisco Sentinel* covered two pages with news
items summarizing simultaneous eruptions of protest in cities across the country. The round-up article showed that the numbers varied from city to city, but
the reflexive reaction of gay people was uniform: 6,000 took to the streets in
San Francisco, 400 in Denver, 5,000 in Houston, 2,500 in New Orleans, 5,000
in New York.[26]

The *Sentinel*'s description of the protest in its own backyard gave readers a
vivid sense of the exhilaration and mass power they could gain if they joined
the movement: "Along the way, runners entered gay bars and restaurants to encourage others to join them. The fast-paced, furious procession swelled its
ranks as people left the sidewalks, the bars, and their homes to join the wildly
yelling throng. The strength of numbers produced a surreal air."[27]

The biggest numbers came in early summer as cities observed the anniversary of Stonewall, most of them with a Gay Pride parade surrounded by dozens of other activities. San Francisco's 1977 parade offered dramatic proof of a rekindled activism, as it drew twice the crowd of the previous year. The *Sentinel's* front-page headline read, simply but powerfully: "250,000!" The story further celebrated the significance of the event, boasting that it was "the largest assemblage of gay people in the history of the world." But the *Sentinel* did not merely *record* the number of people at the parade; its intense coverage of the planning and fund-raising that preceded the event served to *ensure* that the numbers would be noteworthy. Within a few months after one year's parade, the newspaper had already begun to stir anticipation for the next one by placing articles about the most minute of details—from a change in the parade route to the name of a parade marshal—strategically on page one.[28]

Other newspapers also both boosted and boasted of the size of their local high holy day. A month after the *Sentinel* announced that San Francisco had attracted the largest gay crowd in history, *Gaysweek* did the same: "50,000 gay people marched up Fifth Ave. yesterday in the largest celebration of Gay Pride Day held anywhere." *Gay Community News* added up the figures from pride parades around the country to calculate a total figure of 350,000. Many papers created supplements for pride activities; by 1979, the *Blade's* special section numbered sixteen pages.[29]

During 1978 San Francisco gay journalists had even more promotional material to work with than usual because the media spotlight shone brightly on the first member of the community to be elected a city supervisor. If San Francisco was the capital of Gay America, Harvey Milk was president. The ponytailed proprietor of a Castro Street camera store walked into history when he strolled to city hall for his inauguration arm in arm with his lover—and trailed by 150 gay and lesbian supporters. At the end of that year's pride parade, Milk was in his oratorical glory. The *Sentinel* published his inspirational call to action verbatim: "I want to recruit you for the fight to preserve your democracy from John Briggs and Anita Bryant who are trying to constitutionalize bigotry. On this anniversary of Stonewall, I ask my gay sisters and brothers to make the commitment to fight. For themselves. For their freedom. For their country."[30]

No one anticipated on that day of great expectations that five months later Gay America's brightest star would lie in a coffin in the rotunda of city hall. The gunning down of San Francisco's mayor and city supervisor was front-page news in every major paper in the country. For the lesbian and gay press, the tragedy offered the opportunity to canonize Milk. Comparing coverage in Seattle's straight and gay press shows how the devastating event furthered gay journalism's building of a sense of national community. The mainstream

Publications around the country expressed shock when Harvey Milk, the most successful political leader in the history of Gay and Lesbian America, was assassinated in 1978. Courtesy of Seattle Gay News.

Seattle Times reported the slayings on page one, first mentioning Moscone and then Milk, with headshots of the two men. *Seattle Gay News*, on the other hand, led with Milk's assassination but did not mention Moscone until the fifteenth line of the story. The gay paper carried a six-by-eight-inch photo of Milk under the banner headline "Gay Leader Murdered," but ran no photo of Moscone. The paper left no room for doubt that Lesbian and Gay America was a single community unified in its grief at the loss of a magnificent leader.[31]

That sense of unity was reinforced five months later when Milk's assassin was found guilty only of voluntary manslaughter, a crime carrying a maximum of eight years in prison. The *Bay Area Reporter* captured both the frustration and defiance of Gay America with the banner headline "Gays Riot: WHY— WHY NOT?" The paper described the White Night Riots that left parts of the city in shambles and dozens of police officers and gay people in hospital beds, but nowhere in its news coverage or editorial comment did *BAR* condemn the 5,000 rioters. Indeed, the newspaper characterized the men and women as peaceful demonstrators pushed to violence by an unfair judicial system and a homophobic police force.[32]

The *Sentinel* joined *BAR* in pointing the finger of blame first at the court system: "Citizens of San Francisco and countless millions through the state now realize that law cannot always be equated with justice." And then at the police: "As tensions mounted, the police began responding with insulting remarks about the 'F———g queers.'" The newspaper concluded its unforgiving editorial with the statement: "If our justice system allows for a Dan White, it must also allow for rioters."[33]

Gay voices in other cities also refused to condemn the violence. While mainstream papers denounced the riots—the *Los Angeles Times* labeled gay protesters "sick," the *Seattle Times* called them "uncivilized," the *Washington Post* said it was time for heterosexuals "to demonstrate their own displeasure" with homosexuals—the lesbian and gay press simply recorded the details. When newspapers did make judgments, they were not against the gay rioters but against the system. *Seattle Gay News* used the front-page headline "SF Gays Take to Streets," with its lead story criticizing the "all heterosexual jury" for its verdict. The *Washington Blade* began, "San Francisco Gays, convinced that homophobia had been put on trial and let off easy, rioted in front of City Hall after a jury imposed a light sentence on Dan White."[34]

A less controversial event of enormous significance in aiding lesbian and gay journalism's promotion of national unity occurred five months later when 100,000 people converged on the nation's capital for the National March on Washington for Lesbian and Gay Rights. The country's leading news media gave scant coverage to the march. The *New York Times* assigned a stringer and placed the story on page fourteen, devoting half the twelve paragraphs to squabbles over inconsistent estimates of the crowd size. The *Times* did, however, find room for three paragraphs from antigay spokesmen, ending the article with Jerry Falwell denouncing homosexuality as "an outright assault on the family."[35]

The gay press told a different story. After months of promoting the march, newspapers burst with praise. *Seattle Gay News* blanketed an entire page with its coverage, headlined "March and Rally Electrify D.C." *Lesbian News* began its lead story with "The March on Washington for Lesbian and Gay Rights was incredible!" The *Sentinel* wrote, "Treading the same paths which architects of this Republic like Thomas Jefferson and Abraham Lincoln trod before them, gays demanded that repressive laws against gay men and lesbians be stricken from the books." *Lesbian Tide* coverage highlighted a quotation from a lesbian speaker: "In the '80s we are moving from gay pride to gay politics. No longer will we tolerate the violence of our enemies, nor the silence of our friends."[36]

Despite the huge quantity of coverage the *Washington Blade* devoted to the largest gay demonstration in history unfolding in its backyard, coverage of march planning was not all positive. The *Blade* covered such divisive questions as whether the controversial North American Man Boy Love Association would be included in the march, an issue that nearly propelled lesbians to withdraw from the event. But after the march succeeded in rallying Lesbian and Gay America as no event before it, *Blade* pulled out all the stops. A dozen stories reported on the march, while a four-page insert documented it in photos. One item captured the moment by saying: "The air was alive with pride and excitement as group after group of Lesbians and Gay men openly marched down the avenue known as America's Main Street. When ten years ago few open homosexuals would have dared to roam, now tens of thousands of Gays marched."[37]

Journalists as Political Leaders

Beyond promoting national unity, the press provided many of the movement's most able leaders. Number one among them was David B. Goodstein. While living in New York in the 1960s, the multimillionaire had joined Mayor John Lindsay's inner circle. After moving to California in 1974, he remained active in the Democratic party establishment, serving on the State Democratic Central Committee. Goodstein ascended to national prominence as well, joining the Democratic National Finance Council and dining with President Carter at the White House.[38]

These activities provided Goodstein with invaluable political knowledge and

access when conservatives mounted their antigay attacks. Goodstein became
the driving force behind Concerned Voters of California, the gay organization
that formed in 1976 and successfully blocked a petition drive to reverse legislation that had legalized sodomy between consenting adults in California. He
helped revive the organization three years later to assist in defeating the Briggs
Initiative.[39]

Goodstein's forte was his ability to raise money, an essential element in a
battle against the wealthy and well-organized New Right. He established the
treasury of the Concerned Voters of California by making personal donations
as leverage to persuade other wealthy gays to make large financial commitments, eventually raising $900,000 to fight the Briggs Initiative. In 1982 Good-
stein conducted a national tour to create a political network while raising another $600,000. His strategy differed from that of radical activists, as he did not
insist that wealthy supporters come out of the closet—as long as they wrote big
checks.[40]

As with Goodstein's journalistic activities, his political ones were wrapped
in controversy. Many leaders continued to perceive Goodstein, despite his financial and organizational contributions, as a liability to the movement. *Gay
Sunshine* attacked him editorially, stating, "The natural allies of David Goodstein are those who want a society based on everyone's conformity with affluent
white male values." Goodstein received other assaults as well, including so
many bomb threats—from inside as well as outside the gay community—that
he had to hire a bodyguard to ensure his physical safety.[41]

In 1976 Goodstein decided the movement needed a lobbying organization
in Washington to monitor activities at the White House and in Congress. He
called a meeting of sixty-five men and women from around the country who,
he decided, were the movement's most important leaders. The elitist tone of the
"invitations only" conference, which Goodstein chaired at the Hyatt Regency in
Chicago, propelled the national officers of Dignity, the gay Catholic organization, to boycott the event. Gary Aldridge, an openly gay assistant to California
Senator Alan Cranston, opened the conference with a keynote address denouncing Goodstein's leadership style: "To me, a movement implies vitality, creative
force, ambition, and life. A movement dies at the first breath of autocracy or
any other form of undemocratic possession."[42]

By the end of the conference, Goodstein's vision had been realized and the
movement had a national presence in the nation's capital, along with $66,000
in pledges to support it. But the National Gay Rights Lobby was born only after
the conferees vetoed most of the specific proposals Goodstein had wanted. The
organization's name contained *gay;* Goodstein had wanted to avoid the word.

The board of directors consisted of thirty people; Goodstein had wanted only seven. Board members were not asked for financial commitments; Goodstein had wanted the seats reserved for major contributors.[43]

Goodstein countered by denigrating movement leaders. *Gay Community News* quoted him as saying: "Gay 'spokespeople' are disconnected from their constituency. They appear unemployable, unkempt, and neurotic." In another *GCN* quote, Goodstein said, "It is incredible that one movement can have attracted so many angry losers as spokespeople." *GCN* also gave front-page coverage to a New York meeting at which Goodstein's critics attacked him. One charged that Bella Abzug had lost the Democratic nomination for New York senator because *The Advocate* had devoted only two paragraphs to gay support of her campaign and that Goodstein had told Abzug staff members that if they wanted coverage, they should buy ads. The session ended with applause, *GCN* reported, after one activist called out, "*Advocate,* go home!"[44]

Goodstein further alienated many in the community by opposing Harvey Milk. In a move inconsistent with Goodstein's stance that gay people need not wear their homosexuality on their sleeve, he refused to support Gay America's favorite son, dubbing him "the missing person" because Milk often did not raise gay issues when he was speaking to a predominantly straight audience. One *Advocate* editorial opposing Milk stated, "In earlier campaigns he did not speak out on gay rights and his campaign literature in past races did not even mention his being gay." Such comments led to a legendary feud between the community's leading publisher and its leading politician—and their dueling egos.[45]

Other press leaders tended to make their political contributions as grassroots organizers. Jeanne Córdova of *Lesbian Tide* was a strong organizer and gifted orator, appearing on the speaker's platform whenever Los Angeles protesters organized a rally. After the Miami defeat, Córdova helped organize New Alliance for Gay Equality, which helped defeat the Briggs Initiative by educating straights about gays. Córdova was a vocal advocate of lesbian rights during the International Women's Year Conference in Houston in 1977 as well, succeeding in persuading the conference to support several lesbian rights measures. She and two other women then used the momentum of the Houston victory to found the National Lesbian Feminist Organization. Córdova was one of the first leaders to recognize the untapped financial resources of lesbians. In 1978, she wrote, "We are seeing the dawn of lesbian economic power."[46]

The publishers of San Francisco's combined gay voice also emerged as leaders. Bob Ross, publisher of the *Bay Area Reporter,* raised money and support for numerous pro-gay politicians and for Save Our Human Rights, a gay rights group created after the Miami defeat. Charles Lee Morris, publisher of the *San*

Francisco Sentinel, was chairman of the city's Gay Pride activities in 1976. After the riots that erupted in the wake of the Dan White verdict, Mayor Dianne Feinstein turned to Ross and Morris to undertake a joint investigation into the police response to the riots.[47]

Some journalists were more inclined toward public protest. Mark Segal, editor of the *Philadelphia Gay News,* organized a sit-in after the city council failed to enact a gay rights ordinance. After Segal, previously part of the Gay Liberation Front in New York, repeatedly refused to leave the council chambers, security guards finally carried him out of the room. Vito Russo, the film historian who wrote reviews first for *GAY* and later for *Gaysweek* and *The Advocate,* made a similar public statement when the New York City Council rejected a proposed gay rights ordinance. Outraged by the action, Russo disrupted a hearing on the ordinance by jumping from his seat and screaming at council members.[48]

Lesbian and gay journalists from earlier eras contributed their knowledge and leadership skills to the movement. Barbara Gittings of *The Ladder,* Frank Kameny of the *Homosexual Citizen,* and Charlotte Bunch of *The Furies* were three of the seven activists who met in 1973 to form the National Gay Task Force. The task force has remained the primary grassroots lesbian and gay organization in the country. Kameny and Bunch also were among the fourteen activists who went to the White House to meet with presidential aide Midge Costanza in 1977.[49]

Organizing as Professional Journalists

Gay and lesbian press leaders committed their skills to organizing as professional journalists. The catalyst came in 1979 when *The Advocate* published a five-page article about the gay press, including a roundtable discussion with several editors. The article served as an informal "self-study report," prompting the editors to assess the status and potential of the institution they were leading.[50]

One major theme in the article was how the press would define its role as the establishment press increased its gay coverage. Córdova said the mainstream media were not a threat: "They have freed our resources to cover stories they won't touch with a ten-foot pole." Córdova said lesbian mother custody cases and artificial insemination by lesbian couples, for example, remained entirely the province of lesbian publications. The editors were both confident and, ultimately, prophetic about the future. Córdova said: "The gay press will get a lot more commercial and a lot stronger, circulation-wise. And slicker. There will be a recession of radical publications in favor of more middle-of-the-road publications."[51]

The biggest step toward organizing the publications came in 1981 when Joe DiSabato, president of a New York advertising agency, called a three-day series of workshops. Eighty staff members participated in the sessions that ranged from advertising to editorial content to distribution. "We can no longer afford to be just a lot of disconnected local papers," DiSabato said at the time. "We need a way of communicating better, especially given the current political climate." The *New York Times* covered the sessions, saying that the "homosexual press" had achieved increased circulation and "the beginnings of respect from the rest of the journalistic world."[52]

In May 1981 the Gay Press Association was officially born at a meeting in Dallas. DiSabato became president, and a constitution was adopted. DiSabato later recalled: "It was a magical moment in the history of the gay press. Community strength is built on effective communications. We could see that a modern, professional, financially viable gay press could be the glue that would pull the whole country together. We felt a real high."[53]

Many topics vied for a spot on the agenda. Some members wanted a group health plan for gay journalists around the country; others insisted on more how-to workshops. DiSabato's pet project was a national wire service to allow speedy communiques among members of the association. "The Moral Majority was using computers against us. We had to catch up—quick," he recalled. "It was life or death." A dramatic example occurred in 1981 when a bill was introduced in Congress to legalize sodomy in the District of Columbia. Falwell immediately used the Moral Majority's computer network to urge members all over the country to contact their members of Congress, demanding the measure not be adopted. Within days, an avalanche of letters had killed the bill. In that same brief period, most gay newspapers—which published only once or twice a month—had not even had time to alert readers to the rapid-fire events. "Gay newspapers hadn't even heard of the campaign," DiSabato said, "much less had a network to publicize any counter campaign."[54]

Other members of the association feared, however, that a computerized wire service would break their tiny budgets. Members also questioned DiSabato's motives. He was the president of Rivendell Marketing, the first ad agency in the country to market gay publications to Madison Avenue. *The Advocate*'s Randy Shilts recalled: "People were leery about just what Joe had in mind to go across that computer network he wanted so bad. He was in the advertising business, not the news business. They noticed that hidden in the middle of the various goals of the association was the statement:'To promote a healthy business environment.' Some of us who were aware of the perennial conflict between church and state weren't so sure Joe's priority was news."[55]

The Advocate dealt the association a major setback when it refused to join. "Goodstein didn't think we needed it," Sasha Gregory-Lewis, senior editor of the magazine at the time, recalled. "He thought *The Advocate* was perfectly fine on its own—that it was in a class above the rest." Goodstein reinforced his point by digging into his deep pockets to buy a full-page ad in the *New York Times* exactly the same month that the Gay Press Association was born. The ad encouraged businesses to advertise in *The Advocate,* highlighting the high disposable income among middle- and upper-class gay men. Goodstein's haughty tone and seemingly deliberate slap in the association's face by running the ad echoed the theme of editorial acrimony that had reverberated through the history of the lesbian and gay press since the 1950s and clearly threatened future prospects for the nascent Gay Press Association.[56]

Separating Opinion from News

In the late nineteenth century, newspaper icon Joseph Pulitzer of the *New York World* emerged as the master of the journalistic formula to change society: report the news accurately and fairly on page one, while championing a course of action on the editorial page. Throughout its first thirty years, the lesbian and gay press had opted not to follow this route toward shaping the views of its readers. Instead, it had blended news and opinion together into articles written in the tradition of advocacy journalism. It was not until the late 1970s, with the antigay backlash, that this form of the alternative press adopted the formula Pulitzer had established a century earlier.

Anita Bryant presented the publications with an opportunity to demonstrate this one-two punch. In fact, the country's gay activists dismissed the rantings of a fading beauty queen as laughable. Even when the religious zealot stated that proponents of the Equal Rights Amendment were virtually all lesbians, most feminists failed to see her as a serious threat. But *Lesbian Tide* saw Bryant differently. It became one of the first publications to recognize that she was a force to be reckoned with. In May 1977 the news magazine reported Bryant's activities on its first news page. The article was written in a straightforward style that even the most traditional of American newspapers would have found acceptable. The lead read: "The same day the Dade County (Florida) Commissioners passed a pro-gay rights ordinance, singer Anita Bryant led a protest before the Commission pledging she would overturn their 'evil' decision to prohibit discrimination against gays."[57]

The *Tide* did not stop, however, with reporting the facts. On the editorial page, it insisted that Bryant posed a danger to the civil liberties of feminists as well as gays: "We strongly urge our readers to personally TAKE ACTION. We must organize immediately to stop any national anti-gay wave." The editorial urged readers to write letters to their elected officials and checks to gay organizations, boycott Florida citrus products, and convince straight friends that Bryant's campaign endangered progressive thought. For the final item in its list of fourteen proactive steps readers could take, the news magazine called for unison and innovative political strategy: "Share schemes! Readers with ideas are urged to write us so we can share the strength with others."[58]

Lesbian Tide soon had an opponent in its own backyard. Three months after the Miami vote, John Briggs began gathering signatures for the ballot proposition to bar gay people from the public school classroom. *Lesbian Tide* used its one-two punch again. Córdova reported the events in her news pages: "Senator John Briggs has declared war on California gays. If he is successful, a second national gay battleground will form." But on the editorial page, she traded her unbiased tone for an alarmist one: "The country is heading into a reactionary period. We can expect an era that may look something like the McCarthy period. Gays are the 'communists' of the 1970s."[59]

When Congress vetoed the measure to legalize sodomy in the District of Columbia, *Seattle Gay News* published an objective news story on page one, but on the editorial page warned that the setback in Washington had national significance: "Falwell and his minions are serious. They plan to impose their legislation of intolerance on the country. They will succeed if our reaction is to ignore them." The *News* urged Seattle gays to flock to the polls for the next month's local elections. To aid voters in that effort, the newspaper endorsed candidates in each of a dozen races, rating several "actively hostile to gay rights."[60]

At *The Advocate*, the one-two punch was delivered by a man and woman who were responsible for increasing the magazine's news content. Randy Shilts provided the news voice; Sasha Gregory-Lewis, who had hired Shilts, provided the editorial voice. Shilts decided not merely to report which governmental bodies were passing gay rights legislation but also to find out whether gay people in the jurisdictions were actually making use of the rights. Speculating that some people would rather suffer discrimination than publicly identify themselves as gay, he surveyed all thirty jurisdictions where gays were protected. The results were shocking. Not a single complaint had been filed in Portland, Oregon. Only one had been filed in Seattle. Officials in St. Paul, Minnesota, said gays had ignored the city's protective measure. Shilts heard the same story in Ann Arbor, Michigan, and Columbus, Ohio. After he reported his survey results, Gregory-Lewis delivered the knockout punch on the editorial page. She boldly criticized her readers: "If you have been injured by antigay discrimination in a municipality where your rights are legally protected, you have a responsibility to yourself and your community to do something about it. Only cowards take a beating lying down."[61]

Confronting Controversy

As the editorials of the era showed, newspapers did not back away from controversial topics. In fact, they walked boldly into the eye of many hurricanes, even though their actions brought torrents of criticism from inside as well as outside the community.

The most ferocious battle was prompted by articles in *The Body Politic,* whose resulting legal struggles forced the Toronto newspaper into a desperate fight for its life. By the late 1970s, it had evolved into one of the most intellectually and politically sophisticated papers of the era, determined to cover the topics gay people were talking about—even if the issues had never been committed to paper before. Two members of the Body Politic collective said that their priority was breaking the silence: "Suddenly so much had to be written, so much had to be said, and finally there was an audience hungry to read and eager to listen."[62]

The topics cut across a broad spectrum. Historian John D'Emilio celebrated that founders of the first gay organization in the United States included members of the Communist party—a fact previous activists had been reluctant to admit. Mariana Valverde argued that gay people should embrace such bold words as *faggot, dyke,* and *queer,* even though the terms offended conservatives, saying, "We have to take over the house of language." Gerald Hannon assailed gays for mistreating disabled people: "At the back of our first closet we have built another one and into it we have shoved gay deaf and gay blind and gay wheelchair cases."[63]

All such topics paled, however, compared to the one introduced in December 1977 when Hannon profiled three gay men who loved young boys. The description of thirty-three-year-old Simon read: "He is, I suppose, exactly the person that families worry about. He is a primary school teacher, and an active member of several social service agencies that deal with children, including Big Brothers. He has taught for ten years in four different schools and has formed sexual, loving relationships with boys in each of those four schools and in each of the service organizations of which he is a member." Though the article did not directly advocate men having sex with boys, it presented the men and their activities—which included having oral and anal sex with boys as young as seven—with no sense of critical judgment.[64]

Readers were outraged. "By publishing the article, you have demonstrated an immaturity and irresponsibility that is shocking to me." "Why should a gay publication, aimed at helping out ten or fifteen percent of the population, speak out for pedophiles, whose numbers overlap only slightly our own?" "Don't ask me for donations to your cause—you deserve everything you get."[65]

The Body Politic got quite a lot. Five burly members of the Toronto Police Department pornography unit arrived at the newspaper office with a search warrant and announced, "We'll take this place apart." That they did. Four hours later, the officers carried twelve cartons of material down the service elevator. A week later, the newspaper was charged with using the mail to transmit immoral, indecent, and scurrilous material.[66]

The events thrust the paper into the media and legal spotlight as no gay publication before it. The case became front-page news throughout North America, with hundreds of editorials denouncing The Body Politic—but, at the same time, reprinting the most lurid details from the original article. Ironically, many of those same chastising news organizations contributed editorial support as well as money to The Body Politic's legal defense fund because the police had taken from the newspaper office, along with reporter notes, the list of men and women who subscribed to the newspaper. In the minds of many observers, the primary issue became not men loving boys, but men and women valuing a free press.[67]

The trial in early 1979 was sensational, with hundreds of news reporters describing every theatrical legal motion and melodramatic statement by the prosecution. Events then took an incredible turn when Toronto's newly elected mayor, John Sewell, appeared at a Body Politic rally to defend the newspaper. An even bigger boost came a month later when the judge found the publication not guilty.[68]

The elation proved short-lived, as authorities immediately appealed. Although legal fees continued to mount, The Body Politic managed to continue both its fund-raising campaign and publication schedule until it finally was acquitted for a second time in 1982. Despite the $67,000 in legal costs and an enormous commitment of time and energy during the five years of legal wrangling, members of the collective consistently defended their original decision to publish the article, saying, "We helped people to rethink their views on pedophilia and to understand that the central issue was the freedom of a community's press." Nor did they allow the case to chill their editorial content: "The Body

Politic is not about to shut up now. Our task couldn't be clearer: keep warning, keep hoping, keep talking, keep visible."[69]

Other publications also tackled controversial topics. *Leaping Lesbian* angered many readers when it urged lesbians to consider joining forces with prostitutes and pornographers. In a graceful writing style that seemed to conflict with the extremism of her message, Gayle Rubin argued that the sexual fringe had much to offer: "It is a repository for all the varieties of sexual expression which have been rejected by society. While some of that experience should stay in the limbo to which it has been consigned, much of it is worth reclaiming. There is a lot of wisdom, and a lot to learn, out on the fringe."[70]

Other notable editorials came from Harvey Milk, who wrote a political column for the *Bay Area Reporter* before being elected to office. Milk challenged straight politicians who claimed to be "friends" of the gay community. He demanded that activists force such political candidates to go on the record regarding gay rights. Too often, Milk said, politicians avoided the subject or merely hinted they would be favorable toward gay rights—until they were elected. He wrote, "No longer should we allow any candidate to evade the issue because it will 'hurt' them with other voters."[71]

Seeing the Larger Picture

By the late 1970s, the lesbian and gay press was not merely reporting individual events but also identifying *patterns* of events. Leading newspapers traditionally have accepted the responsibility of drawing connections between isolated incidents that, in fact, are not isolated at all. Editors are trained to be alert to dribs and drabs of news that add up to a larger trend.

One such trend that *Gay Community News* identified was the startling rise in antigay violence. The *Ipswich Chronicle*'s headline in August 1977 read "Gang Beats Up Computer Operator." *GCN* saw a different story. It identified the victim not by his occupation but by his sexual orientation, using the headline: "Gay Men Beaten in Crane's Beach Incidents." *GCN* then went on to characterize the attack not as a single event but as the latest in a series of hate crimes. Using the mainstream newspaper's story as the latest piece of evidence, *GCN* wrote in a page-one article, "The story referred to but one of many incidents of antigay violence reported at Crane's Beach in recent weeks." *GCN* also published a statement the latest attacker had made but the mainstream newspaper had opted not to use: "We own this beach and we don't want any faggots here."[72]

Other newspapers identified similar patterns in their cities. The *Bay Area Reporter* ran a front-page article about a local man who had his nose broken during an attack on a city bus. The paper inserted into the article a two-paragraph sidebar that began, "This criminal incident is very, very similar to what many members of San Francisco's Gay community have experienced." Throughout the story, *BAR* referred to the assailant as "the fag-basher."[73]

New York felt the impact of gay hate crimes more than most cities, and *Gaysweek* documented the disturbing phenomenon. In 1978 when two gays were attacked by a group of men in Greenwich Village, the newspaper saw the incident as part of a larger problem, headlining its story: "Two Gay Men Assaulted in Village; Pattern of Anti-Gay Violence Seen." The newspaper expressed incredulity at the fact that police discounted the incident as a random one that could not be identified as gay bashing, because the victims had been walking with their arms around each other. *Gaysweek* put the incident in a larger context by pointing out other incidents of gay men in the Village being attacked and spat on within the month.[74]

The New York weekly was even more alarmed when a fire broke out at the city's oldest gay bathhouse, killing nine men and injuring a dozen more. *Gaysweek* immediately published a four-page extra—the first in gay press history—filled with stories about the tragic fire at the six-story Everard Baths. "We knew it was an extraordinary story. So we made an extraordinary effort," publisher Alan Bell recently recalled. The tabloid framed the tragedy as the latest in a series of fatal fires at bars and bath houses around the country. It was not known if the four-alarm fire was an accident or the work of an arsonist, but *Gaysweek* was not willing to wait for an official report before speaking out. In a dramatic departure from gay papers supporting gay businesses, the lead story pleaded with readers not to patronize dangerous bars and baths: "The wonder is the gay community hasn't suffered more such tragedies considering the fire-traps in the area. Violations are hushed up, and because of a questionable legal status gays crowd into establishments where lives are endangered."[75]

One article in the special edition reported that the fire department had ordered a sprinkling system be installed in the hundred-year-old building twelve years earlier, and an editorial urged readers to come to a rally on the steps of city hall, where activists would demand that Mayor Abraham Beame close the bars and baths that were unsafe. *Gaysweek* continued its crusade for closer scrutiny of conditions at the businesses.[76]

One of the most courageous examples of identifying a pattern in the news occurred in 1981 when the *Philadelphia Gay News* reported a high level of drug and alcohol use among gay men. The series examined the underbelly of life in gay bars, a daring step because most activists saw the bars as hallowed territory that *defined* gay liberation. The *Gay News* saw it otherwise. The newspaper reported that three independent research studies had indicated that one of every three gay people in the United States was addicted to drugs or alcohol—triple the rate in the general population. After interviewing several dozen addicts, the *Gay News* reported facts the community did not want to hear. It concluded, for example, that many men escape into addictive behavior not because of the homophobic society around them, but because of rejection by other gays. One article stated: "Gay males, who use drugs more than lesbians, have high ego levels, and to combat this they may choose a number of outlets. One of these is drugs." The series also criticized the gay community for not developing addiction support groups and for celebrating addictive behavior. The *Gay News*'s bottom line was that, with regard to drug and alcohol use, the community was not so much being victimized by society as it was destroying its own members. The paper admonished readers: "The gay community is virtually blind to the 'problem' of drug abuse simply because it does not see it as a problem."[77]

Randy Shilts discovered another problem facing gay men when he found himself becoming listless and sullen, finding his work dull and his personal life meaningless. None of the signals made sense until the morning he was putting in his contact lenses and noticed that the whites of his eyes had turned yellow. Shilts contacted medical experts in San Francisco, Chicago, Washington, and New York. By the end of the interviews, he had identified a nationwide crisis racing through Gay America: Hepatitis. His *Advocate* stories reported that the frequency of the disease, which can be fatal, in the gay community had doubled during the previous two years, soaring to thirty times the level among the population as a whole.[78]

Investigative Reporting

The concept of the Fourth Estate exposing wrongdoing rose to prominence during the early twentieth century, when muckrakers such as Ida M. Tarbell and Lincoln Steffens disclosed widespread corruption in American industry and government. Investigative reporting gained still more notoriety when the dogged efforts of two *Washington Post* reporters helped to topple President Nixon by uncovering the Watergate scandal. So, later in the 1970s, lesbian and gay journalists adopted investigative reporting techniques for their form of alternative press as well.

Many early articles were small-scale projects uncovering discriminatory treatment by local law enforcement officials. The *Seattle Gay News* exposed harassment of gay prisoners at the King County jail, and the *Philadelphia Gay*

News used internal memos from the Pennsylvania Department of Justice to reveal a systematic effort by state police officers to entrap gay men.[79]

But *The Advocate* soon took the lead. As the only publication wealthy enough to allow a reporter to devote several weeks to following a lead that might not even result in a published story, the magazine was in the best position to undertake major investigations. By holding fast to its strong cultural and entertainment emphasis, *The Advocate* had been largely eclipsed, during the late 1970s, by the news-oriented publications that dominated the genre. But the magazine recognized that certain investigative projects defined the culture of the times while simultaneously making news and attracting readers—and the advertisers that would follow.

Sasha Gregory-Lewis, who championed investigative projects at the magazine, recently recalled: "David Goodstein was infinitely supportive of my investigative work. He felt we needed to know who our enemies were. So he placed no restrictions—not for space, not for money. We were the only paper in the whole universe doing investigative work on gay topics. David liked to be out in front. So he got charged."[80]

One topic that excited Goodstein was domestic surveillance of gay people. In 1977 Gregory-Lewis offered her boss and readers a look inside the federal government's major surveillance operation with an eye-popping story headlined "Inside the FBI: Revelations of a GAY INFORMANT." The series focused on Carl Robert Merritt, a gay man who sold information to the FBI in the early 1970s. Merritt, a high-school dropout, told Gregory-Lewis that the FBI paid him seventy-five dollars a week for information. The agents gave Merritt a long list of men labeled "radical communist sympathizers" and asked him which were gay. The names—all from the Democratic party—included Senator Thomas Eagleton, nominee for vice president in 1972; Senators Hubert H. Humphrey and George McGovern, nominees for president in 1968 and 1972, respectively; and Senators Edward M. Kennedy and Edmund S. Muskie, contenders for president in several races. Disappointed when Merritt said he knew nothing about the personal lives of any of the men, the agents urged him to spend more time in gay bars and bath houses, giving him extra money to pay the membership fees.[81]

The agents clearly realized the increasing power of the gay press, as they were eager to collect information about gay journalists as well. They told Merritt he would be paid bonuses for any evidence he produced to damage the reputation of staff members from the *Washington Blade, The Advocate,* or *The Furies*—apparently not knowing the lesbian newspaper had ceased publication four years earlier.[82]

Much of Gregory-Lewis's investigative work appeared in her recurring column that kept tabs on reactionary political forces. "Right Watch" focused on exposing the work of conservatives such as Phyllis Schlafly, the antifeminist leader who had spearheaded opposition to the Equal Rights Amendment, and Richard A. Viguerie, the "direct mail meister" of the New Right.[83]

To curry sources and obtain information, Gregory-Lewis joined several reactionary organizations, including the Ku Klux Klan and the American Nazi Party. Her work also received a boost from lesbian and gay members of the groups. She said: "When these people found out that they were under attack by the organizations they had spent years building, they came over and helped me expose those very same organizations. Many of these people are still working in their organizations. Some have committed suicide. If the gay issue were left alone, they would be hard-working right wingers."[84]

Antigay forces were not pleased with Gregory-Lewis's work. She received telephone death threats both at the office and at home. Her apartment also was broken into and ransacked, prompting her to begin copying all important documents and placing the originals in a safety deposit box.[85]

Randy Shilts joined Gregory-Lewis in investigative work. The most crucial of Shilts's projects, in light of events that developed in the early 1980s, was one revealing what the country's major health institutions were *not* doing regarding sexually transmitted diseases. Shilts began his blockbuster report by quoting officials at the Centers for Disease Control and other health agencies to document that gay men represented 40 percent of gonorrhea victims and 50 percent of syphilis victims in the country. Shilts then reported that public health officials and medical professionals were systematically refusing to respond to this health crisis.[86]

To support his charge, Shilts reported that the federal government spent $33 million annually on venereal disease control and prevention, but—despite nearly half the cases being among gay men—earmarked only $160,000 specifically for programs for gays. Shilts indicted the public health community at all levels, quoting officials as saying that most doctors treated gay venereal disease patients with outright hostility. Shilts concluded his project by sounding an alarm bell regarding sexually transmitted diseases: "Gonorrhea and syphilis offer grave health hazards. A continuing pandemic in the gay community can reap serious consequences."[87]

The project made quite a stir in the gay community. For the first time, a gay journalist was arguing that the problem was not that sexually transmitted disease was rampant in Gay America, but that the government and medical community were refusing to respond to the crisis. Looking back on his reporting of how venereal disease was being ignored in the late 1970s, Shilts later recalled: "I was saying that this was not a moral issue. I was saying that gay people had to stop blaming themselves and start blaming the system that still refused to recognize gay problems as societal problems. Of course I had no notion, at the time, how that same concept would take on much greater proportions a decade later."[88]

Design Quality and Images

As publications shifted toward a strong professional news orientation, homoerotic images faded somewhat. Readers who had become accustomed to finding page after page of erect penises or bare breasts had to look more diligently to find body parts, and then could expect only to be rewarded with an occasional bare chest or thigh. With regard to advertising, a few newspapers made the decision to steer clear of sexually oriented ads. *Washington Blade* publisher Don Michaels later recalled: "We made a decision back in the late seventies to make it difficult for sex-oriented businesses to advertise with us. Mom and Pop businesses didn't want to be mixed in with the sexually oriented ads. We took a real financial bath for about six months, but we broadened our reach." Most papers continued to publish provocative ads but began placing them in separate sections identified as containing suggestive material. The first page of the *Bay Area Reporter*'s advertising section identified it as an "X-Rated Supplement."[89]

This shift away from homoerotica did not mean, however, that the lesbian and gay press abandoned its emphasis on design and images. The publications merely adapted these themes to their increased emphasis on news. The single photo defining the images of the era was one that entered the news arena on October 14, 1977. On that fateful day, Anita Bryant held a press conference in Des Moines, Iowa, to promote her book about her antigay crusade. As Bryant was discussing her ongoing campaign to wipe homosexuality off the face of the earth, gay activist Thom Archon Higgins jumped up from his seat and—while yelling "Thus always to bigots!"—tossed a pie in Bryant's face. It was a direct hit. As the whipped cream and pieces of sticky fruit dripped down the former beauty queen's face, a bevy of news photographers captured the moment.

The gay press loved it. While a few mainstream newspapers used the photo on their inside pages, gay papers plastered the image everywhere. With unrestrained joy, they competed to find the most creative way to highlight the embarrassing image of the woman that gay men and lesbians most liked to hate. *Gay Community News* placed a photo on page one, under the headline "A Sticky Face for Anita." The *San Francisco Sentinel* quadrupled the fun by running four photographs under the headline "Why Anita Got Pied." But *Gaysweek* carried the day by blowing up a United Press International image of the sticky-faced

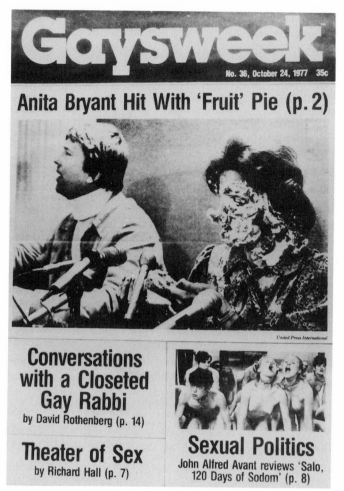

When a gay activist tossed a "fruit" pie in the face of antigay crusader Anita Bryant, the gay and lesbian press had a field day. Courtesy of Alan Bell.

Bryant to fill the entire space above the fold of its front page, highlighted with the banner headline "Anita Bryant Hit with 'Fruit' Pie."[90]

The New York paper held the trophy in the whimsical newspaper war until the *Sentinel* came back with a final blow. In 1980, when Bryant announced her divorce, the San Francisco paper showed no mercy. It rummaged through its files to find a photo of Bryant rubbing her eyes to remove the whipped cream, and ran the image with the page-one story on her divorce. The double entendre headline: "Anita Messes up Her Marriage." While the unorthodox newspaper war reinforced gay journalism's commitment to amusing readers, it simultaneously suggested that the genre's newspapers—even when they worshipped at the fount of professionalism—still were having trouble getting their facts straight. While the newspapers consistently quoted Higgins as saying the Banquet brand pie cost sixty-nine cents, they couldn't agree on the flavor. *GCN* identified the pie as strawberry-rhubarb. The *Sentinel* weighed in with cherry. *Gaysweek* dubbed it banana cream.[91]

The newspapers also used images to maximum effect in their community building. The most frequent page-one visual became an above-the-fold headline flowing over a huge horizontal photograph of throngs of lesbians and gay men carrying a banner at the head of a parade. The contents of the banner changed somewhat—from "Gay Freedom Day" in *GCN* to "Lesbian Feminist Coalition" in *Gaysweek* to "National March on Washington for Lesbian & Gay Rights" in *Lesbian Tide*—but the message remained the same: millions of people are coming together in a powerful social movement. Join it![92]

All occasions calling for strong newspaper images were not so pleasant. As part of its crusade against gay bashings, the *Bay Area Reporter* published numerous photos of attack victims on its front page. A photo of the gay man who was beaten while riding on a city bus was one example. The four-by-six-inch image of the man with a blackened eye and broken nose created a startling visual that pushed the realities of hate crimes into the faces of *BAR* readers. *Gaysweek* took a different tack for bringing the violence home to its readers, searching the city for graffiti and reproducing the angry messages through photos of the hate speak such as "Burn Fags" and "Kill Queers."[93]

The tabloid format of most lesbian and gay newspapers gave them the capability of using large-format photos to maximum effect. The front page of *Gaysweek*'s special issue on the Everard Baths fire showcased a full-page photograph measuring ten inches by twelve inches. The extraordinary photo focused on the decrepit building as thirty fire trucks and 200 firefighters filled Twenty-Eighth Street. As all eyes turned toward the smoke billowing from the upper floors of the old building, the ladders on the fire trucks strained helplessly but could stretch only to the lower floors.[94]

Other images served pro-active roles. With antigay violence soaring, the *Bay Area Reporter* and *San Francisco Sentinel* began a public service designed to help their readers as well as the police. The cooperating newspapers published photos of gay persons who had disappeared, a precursor to the images of missing children that would appear on America's milk cartons a decade later. Articles running with each photograph asked anyone having seen the individual to call the newspaper. The papers also offered a helping hand by publishing, on their front page, police composites of suspected assailants. This service paid off in 1977 when readers saw a composite in the *Sentinel,* recognized the individual being sought, and came forward to identify the man who had killed more than a dozen gay men in San Francisco.[95]

That the results of editorial cartoons published in the papers were not so immediate made them no less important. One clever image published in the *Philadelphia Gay News* aspired to serve as a wake-up call to what the newspaper considered an apathetic gay community. It showed a cluster of pansies smiling pleasantly at each other as a lawn mower labeled "Moral Majority" came racing toward them. To bring home its point, the *Gay News* crafted the hardware on the lawn mower in the shape of a swastika. The cartoon was labeled "Pansies, Arise!" The most memorable image from *Lesbian Tide* also appeared on its editorial page. The news magazine marked the painfully slow march of progress by periodically printing a map of the United States, coloring in only those states that had enacted gay rights legislation. The visual depiction of the entire country—with only a smattering of filled-in spaces in the West and Midwest, while the South and much of the Midwest and East remained devoid of color—dramatically illustrated the huge expanses of the country in which discrimination remained legal.[96]

Winning a Battle

During the late 1970s and early 1980s, lesbians and gay men fought back against a coalition of religious zealots, reactionary politicians, and pure bigots. Gay people proved that, when facing a common foe, they could work together effectively as a unified force. They also showed, particularly through the successful political campaign that defeated the Briggs Initiative in California, that when moderates donated their financial resources and radicals added their energy to unite behind a single goal, Lesbian and Gay America could triumph.

In many ways, the era was a reassuring one for the movement press as well. The victories the community experienced clearly were aided by—and some led by—the network of newspapers and news magazines that had developed across the country. With a rekindled emphasis on news, lesbian and gay journalism had risen to the challenge from the Right to demonstrate a level of maturity and professionalism previously unknown in its thirty-year history. Marching hand-in-hand, the community and the press that helped mobilize it did not merely hold their own or force back the forces of conservatism, but ultimately gained ground in the effort to secure lesbian and gay civil rights. The most dramatic evidence of progress came first in individual cities on Gay Pride days and then in Washington when thousands upon thousands of gay people marched in the nation's capital in an unparalleled demonstration not only of gay visibility, but also of gay power.

And yet, as the 1980s began, the press faced a new barrage of threats and setbacks. Homophobia reared its ugly head when the U.S. Department of Commerce rejected *Gaysweek*'s application to receive a trademark for its name, stating that the newspaper was "immoral and scandalous." California publications felt an additional chafing when a state legislator introduced a bill to ban gay publications from newsstands and vending boxes throughout the state, and again when San Francisco police officers filed a $20 million libel suit against the *Bay Area Reporter* for accusing the force of police brutality. In May 1982 police officers returned to the offices of *The Body Politic* with a search warrant, although the officers left empty-handed this time.[97]

Richard Burns of *Gay Community News* was clearly correct when he said, "Our existence makes many angry and uncomfortable." More devastating proof of that statement occurred in July 1982 when the offices of *Gay Community News,* the newspaper that had emerged as a leader in the resurgence of news and the adoption of professional journalistic standards, was turned to ashes by a seven-alarm fire attributed to arson. The blaze occurred a month after *GCN* staff members had marched on Boston police headquarters calling for disbanding the vice squad. Staff members were convinced the building had been destroyed by off-duty police officers.[98]

Financial difficulties remained another major impediment to stability. During the 1979 editor roundtable discussion, Jeanne Córdova pointed to lack of money as her publication's number one problem. "One reason, of course, is lack of advertisers," she said. "The second is that most of our population—particularly lesbians—are still hidden. They're not subscribing to *LT.* So we don't have their subscription revenue, nor can we charge a high enough advertising rate to make ends meet." One end *Lesbian Tide* met was its own: the country's leading lesbian voice ceased publication in 1980. Another women's publication was silenced the same year, when *Leaping Lesbian* ended its three-year lifespan. Gay publications, although more financially stable than those directed toward lesbians, struggled with finances as well. Though *Gaysweek* was the only major gay publication in the nation's largest city, it did not survive the era, folding after a mere two years. Publisher Alan Bell said recently: "Undercapitalization was certainly one factor. If I had $200,000 to invest, it would have worked." The *San Francisco Sentinel* also teetered on the edge of economic collapse; the newspaper's survival was seriously threatened when publisher Charles Lee Morris declared bankruptcy in late 1981.[99]

Although *The Advocate* had, by the end of the decade, turned the financial corner and begun to make a profit, Goodstein's particular brand of journalism continued to ruffle feathers. Then, in 1978, the brightest star in the lesbian and gay press threw in the towel and shifted to mainstream journalism. Randy Shilts later recalled: "David Goodstein had a narrow view of news. As long as I came up with blockbuster stories that translated into big headlines and splashy art—'Gay Professionals Locked In the Closet,' 'VD: Medicine's Secret Weapon'— news was okay. But when I pitched a story that might threaten ad revenue or didn't lend itself to sensational treatment, his eyes glossed over. For me, journalism had to be more than that."[100]

λ 9

AIDS: Uncovering or Covering Up?

For most gay men, the summer of 1981 unfolded like the carefree season they had come to expect summer would be. In June *The Advocate* reported that bodybuilding had emerged as the pastime of choice in Gay America, with bulging biceps becoming a far more accurate sign of a man's homosexuality than limp wrists had ever been. The magazine announced, "Aspiring hunks can be seen walking around San Francisco with their gym bags—now a *de rigueur* piece of gay equipment—either going to or coming from their daily workout." The men were firming up their muscles so they could pose with appropriate attitude at the bathhouses that had mushroomed into a $100-million industry centered in gay Valhalla. Each week, at San Francisco's Club Baths alone, 3,000 men consumed sex as fast food. And the Bulldog Baths inaugurated a contest epitomizing the values of the times: "Biggest Cock in San Francisco."[1]

Amid such rituals of a hedonistic summer, only a few men were concerned about the smattering of medical stories that began to appear. In May a gay paper in New York reported "an exotic new disease" was striking gay men, and a month later the *San Francisco Chronicle* told a similar story. In July the *New York Times* announced that forty-one cases of a rare form of cancer called Kaposi's sarcoma was attacking the same group. It would be another year before the collective gay consciousness began to acknowledge that something horrible was happening, and longer still before Gay America fully comprehended that it had become the prime target of one of the most catastrophic epidemics in modern medicine. Acquired immune deficiency syndrome would soon make gays long for the distant time when the enemy was an aging beauty queen.[2]

For the gay and lesbian press, the early 1980s was the best of times and the worst of times. Some publications distinguished themselves by relentlessly reporting and crusading against the most heinous enemy in the history of homosexuality. The *New York Native* and *Washington Blade*, for example, performed in noble journalistic tradition, pushing reality into the faces of their readers.

The gay press published the first article about the disease that later became known as AIDS and then continued to cover the epidemic in far more detail than the mainstream news media. Courtesy of Charles Ortleb, *New York Native.*

Such papers acted with courage because the message they carried was one their readers did not want to hear, one that seemed to deny gay men the very foundations of the sexual liberation they had finally begun to enjoy. To close the bath houses and sex emporiums, many activists argued, would be to take a huge step backward. The *Native* and the *Blade* took the heat, forcing readers to sit up and take notice of a disease that, if allowed to continue unchecked, threatened to wipe gay men off the face of the Earth.

Other papers failed to serve their readers. Supporting the argument that full sexual freedom was key to gay liberation while also fearing the loss of revenue they were receiving from bathhouse ads, the *San Francisco Sentinel* and *Bay Area Reporter* campaigned against restricting bath house sex, while *The Advocate* ignored the crisis. All three papers continued to promote unsafe sex despite the medical community's repeated warnings that such activity was spreading the disease with alarming speed. The papers opted *not* to sound the alarm, tacitly allowing thousands of gay men to die.

At the same time, it is difficult to indict the papers. Information about how AIDS was being spread was uncertain, and, after years of enduring government-sanctioned discrimination, gay Americans had good reason to be skeptical of public health officials and government-supported researchers. George Mendenhall, who had edited *Vector* in the early 1970s and reported for *BAR* in the 1970s and early 1980s, said in 1993: "You look back at those days from where we are today, and everything seems black and white. But at the time, there was a helluva lot of gray—uncertainty, skepticism, rumors. Guys looked to the papers for answers, but we didn't know either. We didn't want to print a headline: 'All Faggots Are Dead.' Reassurance is part of what the institution of journalism is supposed to offer its community. We wanted to give readers some hope that they'd outlive this fucking nightmare."[3]

Randy Shilts, however, had no difficulty making an indictment. The gay journalism veteran, whose reporting in the mainstream *San Francisco Chronicle* did more to stop the ravages of AIDS than anything in the city's gay press, later said: "San Francisco's newspapers had what every journalistic institution prays for: the opportunity to save lives. It was the one time in history when the gay press could have proven its mettle once and for all. But it performed miserably. The newspapers in the most important gay city in the country sold out to the almighty buck. The men who made that decision will, unquestionably, burn in Hell."[4]

AIDS quickly demonstrated that it would not be merely a medical phenomenon. For, just as the virus destroyed the entire immune system of its victims, the disease invaded every dimension of gay life. It was those dimensions that would define the major themes of the gay press that struggled—sometimes successfully, often not—to cope with the disease. The most dramatic theme was the degree to which the epidemic challenged the ethical standards of gay sexual behavior. Activists had fought long and hard for gay rights. Relinquishing the right to have sex on demand seemed almost as deadly as AIDS itself. The disease made Gay America ask, quite literally: Is sexual liberation worth dying for? The ramifications of the epidemic extended to the country's most established political and judicial institutions as well, raising perplexing public policy and legal questions. Although it would be trivializing the medical crisis to argue that AIDS had a "silver lining," the epidemic ultimately demonstrated the resourcefulness both of individuals and of Gay America.

The rise of AIDS created a dilemma for lesbians, as well as for the lesbian press. A 1983 essay in the *San Francisco Sentinel* synthesized the predicament. One woman asked candidly, "Where were gay men when toxic shock developed? What support have they offered us for the problem of breast cancer?" Though frustrated by the previous lack of support from most gay men, the author ultimately argued that homophobia was so powerful that lesbians and gay men had to work together if they were to have any hope of securing gay and lesbian rights—with the government earmarking money for AIDS research and treatment now one of those rights. In the same article, the author acknowledged that most lesbians did not live the promiscuous life many gay men did. "But none of us should condemn it," she said. "Lifestyle is not the issue here. Life is."[5]

Despite the overwhelming degree to which both covering and covering up AIDS—primarily a gay male disease—dominated the early 1980s, the lesbian press and gay press did not separate into distinct entities as they had in the mid-1970s. Indeed, with co-gender publications such as *Gay Community News* having evolved, such a separation was, practically speaking, impossible. On a more fundamental level, the attack of the New Right followed by the devastation of AIDS and AIDS hysteria had shown lesbian and gay journalism that it had to remain a united force. Some lesbian publications committed considerable time and energy to AIDS; others concentrated on issues directly related to lesbians. But even when the women's publications focused on issues of their gender, the themes generally paralleled those in the gay male press—health, ethics, public policy, resources.

The largest men's publications continued to be concentrated in urban centers. The latest effort to create a sustained gay voice in the nation's largest city was the *New York Native,* which engaged in a brassy style of journalism similar to the one *GAY* had pioneered a decade earlier. The *Native* was the sassy kid brother of *Christopher Street,* the upscale magazine that for a dozen years had struggled to make a profit by documenting gay life from a sophisticated and literary perspective. On the West Coast, *The Advocate*'s adherence to a cultural focus, despite the emergence of a medical crisis, meant it retained little credibility as a national voice. The two most prominent publications in San Francisco remained the *Sentinel* and the *Bay Area Reporter,* which, during the early 1980s, dropped their cooperative approach to publishing and became bitter enemies. Shilts said of the two papers: "They were after the same advertisers. All they cared about was the almighty buck. So out came the claws. They became the epitome of bitchy queens." Two other influential papers remained the *Washington Blade* and *Gay Community News*, the leftist Boston weekly that continued to provide insightful commentary and remained the only major paper in the country to balance the voices of lesbians equally with those of gay men.[6]

For publications aimed exclusively at women, New York continued to provide fertile ground, as *Big Apple Dyke News* was joined by *Conditions*, a literary magazine. On the West Coast, the most exciting addition to lesbian publishing was *Lesbian Ethics*, an intelligently written publication that struggled with the formidable task of articulating moral principles to guide the lesbian community. Demonstrating the continued diversity of lesbian journalism, *Mom's Apple Pie* in Seattle aimed itself specifically toward lesbian mothers, and *Lesbian Connection* in East Lansing, Michigan, committed itself—as no publication before or since—to reaching the broadest possible spectrum of American lesbians. Though not huge in circulation, these lesbian publications played a crucial role in the lives of their readers. They were creating local, regional, and national networks that were strengthening individual women as well as Lesbian America.

But the overwhelming issue was AIDS. For an alternative press just beginning to achieve financial stability, the disease proved to be a topic that demanded far more resources than most publications were able to muster. In a critique of how the gay press had handled the AIDS story by mid-1983, the *Washington Blade* said, "We know what stories need to be written, but we often don't have the resources necessary to write them." Some of the best publications ultimately made the decision to specialize in one aspect of the AIDS phenomenon. The *Native* focused on medical developments, the *Blade* on public policy issues, *GCN* on legal disputes. *GCN* news editor Sue Hyde said, "To get a national picture, you almost have to read every local paper."[7]

And that was a lot of papers. By 1985 the number of lesbian and gay publications had grown, according to *Our Own Voices*, to seven hundred—twice as many as a decade earlier. Much of the growth continued to be among organizational newsletters distributed to members of the army of social, political, professional, and spiritual organizations gay people had created en masse. *The Advocate*, which in 1984 moved back to Los Angeles, remained the largest single publication; the giant of the gay press was not growing, however, with its circulation remaining flat at 80,000. The combined circulation of all lesbian and gay publications had, by 1985, risen to 800,000—again, double that of a decade earlier.[8]

Because of the enormous impact of AIDS, this chapter is organized differently from the others. It first describes, in one continuous narrative, how the gay press covered—or, in some cases, covered up—the rise of AIDS and its various dimensions. Only after telling that story does the chapter discuss the major lesbian issues of the era.

Taking the Lead in Uncovering AIDS

With a daily circulation of 900,000, a Sunday circulation of 1.5 million, and a staff of 7,300, the *New York Times* in the early 1980s was equipped to cover the globe like no other organization in the history of communication. Despite its enormous resources, however, the *Times* was *not* the first newspaper to report the existence of AIDS, even though early cases were concentrated in New York. That distinction rightly belongs to the city's newest gay newspaper.

The *New York Native* was founded in December 1980 as a biweekly tabloid blending news, entertainment, and erotica. Though published by Charles Ortleb, it was not aimed at the same stratum of sophisticated gay men as Ortleb's *Christopher Street*, which had been sinking deeper and deeper into the red. Instead, Ortleb conceived of the *Native* as a gay *Village Voice* that would pander sufficiently to the gay male desire for smooth flesh and bulging sex organs to pull in the profits needed to supplement the literary magazine that Ortleb otherwise would have to abandon. In the *Native*'s first issue, he said, "We've decided to throw ourselves onto newsprint with a vengeance." A mere five months after its birth, the *Native* delivered on that promise, breaking the biggest story in the history of Gay America.[9]

The *Native*'s pioneering AIDS coverage was the effort of Dr. Lawrence Mass, the first physician to write regularly for the gay press. Mass received the tip for his first article from a friend who had gone to his doctor to be treated for a venereal disease and overheard the doctor talking about an unusually large number of gay men being in the intensive care unit of a New York hospital. The friend called Mass that night. "The rumors were very disturbing," Mass recently recalled. "I knew that they had to be looked into. I had to find out what was going on."[10]

Mass's first article appeared in May 1981. The seven-inch piece stated: "Last week there were rumors that an exotic new disease had hit the gay community in New York." The article was of singular importance because it alerted gay New York—where the disease would do fully half its killing for the next two years— that an evil phenomenon was lurking in its midst. Though the *Native*'s circulation was only 20,000, the gay grapevine quickly spread the story far beyond that number.[11]

The city's gay voice remained far ahead of the *Times* in July 1981 when it pushed "gay cancer," as the disease was labeled, to page one. The *Times* would not give the disease that much prominence for another two years. The *Native*'s huge headline bluntly announced: "Cancer in the Gay Community." Mass's lead pulled no punches either, stating, "Sexually active gay males in several urban centers are currently manifesting a striking, group-specific vulnerability to a relatively rare cancer called Kaposi's Sarcoma." The *Native*'s blockbuster article ran for an exhaustive 170 column inches, allowing room for a question-and-answer interview with Dr. Alvin E. Friedman-Kien of New York University Medical Center as well as two close-up photos of cancerous lesions, designed not only to show readers what to look for, but also to scare them.[12]

Even more astonishing was that the *Native* walked boldly into a buzz saw by informing readers what experts suspected regarding how the deadly disease was being spread. To save the lives of its readers, the *Native*—unlike the stodgy *Times*—did not hesitate to use graphic sexual terms. In its July article the *Native* told readers that "traumatic sex," such as anal intercourse and fist fucking, caused microscopic cuts believed to play a major role in the rapid spread of the disease. In another front-page article, the *Native* raised the possibility that bringing the mouth into contact with the anus through rimming—another taboo term for the *Times*—could be dangerous. For a gay newspaper to challenge these sacrosanct sexual activities was both bold and courageous.[13]

As Mass began to realize, by the winter of 1982, that the disease might decimate the gay male population, he became concerned that the *Native*'s limited circulation meant that only a fraction of the country's gay men were reading about the health crisis. Initially, Mass had hoped to use the country's newspaper of record to disseminate the profoundly important information. "But the *New York Times* during that period was totally homophobic. When I talked to the chief medical writer, he told me the *Times* did not cover the gay community because it was not an advocacy journal." Mass next contacted the city's major alternative publication, the *Village Voice*, which had a large gay readership. Although the *Voice* agreed to commission Mass to write an article, it ultimately rejected the story. "The editor, Karen Durbin, told me, 'It's not a *Voice* piece,'" Mass recalled. "In other words, the dry writing style of a physician did not have sufficient pizzazz, even if it could have saved people's lives."[14]

Mass, who received no payment for his work in the *Native*, was even more disturbed by the rebuff he received from the gay press. After he wrote a question-and-answer piece about the epidemic for the *Native* in the summer of 1982, he persuaded Ortleb to let him try to publish it in *The Advocate*. Mass offered the article for free, but the largest gay publication in the country would have none of it. Mass recalled: "Even when it was clear there was something quite horrible happening to the gay community, *The Advocate* insisted upon distancing itself from the emerging epidemic. They didn't want to publish bad news, for fear of losing readers."[15]

By the end of 1982, the disease had spread to 900 Americans. *Native* coverage totaled fifty-eight articles measuring 2,506 column inches. And yet, by that same point, the *New York Times* had published only seven articles measuring 126 inches. The *Times* was not always so timid about covering medical crises— at least not those affecting straight people. After cyanide was found in Tylenol pain relief capsules on October 1, 1982, the *Times* ran a story every day that month and two dozen more the next month, even though only seven people had died.[16]

Nevertheless, early analysis of news media reportage of AIDS ignored the contributions of the gay press. When a journalism professor published the first comprehensive study of AIDS and the news media in *The Quill*, the journal of media criticism published by the Society for Professional Journalists, he looked at the reporting by dozens of newspapers, magazines, television networks, and local radio and television stations, but he did not so much as mention the gay press. (Ironically, that professor was the same one who has now written this book. I, like most scholars critiquing the news media, focused on the elite news media outlets such as the *New York Times, Newsweek,* and NBC, not even considering what the gay press might have done.)[17]

Media critics who looked at the gay press, however, already were praising the *Native.* In mid-1983, when the *Washington Blade* assessed how gay publications were covering AIDS, it lauded the *Native:* "With its encyclopedic accounts of new developments in the health crisis, the *Native* has set the pace for the rest of the Gay press—and the straight media—on the most important Gay-related story of the 1980s." Randy Shilts agreed: "The *Native's* coverage was exceptional. By the end of 1981 when even the biggest news organizations in the country— *New York Times, Time, Newsweek*—were just starting to see AIDS as a story, the *Native* was bursting with stories about every aspect of the disease."[18]

Shilts was not complimentary, however, of gay press coverage in the other AIDS killing field. The journalist who later wrote *And the Band Played On,* the definitive study of America's bungled response to the epidemic, said: "Throughout 1981 and 1982, the gay community in New York was far better informed about the disease than San Francisco was. All the West Coast papers did was reprint excerpts from Mass's articles—when they bothered to print anything at all."[19]

The three major San Francisco gay papers actually were in a much better position to respond to a major health crisis than was their nascent New York counterpart. But *The Advocate,* with a circulation triple that of any other gay publication in the country, continued to focus on reflecting the gay culture and wrangling in gay politics, rather than fighting the epidemic. Even after *Advocate* associate editor Brent Harris became one of the first men killed by AIDS, the magazine pooh-poohed the disease. *The Advocate's* first article, three paragraphs on page twelve, said that the new form of pneumonia—described as "supposedly" attacking gay men—actually had been around since World War II. Shilts said, "*The Advocate* was not sure what to say about AIDS, and so wrote virtually nothing at all about it until after the subject was picked up by the mainstream press."[20]

BAR, after the libel suit against it was dropped in early 1982, should have been poised to commit itself to responsible journalism, but a new editor opted for sensationalism. In October 1982 Paul Lorch wrote that he considered his paper a gay *National Enquirer.* He said: "The *Bay Area Reporter* was never founded to compete with the *Christian Science Monitor.* To be labeled a 'sleazy rag' has never bothered me; it has always been a given."[21]

San Francisco's third gay voice, the *Sentinel,* began to achieve financial stability in early 1981 when its founder, William Beardemphl, purchased it in bankruptcy court and returned to the publisher's desk. The paper failed, however, to take a leading role in AIDS coverage, opting not to place the disease on its news agenda.[22]

Nor did the Gay Press Association lead its members toward reporting the health crisis. News remained a low priority for the organization, which abandoned its proposal to create a gay wire service because costs were prohibitive. Instead, the association focused on how to increase advertising revenues. Reporting on the third annual convention in 1983, *Gay Community News* editor Cindy Patton wrote, "The twelve workshops reflected a bias toward money making." Patton criticized Joe DiSabato for aligning his advertising agency too closely with the association. She wrote, "GPA is a money making scheme to create a market for Rivendell Marketing [which DiSabato headed] and garner national advertising for publications whose ad bases are more important to them than their politics." With *The Advocate* never joining, *GCN* assailing it, and lesbian publications virtually ignoring it, the association clearly was not an effective leader of the genre.[23]

Debating the Ethics: Give Me Liberation *and* Give Me Death?

For many gay men in the early 1980s, liberation was synonymous with promiscuity. And when men thought of sexual abandon, they thought of San Francisco.

They reveled in the dozens of bath houses, grope rooms, and porn theaters that had proliferated in response to the demands for a cult of ecstasy.

While some men used the baths as a gay community center to meet and socialize with friends, others saw the baths as sexual paradise. After such a visitor entered a bathhouse and placed his street clothes in a locker, he wrapped a towel loosely around his loins and strolled down a long hallway of cubicles with their doors cracked open. Inside each cubicle, a man lay on his stomach. Next to his naked body, the prone figure had placed a tube of K-Y lubricant and a bottle of amyl nitrate that, when inhaled, quickens the heartbeat and intensifies the senses. When the erect man spotted a potential sex partner he liked, he edged his way into the cubicle. If the outstretched man nodded his approval, the visitor quietly closed the door. With no words exchanged, the performance began. It was by no means remarkable for a man to receive the semen of a dozen men in a single night, possibly with a couple showers or steam baths in between. For many gay men, an ideal weekend meant three gloriously full nights at the baths.

By July 1981 the *Native* was reporting the connection between sex and the disease that later became known as AIDS. As coverage evolved, health experts expressed increasing alarm that the gay male propensity for multiple sex partners placed them at high risk and, therefore, jeopardized their lives. Yet gay activists who had won the battle to be allowed to socialize together—replacing the dingy 1950s bars with the comfortable, well-lighted bathhouses of the 1980s—were not eager to take what they saw as a major step backward by shunning either the businesses or the behavior that had come to define their liberation.

Gay newspapers had even more to lose. As the bathhouse industry had mushroomed in the late 1970s, it had provided San Francisco newspapers in particular with the financial stability that had long eluded the gay press. *The Advocate,* which was distributed far beyond the Bay Area, carried many national ads as well, but the *Sentinel* and *BAR* depended on the bathhouses. Club San Francisco's most frequent ad featured a man wearing only cowboy boots as another man sucked his penis; the advertising copy above the image read "Love it." The Watergarden promoted its offerings with an ad dominated by a photo of a man's buttocks as he thrust his penis into the anus of another man. Liberty Baths opted for images of very handsome, very young men frolicking with each other while wrapped in skimpy towels.

George Mendenhall recalled: "The tubs weren't just part of the culture—they *were* the culture. To a large extent, they defined what the gay press was, too. We saw banning sex in the tubs as, with one stroke, losing everything Stonewall did for us. It meant, at the same time, pushing the gay press back twenty years to the

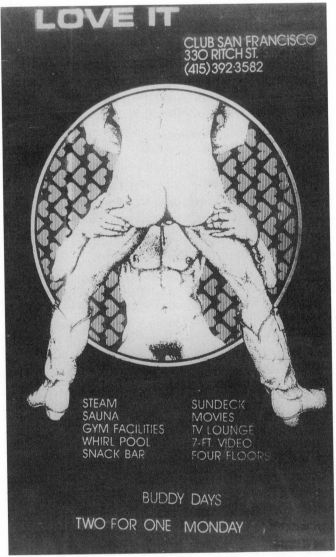

The San Francisco gay press continued to publish suggestive ads in the early 1980s, even after medical experts identified the bars and bathhouses as a gay killing field.

time when we were operating hand-to-mouth. No way we'd let that happen. No way in Hell."[24]

By early 1982 the medical community was describing the baths as death camps. In a front-page article in March, the *Native* stated, "It's probable that sexually transmitted diseases that may be related to the current epidemic are being spread *at* the baths, but not *because* of the baths per se." The *Native* campaigned, therefore, not for sex to be banned from the baths but for gay men to act responsibly by not being promiscuous and not engaging in sexual activity with new partners unless they used condoms—in the baths or anywhere else.[25]

San Francisco papers, on the other hand, continued to promote the glorious sexual abandon of the baths. The *Sentinel* ridiculed the medical research being conducted. As an April Fool's joke, it published a lead story that played off many gay men's fondness for brunch. The headline read "Brunch Causes 'Gay Cancer,'" and the story began, "Scientists seeking to identify the elusive element of the gay lifestyle that causes 'gay cancer' have named gay brunch as the culprit."[26]

While trivializing the crisis, the papers also continued to encourage promiscuity. *BAR* published a series of features highlighting the activities available at the Caldron, one of the paper's most frequent advertisers. A first-person article described the sexual activity available nonstop at the popular bath house: "While Man C is being fucked by Man D and sucked off by man E, Man F places his hand on Man C's left pectoral and starts caressing it. Man C doesn't even look over to see whose hand is touching him. What does he care? It is the experience of raw sexual excitement and sexual pleasure that is of supreme importance."[27]

As the health crisis raced through the gay community, the San Francisco newspapers seemed to go out of their way to mislead readers. A month after running the April Fool's story, the *Sentinel* published the results of a two-month investigation into the safety of city baths and sex clubs. The headline above the lead story proclaimed, "Most Tubs, Clubs Safe." The story began, "A survey of the city's 21 gay sex clubs revealed most have more than adequate safety protection for patrons." An inside headline reinforced the point with "Good Marks on Health," and the lead editorial echoed the theme again with "Safe and Responsible Baths." A reader who looked only casually at the headlines logically would have assumed, with talk of AIDS being spread in the baths, that the investigation had focused on the safety of having sex there. Not so. The persevering reader learned, well into the story, that the *Sentinel* investigation focused not on sex but on fire safety precautions, such as having smoke detectors installed.[28]

The campaign of denial continued. *Sentinel* publisher William Beardemphl wrote an editorial titled "Destroying the Myth of AIDS," which promised his readers, "*The Sentinel* is starting a campaign to clear up misinformation on AIDS." The statements that followed, however, provided textbook examples of distorting the news. Beardemphl's first point—"The homosexual community is over 99 and 99/100 percent free of AIDS. We are more pure than the country's leading cleaning product: Ivory Soap"—ignored the fact that the Centers for Disease Control estimated that, for every full-blown case of AIDS, the virus had infected twenty more victims who were not yet showing symptoms. Beardemphl's second point—"AIDS is already being conquered"—was based on the tendency for many persons with AIDS to go through stages of remission; it ignored the fact that not a single person who had been diagnosed as having AIDS had recovered from it. The publisher's third point—"AIDS is damn difficult to get"—was ludicrous, as cases of the disease were doubling every six months.[29]

Because the San Francisco papers systematically denied the realities of a disease that was decimating their community, it was left to the *New York Native* 2,500 miles away to sound the alarm. That dramatic wake-up call, which came in March 1983, ranks as one of the most significant articles in the history of the alternative press. The blockbuster began in street vernacular: "If this article doesn't scare the shit out of you, we're in real trouble. If this article doesn't rouse you to anger, fury, rage, and action, gay men may have no future on this Earth. Our continued existence depends on just how angry you can get. Unless we fight for our lives, we shall die. In all the history of homosexuality we have never before been so close to death and extinction."[30]

Larry Kramer's angry broadside spread like wildfire across Gay America. Shilts recalled, "Kramer threw a hand grenade into the foxhole of denial where most gay men had been hiding from the growing epidemic." Mendenhall agreed. "Suddenly, gays talked of nothing else. After that one article in the *Native*, gay phone lines to the West Coast were burning up. No doubt about it—he got us talking about AIDS."[31]

Kramer constructed "1,112 and Counting" around the soaring death count. But woven into the facts and statistics was a sense of outrage toward the institutions that were failing to respond to the crisis. Kramer lambasted the National Institutes of Health for funding delays, the Centers for Disease Control for an inability to keep pace with the disease, elected officials for lack of commitment, and the *New York Times* for scant coverage.[32]

Kramer attacked the gay press as well. He singled out *The Advocate* as being particularly irresponsible because of its status as the gay publication whose resources best enabled it to report on the disease: "I am sick of the *Advocate*, one of this country's largest gay publications, which has yet to quite acknowledge that there's anything going on." Kramer continued: "With the exception of the *New York Native* and a few, very few, other gay publications, the gay press has been useless."[33]

Kramer's article influenced other publications. A month after his tirade appeared, *The Advocate* finally broke its silence and quietly suggested, in April 1983, that for gay men engaging in anal intercourse, "Use of condoms may be helpful." The impact of Kramer's article in San Francisco's other gay papers, ironically, ultimately proved to be the opposite of what he had hoped for. In the edition of the *Bay Area Reporter* published immediately after Kramer's article appeared, editor Paul Lorch admitted that he had chosen to be "sparse" in AIDS coverage and then went on to defend his decision: "Each man owns his own body and the future he plots for it. And he retains ownership of the way he wants to die." That philosophy notwithstanding, Lorch then announced a shift in *BAR*'s reporting: "We've made a very deliberate decision to up the noise level on AIDS and the fatal furies that follow in its wake."[34]

The particular focus of *BAR*'s increased attention, however, dismayed Kramer and many others. Rather than attacking the unrestrained promiscuity of the bath houses, Lorch set his sights on AIDS patients and activists. Two weeks after upping the volume on the disease, Lorch denounced patients as freeloaders and activists as fanatics: "The unscrupulous will line up for the giveaway as readily—if not more readily—than the scrupulous. Braying at the government can get quickly tiresome. Already one crowd has *demanded* that the mayor come up with tens of thousands for an AIDS victims' house—or warehouse—as would be assumed under the aegis of a crew I wouldn't trust my sick goldfish to. What a wonderful way to secure a prolonged free lunch."[35]

After a month of attacks, twenty-two AIDS patients wrote *BAR* publisher Bob Ross, criticizing Lorch's coverage and asking Ross to fire his controversial editor. Their letter read, "This sensational approach to reporting only fuels the fires of fear, guilt, homophobia and adds to the everyday stresses patients must face in dealing with this illness." Lorch decided he would respond privately.[36]

But the *Sentinel* had no intention of keeping the issue private. The competing newspaper published both the letter from the AIDS patients and Lorch's private response, both given to the *Sentinel* by one of the patients—on its front page. In his letter, Lorch was neither contrite nor kind to the dying men. He wrote: "I find your letter a sorry document, for its voice is confused, its intent unsure—save to do some punishing. Not liking the message, you scapegoat the messenger. What's more, I sense that your experiences have failed in making you bigger men. The letter reveals a reverse trend, a trend toward peevishness.

What a time in your lives to be without honor. For most of the names on your list, the only thing you have given to the Gay life is your calamity."[37]

Despite the mean spirit and patronizing attitude Lorch displayed in his letter, his private behavior was even more reprehensible. Lorch held onto the letter demanding his termination. Each time one of the men who had signed the letter succumbed to AIDS, Lorch pulled out the letter and drew a line through the dead man's name. One by one, the men disappeared until all twenty-two were dead and Lorch's macabre ritual finally ended.[38]

The *Sentinel* practiced its sensationalism in other ways as well. It began waging a bare-knuckled attack not against the disease, but against an organization the community had created to *fight* the disease. The specific organization the *Sentinel* chose was the National AIDS/Kaposi's Sarcoma Foundation, in which *BAR* publisher Bob Ross served as treasurer. The *Sentinel* filled its front page with allegations that the foundation had inflated the success of a fund-raising event. The *Sentinel* questioned why $60,000 worth of tickets had been given to AIDS patients and why no receipts had been turned in for $15,000 worth of expenses. The paper's charges were so vociferous that the foundation created a committee to investigate them. Even after the committee's three-month investigation cleared the foundation of any wrongdoing, the *Sentinel* still was not satisfied, running an eighty-inch front-page story accusing the investigation of having been flawed.[39]

While the dueling newspapers attacked AIDS patients, AIDS organizations, and each other, they continued to support the bathhouses and the sex that took place there. *BAR* gave bathhouse owners news space to defend their operations. One argued against AIDS educational material being distributed in his bathhouse: "I don't want that going on. People come in here to *forget* what's going on outside." Another said bluntly, "I'm gonna die, I was born to die, and if that's going to be the way, then that's it."[40]

Because the gay press continued to support unrestricted sex at the bathhouses did not mean that gay men did. Bathhouse patronage plummeted. The Caldron, Cornholes, Liberty Baths, Sutro Baths, and Bulldog Baths all closed. When the Hothouse went out of business, *Gay Community News* in Boston quoted the owner as saying he had to close down because the fear of AIDS had cut his business in half.[41]

As the newspapers had feared, the decline of the bathhouse phenomenon had a severe impact on them. After consistently publishing sixteen broadsheet pages, the *Sentinel* had, by the summer of 1983, dropped to ten. The situation was similar at the *Bay Area Reporter*. "We were bleeding. Without the ads for the tubs, we weren't sure we'd survive," said *BAR* reporter George Mendenhall. "Our finances were in the toilet."[42]

In April 1984 public health officials stepped into the bathhouse fracas when San Francisco Health Director Mervyn Silverman announced a ban on all sexual activity in the baths. Silverman said the businesses were so hazardous to the physical well-being of gay men that health inspectors would monitor activities at the baths, much as they monitored sanitary conditions at restaurants, and any business violating the sex ban would be closed.[43]

The San Francisco gay press screamed murder. In an editorial labeled "Killing the Movement," Lorch criticized gay leaders who supported the ban, saying they "gave the green light to the annihilation of Gay life. This group empowered government forces to enter our private precincts and rule over and regulate our sex lives." *BAR*'s editor predicted the restrictions would not end at the baths but would expand to all facets of gay life, including the gay press. He concluded, "The price is but a word. Liberty."[44]

Curiously, *The Advocate* raised its voice in opposition to the sex ban only *after* public health officials made their decision. A month after the ban was announced, David B. Goodstein wrote: "We refuse to behave like Chicken Littles. More of us die from hepatitis, cancer, heart disease and, probably, alcoholism and drug abuse than from AIDS." *The Advocate* also denounced the gay leaders who supported banning sex in the baths: "A significant number of gay men and lesbians acted to urge their city to make criminals of some of their own people."[45]

There were indications that the gay papers had lost touch with their readers. When activists who were outraged by the public health restrictions attempted to stir enthusiasm for a mass protest, they discovered that many gay men supported the sex ban. At the appointed time of the protest, the marchers totaled only twenty-two. Two months later, *BAR* publisher Bob Ross replaced Lorch.[46]

Many of the men involved in the bath house controversy ultimately succumbed to AIDS. Shilts said: "Gay newspapers could have been a leader in banning dangerous sex at the baths much sooner. They could have saved the lives of thousands of gay men. But they didn't lead their readers—except into their coffins. The newspapers were driven not by a noble calling but by greed." Mendenhall added: "We should have done more to warn our readers. When I look back now on my life and think about what I'd do different, that's the first thing that comes to mind. If I could do it over again, I'd have sounded the alarm much sooner and much louder." Shilts died six months after making his statement. Mendenhall died five months after making his.[47]

Although the bathhouse controversy was concentrated in San Francisco, the decisions made in the gay mecca influenced the rest of the country as well. By 1985 cities across the country—from Los Angeles to New York, Atlanta to Newark—also had cracked down on the public sex arenas.

Illuminating Public Policy Issues

As AIDS became a major medical crisis initially fixating on a stigmatized minority group, it raised complex public policy issues. Most of the issues were debated in the nation's capital, which was home to a strong, professional gay newspaper.

By the early 1980s the *Washington Blade* had matured into one of the finest gay newspapers in the country. Beneath its flag, the *Blade* promised readers "Straight facts, Gay news," and it consistently fulfilled that pledge. A mainstream journalism critic who assessed the gay press in 1983 wrote: "The *Blade* knows how to report and write the news. Its news columns are filled with objective accounts of the week's gay-related developments, written by skilled reporters." By developing a clean, well-designed appearance and refusing to publish homoerotic ads, the *Blade* also had the look and feel of a journalistic institution— which, after fifteen years of publishing, it was.[48]

The *Blade* became known for its ability to obtain inside information from confidential government sources, including many closeted gays. That reputation began after a San Francisco baby received a blood transfusion and then developed an immune deficiency disease in December 1982. The widely reported incident prompted concern that the nation's entire blood supply might be contaminated. In late January the *Blade* scooped the titans of daily journalism by reporting that federal health officials would soon ask gay men to refrain from donating blood. Neither the *San Francisco Chronicle,* the *New York Times,* nor the *Washington Post* reported that such a policy was being contemplated. In fact, the papers never even mentioned the voluntary policy until the U.S. Public Health Service released an official statement weeks later.[49]

The case of the San Francisco baby also documented that AIDS no longer could be labeled "gay" cancer. With that reality, mainstream media suddenly became interested in the disease. In the last three months of 1982 the nation's major newspapers and news magazines published only forty stories on the disease; in the first three months of 1983, that figure quadrupled—jumping to 169 stories. In the next three months, the figure quadrupled yet again—this time to 680 stories.[50]

Even when AIDS finally began to receive the coverage a major health crisis merited, the *Blade* continued to beat the country's leading news outlets. When the newspaper wanted to publish up-to-the-minute information on research funding, it initially ran into a brick wall because National Institutes of Health policies precluded releasing any information about the funding of grant proposals until final details had been approved. The *Blade* was not willing to wait. The paper quoted unidentified sources who provided information about the $7 million in grants that would be approved—information not publicly announced for another two months.[51]

Time and time again, the *Blade* scooped the country's leading news organizations. The information that Representative Henry Waxman was drafting legislation designed to speed AIDS research grant proposals through the federal bureaucracy first appeared in the *Blade*. So did the fact that the Centers for Disease Control was designing a mechanism to guarantee anonymity for persons being tested for the AIDS virus. So also did the fact that a House of Representatives report was about to blast the federal response to AIDS. In each case, the *Blade* transformed the information into front-page news before the stories broke in the *Chronicle, Times,* or *Post*.[52]

The *Blade* further served its readers by offering them a healthy dose of journalistic skepticism. In April 1984, when Health and Human Services Secretary Margaret Heckler announced that researchers had discovered AIDS was caused by a human cancer virus and believed they were on the brink of developing a vaccine to prevent the syndrome, the *Blade*'s carefully worded headline communicated both information and prudence: "AIDS 'Probable Cause' Breakthrough Met with Cautious Optimism." Other newspapers embraced the two elements of Heckler's announcement with considerably more surety. The *San Francisco Chronicle*: "Researchers Believe AIDS Virus Is Found; They Hope for Vaccine in Two Years." The *Washington Post*: "Virus Discovery Could Lead to Test for AIDS."[53]

The Washington weekly's biggest coup came in July 1984. By that time, the mainstream news media were providing daily coverage of the AIDS epidemic. Yet, when Assistant U.S. Secretary for Health Edward Brandt, the nation's highest health official, sent Heckler a memo recommending that the recent breakthroughs called for AIDS funding for the year to be jacked up another $20 million, readers first learned the news not in the *Washington Post* but in the *Washington Blade*. Although there was considerable disagreement among Washington insiders as to who had leaked the memo to the *Blade* (it was Tim Westmoreland, chief counsel to the House Subcommittee on Health and the Environment) no one questioned that making the memo public successfully pressured Heckler to approve the supplemental appropriation.[54]

Although the *Blade* had the strongest commitment to illuminating public policy issues, other newspapers covered some of the same issues. *Big Apple Dyke News,* for example, disputed the government's statistics on the number of AIDS patients in high-risk groups. Editor Susan Cavin, basing her argument on the fact that many people considered homosexuality loathsome, said AIDS patients who were both intravenous drug users or hemophiliacs *and* closeted gays were causing the number of gay patients to be deflated.[55]

Fighting AIDS Legal Issues

With AIDS, legal issues erupted as soon as mainstream media began covering the disease—and contributing to AIDS hysteria. Much of the early coverage was sensationalized. One of the worst chapters in that coverage came in May 1983, when the *Journal of the American Medical Association* wrote that AIDS could be transmitted through routine household contact. The *Journal* overstated the likelihood of such transmission, possibly because the editors were frustrated at repeatedly being in the shadow of other scientific journals. But regardless of who was responsible for the sensationalizing, gay people paid the price, as news organizations as well as readers went wild.[56]

The *New York Times* reprinted the Associated Press version of the story straight from the wire machine. The *Times* story began, "Some children may have contracted a deadly disease of the immune system from 'routine close contact' with their families." Within days, newspapers from coast to coast were running photos of firefighters and police officers arming themselves in gas masks and rubber gloves. The photos were soon joined by articles about dentists refusing to provide service to AIDS patients. ABC television added to the hysteria when correspondent Geraldo Rivera announced to 19 million people watching the *20/20* magazine program, "The nation's entire blood supply may be threatened by AIDS." Conservative Patrick Buchanan fanned the flames of fear and hatred through his syndicated newspaper column: "The poor homosexuals; they have declared war upon nature, and now nature is exacting an awful retribution."[57]

Gay journalism had its work cut out for it as it had to struggle on two fronts, informing readers about the disease while also alerting them to the AIDS hysteria that was creating a new wave of discrimination. By August the telephones at gay papers all over the country were ringing off the hook with calls from gay men with tales of ugly encounters with fear and hatred. *BAR*'s Lorch wrote sarcastically: "Everyone has their favorite horror story. We will collect an anthology before it's over."[58]

Gay Community News became a leader in documenting cases of AIDS discrimination. After the "routine close contact" story exploded in the mainstream press, *GCN* published an article headlined "'Casual Contact' Theories Incite AIDS Panic." The newspaper pointed out that, even though there was no body of research to substantiate the suggestion, media reports prompted a flurry of bigoted acts against people with AIDS.[59]

Gay Community News identified one of the most frequent forms of discrimination as placing restrictions on where people involved with the epidemic were allowed to live. In October 1983 the Boston weekly reported that members of a New York co-op had evicted one of the country's leading AIDS researchers. "Tenants were upset that I treated patients with AIDS," Dr. Joseph Sonnabend told *GCN*. "They feared their property values would be adversely affected."[60]

The newspaper also told readers that employers were firing AIDS patients in massive numbers. Compounding both the frequency and difficulty of this particular form of inequity was the fact that people with AIDS desperately needed the medical benefits that came with their jobs—and went when they lost those jobs. Even "enlightened" institutions committed acts of bigotry. A front-page article in *GCN* told the story of a valued employee of the Columbia University music department who took time off to attend graduate school and then was denied his former job because he had contracted AIDS. Employment discrimination was widespread. The *Native* reported that United Airlines had fired two flight attendants diagnosed with AIDS; *Big Apple Dyke News* announced that the American Bar Association had rejected a proposal to ban discrimination based on sexual orientation; and *GCN* wrote an investigative piece on a daylong conference where personnel managers of major corporations paid $395 a head to learn how to get rid of employees with AIDS.[61]

By the summer, AIDS hysteria was manifesting itself in a frighteningly broad variety of ways. *Gay Community News* quoted a member of a Wisconsin county health board saying of gay sexuality, during a public meeting, "With behavior like that, you have to pay the piper," and, "Even animals know better than that." A week later, *GCN* reported that after a gay rights group in Tulsa, Oklahoma, rented a municipal swimming pool, city employees spent an entire day draining and disinfecting the pool. *Big Apple Dyke News* reported that New York City morticians were refusing to embalm AIDS patients. The *Bay Area Reporter* brought the hysteria home to its readers visually when it published a photograph, on the editorial page, of a group of adolescent boys on the subway covering their mouths with handkerchiefs as the train approached the Market and Castro station in the center of the city's gay neighborhood.[62]

Many AIDS patients were not willing to accept the second-class status that bigots were attempting to relegate them to, and those who resisted soon found that fighting back could pay off. *GCN* reported that the Lambda Legal Defense and Education Fund had successfully defended the Columbia University employee, forcing the music department to rehire him. Likewise, the newspaper reported that after gay members of the Wisconsin county health board complained about their fellow board member's antigay comments, the man was removed from his position.[63]

The same San Francisco newspapers that *under*played safety aspects of AIDS ultimately *over*played the level of discrimination it spawned. *BAR*, which AIDS patients already had vilified as spending too much energy attacking AIDS organizations, screamed discrimination in a sensational story headlined "Judge Bumps Juror with AIDS." It was not until seventeen inches into the twenty-inch story that a reader learned that the juror with AIDS actually had *volunteered* to excuse himself from the jury.[64]

Putting a Human Face on an Inhuman Disease

The lesbian and gay press had always defined itself as a form of journalism committed to personalizing the news. Lisa Ben established the theme when she created *Vice Versa* as an extension of her own personality; Jack Nichols and Lige Clarke perfected the technique in the 1960s with their "Homosexual Citizen" column. Continuing this theme, early AIDS coverage communicated a sense of the personal tragedy the disease inflicted.

The *New York Native* offered the earliest perspective on how the disease was affecting the personal lives of gay New Yorkers when Lawrence Mass interviewed one of the original forty-one Kaposi's sarcoma victims. In the interview, the doctor/journalist asked the patient if having the illness made him regret being gay. The man, who had not yet turned forty, responded poignantly: "No. I've *thought* about it. I've once or twice fantasized what it would be like to be straight. But I can't regret being gay any more than I can regret being Jewish, American or human."[65]

That piece was followed four months later by a riveting series that began simply, "I'm Bobbi Campbell and I have 'gay cancer.'" With those dramatic words on the front page of the *San Francisco Sentinel*, a twenty-nine-year-old registered nurse began exposing the intimate corners of his life. Campbell told how, upon returning from a "honeymoon" with his lover, he had removed his hiking boots to find purple blotches on his feet. A month later, he had been diagnosed with KS.[66]

Campbell's "Gay Cancer Journal" took readers through the phases of his debilitating disease. From denial to anger to depression to acceptance, Campbell documented how it felt to be a modern-day leper. Yet his six-part series was infected with neither anger nor bitterness. Even when his lover deserted him and his health deteriorated, Campbell retained an optimistic outlook: "I'm lucky, and happy, because in my time of crisis, I've found out who my real friends are. I'm surrounded by people who love me, who care about me, who follow my progress with interest, and who want me to get well soon."[67]

Campbell labeled himself the "KS Poster Boy" and filled his column with reflections on how people treated him. He juxtaposed the latest research findings with the funerals of his friends. As Campbell became the country's most famous AIDS patient, he also talked about making public speeches, testifying before Congress, and appearing on the *NBC Nightly News*—always wearing a button proclaiming to all the world: "I will survive."[68]

Another human face in the *Sentinel* was that of the paper's former publisher, Charles Lee Morris. One of a long list of gay journalists struck down by AIDS, Morris wrote: "It is very hard for a person to come to grips with his own mortality, especially when the disease is as unknown as AIDS. My God, there are billions of people in the world and only 684 have this illness. How can I be one of the 684? It can't be happening to me!"[69]

Dramatic images of men struggling with AIDS appeared in *Christopher Street*. The upscale literary magazine painted its first portrait of the disease in 1981 with a first-person article written by a man stricken with Kaposi's sarcoma. Three years later, Philip Lanzaratta returned to the pages of the magazine to update readers on his life. Lanzaratta appeared on the cover wrapped in the arms of John Lunning, his lover of nineteen years; the strength and defiance expressed on Lunning's face ushered readers into his lover's inspirational portrait of the resilient human spirit. Lanzaratta refused to go quietly into the abyss of AIDS; he had already outlived everyone who had been diagnosed with the syndrome when he was. Lanzaratta credited his survival to a positive attitude and his determination to take charge of his own destiny. He explored every new treatment program, supplementing chemotherapy with a macrobiotic diet, yoga, shiatsu massages, and acupuncture. The triumphant man completed his piece: "A voice inside me keeps me fighting, intensifying my will to live: 'Life's short! How can I fit everything in? I don't have time to die.'"[70]

Christopher Street's most haunting portrait of the epidemic came from gay literary giant Andrew Holleran, author of the novels *Dancer from the Dance* and *Nights in Aruba*. To capture a sense of the impact AIDS was having on New York, Holleran created "Journal of the Plague Year." The article was the fictional diary of a man as he experienced 1982, the first year the disease was widely talked of in gay social circles: "March 6. S. told me GH has cancer and is in hospital, that John P. died of pneumonia last month, and 4 of EW's ex-lovers died this past year. Imagine how EW feels! And he's still the most handsome man in New York: I used to watch him and R take a rubber raft out every day at sunset on Fire Island and make love far out from shore. Too divine . . . June 17. Found a bruise on the inside of my arm this morning. Was panicked till I realized I hit it against the new overhead-press machine at the gym. Thank God! . . . Nov. 7. Baths have always been a relief from the rest of society. Went hoping I would not find anyone incredible. Tonight I did. It hurt so badly—I wouldn't go into his room—I sat on a bench and got very sad. I thought of sucking his nipple (since it's spread by fluids, what can you get from a nipple?), but I knew that would lead to Everything Else. I miss Everything Else. Left the baths *very* depressed."[71]

Creating Resource Networks

Attacks by the New Right in the late 1970s followed by the devastation of AIDS in the early 1980s made it clear that, if gay people were going to gain their civil rights—indeed, if they were to survive—they had to develop their own resources. The AIDS crisis in particular demonstrated that the gay press would play a central role in constructing that network of resources.

The *New York Native*'s first front-page article about a new disease attacking gay men included an appeal for readers to make financial contributions to support caring for victims and searching for the cause of the disease. The plea, which was set aside as a boxed sidebar to the main article, included an address where readers could send donations. It ended: "Money is desperately needed!"[72]

Such community appeals remained a consistent element of AIDS coverage. Gay Men's Health Crisis, a New York organization Lawrence Mass and Larry Kramer helped to found in 1981, received the most attention and praise. Soon after the group was organized, the *Native* ran a ten-inch "Personal Appeal from Larry Kramer" in which he wrote, "We have often been a divided community in the past; I hope we can all get together on this emergency, undivided, cohesively, and with all the numbers we in so many ways possess." Before the group's first fund-raising event, an item on the *Native*'s front page promoted the event. Afterward, the *Native* gave the organization a full page to thank its supporters. By the end of 1982, the paper had donated a dozen such pages to the organization's cause.[73]

Support for the Gay Men's Health Crisis extended beyond New York. *Gay Community News,* showing its leftist leanings were still intact, praised the volunteers as proof that AIDS had awakened "the least political segment of the gay community, the white middle class." Peg Byron of *GCN* wrote: "In less than two years, GMHC has grown from a vague circle of six men who hammered at their friends about a bizarre-sounding disease, to a highly-structured organization with more than a thousand volunteers pouring their all into support programs, fundraising and advocacy for AIDS victims. The only previous networking done by many GMHC members had been sharing summer houses on Fire Island." She went on to laud the organization's success at pulling in tens of thousands of dollars at private fund-raising events and securing a $200,000 grant from the state of New York to build a net worth of more than $500,000.[74]

Fund-raising became an increasingly important thrust of the crusade against AIDS, and the gay press played an invaluable role in helping to raise money. When the Gay Men's Health Crisis took a big financial gamble by hiring the Ringling Brothers Circus for a fund-raising event, the *Native* exuberantly promoted the event, helping to fill all 17,500 seats—the first time a charity event at Madison Square Garden had sold out in advance—and raise $250,000. The *New York Times,* on the other hand, ignored the circus. *Times* executive editor Abe Rosenthal later apologized, saying: "I really have no explanation for it except one of human error. It was an oversight and that's all I can say."[75]

The gay press helped fund-raising efforts in other ways as well. A particularly vivid example of how AIDS activists used the press came on 1981's Labor Day weekend, the final blowout of the summer season. In that early stage of the disease, when very few men had yet heard about it, Kramer and other activists developed a plan to raise money through a unique "direct mail" strategy. They duplicated thousands of copies of Mass's *Native* article containing the gruesome photos of the KS lesions, and attached a note explaining how people could support research efforts. Then they placed the article and note on every doorstep on Fire Island's two upscale gay communities, Cherry Grove and the Pines.[76]

By mid-1983, when the mainstream media were only beginning to acknowledge that a disease existed, gay and lesbian papers were publishing long lists of AIDS-related services available in their local communities. *GCN*'s "AIDS Resource List," for example, included descriptions and telephone numbers of more than a dozen groups ranging from an AIDS information hotline to a committee coordinating local AIDS fund-raising activities.[77]

Feature articles proved to be a particularly effective vehicle for informing readers of the myriad services available to them. The *Blade* wrote about the phenomenal popularity of safer-sex seminars and AIDS support groups, the plethora of homes being created for people with AIDS, and the record of success being built by gay legal service groups. *GCN* described the Social Security benefits available to people with AIDS and published appeals from AIDS patients who needed places to live. *BAR* documented the creation of the country's first gay funeral home.[78]

At the end of a seven-part series on AIDS, *Blade* editor Steve Martz observed that the network of resources created to combat the disease had given new meaning to the phrase "gay community." He wrote, "One can tell where a true sense of community exists by the way its members treat the weakest among them and, by that yardstick, the compassion that Gays are showing to those afflicted with AIDS is a wonderful sign of strength."[79]

Ironically, the middle of the decade brought gay people the opportunity to demonstrate compassion for one of their arch enemies. In fall 1985 Dan White placed a hose in the exhaust pipe of his wife's car and asphyxiated himself. Gays could have rejoiced in the suicide of the man who had, seven years earlier, gunned down Harvey Milk. They also could have found joy a year later when Roy Cohn, the lawyer who served as Joseph McCarthy's right-hand man during the 1950s homosexual witch hunts, died of AIDS. Instead, Gay and Lesbian America responded to both events with subdued sadness. *GCN* quoted gay supervisor Harry Britt, who had been appointed to fill Milk's term, as saying, "The gay community has seen so much death in the last five years, I don't think anyone is taking pleasure in anyone else's death."[80]

Lesbian Health Issues

While the AIDS epidemic dominated gay men's lives during the early 1980s, new concerns about lesbian health issues also began to surface. Joan Nestle, the driving force behind the Lesbian Herstory Archives, said, "The medical concerns were important, of course, but what was intolerable was the fact that the medical community and most of society seemed to care not at all."[81]

Of particular concern were research studies indicating that lesbians seemed to be at a higher risk for developing breast cancer. Studies were indicating that a gay woman was as much as three times more likely to develop the disease as a straight woman. *Big Apple Dyke News* cautioned readers not to fall into the traditional pattern that women's second-class citizenship had encouraged: "Lesbians should not even consider that this may be some form of retribution by God—or Goddess. Hate mongers like Pat Buchanan and Jesse Helms undoubtedly will preach such heresy soon. Be prepared." The magazine suggested a more logical reason for the high incidence of breast cancer among lesbians was that they were less likely to have given birth to children or, subsequently, used their breasts for nursing.[82]

One venue for discussing such issues was one of the most intriguing publications in the history of lesbian and gay journalism. *Lesbian Connection* was reminiscent of *Vice Versa* because it appeared as single-spaced typed pages stapled together. *LC* differed from its foremother, however, in that it contained the thoughts not of a single woman, but of the broadest collection of lesbians ever assembled. Any lesbian who sent an item to the editorial collective in East Lansing, Michigan, could be assured that it would be printed exactly as submitted. Nestle said: "*Lesbian Connection* became Lesbian America's town crier. It served like a printed town meeting—on a national basis. Lesbian women knew that whatever they wanted to talk about, they could send it to *Lesbian Connection* and ... voila! It was news."[83]

In the early 1980s *LC* readers wanted to talk about health issues. One railed against feminine hygiene products. The woman said that vaginal deodorants were causing serious harm to the 24 million women using them. When the sprays were introduced in 1970, she pointed out, the Food and Drug Administration classified them as cosmetics rather than health-care products, thereby not requiring extensive safety testing. Although women had been complaining for years that the sprays irritated their skin, the product was still available in every drug store and supermarket in the country. The writer opposed women using the sprays to reduce odor, but she was not *entirely* opposed to their use. She concluded her article: "They work very well on roaches."[84]

Lesbian Connection's open submission policy also gave women the opportunity to talk about their emotional as well as physical health. In 1982 a Roanoke, Virginia, woman described events from her past, writing that she had been repeatedly raped by her stepfather when she was an adolescent. She said that the secret had haunted her for years: "I still wake up at night terrified."[85]

Lesbian Ethical Issues

Ethical issues so informed the lesbian press of the early 1980s that the discussions escalated to the point that, in 1984, a woman created a publication focused exclusively on the topic. *Lesbian Ethics*, which was published not only in the format of a scholarly journal but also with substantive content equal to the best of such journals, quickly raised intellectual discourse to its highest level in the history of lesbian publishing.[86]

In her first issue, editor Jeanette Silveira argued that discussing ethical dilemmas was essential for the survival not only of lesbians but of all humanity. The men who historically had ruled the world obviously had never established morality as a guiding principle, she wrote, because they had relegated fully half of the human race to sex objects. Therefore, Silveira said, lesbians faced a daunt-ing responsibility: "Lesbians are in our daily lives building the first true ethics."[87]

Some articles debated such familiar topics as sexual monogamy and lesbians raising male children, but the journal was soon breaking new—and explosive—ground. One series dealt a body blow to lesbian therapists by documenting that many of them abused their clients. Silveira introduced the series by describing a prominent therapist who counseled one of her clients to leave her lover—and move in with the therapist. The anecdote prompted a flood of material from readers who had similar stories to tell. One wrote that she sued her psychiatrist for medical malpractice: "Years have passed and I remain shocked, distraught, and fragmented by the experience. Meanwhile, this therapist continues to treat lesbian patients." Another woman described a therapist seducing and abandon-ing her. The angry woman then spoke directly to her patronizing therapist: "You have said that if there's anything I want to talk to you about, you're willing to listen. Listen to this: Go to hell."[88]

Another bombshell centered on a foremother of the lesbian press. Barbara Grier, former editor of *The Ladder,* owned the largest lesbian publishing house in the country, Naiad Press. In 1985 Grier published *Lesbian Nuns,* an anthology of autobiographies. To increase book sales, Grier sold serial rights to *Forum,* a magazine published by Penthouse International. *Forum* then reprinted the sec-tions that focused specifically on the women's sexual experiences. Although the authors had given Grier the right to reproduce their work, they were shocked when their words appeared in a magazine published to arouse heterosexual men. Grier defended her action, saying a publisher's goal is to increase book sales. *Lesbian Ethics* was not convinced. It blasted Grier as arrogant and her ac-tion as indefensible. One author wrote, "I have grave worries for the future of the feminist movement."[89]

Big Apple Dyke News walked blithely into an ethical minefield in 1981 when editor Susan Cavin accepted a short story in which Joan Nestle described a sex-ual encounter with another woman. A female typesetter working for the com-pany that printed *B.A.D. News* said the story was pornographic and told Cavin she either had to withdraw it or find a new printer. Cavin held the line. She can-celed her contract with the company and located a new one—a Chinese printer whose typesetters did not understand English.[90]

Lesbian Public Policy Issues

Another theme among lesbian publications that paralleled a similar topic in their gay male counterparts was crucial public policy issues. Throughout the first two centuries of American history, lesbians had been largely willing to keep their personal lives hidden from public view. But with the increasing visibility of lesbianism, it clearly was necessary for the country to recalibrate not only its attitudes but also its policies toward women who loved women.

One issue moving rapidly toward center stage was the military's refusal to recognize the huge number of lesbians in its ranks. By 1983 *Lesbian Connection* was receiving so many articles about women being thrown out of the armed forces that it created a section titled "Uncle Sam Doesn't Want You." Specific items described an air force lieutenant from Kansas, an army ROTC student from Maine, and two dozen navy enlisted women from Tennessee being dis-charged because of their sexual orientation, even though the women had been exemplary soldiers and sailors.[91]

An issue that had already secured its place on the national agenda was that of the rights of lesbian mothers. Just as most lesbians had participated in sex-ual activity with men at some point in their lives, a large percentage—some publications estimated fully one half—also had given birth to children. The con-cept of a woman being both a lesbian and a good mother, however, was one the courts did not quickly embrace. So, among lesbians, child custody issues were a major concern.

When the Lesbian Mothers' National Defense Fund was founded in 1974, the Seattle-based organization began producing a mimeographed newsletter titled *Mom's Apple Pie*. In 1980 it became a full-fledged magazine complete with at-tractive artwork and substantive editorial content. Many articles reported the progress individual women were making in the courtroom; others advised women on how to fight for their legal rights as mothers.[92]

Despite some advances during the 1970s, however, the material did not paint a rosy picture. In particular, articles documented that a lesbian mother still faced major impediments to being allowed to raise her children in a household with a lover. Typical was the story of an Illinois woman who was struggling to retain custody of her six-year-old son. The case was complicated by a U.S. Supreme Court ruling that it was immoral for two unmarried lovers, regardless of gender, to live in a household with children. *Mom's Apple Pie* described the details of both the Illinois case and the Supreme Court ruling fairly, exposing its bias only in the headline: "CATCH 22 Alive & Well in Illinois."[93]

Another article analyzed the pluses and minuses of a lesbian mother publi-cizing her courtroom battle. The choice was a tough one. On one hand, public-ity could hold a judge accountable to the public; on the other, a mother could be accused of "promoting lesbianism" and exposing her children to public ridicule. Rather than merely leaving a reader floundering for a decision, *Mom's*

Apple Pie posed several specific questions a woman should ask before making a decision, thereby subtly communicating that a woman had every right to choose to keep her case out of the public eye. One question asked was whether the mother possessed the physical and emotional strength to face crowds of hateful right-wingers cursing and throwing invectives at her—and her children.[94]

Another legal issue combining lesbians and motherhood had to do with women choosing alternative methods of becoming pregnant. Roberta Achtenberg in San Francisco was one of several attorneys exploring the legal ramifications of women conceiving children through donor inseminations. Although the medical procedures were fairly simple, the legal implications were not, Achtenberg told the *San Francisco Sentinel*, because of the uncertainty of the rights of the donor. Achtenberg, a lesbian mother herself, said that the argument most frequently raised by opponents—that lesbians would expose their children only to women—was a minor one. She wrote, "Lesbian mothers recognize that they can't raise their children to be dysfunctional in a heterogeneous society."[95]

Lesbian Resource Networks

The early 1980s was a period during which lesbians intensified their construction of resource networks. Nestle recalled: "We were still feeling the attacks from the New Right, which became more harsh with the chaos over AIDS. We felt under siege. So we did what anyone under attack would do: we looked to ourselves for strength. Our newspapers and magazines created the infrastructure for a guerrilla existence—a whole way of life operating underneath the prevailing landscape. That world was very much built and sustained by our publications."[96]

One of those publications was a magazine printed in Brooklyn and distributed to 1,000 women throughout the country. Produced by a collective, *Conditions* argued that readers were foolish to rely on anyone but each other. "As lesbians we invent our own laws, create and define the bonds among us," the founders wrote. "Is it not difficult, even dangerous, to grant importance to our families of origin, particularly when these families have often rejected or patronized us? Do we not, by the very act of valuing the nuclear family, demean the ties we have chosen?"[97]

Conditions also criticized institutions working against the well-being of lesbians. One article began, "If Hollywood had its way, lesbians would still be very infrequent visitors on the silver screen, invisibility being perhaps the most effective way to control uncontrollable women." The magazine then documented and applauded the works of a dozen independent lesbian filmmakers,

with an emphasis on films encouraging viewers to form alliances for their protection. The article highlighted *Born in Flames,* a 1983 film about a lesbian vig-
ilante motorcycle gang that protected women from physical attacks.[98]

Elly Bulkin, one of the founders of *Conditions,* recently recalled that building
a national lesbian infrastructure was fundamental to the magazine: "*Conditions*
created a network of lesbian writers. It helped establish connections so we got to
know people from all over the country—especially women of different racial
and socio-economic backgrounds—we wouldn't have known otherwise."[99]

Material in *Mom's Apple Pie* also reflected the era's emphasis on support
systems. In lesbian mother custody cases, a woman's former husband and her
parents often became her most strident enemies. So mothers depended on
other lesbians to provide the financial resources necessary to wage their legal
battles. When a Massachusetts judge denied Bunny King the right to care for
her daughters, she appealed to fellow readers of the Lesbian Mothers' National
Defense Fund publication. Two years later, she thanked those readers for helping her pay the $21,000 in attorney's fees that enabled her to win her case. "It is
simply wonderful having my family together once more," King wrote, "and I
know I owe that to everyone who opened their hearts and gave to my case."[100]

Lesbian Ethics's support of networking also called for more pro-active efforts. The California-based magazine criticized hospitals for not expanding
their visitor policies to include the lovers and close friends of gay people. It
raged: "This is homophobia. This is not equality." The journal urged readers
across the country to band together and insist that all hospitals revise their visitor policies, particularly in light of the AIDS epidemic.[101]

The most dramatic demonstration of lesbian publications building national networks was in *Lesbian Connection.* The "Contact Dykes" section came
to epitomize how the press built resources through creative means. The feature
listed names, addresses, and telephone numbers of lesbians—from Alaska to
Florida—who were willing to help other lesbians traveling to their area. If a
woman was planning a trip and wanted to identify "lesbian friendly" hotels
and restaurants, she merely pulled out *Lesbian Connection* and telephoned or
wrote the "contact dyke" nearest her destination. Each woman on the list offered advice, and some provided food and housing as well. Nestle said that the
section liberated American lesbians as nothing before it: "It was very difficult
for any woman to travel by herself, but anti-gay violence made it particularly
threatening for a lesbian. There were no lesbian-owned hotels or bed and
breakfasts back then. 'Contact Dykes' became a wonderful service because it
offered us 'safe houses' virtually everywhere in the country. It opened the whole
country up to us!"[102]

Nestle also continued to be a leader in reclaiming lesbian history as a means of showing the strong foundation that already existed for a nationwide network of lesbians. In one eloquent article in *Lesbian Connection,* Nestle documented the underground world of lesbian bars she remembered from the 1950s. The straight owners of the bars, she wrote, refused to allow more than one woman in the bathroom at a time. So a long line of women stood waiting outside the bathroom door. As Nestle remembered that line, however, she also remembered the deepening strength she and the other women were building: "I stood, a fem, loving the women on either side of me, loving my comrades for their style, the power of their stance, the hair hitting the collar, the thrown out hip, the hand encircling the beer can. Our eyes played the line, subtle touches, gentle shyness weaved under the blaring jokes, the music, the smoke, the surveillance. We lived on that line, restricted and judged, we took deep breaths and played. But buried deep in our endurance was our fury."[103]

The Best of Times, the Worst of Times

The early 1980s offered the gay and lesbian press the opportunity for greatness. Indeed, the time of crisis brought distinction to several news organizations. The *New York Native* merits the most praise. Even though the fledgling biweekly newspaper had minuscule resources compared to those of the mammoth *New York Times,* the *Native* provided the earliest and most comprehensive coverage of the most important medical story of the decade. What's more, the *Native* did not shrink from warning its readers that the promiscuity that was synonymous with gay liberation was spreading the disease.

When James Kinsella wrote the first book-length study of AIDS and the news media, *Covering the Plague: AIDS and the American Media,* he praised the *Native* as "the AIDS paper," saying, "It was the first publication in America to list high-risk behavior, to discuss the potential danger of the disease being spread by a virus." As late as 1984 the *Native* continued to scoop the elite of American journalism by becoming the first news organization in the country to report that French scientists had discovered the virus that caused the disease—a story that did not appear in the *New York Times* until two weeks later. Indeed, the *Native*'s Lawrence Mass had become a source for such leading journalists as Lawrence Altman of the *Times.* Through aggressive and honest reporting, the *Native* displayed journalistic heroism at its finest, saving the lives of an untold number of readers.[104]

The *Washington Blade* also should be commended. It took advantage of its proximity to the federal enclave where public policy makers were deciding the destiny of Gay America. By developing sources inside the government and per-sistently covering the complex issues surrounding AIDS, the *Blade* served both the institution of journalism and its own readership.

Other gay and lesbian publications performed well, too. *Gay Community News* illuminated legal issues surrounding the epidemics of AIDS as well as AIDS hysteria, while *Christopher Street* helped give the disease a human face. Among lesbian publications, *Big Apple Dyke News* was the most committed to tracking the AIDS epidemic, but *Conditions, Lesbian Ethics, Mom's Apple Pie,* and *Lesbian Connection* also served their readers by illuminating the various other issues dominating Lesbian America in the early 1980s.

Three San Francisco publications do not merit praise. The *Bay Area Re-porter* deserves the most criticism. The second largest gay or lesbian publication in the country downplayed the spread of the epidemic in the bathhouses, partly because it saw any attempt to ban sexual activity as a setback for gay liberation and partly because it did not want to lose the revenue it received from bath-house ads. Even when the newspaper finally acknowledged that AIDS could no longer be ignored, the self-proclaimed sensationalistic tabloid focused not on medical details or public policy issues, but targeted—incredibly—AIDS ac-tivists and AIDS patients. News editor Paul Lorch's macabre act of gaining plea-sure from the deaths of the men who had criticized his editorial judgment may mark the nadir in the history of the gay press.

The *San Francisco Sentinel* also rates harsh judgment. Also because of the double fear of losing ground in the gay rights battle and losing revenue from advertising, the newspaper appears to have deliberately misled its readers with front-page news stories and editorials, such as the items headlined "Most Tubs, Clubs Safe" and "Safe and Responsible Baths." The *Sentinel* also ridiculed AIDS research, fabricating "humorous" stories such as "Brunch Causes 'Gay Cancer.'"

The Advocate is the third publication deserving a place in the hall of shame. The era's wealthiest and most widely circulated gay voice—which in 1982 landed Absolut vodka as the first major national advertiser in the gay press—was best positioned to alert Gay America to the epidemic that was threatening to make gay men extinct. But by the early 1980s, David Goodstein was losing in-terest in publishing, while developing new passions. First came his obsession with the self-awareness fad EST. After founding a self-discovery workshop called the Advocate Experience and publishing a regular column about it, Goodstein insisted that his employees complete EST training. This demand conflicted with the independence journalists value; Sasha Gregory-Lewis's refusal to partici-pate, for example, led to her firing. Goodstein's other obsession was with building his own image. In 1983 the egomaniac hired a New York public relations firm to determine whether his connection with the gay press enhanced or detracted from his goal of becoming the national spokesman for all minorities. After interviewing gay and mainstream journalists, the firm concluded, "Not only were many journalists ignorant of David Goodstein, they evidenced no interest in finding out who he was." Both of Goodstein's obsessions became moot in June 1985 when he died of colon cancer.[105]

More important here than telling the stories of individual publications and documenting the frequent irresponsibility of the men who ran them is observing what early AIDS coverage—or lack of it—suggests about the evolution of the gay press. During the early 1980s, the three major gay newspapers in the capital of Gay America failed to alert their readers that a deadly disease was stalking them. The failure of these publications to lead a journalistic battle against AIDS suggests that at least one visible segment of gay journalism was no longer serving its readers, as the genre had for forty years. For the first time, the problematic relationship between advertising and editorial content had slid down the slippery slope to the point where financial gain appeared to be replacing the well-being of readers—at least for some publications—as the driving force behind the gay press.

λ 10

Raging Against the Status Quo

By 1985 many of the country's leading institutions were supporting the virulent antigay backlash that AIDS and AIDS hysteria had spawned. The legal system responded to gay bashings with the mildest possible sentences. State legislatures in Colorado, Indiana, Minnesota, and Texas all considered proposals to quarantine AIDS patients. The armed forces ferreted lesbians and gay men out of their ranks at the rate of a thousand a year.

In the biggest setback of the era, the U.S. Supreme Court ruled in 1986 that states have the constitutional right to outlaw sex acts between consenting adults, even when they are conducted in the privacy of one's own bedroom. The ruling came after Georgia police entered the home of Michael Hardwick to serve a warrant for a minor traffic violation and found him engaging in fellatio with another man. When the Supreme Court upheld Hardwick's conviction, the message was clear: Gay people broke the law every time they had sex—and not even their bedrooms guaranteed them privacy. In fact, the legal system had turned firmly against privacy for straights as well as gays.

Meanwhile, as AIDS patients were systematically fired from their jobs and evicted from their homes, President Reagan refused even to utter the word *AIDS* in public. Watergate reporter Bob Woodward captured the political tone of the era vis-à-vis gay people when he reported a conversation that took place during a meeting of the National Security Council. When the council began brainstorming about what action to take against Libyan leader Moammar Gadhafi, according to Woodward's front-page story in the *Washington Post,* Reagan joked about Gadhafi's fondness for wearing flamboyant clothes, saying: "Why not invite Gadhafi to San Francisco? He likes to dress up so much." With AIDS having already killed thousands of Americans, the punch line Secretary of State George P. Schultz then delivered was grotesque. Schultz quipped, "Why don't we give him AIDS!" The officials in the meeting rolled with laughter.[1]

Gay people were not laughing. Such blatant inhumanity combined with the administration's tepid response to AIDS, the soaring antigay violence, and stalled efforts to enact gay rights legislation transformed lesbian and gay activists into pit bulls. Fed up and fired up, the angry women and men picketed, protested, held "sit-ins" and "die-ins," and pushed their grievances into the faces of American society as never before. Committed to direct political action, the activists sought—and achieved—visibility as they willingly broke the law, even if it meant going to jail, in order to release their fury and shatter the status quo. An *Advocate* editorial shrieked, "The Time for Gay Rage Is Now!"[2]

The new militancy exploded into hand-to-hand combat. ACT UP dramatized the need for more AIDS research and better care for AIDS patients. In a series of kamikaze missions reminiscent of the "zaps" that *GAY* had highlighted during the early 1970s, ACT UP radicals halted rush-hour traffic in New York's financial district and on San Francisco's Golden Gate Bridge, disrupted trading on the New York Stock Exchange, and organized hundreds of other protests to lift gay dissidence to an unprecedented level.

A second group of radicals communicated their defiance simply in naming themselves: Queer Nation. In their first major action, 500 activists marched in Greenwich Village to protest a pipe-bomb attack on a local gay bar. Two months later, the ranks had grown to 1,000 when Queer Nation marched through Manhattan to protest the rising number of hate crimes. Local branches of ACT UP and Queer Nation sprouted in sixty cities, as did independent groups such as OUT! in Washington, CRY OUT! in Pittsburgh, and Queers Action Committee in Milwaukee.

The most massive protest came in October 1987, when half a million people marched on Washington in the largest gay rights demonstration in history. On the same weekend, 600 demonstrators were arrested during a protest of the Supreme Court's anti-privacy ruling. After President Bush had waited until he had been in office more than a year before making his first speech about AIDS, National Gay and Lesbian Task Force Director Urvashi Vaid disrupted his speech by yelling, "We need more than one speech every fourteen months!" Police quickly removed Vaid from the auditorium.

The lesbian and gay press helped lead the eruption of rage against the status quo. *OutWeek* set palpably into print the same message that ACT UP cried from the street: "No more!" The pugnacious weekly did not merely promote the new radicalism, but it made news of its own: *OutWeek* was at the center of the phenomenon of outing. By revealing the homosexuality of closeted men and women in positions of power and prominence, the magazine sought to shake the country into action. Columnist Michelangelo Signorile wrote, "Something big has happened—something from which there is no turning back."[3]

Outing was not the only white-hot issue of the late 1980s. With more than 100,000 Americans—90 percent of them gay men—dead from AIDS by the end of the decade, the epidemic remained pervasive. Along with radicalized lesbian and gay journalism demanding more AIDS research and treatment, it took the offensive on hate crimes, provided a venue for lesbian erotica, and helped redefine the American family. *Gay Community News,* as part of its steady flow of thoughtful political analysis, argued that AIDS and the Hardwick decision left gay people no choice but to become radicals: "The rights we have taken for granted are being questioned by people who would rather we not exist. As long as we remain the invisible minority, the rest of the world will continue to think of us as a small, unorganized group best handled by slow asphyxiation."[4]

Because of the onslaught of challenges, gay people closed ranks. Reflecting this evolution, more publications than ever before straddled the gender line to speak for women as well as men. *OutWeek* in New York and *Gay Community News* in Boston, the most high-profile publications of the era, both were committed to raising the voices of lesbians to a decibel level fully equal to that of gay men. On the West Coast, a Los Angeles weekly that carried the deceptively moderate-sounding name *The News* joined the trend as well.

Among publications that spoke primarily to lesbians, the most notable were magazines celebrating explicit sexual content. *On Our Backs* and *Yoni* on the West Coast and *Bad Attitude* on the East Coast published eye-popping lesbian erotica reminiscent of the gay male images that had filled men's publications a decade earlier. Other important voices included *Lesbian Contradiction* in San Francisco and Seattle, which carried the telling subtitle *Journal of Irreverent Feminism,* and *Hag Rag* in Milwaukee, with the equally descriptive subtitle *New Rage Thinking.* These newcomers joined *Lesbian Ethics* in Los Angeles in expressing Lesbian America's refusal to accept a static social order.

Gay male publications tended to be more moderate in their efforts to change society. The *New York Native* continued to focus on the medical aspects of AIDS but became so erratic in its coverage that new publications, such as Chicago's *Windy City Times* and Houston's *Montrose Voice,* became far more credible sources of information. In 1986 the Houston paper broke new ground by becoming the first gay or lesbian publication in history to appear on a daily basis.

By the end of the decade, the number of publications being produced in the United States, according to *Our Own Voices,* had surpassed 800. A huge number of them continued to be internal newsletters produced by gay people who had organized clubs and associations around shared hobbies or interests; dozens more were newsletters created by people who had tested HIV positive and who wanted to spread information about experimental treatments. Although *The*

Advocate's 80,000 circulation meant that it remained the largest gay publication in the country, that figure had not grown for a full decade; under an arrogant new publisher, Orange County businessman Niles Merton, *The Advocate* became a gay *People* magazine, and making profits remained its driving mission. *Gay Community News*, at the forefront of radicalizing the gay and lesbian press, jumped to a national circulation of 60,000. By the end of the decade, the lesbian and gay press broke the seven-digit mark with a total circulation of more than 1 million.[5]

OutWeek Sets a Radical Pace

Sex had always played a major role in gay life, and no mere pandemic was going to prevent creative gay men from finding ways to express their libidos. As sex in the bath houses faded from the landscape, phone sex ascended. Reaching a sexual climax by talking to another man on the telephone involved the exchange of words, not bodily fluids. By the mid-1980s, gay newspapers were bulging with steamy full-page ads showing men panting with lust as they talked on "976-DICK" and "976-HUNK" phone lines. In June 1989 one of the most successful entrepreneurs, Kendall Morrison, used his phone-sex profits—which totaled at least $4 million—to found a national lesbian and gay news magazine. *Out-Week* debuted in New York exactly twenty years to the week after the Stonewall Rebellion. Indeed, Morrison transformed a Gay Liberation Front poster from 1969 into his first cover.[6]

News filled the front half of the eighty-page magazine that was printed on eight-and-a-half-by-eleven-inch newsprint but carried a glossy four-color cover. *OutWeek* lived up to its co-gender philosophy by maintaining a firm policy of depicting women on at least every third cover, even though sales were consistently less for those issues.

OutWeek concentrated most of its outrage in columns and on the editorial page, which carried the apt title "Outspoken." Targets included the pharmaceutical industry, for gouging AIDS patients with inflated drug prices, and a long list of establishment institutions—Congress, the advertising industry, the White House, police, churches—for supporting or tolerating mistreatment of gay people. *OutWeek* did not confine its rage to heterosexual society, as it also blasted lesbians and gay men for numerous wrongs, including attempts to shunt drag queens and butch lesbians to the edge of the movement.[7]

The volatile magazine's enthusiasm for controversy extended to criticism of the movement press. When the *Washington Blade* reported that ACT UP's disruption of a speech by Health and Human Services Secretary Louis Sullivan

"Outing" exploded into national headlines after OutWeek *magazine exposed the homosexuality of millionaire publishing tycoon Malcolm Forbes in 1990.*

may have done more harm than good, ACT UP demonstrated against the *Blade. OutWeek* loved it. The magazine turned the event into its lead story, savoring every detail of how *Blade* publisher Don Michaels had called the police to remove the activists—Michaels castigated them as "Nazi brownshirts"— from his office and how *Blade* editor Lisa Keen ultimately had backpedaled on her story about the Sullivan speech, admitting, "The story was not perfect."[8]

OutWeek threw a much bigger hand grenade at the gay press when it criticized publications such as *The Advocate* and *New York Native* for advertising gay porn videos that placed the stars of the videos in harm's way. Porn videos had soared in popularity because of AIDS, as they offered viewers a safe sexual outlet. Making the videos placed the performers in grave danger, however, as the men acted out sexual fantasies for viewers by casually participating in anal intercourse, oral sex, and rimming with a variety of partners without condoms. Video producers largely avoided condoms for fear they would reduce the erotic impact. Even as the list of stars struck down by AIDS grew longer—Val Martin, J. W. King, Bob Shane, Casey Donovan, John Holmes, Johnny Dawes—the gay press remained thunderously silent on the situation, not only ignoring the issue but also running ads for the videos. Not so *OutWeek*. Publications should not only stop advertising videos that do not use condoms, *OutWeek* argued, but they should also raise the issue through editorials and news stories, thereby pressuring the industry to incorporate safer sex measures. *OutWeek*'s fundamental question: "Is a press purporting to serve its community acting responsibly when it fails to expose and campaign against practices that are killing the sexual icons that same community reveres?"[9]

Staff members at the mercurial *OutWeek* did not find their own publication perfect either. The two dozen full-time employees, as well as the stable of freelancers, grew displeased with how poorly the magazine was managed, particularly with its spotty record regarding payment. Donna Minkowitz, who also wrote for the *Village Voice*, lambasted *OutWeek* for not paying her or other writers. She wrote in *The Advocate*, "*OutWeek* is known for nonpayment, low payment, and refusing to make up its mind about submissions."[10]

The management problems evolved from Morrison and his editor, Gabriel Rotello, coming to the magazine as activists—Morrison was HIV positive; Rotello had lost a lover to AIDS—rather than from business backgrounds. So Morrison entered into a partnership with three men, led by Florida real estate investor Steven Polakoff, who managed the magazine in exchange for stock in Morrison's phone-sex company. Although Morrison was perfectly willing to pay *OutWeek*'s weekly losses of $10,000 to $15,000, his business partners were more interested in pouring the phone-sex profits back into that business than in raising a militant voice through an unprofitable magazine. Those partners ultimately maneuvered their way into full control. Morrison later recalled: "I did what they said. They were my lawyers." The publisher admitted he was naive and inept at business: "Sometimes they sent me a stack of just the back pages of agreements, not the actual agreements. And I'd sign. I was really stupid."[11]

Although the outing phenomenon brought *OutWeek* enormous media coverage, it did not attract a comparable number of readers or advertisers. The magazine's circulation never exceeded thirty thousand and its efforts to attract mainstream advertisers failed miserably. Most companies had no interest in promoting their products in a publication committed to radicalism. Kit Winter, whose job it was to sell ads for the magazine, called outing "a torpedo" when it came to selling ads. Winter said bluntly, "The business community was outraged."[12]

OutWeek was not an all-news publication. In keeping with the New York journalism tradition established by *GAY* in the late 1960s and continued by *Gaysweek* in the 1970s, the new kid on the block amused while it informed. *OutWeek's* arts section was edited by Sarah Pettit. During her undergraduate days at Yale, the talented young woman had led the school's lesbian and gay student organization and was instrumental in expanding the university's antidiscrimination policy to include sexual orientation. Through *OutWeek,* she hoped to attract readers to the movement: "For many people, the connection between their lives and these publications has remained nebulous." To change that, Pettit created an arts section filled with film, theater, and opera reviews, as well as descriptions of the entertainers performing in bars and cabarets.[13]

The magazine's "Dykes to Watch Out For" cartoon strip quickly became a popular feature. Indeed, the insightful wit and intellect of cartoonist Alison Bechdel ultimately were to endure far longer than the publication itself. Bechdel blended lesbian satire with serious discussion of important issues to create a comic strip that could have been required reading for Lesbianism 101. "Comics have great power for good or evil," she said. "They get absorbed directly into your bloodstream." The premier edition of Bechdel's strip in 1989 introduced a "domestically challenged" woman who tried to turn leftover lasagna into soup and a stridently radical woman whose given name was Phyllis but who insisted on being called "Milkweed Moongarden." While making readers smile, that first cartoon simultaneously encouraged lesbians to unite with each other to fight back against antigay violence.[14]

Terms such as *dyke, queer, fag,* and *lezzie* were commonplace in the magazine, as the editors fully endorsed gay people defiantly appropriating terms of antigay oppression and giving them positive meanings. *OutWeek* spoke in other colorful words as well, particularly in the personal columns that became its signature. When Signorile became enraged at *New York Daily News* gossip columnist Liz Smith drooling over jet-setting New Yorkers, he exclaimed: "Fuck you, Liz! Fuck you! Fuck you! Fuck you! Fuck you!"[15]

Outing Rages Through the Closet

After Michelangelo Signorile earned his journalism degree from Syracuse University, he worked for a Manhattan press agent. His specific job was to feed tidbits of scandal to gossip columnists. In exchange for the juicy items, the columnists published favorable comments about the clients who paid Signorile's boss to keep them in the public eye. After two years, Signorile grew angry with the incestuous arrangement, later saying, "The whole system was totally corrupt, like the media in general."[16]

So he quit. Signorile then began earning his livelihood by freelancing for *People* and *Women's Wear Daily*, while also joining ACT UP and helping found Queer Nation. When *OutWeek* appeared, Signorile became features editor and wrote a weekly column. "Gossip Watch" chatted about New York and Hollywood celebrities, with an emphasis on attacking the media elite for failing to place AIDS on the national agenda.

Outing burst into the national news spotlight in August 1989 when *OutWeek* published a provocative item on the page opposite "Gossip Watch." Under the ambiguous headline "Peek-A-Boo," the item listed—without comment—the names of sixty-six men and women. The names had long been bantered about in gay and lesbian gossip circles but had never before appeared in print. Illinois Governor Jim Thompson and superstar Michael Jackson led the list, followed by such "notables" as singer Whitney Houston, actors Tony Randall and John Travolta, and political figures Ronald Reagan Jr. and New York Mayor Ed Koch. A month later, a second "Peek-A-Boo" listed thirty-two more names, including Senator Barbara Mikulski and Governor William Donald Schaefer, both of Maryland.[17]

Although the "Peek-A-Boo" label was ambiguous, there was no equivocation five months later when Signorile outed Malcolm Forbes, the millionaire publishing tycoon who had died three weeks earlier. *OutWeek's* cover showed the flamboyant Forbes wearing a leather jacket and sitting astride his purple Harley-Davidson. Inside, Signorile quoted a score of waiters, chauffeurs, and *Forbes* magazine staff members who had allowed Forbes to caress and perform oral sex on them in return for one-hundred-dollar bills. Signorile also blasted gossip columnists for portraying Forbes as actress Elizabeth Taylor's lover.[18]

On the editorial page of that fateful issue, *OutWeek* said it exposed Forbes's sexual orientation to dramatize that prominent gay people should no longer hide in the closet: "The fears of social and professional catastrophe that motivated people like Malcolm Forbes to remain hidden may have been well-founded in 1950 or 1970; they're wildly exaggerated in 1990." The editorial then spoke directly to gay youths. "There are thousands of invisible paragons you aren't allowed to know. There are lesbian movie stars and gay sports stars and famous gay writers and famous lesbian singers and gay scientists and lesbian poets and gay politicians and lesbian and gay geniuses. And for your futures we claim them all."[19]

The Forbes article catapulted *OutWeek* into the national news spotlight. *Newsweek* reproduced the Forbes cover, *Time* coined the term *outing*, and Signorile was quoted and requoted in a blizzard of stories in the *New York Times, Washington Post, Time, Boston Globe, Philadelphia Inquirer, Chicago Tribune, Los Angeles Times,* and *San Francisco Chronicle.* The publications shook their self-righteous fingers at the concept of outing.[20]

In response to the blistering attacks, Signorile argued that the closet was destructive rather than protective. Concealing a person's homosexuality was tantamount, he said, to indicting all lesbians and gay men as sexual deviants. He wrote: "When straight people's sex lives are written about, it's considered 'news' in every publication from *People* to *The New York Times.* But if gay people's sex lives are written about, it's an 'infringement of privacy.' Well, I call it homophobia. When we say that our sex lives are 'private,' we immediately are opining that homosex is disgusting, vulgar and distasteful." Lesbian and gay journalists, Signorile insisted, not only have the right to make other gay people's sexuality public, but are *obligated* to. Not outing a person, he argued, meant acknowledging that homosexuality is an abomination. He wrote, "We must sensitize society, NOW."[21]

Most gay and lesbian journalists did not agree. When the managing editor of the *San Francisco Sentinel* outed the city's superintendent of schools, publisher Ray Chalker fired her. *Washington Blade* editor Lisa Keen denounced outing, saying, "Privacy is supreme." Randy Shilts, after initially supporting outing, ultimately denounced it as well, stating: "It's doubly hypocritical to seek the right to privacy in courts and then wantonly violate others' rights to privacy in the gay press. . . . It's a dirty business that hurts people."[22]

Despite such criticism, Signorile continued to live up to the sobriquet the mainstream press bestowed upon him: "Mr. Out." He dynamited columnists Liz Smith of the *New York Daily News* and James Revson of *Newsday* out of their respective closets, and then did the same with Barry Diller, the head of Twentieth Century-Fox, and Merv Griffin, the talk show host and entertainment mogul. Signorile thrived on the controversy, gloating: "EVERY bigtime queer actor and actress in Hollywood is petrified—as in *scared shitless*—of *OutWeek,* of this column, of *moi.*" But Signorile was not all narcissism. He continued: "Instead of sitting around cowering, these pea brains could all come out, stand proud and do the right thing for humanity. These people are selfish sewer rats, pursuing their own gluttonous needs, lying around in the sun and waiting for another million-dollar check, while their own friends die."[23]

By August Signorile had become so identified with outing that the country's leading news organizations turned to him when they suspected President Bush's nominee to the U.S. Supreme Court, David Souter, of being gay. The *New York Times, Washington Post,* and *NBC Nightly News* all asked Signorile if he was going to out Souter. With the bravura that was becoming commonplace in Gay America, the columnist screamed: "What could be next?! Would I soon look up from my desk to find Tom Brokaw offering me a blow job in exchange for the right info?"[24]

Such comments fueled Signorile's campaign. After *Silence of the Lambs* opened to huge audiences and rave reviews, "Mr. Out" exploded. While the vast majority of serial killers are straight, Signorile wrote, Oscar-winning actress Jodie Foster and the other persons involved in the film chose to portray a psychopathic killer as gay. Signorile set his sights on Foster, who had long been rumored to be a lesbian: "Jodie Foster, TIME'S UP! If lesbianism is too sacred, too private, too infringing of your damned rights for you to discuss publicly, then the least you can fucking do is refrain from making movies that insult this community!"[25]

Greed Triumphs

Like so many lesbian and gay publications before it, *OutWeek* died from fractious infighting. Founder Kendall Morrison wanted to raise a radical voice; the businessmen who managed the magazine's financial affairs knew their profits would be much larger if all energy was committed to the phone-sex side of the business. In the end, greed triumphed. When AIDS forced Morrison into the hospital in July 1991, his partners locked the front door, and staff members lifted the fax machine and computers in lieu of the final paychecks they knew would never come.[26]

In his colorful style, AIDS activist Larry Kramer cut to the chase when he said: "It was killed by these assholes who thought more of their own greedy needs than of this precious child they'd brought into the world. Instead of acting like respectable businessmen, they all became vicious queens." The death of the whirling dervish in July 1991 placed yet another granite marker in the crowded graveyard of the New York gay press.[27]

OutWeek arts editor Sarah Pettit, whose contributions to the lesbian and gay press would soon continue through a new magazine, cast the demise in more theoretical terms: "The real lesson in *OutWeek* is what happened when you got this diverse network of gay and lesbian viewpoints, most of them pretty volatile, and placed that within a traditional magazine hierarchy. You're forcing into a capitalist framework ideals that are by nature its exact opposite." This time, as often had occurred in the past, avarice defeated activism.[28]

The phenomenon that had become *OutWeek*'s cause celebre ultimately lived longer than the journalistic pit bull itself. When conflict in the Persian Gulf began placing Pentagon spokesman Pete Williams on television news night after night, Signorile began investigating rumors that Williams is gay. By the time the columnist was prepared to out him, however, *OutWeek* had ceased publication. Signorile took his story to *The Advocate*. Although the magazine earlier had criticized the outing phenomenon, it eagerly covered eleven pages with the latest revelation. Signorile's article relied on interviews with men who had slept with Williams and others who had socialized with him at Washington's gay watering holes. Signorile also quoted Massachusetts Democrats Barney Frank and Gerry Studds, the two openly gay men in Congress, to establish that Williams was not merely a mouthpiece but also a Pentagon and White House policy adviser.[29]

Signorile framed the dramatic outing in the context of the federal government's relentless effort to purge the military of lesbians and gay men. That the Defense Department had spent millions of taxpayer dollars collecting details on the sex lives of military personnel at the same time that a major defense policymaker was gay created exactly the kind of supreme irony Signorile abhorred.

Promoting Radicalism

In the late 1980s, an increasing number of Americans began to think of lesbians and gay men as angry activists shrieking at the top of their lungs: "We're here! We're queer! Get used to it!" For much of the community had become radicalized, raging against a system that continued to deny gay people equal rights. And the movement press fully supported the radical shift.

The headlines in *OutWeek* changed each week, but they consistently communicated the frustration and scorn that boiled in much of Lesbian and Gay America. Week 1: "Activists Seize . . ." Week 2: "Activists Denounce . . ." Week 3: "Riot Erupts . . ." Week 4: "Activists Clash . . ." The magazine further communicated the intensity of that fury with commentary pieces carrying headlines such as "How to Fuck the Patriarchy" and photos of protesters burning the American flag.[30]

Immediately behind *OutWeek* in promoting radicalism stood *Gay Community News*. Defying the establishment was not a new role for the Boston weekly, as a leftist philosophy had been its driving force since its founding fifteen years earlier. The *Washington Blade* said of *GCN*, "Its staff of writers and editors are the dedicated radicals of the Gay and lesbian feminist movement." *Gay Community News* differed from *OutWeek,* however, in the breadth of its radicalism. While the New York magazine focused exclusively on gay and lesbian issues, *GCN* embraced a wider agenda. Whether Bostonians took to the streets to protest apartheid, racism, or threats to a woman's right to have an abortion, *GCN* highlighted the event on the front page—each time including an estimate of how many gay people had joined the march.[31]

Lesbian Contradiction, with dual bases in San Francisco and Seattle, adopted a broad agenda as well. To illustrate an article about the impact of AIDS on lesbians, the radical paper ran a photo of protesters carrying signs with messages reading "NO to AIDS Hysteria," and "NO to Increasing Anti-Gay Attacks." While the women carried the signs, wire coat hangers—the symbols of abortion rights advocates—dangled from their collars and belts.[32]

Hag Rag in Milwaukee wore its radicalism on its sleeve by titling the column of news briefs appearing in each issue "Read It and Revolt!" The directive seemed entirely appropriate for items that told of skinheads in San Diego raping a lesbian, and gay leaders in Houston instructing women not to wear visible bras or panties to the city's annual pride parade—an item prompting *Hag Rag* to scream: "A Fucking Dress Code!"[33]

Lesbian Ethics also advocated revolutionary acts. The editor created a section titled "Guerrilla Feminism." Items described lesbians throwing rocks through store windows and spray-painting storefronts with angry words such as "Dead Men Don't Rape." The Los Angeles magazine encouraged terrorism by publishing lists of pointers for lesbians who were novices at committing covert acts. One list gave practical advice to women wielding cans of spray paint: "Wear gloves or paint your finger tips with clear polish" and "The inside of plastic/latex gloves is a prime spot for finger prints, so never leave gloves at the site." Other advice was more broad: "Never admit to anything, no matter what you're caught with or what they (cops, etc.) say to you. They lie." Still other items were clearly designed to give readers a final nudge toward warfare: "It's not as scary as it seems."[34]

The conventional name and appearance of a Los Angeles publication belied its underlying radical nature. *The News* looked like an establishment news organ, with the top of the front page carrying a drawing of a stately lion holding a heraldic shield and depicting the name of the paper in an Old English typeface. News content, however, championed open defiance of the social order. When activists crashed a $1,000-a-ticket cocktail party at a mansion in tony Bel Air, the *Los Angeles Times* did not so much as whisper that the protest had taken place, even though the Secret Service had to call in local police reinforcements to protect then–Vice President Bush. *The News,* on the other hand, blanketed the top half of page one with a photo of protesters carrying signs that read: "Republicans Get AIDS Too." Publisher Sandy Dwyer crafted a lead predicated on the belief that the government had not responded adequately to AIDS. Her story began, "Concerned that the battle against AIDS will continue to be inadequately addressed by the federal government, ACT UP/LA demonstrated June 5."[35]

Regarding specific targets of the radicalized press, the government's half-hearted response to AIDS received the most venom. *OutWeek*'s first issue carried a full-page article portraying ACT UP's takeover of an AIDS conference in Montreal as a strategic triumph of heroic proportions. The lead read: "More than 300 members of ACT UP/New York commandeered the escalators, took over the stage, demanded that the microphones be turned on. Montreal and Royal Canadian Mounted Police seemed unprepared for the rowdy, U.S.-style activism, and took no action." The magazine further celebrated the radical act with photos showing protesters screaming and raising clenched fists. The most prominent message on the placards: "Silence = Death."[36]

Later issues continued to highlight militant activities in an effort to speed and strengthen the country's response to AIDS. When members of ACT UP chained themselves to the front door of a Chicago hospital, *OutWeek* published a full-page article explaining that the activists wanted Astra Pharmaceuticals to release an experimental treatment for the retinitis that causes blindness in AIDS patients. The magazine found room for a photo of protesters holding signs reading "Queers Against Profiteers," but the *Chicago Tribune* did not so much as mention the protest. Similarly, when activists blocked the door to the District of Columbia's main governmental office building to protest District officials failing to spend half the money set aside for AIDS programs, *OutWeek* ran a two-page story and a photo of a lesbian activist being arrested. *OutWeek*'s story pointed out that the officers who arrested the protesters were wearing rubber gloves, but the *Washington Post*'s brief item about the protest had no room for such detail.[37]

The Supreme Court decision in the Hardwick case was a second target of journalistic fury. *Gay Community News* kept the decision on the minds of its readers by covering annual demonstrations against the decision. Even though a paltry forty activists turned out for the 1987 protest in front of the U.S. Supreme Court Building, *GCN* devoted forty-two column inches to the event. Coverage included a two-column photo of picketers and their clever messages, including a T-shirt that read "I Violate Section 553-4 of Maryland's Annotated Code. Safely. And Extremely Well."[38]

Mainstream media were a third consistent butt of gay press invectives. When *Cosmopolitan* advised readers that so few women had been infected by the AIDS virus that they should "not bother" using condoms, *Gay Community News* denounced the magazine. When New York Mayor David Dinkins repeatedly referred to lesbians and gay men in an impassioned speech about the rise of hate crimes but the *New York Times* omitted all references to gay people in its coverage of the speech, *OutWeek* condemned the nation's leading newspaper as "insensitive" and "homophobic." When NBC announced it would broadcast a film about a bisexual man with AIDS who intentionally infected women, the *New York Native* shrieked in protest.[39]

The lesbian and gay press also covered the brouhaha over Robert Mapplethorpe's photography, which evolved after conservative members of Congress denounced the National Endowment for the Arts for supporting projects they deemed offensive. At the center of the debate were Mapplethorpe's homoerotic images with overtones of sadomasochism. When Washington's Corcoran Gallery of Art canceled a Mapplethorpe retrospective, activists donned pig masks and paraded in front of the gallery carrying signs reading "Jesse Helms Is a Pig." *OutWeek* was there to record the protest. Coverage highlighted the demonstrations, which included projecting Mapplethorpe's photos on an exterior wall of the Corcoran.[40]

Searching for the Root of the Pandemic

Although gay people had many reasons for raging against the status quo, none compared with the government's inadequate response to the deadly disease that continued to ravage the community. Unfortunately, in one of the many vicissitudes that have defined the history of the gay press, the publication that initially had distinguished itself for identifying and tracking the rise of AIDS had, by the mid-1980s, veered off in a direction that can only be described as bizarre. The *New York Native*'s AIDS coverage became the ravings of a mad man rather than the protests of an angry one.

Dr. Lawrence Mass's pioneering coverage of the medical aspects of the pandemic had collapsed by mid-decade. A sensitive man who became overwhelmed by the human devastation of the disease combined with the complexities of his personal life, Mass suffered from anxiety and exhaustion that became so severe he had to be hospitalized for depression.[41]

Native publisher Charles Ortleb, whose lack of medical knowledge was outweighed by his abundance of ego, then assumed responsibility for reporting on the disease. Ortleb's worldview had been shaped by his experiences as a college student in the turbulent 1960s and as a gay man in the reactionary 1980s—so he did not trust government. Indeed, Ortleb was convinced that the country's leading health officials were intentionally murdering gay men. Although Ortleb was correct in believing that AIDS was not the top priority among health officials that their public pronouncements claimed, his paranoia moved the *Native*'s AIDS coverage from probing to provocative to preposterous. Mass recently recalled: "Chuck has to be given credit for seeing the seriousness and importance of this epidemic in its early stages. But it's downhill from there. He was very attracted to the idea that the epidemic was some kind of big political plot—like chemical or biological warfare—by the government. Chuck became fanatical, irrational, psychotic."[42]

By 1985 the *Native* was insisting that AIDS was not caused by the human immunodeficiency virus, even though the world medical community had been focusing almost exclusively on HIV for a year. In fact, Ortleb rejected the entire premise that AIDS was a disease at all. He placed quotation marks around the terms *AIDS* and *AIDS virus* as a gesture of derision. In keeping with his distrust of the government, he also downplayed all government-approved AIDS treatments. Ortleb referred to the most widely used of the drugs, AZT, as "Draino" and a "government-approved killer." When city officials made AZT available to prisoners who had tested HIV positive, Ortleb translated the action into sensationalism with a huge front-page headline: "City Planning to Poison Prisoners."[43]

Ortleb focused on trying to prove a relationship between AIDS and the African swine fever virus, which mainly attacks pigs. While both diseases destroy the same cells in the immune system, the vast majority of scientists had determined, by 1985, that the two diseases were not related. By that time, scientists in the United States, Belgium, and the Netherlands all had searched for a connection but had concluded that further study of the topic would waste valuable time that could be devoted to pursuing more productive leads. Not Ortleb. The erratic publisher pummeled his readers with front-page articles such as, "Is African Swine Fever Virus the Cause?" and "Antibodies to African Swine Fever Virus Found in City's Blood Bank."[44]

Ortleb's second obsession was with government conspiracy. In a series carrying the eye-popping title "AIDSGATE: The Medical Scandal of the Century," he accused the government and medical community of plotting genocide against gay men, arguing that every straight scientist was driven by homophobia. In particular, he attacked National Institutes of Health official Dr. Robert Gallo, the country's leading AIDS researcher. In a rabid campaign of character assassination, Ortleb described Gallo as a demonic creature who was "fraudulent," "vindictive," "arrogant," "anti-gay," "xenophobic," and "racist."[45]

While Ortleb doubted government authorities, he firmly believed in himself. Indeed, he became so convinced that he had turned the *Native* into a jour-nalistic legend that he became the first publisher to nominate a lesbian or gay newspaper for a Pulitzer Prize. Although the *Native* did not win, Ortleb had a trophy he displayed as others might a Great Northern pike. Ortleb's bounty, which he proudly mounted on his office wall, was the postcard Pulitzer officials had sent him to acknowledge that his entry had, indeed, been received.[46]

Ortleb also employed gay camp. To illustrate his feelings toward the coun-try's best-known scientist researching AIDS, the eccentric publisher covered one front page with a huge image of the flamboyant Latin dancer Carmen Miranda—complete with ruffles, bare midriff, and dangling earrings—but with her face cut out and replaced with Gallo's.[47]

Such sophomoric pranks were one of the forces that motivated Kendall Morrison to found *OutWeek*. His first editorial spoke specifically of the *Native*'s "editorial bias concerning the cause of AIDS. Its unwillingness to print health news which conflicts with that bias has often resulted in slanted, inaccurate articles." Larry Kramer picked up the bayonet. He attempted to change the *Native*'s approach to AIDS reporting by writing an open letter. In the letter, published in *OutWeek*, Kramer told Ortleb: "You have squandered the good will so many of us once felt for you. . . . I want the *Native* that now comes out each week to disappear. I want the old *Native* back."[48]

The bizarre notions the *Native* showcased, combined with the criticisms in *OutWeek*, propelled ACT UP to launch a boycott against the *Native*. The protests did not, however, seem to have any impact on Ortleb's idiosyncratic behavior. During a panel discussion, when a man with AIDS charged that the *Native*'s ir-responsible reporting was killing people, the publisher responded with neither compassion nor grace, replying with the snide comment, "Maybe you'd just better start your own paper."[49]

Ironically, the *Native*'s circulation did not plummet but actually increased during this period, rising from 20,000 to 25,000 between 1985 and 1989. In ad-dition, the tabloid continued to attract not only new readers but also more ad-vertisers. In the same time period, it jumped in size from a forty-page biweekly to a seventy-two-page weekly. Lawrence Mass, who has lived in Manhattan for fifteen years, said that gay New Yorkers were far too sophisticated to believe Ortleb's bizarre medical and conspiracy theories: "By the second half of the decade, we knew better than to take the *Native*'s ravings seriously. We saw its AIDS coverage as a joke—a very bad one." But readers saw much more merit in the paper's cultural coverage. For the *Native* clearly had its finger on the pulse of gay New York. "If you were gay and you lived in New York, you had to read it to know what was going on," Mass said. "It provided the best entertainment news in town. So we laughed at the AIDS 'news' and absorbed the extensive cultural material."[50]

Taming of the Scourge

Fortunately, as the *Native* sacrificed its position as the country's leading source of AIDS information on the altar of Ortleb's oversized ego and irrational obsessions, other publications stepped forward to fill the gap. Gay newspapers generally accepted the medical community's explanation for the cause of AIDS and focused their energies on telling healthy readers how to avoid the disease and infected ones how to improve the quality of their lives.

In their information about how the disease was spread, gay publications—unlike mainstream ones—spoke in the sexual terms that had to be used if this modern-day scourge was to be slowed. While mainstream publications still debated whether it was too risqué to use such vague terms as "bodily fluids," *OutWeek* was writing in straightforward language that saved lives: "USE A CONDOM DURING ORAL SEX. If you don't, avoid placing the head of your partner's cock in your mouth. HIV-infected cum can enter your bloodstream through cuts, tears or ulcers in your mouth."[51]

Lesbian publications illuminated how lesbians could be at risk, even though the mainstream media ignored this threat. *Hag Rag* warned readers that sharing dildos or vibrators could spread AIDS, bluntly stating: "Blood, semen, and vaginal juices transmit the virus. Vaginal and anal fisting can draw blood, which may come in contact with hand sores, cuts and rashes." The magazine also pointed out that cunnilingus is dangerous during menstruation because menstrual blood frequently carries the AIDS virus.[52]

Gay men's publications devoted huge quantities of editorial space to helping readers treat the disease. *Montrose Voice* publisher Henry McClurg said at the time: "When you're a community newspaper like we are, you can't cover everything. So I leave the heavy-duty scientific reporting to the *New York Times* and *Newsweek*. I concentrate on helping guys here in Houston figure out how to stay alive to see another Christmas morning."[53]

McClurg and other gay journalists published material about a variety of alternative treatments. Their efforts played a singular role in helping readers because mainstream media waited until a drug trial was completed and the federal government approved a new medication before reporting on it. The gay press didn't wait. McClurg said: "If I don't talk about new drugs until they get through the federal bureaucracy, half my readers will be dead." The gay press labeled the drugs "experimental" and published all the details it could find.[54]

Typical was an article based on interviews with doctors at Northwestern University Medical School. While testing a drug developed to treat breast cancer, doctors noticed that the women who took the drug developed voracious appetites and, therefore, gained weight. Knowing that many AIDS patients suffer severe weight loss, the doctors gave the drug, megestrol acetate, to a dozen AIDS patients. Within two weeks, the article reported, the patients had regained an average of fourteen pounds. Megestrol acetate purchases in Houston soared—as did hope. Other articles in the *Voice* discussed such alternative treatments as typhoid immunization and penicillin injections. Also among the mix of articles overflowing the pages of the newspaper were those that simply gave the location of guerrilla treatment centers where people with AIDS would brew up their own remedies from makeshift supplies that government officials would never even consider approving.[55]

OutWeek's "AIDS Treatment News" column swelled larger each week. Many people infected with the virus literally committed their lives to investigating alternative treatments, often developing more expertise than their physicians. *OutWeek* responded with precise, highly technical information that read like a medical journal. One item began: "Fluconazole is a very good antifungal which is taken by mouth; it is effective for cryptococcal meningitis." The item went on to describe the cost and side effects of the drug and to compare it to other treatments of fungal disease. The author treated as incidental the fact that federal health officials had not approved the drug but ended the item with the phone number of the guerrilla treatment group that had provided the information— a not-so-subtle hint about how the reader might obtain the illegal drug.[56]

Gay Community News published safer-sex guidelines every week. The paper also created a weekly column written by people with AIDS and publicized the slew of newsletters that AIDS patients had developed to share information. One *GCN* feature profiled the 10,000-circulation *PWA Coalition Newsline* in New York, also listing the names and addresses of dozens of other newsletters that had emerged.[57]

Unfortunately, a medical crisis that creates desperate people also creates opportunists. So gay and lesbian publications assumed the responsibility of exposing such unpleasant truths as the fact that pharmacies charged as much as $3,000 for a one-month supply of AZT that had a wholesale price of $750. Other articles reported that some substances being promoted as safeguards against the virus were unsafe. *Gay Community News* stated, for example, that a particular sex lubricant was extremely dangerous, even though it was being advertised in the gay press. "Lubraseptic may kill HIV in a test tube," *GCN* said. "So do battery acid, Chlorox and household lye. But are any of them safe to use

in a vagina or rectum?" The lubricant contained a hazardous mercury compound that health officials had barred from spermicides, *GCN* reported, and if
the compound was not safe for the relatively nonabsorptive vagina, it certainly
could not be safe for the highly absorptive rectum.[58]

McClurg was so determined to keep up with treatment options that in
mid-1986 his *Montrose Voice* became the first lesbian or gay publication to subscribe to the United Press International wire service. In November of that year,
McClurg scored another first by transforming his weekly newspaper, which
circulated only in the Houston area, into a daily. It had taken gay and lesbian
journalism forty years to reduce the gap in its publication schedule from once
a month to thirty times a month. McClurg said: "Gay people have always had
visions of grandeur, and I'm no different. I just couldn't see how I could call
my publication a *news*paper without at least trying to provide my readers with
a daily source of news."[59]

With five full-time employees, having sufficient news content to fill a daily
paper was not a problem; having sufficient advertising was. "We've still got the
stigma of homosexuality, at least in Houston," McClurg said. "And because of
that, we're limited in the kinds of ads we can get." Half the *Voice*'s advertisements were from gay bars, while the rest promoted stores and other businesses
catering to gay people. McClurg had hoped that daily publication would entice
more advertisers, but he soon acknowledged that his foray into daily journalism was doomed. After only one week of publishing daily, McClurg cut back to
twice a week. After six more months, he reverted to weekly publication. Although the *Montrose Voice*'s time in the journalistic spotlight had been brief, it
still had made history. McClurg was not distressed: "It was like a premature
ejaculation. You wish it wasn't over so quick, but, well, it still felt pretty good."[60]

Waging the Lesbian Sex Wars

A decade after lesbian publications broke new social barriers by discussing lesbian sex, a new generation of assertive women of the late 1980s demanded that
the conversation be further expanded. Former *Ladder* editor Barbara Grier recalled: "We began to say, 'You know, we own businesses and live in male-free
households. We should be in charge of our sex lives, too. Go screw yourself.'" As
part of the expression of their rage against the status quo, several lesbian publications expanded coverage to include erotica. That expansion soon loosed a
maelstrom of debate among lesbians that wiped out all memory of the sense of
sisterhood that had permeated earlier phases in the history of the lesbian
press.[61]

This woman's bare skin and black leather outfit appearing on the premiere issue of On Our Backs *fired an opening salvo in the highly charged lesbian sex wars.* Courtesy of Bayla Travis, *On Our Backs.*

When *On Our Backs* hit the streets of San Francisco, readers immediately knew the magazine's title was a direct challenge to the politically correct voice of feminism, *Off Our Backs.* The opening headline of the slick *On Our Backs* brazenly proclaimed, "Year of the Lustful Lesbian!" Surrounded by photos of sensual beauties in various stages of undress, the editorial continued the sassy tone: "Yes, finally a sex magazine for lesbians! Lesbian sexuality is a vibrant and powerful aspect of our growth. It is as diverse and multi-flavored as all the parts of our lives."[62]

The founders of a second Bay Area erotic magazine chose the name *Yoni*, which means *vulva* in the Indian and Tibetan languages. The first article in the premier issue said that the staff was not entirely certain what lesbian erotica was, posing the rhetorical question "Is it sexuality, sensuality, or some sort of in-depth bonding?" Later in the piece, the staff responded to its own question with a statement that launched the publishing venture: "All we know for sure is that we want to know!"[63]

A third forum for lesbian erotica, *Bad Attitude,* placed the motivation for its founding in the context of lesbian liberation. Editor Cindy Patton, formerly of *Gay Community News,* pointed out that the leading lesbian activists of the 1970s had called themselves "woman-identified women," stressing the mind rather than the genitals. Patton continued: "With our tightly circled wagons of lesbian separatism, the Amazon army had won, but we didn't quite know what to do with our cunts and their special pleasures: they had spent too long with the enemy, and we didn't know how to re-educate them." Through the text of Patton's article as well as the accompanying photo of a woman masturbating, the Boston magazine clearly intended to play a role in that reeducation.[64]

Long-time *Advocate* columnist Pat Califia, sometimes dubbed "the high priestess of lesbian S&M," already had been educating lesbian as well as gay male readers through her advice column in which she responded to intimate questions about sex and relationships. She wrote: "I identify more strongly as a sadomasochist than as a lesbian. If I had a choice between being shipwrecked on a desert island with a vanilla lesbian and a hot male masochist, I'd pick the boy."[65]

The lesbian erotica magazines and Califia's column were polar opposites of *Off Our Backs* and many other feminist publications that scorned all pornography. According to this view, erotic films, magazines, and other materials exploited and degraded women. So these feminists believed that lesbian erotica perpetuated the same offenses, merely shifting the genders of the exploiters from men to women. They also argued that lesbian erotica imitated the dominant-submissive roles that had traditionally subjugated women. Rather than using those roles as models, anti-lesbian-erotica activists said, lesbians should develop new roles in which neither partner was dominant or submissive. They also repeated the anti-dildo arguments raised by some lesbian publications of the mid-1970s, saying that to use such devices suggested that women could not achieve sexual pleasure unless they simulated male body parts.

The most striking element in the trio of new lesbian sex magazines were the images. Dozens of photos showed women licking each other's clitorises and inserting hands into rectums, dildos into vaginas. Other photos showed women wearing handcuffs or otherwise participating in bondage. Ads showed women in chains and leather harnesses, as well as close-up photos of vulvas that had been pierced with metal rings.

Editorial content spanned fiction as well as nonfiction—all sharing a tone of defying traditional social and sexual boundaries. An autobiographical short story by Joan Nestle in the premier issue of *On Our Backs* described a sexual encounter with a handsome butch lesbian. Nestle wrote without shame or embarrassment: "I am wearing a long dress that hides my body, my body that I have hated so long for not being lean, hard, hated it for its flesh, thighs without muscles, large buttocks that want penetration by this woman's hand, her erotic acceptance that will free me from the crime of being a big assed woman." The story continued with not only a graphic description of the two women's lovemaking but also an argument that their actions represented a political statement.[66]

The magazines also contained selected news articles. The premier issue of *Yoni* contained a piece explaining a California ballot initiative to require all persons with AIDS to tell public health officials the names of their previous sex partners. The piece made no pretense of being objective, bluntly stating, "Proposition 64 is an attempt to erode the civil liberties and rights to privacy of all persons in California." A news items in *On Our Backs* reported that a new group called Lesbian Agenda for Action was focusing on decriminalizing sodomy and fighting the political battles surrounding AIDS.[67]

Most editorial content remained tightly focused on lesbian sexual themes. A feature in *Yoni* profiled a woman who created exotic dildos for women. The entrepreneur said: "People aren't as afraid of dildos now as they were during the 70's. All dildos then were penis-shaped. I wanted to offer women an alternative." A full-page photo of the woman showed her displaying silicone dildos shaped like dolphins, tongues, and corn cobs. The article also included the woman's reasoning on why lesbians should feel no embarrassment about using objects other than their own body parts to achieve sexual pleasure: "These things don't have a mind of their own, you know. They can go fast, slow—it's great! But it's your partner that makes them go."[68]

On Our Backs immediately dispensed with the question of whether lesbians should use human-made sex toys by creating a standing column titled "Toys For Us," playing off the name of the popular chain of children's toy stores. The column stated authoritatively: "Ladies, the discreet, complete and definitive information on dildos is this: penetration is as heterosexual as kissing! Fucking knows no gender." It continued: "We're beyond finding our clits now. So much lesbian sex education has focused on this—You part your lips, find your clit, and boom, you're liberated. The sex magazines are about what images turn you on, not what makes you feel safe."[69]

Bad Attitude staked out its position on dildos when Sue Hyde, an editor of *Gay Community News,* described how she and her lover created a customized harness that held two different dildos—a small one for anuses, a large one for vaginas. She said: "Dildos keep fucking for hours. They never go limp, they never get tired, they're not petulant, bratty or subject to anyone's whims or hard days at the 'orifice.'" Accompanying photos showed women thrusting their harnessed dildos into each other's anuses and vaginas.[70]

The dildo debate paled in comparison to the rhetorical attacks from women who opposed lesbian erotica. *Gay Community News* synthesized the arguments: "Some women maintain that women who enjoy porn, have non-relational sex, do kinky sex or s/m have adopted male-identified behaviors and values. According to this theory, such women exploit other women, objectify other women. They don't have egalitarian relationships, they are hedonistic and callow, and they commit violence or promote violence against other women." But the straightforward summary belied the passion with which many lesbians approached the topic. A second *GCN* article came closer to capturing the intensity when it pointed out that the anti-lesbian-erotica arguments touched the same emotions as those aroused by why women should oppose pornography. The article said, "The controversy within the women's movement about the lesbian sex magazines represents the newest battle of the sex wars."[71]

GCN again played a pivotal role in the warfare when it reported that several feminist bookstores refused to stock *Bad Attitude* and *On Our Backs.* To provide an unbiased summary of the arguments on the highly incendiary topic, *GCN* reproduced verbatim a letter from a bookstore owner. The letter articulated why some lesbians saw erotic magazines as working against feminism: "The material often utilizes the traditional pornographic format in that it stereotypes women as enjoying violence and degradation and perpetuates an industry that exploits all women. We as a bookstore will not promote the commercialized exploitation of women."[72]

Joan Nestle raised an articulate voice in support of lesbian erotica. Just as the First Amendment's guarantee of free speech allows male pornography, Nestle argued, it also allows for lesbian erotica. Nestle's stand was controversial. In a 1985 *Bad Attitude* article she described how other lesbians attempted to censor her writing on sexuality. "If I am writing about them in any positive way," she said, "I am on the 'enemy list.'" Nestle told of other lesbians telephoning her in the middle of the night and calling her a traitor for promoting traditional heterosexual roles. In the article, Nestle said that such attacks reminded her of Joseph McCarthy's antihomosexual witch hunt, which was taking place when she came out in the 1950s. Combining the graceful style of a fiction writer with the rhetorical power of an activist, Nestle said: "Little by little we are being rounded up. First we are distanced and told we are not feminists—even though many of us have spent years building the movement. Then we are told we are patriarchal, that we are the voices of submission and dominance, that we are heterosexual lesbians."[73]

Nestle and her arguments won the day, as the erotica magazines thrived. Their success indicated that many lesbians were no longer willing to repress their sexual desires. Lesbians clearly were pressing beyond the perimeters of what had previously been considered acceptable sexual expression. The magazines had secured their beachhead as a vibrant part of the lesbian and gay press.

Redefining the American Family

After historically being forced to adapt their lifestyles to the traditional relationship models established by straight society, gay people increasingly rejected those limited—and idealized—definitions and reshaped the American family according to their own rules. This redefinition was particularly salient because it coincided with the ascendance of "family values" during the Reagan-Bush era.

The most dramatic change involved lesbian mothers. After decades of struggling in the courtroom to retain their rights to raise the children they had given birth to while married, lesbians defied the dictates of society by creating new methods of becoming mothers. And lesbian magazines and newspapers were crammed with articles to help them.

Gay Community News was a leader in this form of shattering the status quo. The newspaper routinely wrote about the network of lesbians who were choosing to become mothers through alternative insemination, often in cooperation with gay men. Indeed, by 1986 the Boston weekly documented a "lesbian baby boom." In keeping with its leftist orientation, *GCN* applauded the phenomenon as a "profound and exciting" development in the larger movement toward women winning reproductive rights. The newspaper pointed out that children conceived by lesbians were always wanted and loved; while the children of straight women sometimes were the unwanted results of "accidents."[74]

While supporting lesbians choosing to become mothers, publications did not ignore the complex medical, social, legal, and economic issues involved. *Lesbian Contradiction* published articles aimed at helping a woman answer questions such as how to locate a semen donor and how to impregnate herself—including using a turkey baster. Other articles contemplated the question of whether a radical lesbian who gave birth to a child would become more politically conservative, fearful her activism would jeopardize her ability to protect and care for her child. Ultimately, authors concluded that motherhood should make a woman even more committed to radicalism. One wrote: "The status quo in our society means something very unhealthy indeed, physically unsafe, insecure and sick in the soul. Maybe the way to protect our children's interests is to *change* everything."[75]

The West Coast newspaper also discussed the myriad legal complexities of becoming a lesbian mother. Although a semen donor might initially have no intention of being involved in a child's life, for example, if he later decides to assume the role of father, a court is likely to recognize that right. Another area of concern involves the role of the lover of a lesbian mother, as most courts recognize only the rights of the biological mother; if a mother dies or her relationship ends, the lover may be left with no rights regarding the child.[76]

Another battlefront in Lesbian and Gay America's effort to redefine family relationships focused on domestic partnerships. Although same-sex couples had been sharing their lives for many decades, legal and political institutions ignored such unions. AIDS intensified concerns about this lack of recognition because of increased attention to medical benefits for spouses and policies regarding an employee's rights to be released from work to care for a spouse. Activists across the country sought domestic-partner rights, and by 1988 legislation was beginning to be adopted in a handful of California cities.[77]

The highest profile domestic-partner case was that of Sharon Kowalski. Every lesbian and gay publication in the country carried wrenching stories about the thirty-year-old Minnesota woman who was partially paralyzed and suffered brain damage when a drunk driver struck her car in 1983. Even though Kowalski and her lover of four years, Karen Thompson, had owned a home together and had named each other beneficiaries of their life insurance, the courts awarded guardianship of Kowalski to her father. Donald Kowalski placed his daughter in a nursing home that provided no rehabilitation and refused to allow Thompson, a physical education professor, to visit her life partner. Thompson and Kowalski began the battle to prove the validity of their relationship, as well as Kowalski's right to make her own decisions. "As long as I can fight, I will be fighting to get Sharon back," Thompson told *GCN*. "I could never leave her."[78]

The lesbian and gay press, seeing the case as a dramatic means of forcing the country's legal system to accept the emerging dimensions of the American family, provided a dual service to Kowalski and Thompson. Not only did publications doggedly follow the case through the courts, but they also appealed to readers to send financial contributions. Regardless of whether an article appeared in *Lesbian Contradiction* in San Francisco/Seattle or *Hag Rag* in Milwaukee, the final paragraph was identical: "Donations to help pay legal costs may be sent to ..." The story of the women's struggle against a homophobic society also contained elements of the human spirit. When Kowalski learned to use an electric typewriter, publications broadcast her plaintive three-word message across the country: "Help me, Karen."[79]

After six years of struggle, court officials agreed to move Kowalski to a rehabilitation facility and allow Thompson to visit without restriction. When Kowalski saw her lover after their many years of separation, she typed out another poignant three-word message: "I love you."[80]

The future of all gay people looked bright in October 1987 when a new kind of family reunion took place in the nation's capital. For more than three and a half hours, women and men participating in the National March on Washington for Lesbian and Gay Rights walked boldly past the White House. People with AIDS—hundreds of them in wheelchairs—led the 400 marching units. The Metropolitan Community Church had the strongest presence, with some twenty separate congregations marching down Pennsylvania Avenue. In keeping with the tradition established eight years earlier with the first large-scale gay demonstration, mainstream media devoted most of their coverage to squabbles over the crowd size estimates, with organizers saying 500,000, Park Police saying 200,000.[81]

Straight and gay media alike focused much of their attention on the stunning quilt unfolded on the National Mall. By the date of the march, the Names Project had grown to some two thousand individual panels created in such a rainbow of colors and textures—denim, feathers, leather, sequins, fur, teddy bears, flags, cremation ashes—that it truly had become a mosaic of the men and women who had been felled by AIDS. The 7,000-pound quilt was flown from San Francisco to Washington to become the colorful centerpiece of the weekend of activities. Another emotional moment came when 2,000 same-sex couples gathered for a massive marriage ceremony in front of the Internal Revenue Service. Lesbian couples wore full-length wedding gowns, while gay couples donned tuxedos in a huge public display.[82]

The saddest element of lesbian and gay journalism's coverage of the reconstituted American family was the obituary sections that mushroomed in the news-oriented publications with the rise of AIDS. Yet, despite the tragic content of the articles, most publications worked to avoid making them maudlin. *The News* told readers submitting obituary material: "Don't assume any detail or accomplishment is too small to include. *The News* wants to offer as accurate and complete a profile on the deceased as possible."[83]

The obituary sections chronicled the lives of citizens of Gay and Lesbian

America—both remarkable and ordinary—with dignity and grace. David Fields loved films and developed a discerning ear for sound. His obituary in *The News* stated: "His living room became a mini screening room with a seven-foot Novabeam video screen, eight speakers with surround sound and a large selection of movies." Fields died at thirty-four. Anthony Thompkins danced in the film *Grease* and was a featured player on television's *Love Boat*. Thompkins died at thirty-three. Gary Pushard worked as an attendant at a Texaco gas station and was survived by his companion, Larry Vold. Pushard died at twenty-nine. The obituary for G. William Cox contained a statement he made while he was managing editor of the *Honolulu Star-Bulletin:* "I have spent my career trying to shed light in dark corners. AIDS is surely one of our darkest. By writing about AIDS, I am following a tradition of journalists who have written about their illnesses to help educate and, if blessed by finding the right words, to help others with the disease feel less alone." Cox died at thirty-nine.[84]

Stanching the Flow of Gay Blood

In 1987 Jeff McCourt was leading the lesbian and gay newspaper he published, the *Windy City Times,* in exposing the activities of a local neo-Nazi group that had attacked a number of gay men. McCourt was alone in his office on a Sunday afternoon when two young men with shaved heads entered his office and began swinging baseball bats. By the time they left, McCourt lay on the floor with several broken bones. "It was brutal," he later recalled. "But there was no chance I was going to let those punks stop me from my work. They won the battle that day—no question. But I was going to win the war."[85]

McCourt's Chicago newspaper became a leader in gay and lesbian journalism's crusade against hate crimes. Physical attacks had always been a given for gay people. Hundreds had been killed and thousands more had been kicked, beaten, and spat upon. The violence had escalated with the assaults from the New Right in the late 1970s and then risen even higher with the anti-AIDS backlash. By 1987, 7,000 lesbians and gay men a year were reporting incidents of violence or harassment. Although newspapers and magazines had, since the 1950s, documented the violence, it was not until the late 1980s that their rage burst into an offensive journalistic campaign to stop the violence and stanch the flow of gay blood.[86]

McCourt came late to journalism, but he brought an impressive record of accomplishment. In the 1970s and early 1980s, McCourt had ascended quickly up the ladder of success in the world of finance. Specializing in stock options, he managed Merrill Lynch's corporate finances and earned a seat on the Chicago

Board of Trade. But he grew bored with that world and wanted to combine journalism and activism. He found that marriage by creating the *Windy City Times* in 1985. "I wanted to bring an uptown professionalism to the gay press," McCourt said four years later. "I believe I've succeeded. I've expanded the boundaries of what the gay press can do."[87]

The Chicago weekly grew into one of the largest, most respected, and most influential gay papers in the country. Much of the success came from McCourt's ability to persuade advertisers to buy space in his paper. Building on the knowledge he had gained during his career in finance, McCourt broke new ground by attracting major national advertisers. Within two years, the *Windy City Times* bulged with ads for Twentieth Century-Fox, Budweiser, and True Value Hardware, as well as a long list of local companies advertising everything from opera to smoke alarms. In 1988 the *Times*'s Gay Pride issue set a new record for the largest single gay or lesbian publication in history—156 pages.[88]

But McCourt's pages were bulging with arresting editorial content as well. In particular, he consistently used the pages of his newspaper to demonstrate that police, courts, and law-making bodies were all contributing to the epidemic of violence. This effort included using investigative reporting techniques as well as internal government documents to show a pattern of discrimination against gay people. Specific articles documented that police officers refused to accept gay-related harassment complaints and district attorneys impeded prosecution of people charged with antigay assaults. Another reported that the wife of Representative Robert Dornan of California had verbally attacked a gay activist when she screamed, "Shut up, fag!"[89]

The editorial page served as another battlefield in McCourt's war against violence. When his newspaper's third birthday coincided with the Chicago city council's rejection of an ordinance that would have protected his readers, McCourt wrote: "We at *Windy City Times* would like to celebrate a tradition that has been, historically, the hallmark of gay/lesbian community journalism. The tradition of activism." He then asked readers to express their support of the newspaper by sending letters of gratitude and financial contributions to council members who supported the ordinance and, "To the others, perhaps a good memory come next election time should suffice."[90]

McCourt may have been the only gay or lesbian journalist of the era to feel the force of a baseball bat against his ribs, but he was not the only one to fight a war against gay hate crimes. *The News* established a standing feature labeled "Violence Hotline" to document the number of attacks against Los Angeles gays since the previous issue—eleven people kicked, ten threatened with a weapon, the homes of four vandalized. The newspaper also went out of its way to inform readers of the activities of their enemies. When the Ku Klux Klan elected a new Imperial Wizard and the Los Angeles media failed to document his position on gays, *The News* called the man. Getting that position on the record proved to be worth a long-distance telephone call. *The News* reported that the new KKK leader favored all lesbians and gay men being imprisoned.[91]

Some publications struggled with the question of whether an activist was justified in employing violence to stop violence. *Lesbian Contradiction* editor Jane Meyerding ultimately concluded that such action was justified: "When one is empowered by commitment to a powerful action/movement for real social change, one can face the prospect of jail or prison with little concern." The radical *Hag Rag* expressed no ambivalence whatsoever, urging its readers to buy guns: "Since men are trained early on how to use guns, how to hunt and kill, how to use karate and other 'self defense' martial arts, shouldn't we embark on a 3000-year program to condition men to recoil from violence as wimmin have been conditioned to?" *Hag Rag* advocated nonviolent offensive tactics to end violence against lesbians as well. Among them: painting billboards, occupying the offices of powerful corporations, and organizing protests at Elk, Moose, and American Legion posts.[92]

Lesbian Ethics offered pointers for lesbian resistance groups. Specific tactics included throwing glass Christmas ornaments filled with paint at offensive billboards and posting fabricated proclamations from the mayor, stating that a curfew had been instated because of the surge in violence. Writers acknowledged that such actions were illegal but insisted that they were justified to prevent anti-lesbian violence. One wrote, "Street action is essential." The Los Angeles magazine further promoted civil disobedience by reporting that angry women all over the country were fighting back. The magazine published items telling of women barring the doors of the New York Stock Exchange, disrupting a lavish open house at an Illinois newspaper, and conducting massive marches and sit-ins in Ohio and Massachusetts. To make perfectly clear how the magazine felt about performing violent acts as a response to hate crimes, the editor reprinted a flyer distributed at "Take Back the Night" demonstrations. The flyer identified the courts, police, and churches as primary targets, concluding: "Spray paint is cheap. Bricks are cheaper."[93]

Lesbian and gay publications adapted the genre's long-standing emphasis on images to their campaign to combat hate crimes. When Boston lesbians picketed outside the courtroom where a man was being tried for attacking one of their own, *Gay Community News* ran a page-one photo that focused on two of the signs carried by protesters: "LESBIANS REFUSE TO ACCEPT ABUSE— END VIOLENCE" and "WE WILL NOT BE SILENT." When 1,000 New York activists marched through Greenwich Village carrying a banner that read "LES-BIANS AND GAY MEN FIGHTING BACK," and again when 1,500 activists covered the same ground toting a banner reading "BASH BACK," *OutWeek* spread photos of the banners across the entire width of its first news page. Captions reinforced the message: "TAKE IT AS A WARNING."[94]

Testimony to the impact the crusade was having came in the spring of 1990 when the National Gay and Lesbian Task Force was given seven invitations to the White House for the signing of the most crucial—some would say *only*—pro-gay act of the twelve-year Reagan-Bush administration. The Hate Crimes Statistics Act ordered the Department of Justice to collect and publish statistics on crimes motivated by bias based on race, religion, ethnicity, or sexual orientation, marking the first time that civil rights legislation included lesbians and gay men. The signing also marked the first time that openly gay people were invited to a public event at the White House. *OutWeek* added a telling footnote, however, when it reported that Urvashi Vaid, the outspoken director of the task force who two weeks earlier had disrupted a speech by President Bush, was barred from attending the function.[95]

On the Offensive

During the second half of the 1980s, lesbian and gay journalism was on the offensive. Whether the issue was AIDS or anti-gay violence, publications were not willing to allow homophobia to set the country's agenda. Outing, more than any other phenomenon, defined the era. Ripping a person from the security of the closet certainly is an extraordinary act that is difficult to defend, but, then again, so is a police officer invading the privacy of a person's bedroom—not to mention the courts sanctioning such action. Also unjust was the government's slow and halfhearted response to a medical epidemic that was continuing to devour Americans, most of them young gay men. Against the backdrop of these heinous affronts to Lesbian and Gay America, outing did not seem such an outrageous act but merely another example of the gay and lesbian press redefining the term *unspeakable*.

Regardless of the morality of outing, it is difficult to sustain such an intense and controversial act for long. The vehicle for outing, the whirling dirvish *Out-Week*, survived a mere two years, a victim of a clash between activists eager to support radicalism and businessmen more interested in larger profits—with the businessmen carrying the day. Radical voices in other parts of the country burned out as well. *Yoni* and *The News* in California and *Hag Rag* in Wisconsin all ceased publication, and Boston's *Bad Attitude* stayed alive only by transforming itself into a magazine of erotic photography and fiction with virtually no news content, much as the gay male pornographic magazine *Drummer* had in the 1970s.[96]

As had been the case in the revolutionary period immediately after Stonewall, the publications that survived the era of radicalism tended to be those that did not screech at the highest decibel level. Yet publications such as *Gay Community News, Lesbian Contradiction,* and *On Our Backs* could hardly be classified as meek. Support for the lesbian and gay press clearly had grown since the early 1970s, allowing for a broad range of publications, including radical ones.

Three developments among late 1980s publications foreshadowed the evolution of the press of the 1990s. The first took place at the *Windy City Times.* After Jeff McCourt founded the Chicago weekly in 1985, he used his background in the world of finance to build one of the biggest gay papers in the country. McCourt attracted an impressive stable of national as well as local advertisers, including such blue-chip companies as Budweiser and Twentieth Century Fox. Major advertisers clearly were no longer turning their backs on the gay dollar.[97]

Another development was more ominous. As the *New York Native*'s coverage of the AIDS epidemic became increasingly bizarre, instead of the newspaper shrinking, its circulation and size both mushroomed. Even though publisher Charles Ortleb was obsessed and his newspaper became irresponsible in its coverage of the most important story in the history of the gay press, readers continued to buy the newspaper because of its excellent coverage of gay culture. This disturbing phenomenon suggested that readers were willing to overlook a publication's failure to provide accurate and meaningful content as long as it offered first-rate lifestyles coverage. Perhaps readers were beginning to believe that as the gay and lesbian profile rose—thanks mainly to AIDS forcing straight America to acknowledge gay people—they could look to the mainstream news media for information about the major events influencing their lives, while turning to their own publications primarily for coverage of cultural events and trends.

A third portentous development evolved from an article in the pages of the publication that defined the era—*OutWeek.* When the short-lived news magazine lambasted the gay press for not forcing the gay porn industry to protect the community's sexual icons, it did not succeed in its mission. The gay press continued to run ads for videos that did not include condom use among their stars, and the handsome young men in the videos continued to die. Because the issue was hauntingly reminiscent of the one revolving around unsafe sex in the bath houses earlier in the decade, it suggested that the gay press was not always learning from experience. Once again, some gay publications seemed to value making a profit more than saving lives.

These developments signaled that gay and lesbian journalism faced profound and complex issues as it approached its fifth decade. Indeed, the genre was on the brink of entering yet another distinct chapter in its mercurial evolution.

λ 11

Marching into the Mainstream

America's alternative media have evolved because groups of people outside the mainstream of society—most notably African Americans and women—historically have been denied a voice in conventional media networks. Eager to communicate with each other as a step toward changing the social order that discriminates against them, these repressed groups have created their own media. Advocacy journalists have sacrificed time, energy, and personal resources, for along with being denied a venue in the marketplace of ideas, outsiders also have been denied economic power. Thousands of alternative publications have spoken boldly and loudly...but soon have been silenced because they have failed to attain fiscal stability. For example, *Freedom's Journal,* the first African-American newspaper, was founded in 1827 and ceased publication in 1829; and *The Revolution,* the first women's suffrage journal, was born in 1868 and died in 1870. One scholar of advocacy journalism has even argued that fiscal security *prevents* an alternative publication from being politically effective.[1]

Lesbian and gay journalism initially suffered a similar fate, as *Vice Versa* lasted only from 1947 to 1948. By the late 1960s, however, the genre had veered from the standard course of alternative media. From the vantage point of the 1990s, one of its unique themes is that gay and lesbian publications have not only raised the voices of a demonized minority, but also have achieved fiscal solvency. Indeed, some have pulled in big bucks. Dick Michaels founded the *Los Angeles Advocate* in 1967; he sold it seven years later for a handsome $1 million. In the history of alternative presses, such a financial return was unheard of. David Goodstein then poured $3 million of his personal fortune into redesigning and redirecting the publication, and by the end of the 1970s his lifestyles magazine was turning a tidy profit. During the 1980s, the *Windy City Times* further contributed to the trend when founder Jeff McCourt used his fiscal know-how to corral an impressive list of national as well as local advertisers.

By 1995 it was clear that the latest chapter in the history was the emergence of a bumper crop of slick, upscale magazines brimming with the same full-page ads appearing in tony mainstream magazines. What was *not* clear was whether this development was an advancement. Most of the editorial content wrapped around the ads was decidedly moderate in tone, reading like the inoffensive articles some advertisers demand that magazines publish if they expect to secure long-term contracts. Largely absent from the glossy gay magazines were the sexually explicit images, unique lexicon, and defiant editorial stances that had defined earlier generations of the genre.

Major topics of discussion became what young, beautiful, fashion-conscious gay people were wearing as they stepped out into the social whirl of the rich and famous. Other articles, combined with the ads surrounding them, focused on how gay DINKS—double income, no kids—could transform their city residences and country cottages into perfectly precious showplaces; still others described the most desirable destinations for Gay Nineties vacationing. Most editorial content was written by freelancers who were hustling their flashy words and insider knowledge of the latest fads simultaneously to gay and mainstream magazines.

Breaking news was devalued, often packaged into columns of news briefs reminiscent of those in *The Ladder* and *Mattachine Review* in the 1950s. The biweekly *Advocate* was the only 1990 glossy to subscribe to a wire service, but the magazine's commitment to covering the news was ambiguous at best, as it lacked the "fire in the belly" an aggressive news outlet must possess. In late 1994, cocky new *Advocate* editor Jeff Yarbrough, whose previous experience had been at *People* and *Interview* magazines, told the National Lesbian and Gay Journalists Association he had redesigned *The Advocate* not to enhance its ability to report the news, but, "We needed to clean up our act and get a little more happy and shiny to attract advertisers." Yarbrough went on to say that he lived in "constant fear" that another gay magazine might shift from monthly to biweekly "and force me to go weekly, which I'm dreading." Such statements—hardly the comments of a hard-driving newshound—suggested that *The Advocate* continued to be motivated by a desire to attract advertisers, not inform readers.[2]

When substantive topics surfaced amid the sea of narcissism and timidity that filled the magazines, they tended to be the same topics mainstream media were covering, such as lifting the ban on gays in the military. The era's dramatic political shift to the Right was reflected in the new generation of lesbian and gay press, with the glossies showcasing gay conservative views such as those espoused by Bruce Bawer, who became an *Advocate* columnist.

Editorial content in the slick magazines was not militant, as the men and women responsible for the new generation of publications were neither activists nor journalists but a new breed called "publishing people." The founding editor of *Genre*, the first of the new glossies, expressed unbridled relief that the genre was no longer dominated by individuals fighting for social change. "You have a lot of people who came up through the ranks of magazines, not as political activists," Michael Jones boasted. "Gay publishing is now being treated like a business—for a change." Jones went on to express his delight that gaining civil rights was no longer the paramount issue for the new generation. Clearly, that position had been taken over by the pursuit of financial profit.[3]

"Publishing people" were not embarrassed by their pursuit of profit, but praised themselves for assiduously *avoiding* taking stands. Alan Bell, founder of a slick magazine targeted toward gay African Americans, said, "There's no editorial page in *BLK*, and that's purposeful, because I don't have anything I particularly want to say. There's not a point of view that I want to push." *Lesbian News* editor Katie Cotter echoed the same nonpolitical sentiment. "There is no effort to get people to do anything whatsoever. We're a mirror, not a cattle prod."[4]

In fact, "publishing people" castigated their militant predecessors who had pioneered in lesbian and gay journalism not just because of their lack of business acumen. After bragging that he was well versed in the history of the gay press, Yarbrough grossly overstated the importance of his magazine: "*The Advocate* was, for twenty-five years, the only 'serious' publication and the only publication of any note in America"—in one sentence insulting literally hundreds of pioneering publications such as *Amazon Quarterly*, *Gay Community News*, the *Washington Blade*, *Lesbian Tide*, *Lesbian Ethics*, *GAY*, *The Furies*, and *OutWeek*.[5]

The new glossies were based almost exclusively in the three urban centers—Los Angeles, San Francisco, New York—that had led the evolution of the genre, and many of them targeted both lesbians and gay men. *Square Peg* in Los Angeles as well as *OUT/LOOK* and *10 Percent* in San Francisco aimed at both sexes, as did *Out* in New York. When the shift toward lifestyle magazines swept *The Advocate* back into vogue, Gay America's venerable voice also made a renewed effort to appeal to women, although lesbian readership still did not exceed 5 percent.

Among single-sex publications, *Deneuve* in San Francisco for women and *Genre* in Los Angeles for men set the pace. Two other L.A. magazines, *Lesbian News* and *Frontiers,* joined the trend toward slick magazines by dressing themselves up in shiny new covers. Other new glossies defined their audiences more narrowly—*BLK* focusing on African Americans, *Victory!* on business entrepreneurs, *POZ* on people who had tested HIV positive.

The glossy magazines increased the total number of gay and lesbian publications only slightly, to about 850. But they caused the total circulation to explode. The newcomers alone boasted a circulation of more than 900,000. That figure nearly matched the 1 million aggregate total of newspapers and magazines as it stood in 1990. Spectacular growth of the glossies coupled with continued modest growth of the long list of news-oriented publications—such as the *Washington Blade* and *Philadelphia Gay News*—propelled the genre over another circulation hurdle. By 1995 the gay and lesbian press, which was approaching its fiftieth birthday, boasted an aggregate circulation of 2 million.[6]

The rise of slick, upscale magazines reflected a larger change in society's attitudes toward gay people. In cities such as New York and Los Angeles, it had become desirable for the place cards at chic dinner parties to include the names of a few "guppies"—upwardly mobile, well-educated, and *gay*. *OUT/LOOK* observed, "In a few areas of the nation, and increasingly among the young, hip, and artsy, it's almost cool to be queer." Ironically, AIDS—with the number of cases in the United States nearing 500,000 by 1995—deserves much of the credit for accelerating the visibility and progress of gay people, as it was proving to be a disease so pervasive that neither it nor its favorite prey could be ignored.[7]

Such major publications as *USA Today, Newsweek,* and the *Washington Post* reported on the rise of the slick magazines, propelling the gay and lesbian press into the spotlight as never before. In 1992 the genre made its debut in the ultimate position in the American news media: the front page of the *New York Times*. After four and a half decades, the country's newspaper of record acknowledged the existence of the gay—though not the lesbian—press. The lead of the forty-inch story read: "The gay press is emerging from the shadows to claim a place in the mainstream. After years of being distributed without charge in bars and being dependent on sexually oriented advertisements for revenues, gay publications are changing their image and their aspirations."[8]

Out: Gay and Lesbian America's *Vanity Fair*

The biggest success story was *Out*. In keeping with the values of the new glossies, that success was measured not by the quality or impact of editorial content, but by the magazine's ability to secure blue-chip advertisers. When *USA Today* reported on *Out*'s birth, the lead moved quickly to the advertising angle: "The premier issue of *Out* magazine is on newsstands nationwide today. Its 104 glossy pages contain 20 pages of ads, including 18 pages from national advertisers such as Benetton, Absolut vodka, Opal Nera liqueur and Geffen records."[9]

Out appeared on the streets of New York City in June 1992, dubbing itself the *Vanity Fair* of gay publishing. *Out* also directed attention to itself by nabbing top designer Roger Black, who had shaped the looks of such titans of the magazine industry as *McCalls* and *Premiere*. *Out*'s sophisticated look helped attract its large stable of advertisers, as did "launch parties" in several cities and T-shirts at Gay Pride parades—all part of a nonstop marketing campaign. *Out* also made history as the first gay or lesbian publication to participate in Publishers Clearing House. After *Out* secured its place in that mass mailing operation, all a consumer had to do to guarantee a discounted subscription rate was lick the stamp and mail it in—right along with the stamps for *Reader's Digest* and *TV Guide*.[10]

Out editor and president Michael Goff, who had written a column for *OutWeek*, said, with the high degree of immodesty characterizing his generation, "With *Out*, we brought a level of professionalism to a gay publication that hasn't been there before." A sizable bankroll helped, too. A group of investors, led by Boston's Robert Hardman, committed $500,000 to their new enterprise. They expected the magazine to turn a profit by 1996.[11]

Goff hired the hottest writers and photographers of the day because the names were already familiar to the young, upscale readers *Out* wanted to attract. Bylines included such "notables" as Lindsy Van Gelder from *Allure*, Ray Rogers from *Interview*, and Peter McQuaid from *Us*. The words and images of dozens of other writers and photographers had appeared in *Entertainment Weekly*, *People*, *Spin*, *Variety*, *Billboard*, *Vanity Fair*, *Playboy*, *Vibe*, *Details*, *Elle*, *Travel & Leisure*, *Mirabella*, *Essence*, *Architectural Digest*, *Harper's Bazaar*, *Gentleman's Quarterly*, and more. In case a reader failed to recognize a name, *Out* highlighted each contributor's publication credits in a box on the first page of major features, as well as in biographies at the front of the magazine.

The upscale magazine did not, however, find room for the explicit sex ads that had been the bread and butter for generations of its ancestors. Indeed, the "publishing people" at *Out* spoke of such ads with derision. Public relations director Michael Kaminer told *Marketing News*: "It's a simple fact of life. You're not going to attract major advertisers with *those* in your magazine."[12]

Out's breezy writing style matched the trendy topics it promoted. When Chiqui Cartagena piloted readers through the troubled waters of lesbian dating in a piece titled "Sex and the Single Girl," she wrote: "Like a lot of things, dating isn't as simple as it used to be. To some of us it's one of the no-no words of the '90s, almost as threatening an idea as the C word—commitment. To others, however, dating in the '90s is just another word for seeing a friend, even if you see that friend in bed."[13]

The dating article appeared under the standing headline "Love." Other recurring departments were labeled "Bodies," "Horoscope," "Parties," "Acquiring Taste," and "Out Front," a roundup of gossipy tidbits such as a New York drag queen starting a cable TV cooking show titled *Come 'n Get It*.[14]

Each issue also contained half a dozen free-standing features. Topics ranged from the cowgirl mystique ascending into the pop culture to a lighthearted discussion of the intuitive sixth sense gay people use to identify each other, from the how-tos of throwing a successful party to the new Hollywood game of racking up how many celebrities you had slept with—singers Madonna and Elton John came with the most points.[15]

With such fluff dominating the new flagship of lesbian and gay magazines, not everyone was joining the *Out* pep squad. Executive Editor Sarah Pettit acknowledged that many members of the community greeted the magazine with criticism: "We were perceived to be hideous sellouts." But Pettit, formerly arts editor at *OutWeek,* defended *Out*'s nonpolitical editorial content as reflecting the values of Generation X: "If we look realistically at what most gay men and lesbians do with their time, they're probably more likely to be watching 'Melrose Place' or MTV than to be in a gay and lesbian bookstore."[16]

Despite the thin editorial content, advertising continued to spell success. In a year and a half, advertising revenue increased fivefold, soaring from $52,000 in the June 1992 issue to $271,000 in the December 1993 issue. And the ads just kept coming. *Out* itself became the first gay-oriented product advertised on national television, sponsoring the first all-gay comedy special, "Out There," on the Comedy Central cable network in 1993. The magazine also made history as the first gay publication to enter the computer age, sending its table of contents and best articles across the country via the America Online service. Its full-time staff increased from five to thirty, and it opened a Los Angeles office to increase the presence of film, television, and entertainment coverage—and advertising. *Out* sold so much space that it shifted from quarterly to bimonthly to ten issues a year, each containing a hefty 166 pages. Again, the driving force was not providing timely information but attracting more ads. Publisher George Slowik said, "With greater frequency, we will be able to catch timely ads for movies and home videos."[17]

Circulation figures soared as well. *Out*'s all-out marketing campaign paid off, helping the magazine's circulation to double in its first two years, a feat the *New York Times* announced with a major story in its financial section. By mid-1994, *Out* passed *The Advocate* to boast the highest circulation in the history of the lesbian and gay press—100,000.[18]

Advertising Takes the Driver's Seat

The driving force behind businesses filling the pages of the gay glossies had little to do with a sense of justice and everything to do with capitalism. Faced with a severe economic recession in the late 1980s, American business was struggling. So it shifted away from trying to appeal to the broad audience and entered an era of niche advertising. When aggressive marketers representing the gay press convinced companies with slumping sales that they were overlooking an affluent segment of the population, prejudice took a backseat to profit making.

In 1992 jaws in advertising agencies all over the country dropped when a research firm attached a specific figure to how much America's estimated 18 million gay and lesbian adults were pumping into the nation's economy each year: $514 billion. Although advertisers knew that such marketing-survey figures are always inflated, this number was too high to ignore completely. Overlooked Opinions, Inc., produced that figure by surveying gay people nationwide. The study also compared incomes of 7,500 same-sex couples with U.S. Census Bureau figures for straight couples. The results were astonishing. The average gay male couple earned $51,600 a year, while the typical married couple made only $37,900—a difference of 36 percent. "When you have two well-educated, ambitious, career-minded men in the same household, they pull down huge salaries," said New York advertising agency executive David Mulryan. "They send the figures clear off the charts." Although the figure for lesbian couples was not *as* spectacular, their $42,800 average household income was still 13 percent higher than that of married couples. Even these impressive figures failed to reflect the huge proportion of gay household income that is disposable because 85 percent of the couples do not have to pay for childcare, braces, or private school.[19]

Genre was the first to reap the benefits of Madison Avenue's eagerness to reach the gay market. Founded in the spring of 1991, the magazine targeted affluent gay men. Editor Ron Kraft said, "I took the magazine out of the gay ghetto." With its narrow focus clearly in sight, *Genre* quickly attracted national advertisers. Absolut vodka, which had been advertising in *The Advocate* since 1982, was the big success story. Kraft said: "When Absolut took the risk of placing ads in gay magazines, no gay man would serve anything but Absolut. Those ads took Absolut from fifth place to the number-one selling premium vodka in the country." Liquor ads quickly became a staple in *Genre,* with full-page color ads from Hiram Walker, Bud Light, Courvoisier cognac, and Southern Comfort. Entertainment products followed, with ads for national record companies such as Epic, MCA, Sire, and Arista. In 1994, the magazine's 70,000 circulation allowed it to expand from a quarterly to a monthly.[20]

Later that spring, a second magazine proved that national advertisers were not interested solely in gay men, but were ready to court the lesbian market as well. *Deneuve,* a bimonthly, initially struggled to find a financial backer. Founder Frances Stevens recalled: "Banks wouldn't even talk to me. Lesbian publishing was an unproven market." After Stevens put up her own money to start the magazine, she next struggled to convince advertisers that high disposable incomes were not exclusive to gay men. "I finally had to go with just two ads in the first issue," she said. The break did not come until 1993, when *Deneuve* shifted to glossy paper and began printing in four color on some inside pages. That upgrade enticed Budweiser and Warner Brothers to take a chance on the magazine, whose 50,000 circulation became the largest in the history of the lesbian press. Those advertisers begot others, such as Pusser's rum and Community Spirit long-distance telephone service. Bud Light took up residence on the back cover.[21]

Out pushed the trend giant steps forward in June 1992 by cracking the upscale clothing market, becoming the first gay and lesbian publication to advertise Banana Republic, Calvin Klein, Giorgio Armani, Tommy Hilfiger, and Benetton—often in stunning, two-page ads in the vibrant colors the company is famous for. Other upscale companies plunged into the lesbian and gay media through *Out*: Apple Computer, American Express travelers checks, Matsuda Eyewear, Walt Disney, Virgin Atlantic Airways, and L.A. Eyeworks.

10 Percent caught the wave soon after it was founded in the fall of 1992. Editor Carlos Stelmach characterized his magazine as less trendy than the competition: "Our readers are professionals, not necessarily as interested in the trends of the moment. They're more likely to attend dinner parties with friends than go out to clubs. They're more integrated in society and not living in gay ghettos." Translation: older, richer. *10 Percent* secured ads from upper-end alcohol companies such as Remy Martin cognac, Dewar's scotch, and Bombay gin.[22]

The Advocate, the grandfather of gay magazines, benefited from the surge in advertising as well. Threatened by the spate of youthful new competitors, *The Advocate* unveiled a slick new look, in 1992, designed specifically to attract more ads. The switch from newsprint to glossy paper and the addition of flashy graphics immediately reeled in three new national advertisers—Academy Entertainment, Naya spring water, C.J. Wray rum. Two years later, when AT&T began advertising its corporate calling card in the magazine, the *New York Times* devoted an entire story to the development. Editor-in-chief Richard Rouilard pointed out that an ad in his magazine cost one-twentieth as much as one in a mainstream publication, such as *Vanity Fair,* aimed at a straight market with similar demographics. *The Advocate*'s 1990 total advertising revenue of $1.9 million doubled to $3.8 million in 1992. Rouilard had no illusion, however, that the shift was a result of an awakening to human rights. He told *Marketing News*: "This is a very rich niche. My readers are richer, smarter, and more informed. They are the divine DINKS."[23]

After *The Advocate* tried for several years to crack the extremely desirable automobile industry market, the prize ultimately went to *Out*. In the fall of 1994, Saab began urging gay and lesbian readers to put "someone you love" inside one of the upscale car manufacturer's sporty convertibles.[24]

By the mid-1990s, dozens of major companies had jumped on the bandwagon and were emblazoning their names on the glossy pages of one or more of the magazines...Xerox, Continental Airlines, Benson & Hedges, Philip Morris, Parliament Lights, Hennessy cognac, Glenlivet scotch, Drambuie and Kahlua liqueurs, Smirnoff vodka, Tanqueray gin, Campari Aperitivo, Seagram whiskey, Evian and Calistoga mineral waters, Sony Electronics, Diesel jeans, Cignal and Body-Body-Wear menswear, Kenneth Cole shoes, Physikos and Raymond Dragon clothing lines, Swatch watches, Silhouette Eyewear, Joseph Abboud and Nautica colognes, New Line Home Video, Tables & Chairs furniture, Waldenbooks, Viking Press, Anchor Books, HarperCollins, Dutton, Simon & Schuster, Atlantis and Empress travel companies, MCI long-distance telephone service, and a slew of music companies—Geffen, Elektra, GRP, Virgin, and Tower.

The advertisers acknowledged that their decisions were based purely on dollars and cents. When asked what drew them to the gay glossies, spokespersons for the various businesses made no mention of civil rights. Remy Martin cognac: "Gays have a high disposable income. They fit the demographics of income and education we are looking for." C.J. Wray rum: "It's a market that has money." Virgin Atlantic Airways: "They're an audience that we believe will give us a great return on our advertising investment." Nora Beverages: "This was not a political decision. It was a business decision." Hiram Walker liquor: "Knowing detailed information about the gay market is like wondering how many trees there are. Does it matter? They're all green."[25]

The largest of the magazines launched a joint marketing campaign—proving that visions of dollar signs even overcame the fractious infighting that had plagued earlier gay press editors. The glossies introduced a discount service offering subscribers multiple magazines at 75 percent off the cover prices. Promotional material featured a rainbow logo and boasted that the service was 100 percent gay and lesbian owned. The service included five titles—*The Advocate*, *Deneuve*, *Genre*, *Out*, and *10 Percent*—along with three dozen mainstream ones, including *Time* and *Newsweek*.

Not everyone was thrilled that national advertisers were adding revenues to gay press coffers. The New Right set its sights on the companies, warning them that their ads could have negative repercussions. Robert Knight of Family Research Council told the *Washington Post*: "Companies may risk alienating a larger market. I am not so sure all advertisers will think it is worth it."[26]

The threats, however, proved unsuccessful. After Boy Scouts of America banned gay men from working with the organization, Levi Strauss Co. dropped the organization from its corporate-giving list, prompting conservative forces to boycott the jeans manufacturer. A Levi spokesman said: "Their boycott has not had any effect at all, and we had all-time record sales and earnings this year." In 1994 the Christian Right admitted it was losing the war against homosexuality. An aide to Reverend Jerry Falwell told *Advertising Age*: "There's a pretty apparent trend in media and in entertainment and even in government towards greater acknowledgement of gays and lesbians as a legitimate minority, and I think the tide has certainly gone in that direction."[27]

The Gay Nineties magazines, like their straight counterparts, tailored their editorial content to please advertisers, as the new generation carried the gay press proclivity for blurring the line between editorial and advertising into a marriage of convenience and profit. A six-page article in *Out* purported to document the lesbian's rise to "cover girl" status in mainstream magazines. One full-page photo showed a woman clutching a *Playboy* with lesbian actress Sandra Bernhard on the cover. The editorial comments clearly were secondary, however, to the major purpose of the feature: to advertise the clothes the models were wearing. A la *Vogue* and *Mirabella,* each spread included a block of copy describing the items. And a line on the final spread told readers, "For store information see page 144." That page gave the manufacturers and prices—including a Jil Sander sweater for $920 and suit for $2,210, both available at Barneys in New York.[28]

Some editors appealed directly to their readers to support advertisers. Jeanne Córdova, editor of *Lesbian Tide* in the 1970s, distributed her slick new magazine, *Square Peg,* free of charge. So she depended on ads for all her revenue, begging her readers to buy the products advertised in the magazine: "I ask you to kindly read the advertisements here in *Square Peg.* See if there isn't some purchase, no matter how small, you can make." Frances Stevens of *Deneuve* was convinced that her readers were committed to companies supporting her magazine. She told *Advertising Age,* "They see an ad for a tampon in *Deneuve,* they'll change their tampon brand."[29]

Other efforts to persuade readers were less direct—and, therefore, more insidious. A four-page travel article in *Out* lauded the glories of vacationing in Lesbos, the Aegean island that gave lesbians their name. The positive article

focused specifically on a recent all-women tour of the island arranged by Olivia
Cruises, the same company that ran an ad later in the issue. Similarly, the same
issue of *10 Percent* that featured Elton John on its cover and devoted seven
pages to an article about reviving his pop music career also carried a four-
color ad from MCA Records promoting John's latest album. And when *Victory!* ran a glowing story about Tim Gill parlaying a $4,000 investment into a
business with annual revenues of $120 million, the magazine did not mention
that Gill's software company ran an ad on the back cover.[30]

Redefining AIDS Coverage

No topic better illustrated the editorial direction of the slick new magazines
than the one that had dominated the gay press for the previous decade. AIDS
and its devastating impact on the community were the dual forces that had
moved gay and lesbian issues out of the shadows and onto center stage—a steep
price to pay for public visibility. By the early 1990s most gay men understood
the dangers involved in the various types of sexual activity and were taking precautions to avoid them. For many gay men, in fact, far too much of life had become devoted to visiting sick friends, attending memorial services, and reading
about the latest research dead end.

For Richard Settles, founding editor of *Genre*, the disease had hit very close
to home, taking his brother's life. Settles recalled the impetus for creating his
magazine: "I was sick and tired of reading one depressing AIDS story after another. So I decided that *Genre* would focus on the other areas of life in the gay
1990s—fashion, travel, arts, entertainment, health, fitness. *Genre* became a
breath of fresh air."[31]

The magazine redefined AIDS coverage in positive terms. Typical was a
feature boldly headlined "Being Alive!" The article profiled half a dozen gay men
living active, vital lives as long as ten years after being diagnosed with full-blown
AIDS. *Genre* also promoted the national prescription service owned and operated by gay men who had tested positive for HIV. Community Prescription Service cofounder Stephen Gendin said: "We have the latest information about
alternative therapies. And we know about the drugs you're taking because
chances are we take them, too."[32]

Other magazines imitated *Genre*'s optimism. *Out* ran articles about how
men could continue dating despite being HIV positive. *Victory!* assured positive readers that with a bit of creativity they could still travel anywhere in the
world. *Frontiers* downplayed the impact the virus played in people's lives—a
profile of an artist who painted dancing octopi and alligators on wheels did not

mention that the artist was HIV positive until ten inches into the story. *OUT/LOOK* published the full script of the first play to take a humorous look at AIDS, Robert Patrick's *Pouf Positive*. The comedy contained one-liners such as a vain man being told he has the disease and immediately responding: "AIDS! Oh, doctor, thank God. I thought you said, 'Age!'"[33]

The upbeat approach to AIDS coverage reached its zenith in 1994 when another slick New York–based magazine joined the burgeoning gay and lesbian market. The title *POZ* carried a double meaning. The magazine targeted the country's 1 million HIV *pos*itive men and women, as well as their families and friends; its editorial content was consistently framed in a *pos*itive tone. Publisher Sean O'Brien Strub, a direct-mail expert who had survived HIV for fifteen years, said: "If we believe ourselves to be terminally ill, we void everything else about our lives. Our love, passion, vision and vitality. Our hopes and dreams. We might as well just plan the funeral and wait to die. But if we are survivors, we have a future. Something to survive for. Places to go. People to meet. Things to do. Love to share."[34]

POZ envisioned itself as a cross between *Details* and the *New England Journal of Medicine*. Vibrant features considered topics such as how AIDS was being depicted in contemporary art and music as well as what Hollywood might do with the subject after the film *Philadelphia* had succeeded at the box office. But the magazine also printed timely news such as progress toward creating a home HIV test and detailed, technical descriptions of recommended treatments for diarrhea and toxoplasmosis titer. Each issue also published Strub's most recent blood work along with analyses by two doctors—whose prognoses often totally disagreed.[35]

POZ profiles quickly became the magazine's trademark. By sketching vivid portraits of people who carried the virus but remained active and productive, the magazine inspired readers to approach their own lives with healthy attitudes. Each issue bulged with role models: Fred Bingham, diagnosed with AIDS three years earlier, had gone into remission after he experimented with herbs and organic materials. . . . Teddy Kalidas, whose body was covered with Kaposi's sarcoma lesions when he competed for the bodybuilding title at Gay Games IV. . . Florent Morellet, a restaurateur whose Manhattan bistro had grown more popular each of the eight years since he had tested positive . . .[36]

Advertisers waited in line. Calistoga and Perrier mineral waters purchased full-page ads in the first issue; Benetton bought the first two inside pages for an ad featuring two handsome men embracing. The biggest advertisers in the magazine, however, were the numerous businesses eager to reach the specific niche the magazine occupied. Viatical Settlements, Inc., told readers it would pay cash now to become the life insurance policy beneficiaries of persons with AIDS; Advera promoted its nutritional supplement specifically designed for people with AIDS.

POZ did not receive positive reviews from all sectors of the gay community. In the latest example of the internecine feuding that has been part of the gay press since the 1950s, the New York Native ridiculed the new publication by suggesting that someone next would create a magazine called NEG for people who have tested HIV negative and another called GAZ for survivors of Nazi death camps. Other critics said that POZ glamorized AIDS while ignoring the tragic elements of the disease.[37]

But the strongest attacks came in the area of advertising. Some critics accused POZ of being ghoulish in accepting ads from viatical companies. Publisher Strub defended his magazine, pointing out that many people with AIDS benefit greatly from finding a company to buy their life insurance policies because they desperately need money to pay for medical care. Others charged that the magazine was tacitly endorsing drugs that were not effective by publishing ads for them. An example came during a National Lesbian and Gay Journalists Association panel discussion titled "HIV Magazines: Help or Hindrance?" A member of the audience said that an ad for rifabutin, which treats mycobacterium avium complex (or MAC), was deceptive because laboratory tests had not determined whether the drug prevented MAC or only held down the levels of bacteremia, the substance in a person's blood that indicates whether he or she has MAC. Strub responded: "We respect the intelligence of our readers. We present the information; the reader makes the decisions."[38]

Living the Good Life

When the founders of lesbian and gay glossies conceived of publications to appeal to guppies, they did not have to look far to find magazines to mimic. In the 1990s dozens of slick monthlies were reflecting the good life the country's young, upwardly mobile population was living. The gay versions merely adopted the specific topics gay people were interested in—which meant virtually all of them.

Square Peg joined in depicting the lesbian and gay good life. Long-time journalist Jeanne Córdova founded the co-gender magazine with newsprint on the inside but a slick cover out front. Now a successful businesswoman with her own publishing firm, Córdova hired two psychotherapists—one lesbian, one gay—to dispense advice to readers about their love lives. She also created a calendar to promote the soaring number of gay dance clubs in Los Angeles.

The bevy of slick magazines of the early 1990s placed a higher priority on pleasure and profit making than on politics and fighting for civil rights. Courtesy of Frances Stevens, *Deneuve.*

The departments appearing in other magazines further reflected the eagerness of the newest generation to respond to the values of upwardly mobile readers. *Deneuve* created a column on dating called "Dyke Drama [!?]" and another on music called "Hot Licks from Cool Chicks." *Out* printed gourmet recipes and top-ten lists such as "Tips on Getting Picked up in a Nightclub" and "Reasons You're Not Having Sex with Your Partner." *BLK* published snippets of gossip about gay African Americans under the heading "Read My Lips." *Lesbian News* printed a horoscope column called "Star Talk!" *10 Percent's* "Just the Facts" offered tantalizing tidbits for readers to ponder—28 percent of lesbians have been unfaithful to their lovers; the comparable percentage for gay men: 82.[39]

The rich and famous have always been popular among upscale readers, regardless of sexual orientation. *Genre* pioneered among the gay glossies in this area by creating "On the Circuit," a *Town and Country*–style feature crammed with snapshots of celebrities wearing tuxedos and sequined gowns; gay people such as playwright Tony Kushner, who won a Pulitzer Prize for *Angels in America,* and Assistant Secretary of Housing and Urban Development Roberta Achtenberg, the highest ranking openly lesbian or gay federal appointee in history, shared space with straight luminaries such as superstar Barbra Streisand and First Lady Hillary Rodham Clinton. *Deneuve* followed suit with its "Lesbofile" gossip column reporting, for example, when Texas Governor Ann Richards went on *The Tonight Show* and allowed as how, yes, singer Dolly Parton had spent some time at the governor's mansion in Austin. "We're buddies," Richards told curious host Jay Leno. "We share secrets, which we will not share with you."[40]

The periodicals also secured their celebrity quota through feature stories on the entertainment industry. When Mariel Hemingway kissed Roseanne Arnold during a controversial segment of ABC's television comedy, *Deneuve* used the smooch to launch into a tribute to Arnold. Calling her top-rated show "the dykiest show on television," the magazine praised the megastar for depicting the courage of the ordinary American working woman. *Deneuve* also depicted the star's quick wit as she displayed it at a San Francisco book reading. A member of the audience asked Arnold, "Is Hillary Clinton a lesbian?" Arnold deadpanned, "I don't think that Hillary is a lesbian. You shouldn't assume 'til you're told."[41]

The magazines grabbed every opportunity to profile the increasing number of gay performers rising to the top of the entertainment world. Singing sensation k.d. lang was a frequent subject; an *Advocate* cover story on her, which launched the magazine's new look, ushered her out of the closet with her quote: "When I'm up there on stage, I'm certainly not singing about the Marlboro Man!" When former *OUT/LOOK* editor Debra Chasnoff won an Oscar for her documentary on General Electric's negative impact on the environment, *Square Peg* quoted verbatim the statement she made live to 1 billion TV viewers: "I am very grateful to family and friends, to Kim Klausner, my life partner, who always had faith in me, and to our son, Noah." And after Jodie Foster won her Oscar for *Silence of the Lambs, Square Peg* tracked her down and asked her to comment on her sexuality. Foster remained evasive.[42]

The magazines championed the new prominence of lesbian comics. *Square*

Peg spiced up a feature about half a dozen of the women by reproducing their best jokes. When people ask Suzanne Westenhoefer how a person gets to be homosexual, she goes into her best Valley-girl talk with a Jersey accent: "Like, homosexuals are chosen first on talent, then, like, interviews. The swimsuit and evening gown competition eliminates the rest of them." The magazine devoted the most space to "beyond bodacious" Lea DeLaria, who appeared on the *Arsenio Hall Show* wearing a man's suit and lipstick. When Hall announced her arrival, DeLaria raced madly onto the stage yelling, "Yes, we are in the '90s! And it's hip to be queer! Yes!" She then jumped on Hall's lap and started pumping his crotch. *Square Peg* also reported the comic's comments about the First Family: "I like this administration. I like them because finally in this country we have a First Lady you can BOINK!"[43]

BLK highlighted African-American drag sensation RuPaul with a flashy cover showing the six-foot-five-inch bombshell wearing her signature blond wig and a hot pink miniskirt. The interview glorified Gay America's reigning diva, who played virtually every gay club in the country on his way to national fame. *BLK,* however, focused on the burning questions previous profiles in the *New York Times, Esquire,* and *The New Yorker* had somehow missed: "If RuPaul were a hairdresser and could do anyone's hair, who would you do?" "If you could give anyone a makeover, who would it be?" "What color toilet paper do you use?" The answers: Diana Ross's hair, Whitney Houston's look, and white—Charmin, to be exact.[44]

Lesbians and gay men living the good life did not spend all their time being entertained, as creating the perfect home also was a priority. The glossies published myriad feature stories and photo essays on home decorating, architecture, and trends in furniture styles. *Out* placed such stories in its "Acquiring Taste" department. Some articles raved about the latest lesbian- or gay-owned businesses, such as Manhattan's new East Village furniture store ReGeneration, which specialized in vintage 1950s items. Other articles kept tabs on avant-garde furniture such as the latest in loveseats—fiery red damask with French tassles and turned-wood feet. *10 Percent,* in keeping with its goal of appealing to the well heeled, concentrated on describing the homes of the rich and famous. With the same rhetorical flourishes that run rampant through the pages of *Architectural Digest, 10 Percent* captured the essence, for example, of Villa Zaragosa, the 5,500-square-foot Hollywood Hills home of entrepreneur Tess Ayers and playwright Jane Anderson, complete with its "thick muscular walls," "painted wood assemblages," and "al fresco living."[45]

Reflecting the fact that upper-class gay people had no reason to confine their lives to their perfect homes, the magazines also anointed vacationing hot spots. *Deneuve* pointed to Toronto and *Genre* to Provincetown, while *Out* called, "Viva Barcelona!" Broader travel features dotted the pages of the magazines as well. *10 Percent* described the growing number of travel-obsessed men who transformed accumulating frequent flyer miles into a way of life.[46]

Cartoons remained a popular medium, the 1990s versions snickering at life as a guppy. A *BLK* cartoon depicted an African-American lesbian with a huge stomach trembling with fear as her lover tried to console her: "It was just a nightmare. But you are going to have to face the fact that our baby *might* be straight." *Deneuve* cartoons often focused on changing lesbian lifestyles. The first frame of one showed a woman whining to her lover, "Every queer and their cat is having kids or ceremonies." And by the final frame, the couple was in place at the wedding of the woman's mother, whose hair was streaming in the wind as she rode off on the back of a motorcycle with her own new partner, "Biker Bette."[47]

Looking Good

Gay publications had long reflected the high value many gay men place on appearance, with *The Advocate* introducing its body-building column, "Body Buddy," in the early 1970s and tracking men's fashion trends later that decade. But it was not until the 1990s that a critical mass of lesbians embraced that same value. More "lipstick lesbians" were wearing high heels, panty hose, short skirts, jewelry, and makeup. Reflecting the pivotal role that looking good played in the lives of many lesbians as well as gay men, the magazines veered away from trying to look and read like the *New York Times,* replacing that role model with such fashion and grooming icons as *Elle* and *GQ*. Editors made no apologies. *Genre's* Ron Kraft, who took over as editor in 1994, said: "We're a lifestyle magazine. We're not looking to do a whole lot for the political movement. We help our readers preserve their summer tans into the fall, not change the world."[48]

Fashion spreads became the largest single editorial element in the new magazines, accommodating to the upscale clothing designers lining up to buy ads. Lavish fashion spreads stretched to as many as ten pages, each unabashedly promoting the name-brand items featured in the photos. Prices and store locations often were listed as well. *Out* led the pack, adopting a standard of three fashion spreads per issue. *Victory!* created a column on how to dress for success in the business world. *Genre* borrowed a successful concept from *Sports Illustrated* and gave its male readership a men's swimsuit issue each spring.[49]

Product promotion was rarely strident, however, as the magazines followed the example of their straight counterparts and opted for the soft sell. *Deneuve's*

"A Date with Spring," for instance, contained lots of white space, soft lavender type, bunches of white tulips, and two photos of beautiful white-clad women on the first two-page spread. By the fourth page, the women had come together in a romantic embrace, and the bottom of the page listed the prices and store locations for the Ann Klein pleated skirt and Calvin Klein jean shorts the women wore. The photos were not explicit but carried a sexual subtext.[50]

Many lesbians found fault with the magazines for mirroring the tastes of women likely to buy the high-style clothing and costly grooming products advertised in their pages while having no images of women who opt for flannel shirts and hiking boots. *Out*'s Sarah Pettit acknowledged that the critics had a point—"Yes," she said, "we are creating an image of the gay community that may or may not be accurate." She neither apologized nor suggested any change.[51]

Frontiers covered fashion as well. Though carrying the coverline "the nation's gay newsmagazine" and printing on newsprint, the Los Angeles biweekly sported a slick cover that often highlighted men's clothing trends. One issue featured the coverline "Style" above a color photo of four handsome young men—Asian, black, blond, brunette—wearing loose-fitting shirts and shorts in shades of white and gray linen.[52]

Lesbian News dressed itself up with a slick cover, even though it, too, printed inside pages on newsprint. The monthly emphasized another form of looking good in the 1990s: physical fitness. To promote Gay Games IV, for example, *Lesbian News* blanketed its cover with a four-color photo of Jennifer Stary, a local woman competing in the international event, poised to throw a javelin. The cover placed Stary against an orchid sky and pink clouds with the coverline "Field of Dreams."[53]

Publications encouraged all readers, not just athletes, to tone their bodies as a step toward looking good. *Out*'s "Bodies" section advised readers on exercise programs suited to their needs and lifestyles. *10 Percent*'s "Health" column illuminated a variety of exercise programs, from step aerobics to yoga, body building to *tai chi*. *Deneuve*'s "Brownworth" column reflected the pivotal role of sports in many lesbian lifestyles.

Genre assumed the role of arbiter of what looking good meant for the affluent gay man. Its "Who's That Guy?" photo feature offered candid shots of nameless hunks whose well-defined chests turned heads. For readers who wanted to transform that second look into a livelihood, *Genre* offered "10 Ways to Trap a Sugar Daddy"; the list began with "Go to the gym and get a body" and continued through "If, and only if, you're pretty enough, try to get on the cover of *Genre*." Another feature provided details on the various forms of cosmetic surgery that had become a way of life for many gay men; the article reported that the going rate for a face lift was $2,500, and a penis enlargement would set a guy back $5,000.[54]

The strongest statement on how central appearance was in modern Gay America came with the prominence *Genre* gave to men's grooming. The magazine created the position of grooming editor and hired a twenty-year veteran of Elizabeth Arden to fill it. For his full-time job, Brad Johns helped stunning women such as Lauren Hutton and Claudia Schiffer appear even more beautiful; as a magazine editor, he counseled gay men on how to achieve the look they wanted. His first article introduced the topic of hair coloring, beginning with the subtitle: "How not to end up looking like a canary." Other pieces raved about the benefits of exercising facial muscles and bleaching one's teeth.[55]

Competing magazines followed *Genre*'s lead. When *BLK* reported on national meetings of gay African Americans, it looked to the events not for their political messages but for what they said about trends in men's grooming: "The fashion watchword for this year's National Black Gay and Lesbian Conference was dreads. They were everywhere, in all configurations, and particularly on Gary Paul Wright of New York. Yum." *Victory!* introduced a "Gay Friendly" column with a profile of a Southern California hair replacement business. The man-and-wife team created high-quality hairpieces. Only toward the end of the article did the reader learn just why the profile was appearing in *Victory!*— 90 percent of the company's clients were gay men.[56]

Making the Bucks

Most of the activities and values promoted in the pages of the slick magazines required the laying out of major quantities of cash. So the highly visible voices of 1990s Gay and Lesbian America committed themselves to helping their readers secure the incomes to enable them to partake of the good life and look good, while—of course—paying for the abundance of consumer goods advertised in the magazines.

The epitome of this phenomenon occurred in December 1993 when *Victory!* was founded as a monthly magazine carrying the subtitle *The National Gay & Lesbian Entrepreneur Magazine*. The founder of the genre's first business publication, M. J. McKean-Reich, was a twenty-seven-year-old novice with experience neither in publishing nor in business. Speaking with the pompous attitude rife among the new generation of publishers, he boasted: "My whole life has been a success story so far. So I get turned on by other people achieving success." With that vision in mind, McKean-Reich set out to show readers how successful gay business people had made their fortunes and, therefore, how others could do the same.[57]

One successful feature splashed onto the newsstands in early 1995 when he published his first annual list of the fifty fastest-growing businesses owned by lesbians and gay men—from the Big Hair/Big Art hair salon and art gallery in Sacramento with annual gross revenues of $82,000 to the Denver-based software giant Quark, Inc., with earnings of $110 million.[58]

McKean-Reich deserved credit for his personal rise as well. An African-American man who grew up on government assistance in Pittsburgh's inner city, he was spared the trials of urban gang warfare only because he was, in his own words, "too effeminate" to be accepted into a gang. He escaped from poverty by way of an Ivy League education at Yale University.[59]

Unlike many publishers of the era, McKean-Reich was committed to social activism, helping to establish AIDS education programs while still in college. He saw publishing *Victory!* as a form of activism as well, insisting that economic vitality was crucial to gay people securing civil liberties. "The only way things are going to change is if we own businesses," he said. "The next step for the civil rights agenda for the gay community, in my opinion, is economic stability."[60]

Although McKean-Reich's magazine was the leading vehicle for telling gay and lesbian readers how to make money, this message was not entirely the province of *Victory!* The magazine had its own personal finance column called "Power Investing," but similar features also popped up in other magazines, with only the names changing—"Checks and Balances" in *10 Percent,* "Risky Business" in *Genre.*

By profiling successful entrepreneurs and business trends, other publications highlighted how readers could make money. *Deneuve,* as the most visible glossy magazine for lesbians, was particularly committed to such stories. Reviving a technique Barbara Gittings had invented in *The Ladder* thirty years earlier, Frances Stevens of *Deneuve* profiled composer Kay Gardner and Stanford University medical school professor Kate O'Hanlan. The magazine also spotlighted trends such as the rise of lesbian television. After describing the successful *Dyke TV* in New York and *One TV* in Houston, *Deneuve* crowed: "While there's a black hole of queer programming on network TV, cable is a brand new galaxy."[61]

Celebrating the Youth Culture

Personalities are an important element in the formula for creating a successful slick magazine. In the American culture where the search for the Holy Grail has been supplanted by the search for the Fountain of Youth, the people many readers most want to look at and read about are those who are young and attractive, young and vibrant, young and successful, and just plain *young*. The lesbian and gay glossies responded by focusing on women and men who had no wrinkles, no love handles, no bags under their eyes, and—thanks to the wonders of air brushing—no pores.

Such glorifying of youth had positive elements. As lesbian and gay teenagers of earlier decades had struggled to discover their sexual selves, the only role models they could find were from the mainstream media . . . and that meant straight couples only. For the first time, thanks to the gay glossies, teenagers had a whole new set of images to consider.

Many of the people who became driving forces behind the magazines were young. After earning a degree in chemistry and microbiology from San Francisco State University, Frances Stevens opted not to spend her life in a lab. So, at twenty-three, she gave magazine publishing a shot. She recalled: "I wanted a magazine like *Deneuve* and no one else was doing it. So I did. I'm not much of a whiner; I'm more of a doer. You say the word 'overachiever' comes to mind? I wouldn't argue with that."[62]

Stevens expressed her youth in her magazine. A typical feature surveyed teenagers about the issues weighing on their minds. The article discussed topics ranging from dating to drinking to using drugs, repeatedly pointing out that being lesbian puts a different spin on every issue—and not always a positive one. The story counseled: "We need to tell these kids, 'There's a life for you. Everything's going to be OK.'" *Deneuve* did not, however, allow the article to get too heavy. The photo on the first spread showed one young woman quoted in the article wearing only jeans and a black lace bra. The caption: "Amanda Hill bares all . . . almost."[63]

When there was a groundswell of interest in the feature on teenage lesbians, Stevens located a twenty-one-year-old "babydyke" to write a "Hey, Baby!" column in each issue. Bree Coven reassured her readers that they were not alone, using the steady stream of "Dear Babydyke" letters as proof. Coven wrote: "If the same sentence 'I must be the only babydyke in my school, town, state, the world' comes from all these different people, guess what? You must be wrong!" Her column covered issues ranging from how lesbian teenagers can locate other lesbian teenagers to how a young lesbian can tell aggressive male suitors . . . "It's not going to happen!"[64]

Stevens was not the only young editor who became a principal in a magazine. When *Out* debuted, president and editor Michael Goff was twenty-six. Goff had graduated from Stanford and passed the exams to follow in his parents' footsteps as a diplomat, until the State Department rejected him because of his sexuality. He then brought his youthful energy and creativity to publishing. Goff shared responsibilities with executive editor Sarah Pettit. Only twenty-five when the magazine got off the ground, she already had a degree from Yale and publishing experience at St. Martin's Press under her belt. The youthful overachiever said, "I wanted to prove how irresistible a top-notch gay publication can be."[65]

A vivid example of how the editors' own youth translated into content came when *Out* showcased "Mr. and Mr. Bob and Rod Jackson-Paris." The cover photo showed the two twenty-something body builders holding a pitchfork between them with a white clapboard farmhouse in the background, à la American Gothic. The spread inside showed them—one a former Mr. Universe, the other a model whose attributes had been featured in *Playgirl*—in various poses to highlight their massive chests. The text, which paled in comparison to the photos, concentrated on the minutiae of the couple's eight-year relationship, which also happened to be the subject of their book, *Straight from the Heart*, which had just been released.[66]

The magazines were reassured that their emphasis on youth was fully in sync with their targeted readership when the Jackson-Paris cover sold more than any other issue of *Out*. The *Advocate*'s experience reinforced the phenomenon, when the biggest-selling cover in the magazine's 700-issue history proved to be the one featuring the youthful, hard-bodied model Marky Mark.[67]

The magazines glorified youth in their features articles. They swooned when *Melrose Place,* the prime-time soap opera crafted to capture teenage viewers, added a gay character to the cast. When *Square Peg* wanted to talk about gay Asians, it looked through the eyes of a twenty-four-year-old Filipino. *10 Percent* examined the social and political climate for college students in lesbian nirvana, titling its article "Northampton: 10,000 Cuddling, Kissing Lesbians." Barry Goldwater's grandson was only thirty-one when *POZ* placed him on the cover of its premier issue. Tracy James was twenty-five when *Out* crowned him "the sexiest go-go boy in America"—complete with two full-page photos of the young man doing what he did best. Models in the ubiquitous fashion layouts were uniformly young, sleek, and gorgeous as well.[68]

Victory! reinforced the message that all successful lesbian and gay entrepreneurs were not graybeards. Matt Marco had just turned twenty when the business magazine praised him for founding a publication for gay young people titled *YOUTH* (Young Outspoken Ubiquitous Thinking Homo). And a profile of a digitized media business focused on Clinton Fein, who was only twenty-nine when he acquired the CD-ROM rights to Randy Shilts's best-selling *Conduct Unbecoming: A History of Gays and Lesbians in the U.S. Military.* The finished product included the book's complete text along with video interviews and still photos of people profiled in the book.[69]

The most poignant article about gay youth appeared in *10 Percent*. It consisted of photos of young men and women who had tested HIV positive. The only text was quotations from the young people: "'It was my first sexual experience. He was older and experienced, so I left it up to him. That's what a lot of young people do because they have no self-esteem,' Johnnie Norway, tested positive at 19. . . . 'I know a lot of young lesbians who are in denial about HIV,' Antigone Hodgins, tested positive at 22. . . . 'I was going to be an architect and live in a nifty house and have somebody to share my life with, and that would have been really nice. Now I find myself spending more and more time at the hospital. I started chemotherapy about a month ago and I'm losing my hair. I shouldn't have to think about things like losing my hair,' Scott Miller, tested positive at 18."[70]

Designing for the Mainstream

As veterans of mainstream magazines, many staff members had been schooled in the belief that how their magazines looked was at least as important as how they read. The glossies strived for the image of class and sophistication that would persuade young, upwardly mobile men and women first to plunk down five bucks for a copy—and then to buy the products advertised inside. The challenge was a formidable one, but the gay and lesbian press had demonstrated a commitment to design for nearly half a century. In the 1990s that commitment mushroomed to an unparalleled magnitude.

The magazines opted not to pack their pages with hard-hitting news content but to explode with visual stimuli—vibrant colors, stunning photos, bold graphics, varied typography. In fact, the first of the new magazines set a design standard that remained unmatched despite the spate of imitators that followed. From the beginning, *Genre* successfully balanced its desire to engage readers with its commitment to taste and style. When announcing its first annual Gay Hall of Fame, for example, *Genre* presented its lowercased "men we love" headline not in the primary colors such a bold venture might suggest, but in subtle shades of mauve and olive. The full-page photos of the eight men that followed maintained the restrained tone. The first pictured "Friend of Bill" David Mixner in a conservative navy blue suit; the last depicted veteran drag queen Charles Busch wrapped not in a sequined gown and scarlet boa but in black trousers and sweater.[71]

At the same time, *Genre* established a unique style distinct from both gay and mainstream competitors. Most notably, it broke from the conventional wisdom of publishing by printing most of its text in sans serif typefaces, which are generally avoided because they are difficult to read in large blocks. *Genre* defused the readability issue by placing ample space between the lines and maintaining broad expanses of white space at the outer margins of the page. The effect became one of a crisp, clean image fully in concert with the sense of refined sophistication the magazine sought to communicate.

By contrast, "restrained" did not appear in the dictionary Roger Black used when he designed *Out*. With creating the mainstream looks of such major magazines as *Esquire* and *House Beautiful* already to his credit, Black said: "I take a look at most gay magazines, and I find them either drab or boring. What we feel is needed is an alternative that is entertaining." Black translated that concept into constantly jolting the reader with nonstop design surprises. He began with high-gloss, stark-white paper that transformed blocks of tightly set type into mere design elements to set off the magazine's bold images. The magazine so gloried in breaking from the rigidity of the grid format that readers rarely found examples of that layout in its pages, even though it remained standard in the magazine industry. To give *Out* a three-dimensional quality, Black created huge blocks of primary color that jumped off the page. For an article about body piercing, for example, he placed a photo of a festooned lesbian and gay man against a block of fire-engine-red ink bleeding across the gutter, overwhelming the ribbons of type that seemed to be an afterthought squeezed onto the edges of the page.[72]

10 Percent, aiming at the more established reader, settled in with a look between *Genre* and *Out*, mercifully leaning toward the former. Printed on slightly off-white paper and with ample white space between the lines of text, *10 Percent* avoided primary colors in favor of muted earth tones. A profile of lesbian author Lillian Faderman opened with a full-page, black-and-white portrait of the historian, balanced against the first page of text set in white type against a brown background bled to all four edges. *10 Percent* also used typographical techniques to help readers grasp the major themes of an article. When the magazine persuaded John Schlafly, the conservative gay son of antifeminist crusader Phyllis Schlafly, to be interviewed by Dee Mosbacher, the liberal lesbian daughter of former Secretary of Commerce Robert Mosbacher, it broke up the sea of gray type by printing selected words from the text in maroon ink. The enhanced words jumped off the page, graphically alerting the reader's eye to the major themes in the interview—"Republicans," "hypocrisy," "right-wing."[73]

While generous use of color and high-quality paper helped *Genre, Out,* and

10 Percent create their distinctive looks, *Deneuve* proved that design quality does not have to come with a high price tag. Rarely able to afford four-color photos, the lesbian magazine turned the use of a second color into a fine art. To commemorate the quarter-century anniversary of Stonewall, the magazine coupled statements from lesbian foremothers with portraits rendered not *less* but *more* effective by the faded quality achieved with a second color—Phyllis Lyon in sepia. All the colors in the rainbow could not have added more impact to the grainy black-and-white image of a youthful Martha Shelley with a fist raised and a peace medallion dangling from her neck. *Deneuve* wisely enlarged the magnificent photo to cover an entire page bled to all four edges.[74]

Compared with this quartet of newcomers, *The Advocate* looked like a country cousin who had not yet discovered the world beyond rural Kansas. Even after its 1992 redesign, the grandfather of gay publishing lacked the design sophistication and artistry of the new kids on the block. Much of the problem could be blamed on the lightness of *The Advocate*'s paper, as even its occasional high-quality color photo washed out because of the thin, almost translucent, paper the magazine used.

The rigid boundaries of establishment publishing continued to try to limit the lesbian and gay press in its use of images, as had been the case in previous eras. Before the editors of *OUT/LOOK* hired a printer, they explained that they occasionally would run sexually explicit graphics. Sheridan Press in rural Pennsylvania assured the editors that such content would not be a problem. Upon receiving the first set of production boards, however, the company called to say that two graphics were "too immodest." A photo with a feature on lesbian fashion showed bare nipples; a cartoon depicted a cheerleader—who bore a striking resemblance to First Lady Nancy Reagan—whose pom-poms were made of pubic hair. The company refused to print the material. *OUT/LOOK* publisher Kim Klausner was furious. She told *Gay Community News*: "It's appalling that playful images about women's sexuality are still so threatening that a printer would break his contract and try to censor them." The magazine dug in its heels, although finding another printer meant delaying the first issue for several weeks. An editorial stated: "We're more determined than ever to stick to our original mission: to create a national forum for men and women that showcases the erudite and the sublime in the same setting."[75]

OUT/LOOK again found itself in hot water—this time from within the lesbian community—when it published an essay on gay pornographer Tom of Finland, known for his explicit drawings of men with oversized genitalia. A North Dakota woman wrote: "Calling *OUT/LOOK* a lesbian and gay quarterly and feeding the stereotype of gay men's massive penises as their only vital organ is offensive." A Massachusetts woman said that the article caused her to abandon her plans to give subscriptions to the magazine as Christmas gifts. The editors stood by their decision, arguing that pornography is a formative influence on gay men. "As a forum for both gay men and lesbians," an editorial stated, "*OUT/LOOK* articulates the spectrum of experience in both communities, whether or not they are 'acceptable' to us or to other sectors of our readership."[76]

Reporting the News

The major thrust of the slick new magazines was toward securing ads and creating benign editorial puffery to enhance them, but substantive news and commentary were not entirely absent. Most of the glossies carried columns of news briefs. In addition, several covered the controversial issues of the day, reassuring gay people that finding one's best hair color and selecting the perfect shade of damask for the slipper chair in the library were not the *only* dilemmas of the age.

OUT/LOOK, the most substantive of the magazines, raised a controversial issue when it asked bluntly, "Why don't gay and lesbian leaders last?" The seventeen-page article dissected the political careers of past leaders—Del Martin, Frank Kameny, and David Goodstein among them—to analyze why the movement had yet to find a leader comparable in stature to the Reverend Martin Luther King, Jr. Unity within the movement had always been tentative, the article argued, because being gay differs for various subgroups: "If the leader promoted by one faction exemplified the wrong qualities in the eyes of another faction, say the left-feminists running *Gay Community News,* the dissidents not only refused to follow him, but also considered it necessary to repudiate him." The article concluded that the person who ultimately would lead Lesbian and Gay America to freedom would be someone whose personal appearance and style did not alienate any major faction.[77]

The magazines contributed to the rising public profile of openly gay men and women. No publication embraced the concept of outing as stridently as *OutWeek* had, but several published articles about prominent women and men whose sexuality already had been publicly divulged. *The Advocate* ran cover stories about gay staff members at the *New York Times* and NOW president Patricia Ireland's personal life with a husband as well as a female companion, and another piece lambasting Anne-Imelda Radice, the conservative President Bush appointed acting chair of the National Endowment for the Arts, labeling her a "lesbian Clarence Thomas" and "lesbian from hell." *10 Percent* profiled singer Melissa Etheridge after she came out during the first lesbian and gay inaugural ball in 1993.[78]

Two of the biggest events of the era unfolded when hundreds of thousands of gay people descended first on Washington in 1993 and then on New York a year later. As with the two previous marches, the body count for the 1993 March on Washington varied with the source—organizers said 1 million; the Park Service said 300,000—but everyone agreed that the mainstream media gave extensive coverage to the march this time. So lesbian and gay magazines opted for different angles. *10 Percent* committed its editorial energies to describing vacation sites near the nation's capital; *The Advocate* played the cynic by questioning the long-range impact of mass demonstrations. *Square Peg* selected the best "girl" chant—"We're here. We're queer. We can't find Jodie Foster."[79]

There was even more discrepancy in the crowd estimates in 1994 when men and women from all over the globe converged on Greenwich Village to mark the twenty-fifth anniversary of Stonewall, which coincided with Gay Games IV and its 10,000 participants from forty countries. Organizers boasted a total figure of 1.1 million; New York City police said 100,000. Mainstream media published and broadcast eye-catching images of the mile-long rainbow flag marchers carried down First Avenue; while their accompanying articles made much of the dispute that resulted in two distinct parades. The splinter group was led by Sylvia Rivera, a drag queen who had fought at Stonewall and returned in black pumps and gold dress for the celebration, announcing, "I'm here to see that we still have the guts to take Fifth Avenue." Establishment media squabbled over who to blame for the division into two parades—the *New York Times* said that the "rebel contingent" was displeased that organizers had not paid more attention to AIDS; the *Washington Post* insisted that the issue was man/boy love.[80]

One institution *not* embracing the spirit of Stonewall was the American military. The gay and lesbian press played a singular role in attempting to end banning gay people from serving in the armed forces when candidate Bill Clinton told *The Advocate,* in February 1992, "If elected, I would reverse the ban." But after taking office, Clinton was stunned at vehement congressional and military opposition. *Frontiers* editorialized: "What we have is a mix of mostly older, straight white men, holding the highest offices in the world's most powerful nation, who hang onto old stereotypes and prejudices. The defining term is *bigot.*" Six months after taking office, Clinton—in the first instance of waffling that would define his presidency—announced a compromise prohibiting officials from asking new recruits about their sexual orientation but continued to allow soldiers to be discharged merely for letting their orientation be known.[81]

Deneuve kept the ban issue on the front burner by saluting Colonel Margarethe Cammermeyer, a thirty-year veteran who was decorated for service in Vietnam before she publicly announced she was a lesbian. Calling Cammermeyer "an officer and a lesbian," *Deneuve* quoted her as saying: "This is America. We fight for the freedom of everyone—unless you're gay or lesbian."[82]

Defining the Limits of Mainstream

In 1977, *Gay Sunshine* stated in a trembling voice: "Gay periodicals have had an alarmingly high casualty rate, and it's unpredictable how many of the new crop will last." A decade and a half later, the trembling had subsided somewhat. The Gay Nineties generation had lifted lesbian and gay journalism to a new height— at least as a business enterprise.[83]

Out epitomized the generation. The principals behind the upscale magazine used the half million dollars they raised from investors to promote their magazine as none had before it. Their marketing strategy was sophisticated and comprehensive, from well-placed publicity to compact discs as gifts for new subscribers. Results were equally impressive. In two years, circulation reached six figures and advertising revenue quintupled, with major companies standing in line to appear in the gay *Vanity Fair.*

Although entrepreneurs cannot argue with such success, activists can. Insisting that the money used to publish the magazines would have been better spent on AIDS research or the ongoing gay human rights campaign, activists denounced the slick magazines—particularly the meekness of their editorial content. ACT UP spokesman Robert Rafsky sarcastically pointed out that the rise of the glossies proved one thing only: "Gay people can turn out totally worthless lifestyle magazines." Indeed, their editorial content was diluted. As voices for change, the magazines barely whispered.[84]

What's more, the magazines took advertising that otherwise might have gone to strengthen more assertive, news-oriented publications. "There is a bias among Madison Avenue agencies," *Washington Blade* publisher Don Michaels said. "They like to go with the slick glossy stuff." The advertisers knew that the glossy magazines attracted a more affluent readership, reproduced ads more attractively, and were less political than general gay and lesbian newspapers such as the *Blade* or *Windy City Times.*[85]

The "publishing people" who created the glossies were critical as well, reinforcing that editorial acrimony remained a lodestar of the gay and lesbian press. Despite the slick new magazines' large circulations and ever-growing stables of advertisers, the gay grapevine was alive with rumors of financial uncertainties and impending collapse of even the largest of the magazines, with *The Advocate, 10 Percent, Out,* and *POZ* the most often whispered about. *The Advocate's* Jeff Yarbrough reflected the unsympathetic spirit that had characterized gay and lesbian editors for decades when he publicly stated: "If magazines are bad, they deserve to die. Some of the magazines that are out there *aren't any good.*"[86]

In marching into the mainstream of American publishing—not to mention marching to the bank—the magazines sacrificed several principles on which the gay and lesbian press had been built. Largely absent, for example, was the concept Lisa Ben inaugurated when *Vice Versa* created an open forum for a variety of views. If a writer's byline had not previously appeared in magazines such as *Allure* or *Gentleman's Quarterly,* she or he stood little chance of getting the big break in *Out* or *10 Percent.* Gone as well were the unique lexicon and graphic sexual images that had come to define the genre. The language and visuals appearing in the glossies were as mainstream as their ads. Indeed, the unremitting effort to attract those mainstream ads dictated timidity in language and images. Nor did the magazines advance the creation of a national community to the degree that their predecessors had. The glossies were more interested in showing how readers blended into mainstream society than in helping them strengthen Lesbian and Gay America.

Postmortems on the pair of publications that already had failed by mid-decade reinforced the formula for success among the slick new magazines. *OUT/LOOK,* with a dearth of major advertisers and a circulation of only 15,000, ceased publication in 1992. The quarterly died, in part, because its commitment to editorial substance and its willingness to publish "offensive" material scared advertisers into the arms of more accommodating competitors. Articles such as the seventeen-page analysis of why gay people had failed to identify a Reverend Martin Luther King, Jr., and provocative visual images such as a woman's bare nipple and the artwork of Tom of Finland were out of step with the new era. *Square Peg,* which also lacked national advertisers and peaked at a circulation of 13,000, died in 1993. Publisher Jeanne Córdova lamented: "We printed more substantive stories than fluffy features and graphics. So we never appealed to big advertisers. Besides, those companies won't print their ads on newsprint, and we didn't have half a million bucks to go to slick paper."[87]

So what's *wrong* with glossy magazines covering fashion and entertainment rather than news and politics? Few would attack *Mirabella* or *Details* as doing a disservice to the country. The difference is that those publications are not part of the alternative media. They have never played a role in a social movement to eliminate second-class citizenship for a minority group that continues to be repressed and demonized. Until a cure for AIDS is found, lesbians and gay men are allowed to serve in the military, federal law prevents employers from firing gay people because of their sexual orientation, and gay bashing is no longer running rampant across the country, it is difficult to applaud gay and lesbian journalism that concentrates on documenting the joys of owning a red damask loveseat and that has editors like *The Advocate*'s Jeff Yarbrough "dreading" the time when his magazine has to be published more frequently. As long as homophobia continues to relegate gay people to second-class citizenship, lesbian and gay publications are intrinsically part of the movement. By becoming mainstream in their editorial content, design, and advertising, the gay glossies slipped away from the most fundamental purpose of a movement press: securing equal rights for their readers.

Dramatic evidence of just how mainstream the gay glossies had become surfaced in 1994 when Time, Inc., announced it was considering starting a magazine to compete with the likes of *Out* and *Deneuve*. The gay man who took the idea to Time argued that the media powerhouse could attract a huge readership because—ironically—gay publications were ignoring the needs of their readers. Specifically, Maer Roshan said that the glossies were too concerned about advertising: "The gay community needs a magazine that is focused on readers rather than advertisers. We are living in gritty times, and they call for journalism that comes from the soul, rather than articles that consider what Calvin Klein might think." Time invested $75,000 and six months of effort to develop three prototype issues of a gay magazine called *Tribe*.[88]

Then newspapers began reporting that the Reverend Donald Wildmon, whose American Family Association had attacked television programs with gay themes, was pressuring Time to kill the project. A week later, the media conglomerate that built its empire by speaking primarily to conservatives pulled the plug on *Tribe*, saying that the proposed magazine's 250,000 potential circulation was not large enough. The "publishing people" in the lesbian and gay press were, however, not discouraged—partly because they did not welcome the competition and partly because Time's mere consideration of such a project sent a positive message about the future of the genre. *Out* associate publisher Harry Taylor told the *New York Times*: "For such a large conglomerate to even consider a general-interest magazine geared toward gay men and lesbians only validates the market." Comments from Time, Inc., editor-at-large Gil Rogin were encouraging as well: "I call *Tribe* a cryogenic magazine—it's going to thaw, one way or another. It's not going to die."[89]

λ 12

Looking Back to See the Future

Gay and Lesbian America will win. Absolutely. In a country founded on the principle of equality, justice ultimately will prevail over homophobia and bigotry. The ban will be lifted. A cure will be found. Gay marriages will be performed openly and with glorious ceremony that puts Martha Stewart to shame. Employers will seek out lesbians and gay men to diversify their personnel profile. The country's new president will borrow her lover's panty hose before making her Inaugural Address.

In the context of this book, then, the question becomes How much will the lesbian and gay press help in attaining this full freedom that lies somewhere in the future? Based on the events of the past half century, that question can be answered in two opposing ways: "A lot" or "Very little."

Either response may apply because the history of this intriguing form of the alternative media has not been one defined solely by advancements, but also by setbacks. Periods during which the gay press has propelled the movement forward toward civil rights have been followed by periods in which the leading publications of the day seemed more intent upon marching to the bank than marching to freedom. Reading the history of the lesbian and gay press, as detailed in the eleven preceding chapters, is like taking a ride on a roller coaster.

The story began in 1947 when a spirited young woman with empty space on her dance card found a creative solution that launched a new genre of American journalism: *Vice Versa*. The story continued its positive climb in the 1950s as *ONE*, *Mattachine Review*, and *The Ladder* raised their voices for "the love that dare not speak its name," even as postal authorities, FBI agents, and the shadow of Joseph McCarthy loomed over them. Militancy held sway in the turbulent 1960s. Early in the decade, editors simultaneously organized and promoted the first public demonstrations by gay people; later in the decade, editors adapted the themes of the counterculture to provide palpable evidence that the times were, indeed, changing. Perhaps even more important, the late 1960s press already had pioneered unique themes that distinguished—then as well as now—the genre not only from establishment journalism but from alternative journalism as well.

The path continued upward after the Stonewall Rebellion ignited the modern Lesbian and Gay Movement. The fumes of liberation created a generation of "wild and woolly" tabloids and street papers that debated such fundamental issues as the role drag queens and "dykes on bikes" would play in the movement. The cultural phase of the mid-1970s followed, led by such legendary publications as *Amazon Quarterly* and *Fag Rag*.

But then came some tough times. The cultural emphasis left the genre vulnerable to virulent assaults by the New Right at the end of the 1970s. Although lesbian and gay journalism recovered by reviving its emphasis on news and becoming more professional, the genre again suffered a severe setback when AIDS chose gay men as its favorite prey. The early 1980s witnessed a dark chapter in the history of the gay press as the leading voices in the capital of Gay America—the *Bay Area Reporter, San Francisco Sentinel,* and *Advocate*—failed to alert their readers to a murderer in their midst, even while other publications—the *New York Native* in particular—served their readers with commitment and integrity.

In the second half of the 1980s, the lesbian and gay press led a period of radical resurgence against the status quo, with *OutWeek* and several militant lesbian voices setting the pace. Those demands for reform were eclipsed in the early 1990s by a gaggle of glossy magazines that diluted their content to attract deep-pocket advertisers and give new meaning to the term *superficiality.*

Despite the revolving cast of characters and mind-numbing waves of ups and downs, the lesbian and gay press most certainly has, in fact, risen. In 1947 the genre's single voice had a circulation of exactly one dozen. A quarter century later, some 150 publications had a circulation of 250,000. Today, some 850 boast a total circulation of 2 million.

Indeed, Lisa Ben's quixotic foray into publishing had proven to be a remarkably fertile foremother. Ben wrote blithely in 1947: "Perhaps VICE VERSA might be the forerunner of better magazines dedicated to the Third Sex which, in some future time, might take their rightful place on the news stands." With 2,600 publications having followed in its precarious path, how right she was.

Tiny magazines that began as fragile lifelines to frightened and isolated individuals have evolved into a powerful force that has played a vital role in constructing a strong, visible, politically enfranchised national gay and lesbian community. Fifty years ago topics of fundamental interest to gay people were unspeakable. Today publications speak openly about a wide range of topics, consistently offering positive images of an array of lifestyles while constituting a unique genre that has not only taken its place at the table of American journalism but has redefined what the alternative media in this country can be. Gerald Hannon, a longtime member of the collective that produced *The Body Politic,* had it right when he articulated why he had committed his energy to the lesbian and gay press: "I got hooked on empowerment, the transformation of The Helpless Queer with no history and an unlikely future into Someone, into a *group* of Someones, who uncovered a history, who found heroes, who grabbed today and shook it till tomorrow fell out of its pocket and there was a place there in it for us."[1]

Even before the Stonewall Rebellion ignited the modern phase of the Lesbian and Gay Liberation Movement, the movement press had already established the themes that ultimately came to define its later chapters. The genre's penchant for expressing itself in a unique lexicon came into sharpest focus in the era immediately after Stonewall when publications communicated their revolutionary fervor by defiantly using terms—such as *dyke, cunt,* and *clit*—that previously had been terms of derision. The controversial theme of blurring the line between news and advertising intensified during the same period as the proliferation of gay bars and bathhouses caused some publications to limit their reform efforts.

Several themes reached their zenith in the 1970s. Editorial discord soared in 1974 when David B. Goodstein's transformation of *The Advocate* into an upscale lifestyles magazine so aggravated Gay America that he had to hire a personal bodyguard. This was also the era when the commitment to amusing readers rose to new heights, as the cultural phase emphasized such pastimes as playing softball and attending music festivals for women, bodybuilding and feasting on sex for men. Likewise, it was in the 1970s that the genre's long-standing emphasis on visual images was most palpable with the beefcake that became a staple of the gay press. Finally, the commitment to design quality was dramatically reinforced by the high style of the gay glossies in the 1990s.

Now that each of these half dozen themes has worn the test of time for thirty years—some of them for fifty—it seems likely that they will continue to shape the lesbian and gay press as it enters the twenty-first century.

An alert reader might challenge that last statement, pointing out that the lifestyle magazines of the 1990s do not, for example, speak in a gay lexicon as much as they speak in the language of the young and the beautiful of mainstream society. This is true, but while the gay glossies were the *biggest* story of the early 1990s, they were not—thank God and Goddess both—the *only* story. For gay and lesbian journalism has continued to grow ever more diverse. A tabloid newspaper such as *The Weekly News* in Miami is light years away from *CTN* magazine (originally *Coming Together Newsletter*) for deaf gays or *Black*

Lace for African-American lesbians or *Lesbian Connection,* the mimeographed bimonthly in East Lansing, Michigan, that for twenty years has remained Lesbian America's town crier, appearing on typing paper in a rainbow of gold, blue, green, yellow, pink—whatever is available. 'Zines are cutting another wide swath across the Gay Nineties landscape because all it takes is one or two creative minds and a computer to make a single original that is then photocopied and sent on its way. Punk rhetoric and explicit sex dominate the dozens of 'zines that range from *Up Our Butts* and *Taste of Latex,* to *Meandyke, teen fag* and *Dragnett: The Feminist Militant Drag Queen Superhero Comic with a Mission.*

The biggest explosions of all will be along the information superhighway. In a community where creativity is valued almost as highly as good sex, technological boundaries are bursting. While the emphasis so far has been on cultural material, programming is expanding rapidly and would be an excellent topic for another book on gay and lesbian media. In 1992 KGAY became, for one frenetic year, the first twenty-four-hour gay and lesbian radio station, using satellites to broadcast its signal throughout the United States. The syndicated radio magazine show *This Way Out* broadcasts interviews to eighty stations in six countries. *Our World Television* brings gay public affairs and cultural programming to 300,000 cable subscribers in Southern California. Gay Entertainment Television uses satellites to beam programming, including the talk show *Inside/ Out,* from New York to 7 million homes nationwide. Network Q subscribers receive a two-hour video in their mailboxes each month, keeping them informed about gay cultural events.[2]

After piloting the reader through half a century of gay and lesbian journalism history, I feel compelled to share a few broad observations about this genre that has dominated my life for the last three years. These forces have helped make the genre what it is today and, therefore, very well may shape its future as well.

▼ I am struck by how many gay press pioneers were catapulted into the field by their own personal bouts with discrimination. Dale Jennings proposed creating *ONE* in 1952, and Dick Michaels founded the genre's first true newspaper in 1967 after being wrongly arrested on morals charges—both were later exonerated. Franklin E. Kameny founded the *Homosexual Citizen* in 1966, and David B. Goodstein used $3 million of his personal fortune to build *The Advocate* into the premiere gay publication of the 1970s after they had been fired from their respective jobs because of their sexuality. Discrimination is not the stuff of the distant past. Michael Goff became founding editor of *Out* in 1992 after passing the exams to become an American diplomat, but then having the

State Department reject him because of his sexuality. Each of these men turned to journalism because he saw it as the vehicle that ultimately could end the bigotry he had suffered firsthand. Jennings spoke for them all when he said recently, "In a nation founded on the cornerstone of free expression, the press seemed to me like the little guy's only salvation—it still does."[3]

▼ Bigotry did not evaporate, however, when these determined individuals committed their energies to advocacy journalism. In fact, for many pioneers, the lesbian and gay press meant not only donating huge quantities of time with zero financial reward, but also becoming victims of hate crimes. After Phyllis Lyon founded *The Ladder* in 1956, her nights were repeatedly disrupted by telephone death threats, and when Sasha Gregory-Lewis investigated the New Right as part of her work for *The Advocate* in the 1970s, she not only received death threats but also had her apartment ransacked.

Hate crimes against gay male journalists have extended to physical violence. While distributing his *San Francisco Gay Free Press* soon after Stonewall, editor Charles Thorp had his face slashed with a knife and was struck in the head with a baseball bat. George Mendenhall suffered similar abuse when he reported on the repeal of the gay rights ordinance in Miami for the *Bay Area Reporter* in 1977. And in 1987 Jeff McCourt was leading the *Windy City Times*'s effort to expose a neo-Nazi group that targeted gay men. McCourt was alone the Sunday afternoon when two skinheads entered his office and began swinging baseball bats. By the time they left, McCourt lay on the floor with several broken bones.

▼ Lesbian and gay journalism has been on the front lines of the war for civil liberties because for half a century it has been the movement's most visible and most vulnerable institution. While other arms of the movement have remained underground, publications have been out on the streets every day. The pioneers of the 1950s were the first to pay the price for this visibility when the U.S. Senate, Post Office, and FBI all investigated their magazines. In addition to the grueling interrogations and constant acts of intimidation, those courageous men and women also suffered in their employment and career advancement. During an era when people even rumored to be homosexual were summarily fired from their jobs, FBI agents sent the names of the editors to their employers, routinely describing them as "perverts," "deviants," and "security risks." Martin Block, founding editor of *ONE*, said: "None of us can prove it, but obviously those conversations and those letters did severe damage to all of our careers. The authorities did all they could to keep the queers in their place."[4]

The price of sitting atop the gay lightning rod continued in later decades. In

1967 gay press veteran Jack Nichols appeared on a CBS television documentary one day and was fired from his job the next. After the Stonewall uprising in 1969, FBI Director J. Edgar Hoover—a closeted gay man who felt contempt for gay rights advocates—stepped up his investigation of the movement press, eventually amassing 6,800 pages of material on men and women such as John O'Brien of *Gay Times* and Martha Shelley of *Come Out!*. By 1977 the FBI recognized the increasing power of the gay press, as shown by agents offering a paid informant bonuses for any evidence he produced that would damage the reputations of staff members from the *Washington Blade, The Advocate,* or *The Furies*—apparently not knowing that the lesbian newspaper had ceased publication four years earlier. In 1978, authorities shifted their intimidation campaign to *The Body Politic*; it took five years in court for the newspaper to confirm that press freedom extends to gay newspapers. *Gay Community News* paid the price for visibility in 1982 when, a month after the staff had demanded that Boston's vice squad be disbanded, arsonists burned the *GCN* offices to the ground.

▼ Such sacrifices have reaped rewards. One major victory came in 1958 when the U.S. Supreme Court finally ruled, after a four-year legal battle, that gay-oriented materials could legally be sent through the mail. The battles against censorship have continued. In 1981 a printing company refused to publish an issue of *Big Apple Dyke News* because it contained a Joan Nestle article about a sexual encounter with another woman; editor Susan Cavin shifted to a printer whose Chinese typesetters could not read English. Again, in 1988, a printer told *OUT/LOOK* publisher Kim Klausner that her images were "too immodest." Klausner dug in her heels and found another printer. Each of these efforts to censor the lesbian and gay press ultimately failed. So will future ones.

▼ On a more personal level, the genre has launched the careers of some extraordinary writers. Rita Mae Brown, who has published more than a dozen best-selling books, first set pen to paper to write poetry and fiery essays for *The Ladder* and *The Furies*. Randy Shilts, who became the most famous gay journalist in history, got his start at *The Advocate*. Shilts ignored the journalism professors who said that working for the gay press would destroy his career. He later said: "I worked my ass off to prove them wrong. I was determined to make gay journalism something to be proud of." He did, in fact, redefine what being a gay journalist could mean.[5]

▼ Advertising in the gay and lesbian press has forged a history every bit as gripping as that of the genre itself. This story began in 1954 when *ONE* printed an ad for men's satin undershorts, modeled by a handsome man. Throughout the 1960s the only businesses consistently willing to advertise in the gay press were mail-order companies specializing in homoerotic books and films; while lesbian publications continued to struggle for advertising throughout the 1970s and 1980s.

For the gay male press, the big break came in the mid-1970s when Goodstein aimed *The Advocate* at the affluent gay middle class. Suddenly, advertising took on a life of its own. Dozens of full-page ads promoted San Francisco's bar and bath house culture, and forty pages of personal ads became a lucrative source of revenue. The sexual nature of the ads created a crisis with the advent of AIDS in the early 1980s, with ads becoming a villain in one of the worst tragedies in the history of the genre. Creative gay entrepreneurs eventually found a solution when newspapers began to bulge with ads showing hot, sweaty men panting with lust as they talked on "976-DICK" and "976-HUNK" phone lines.

The *Washington Blade* and *Windy City Times* broke into mainstream advertising in the 1980s, foreshadowing the explosion of national ads that became the driving force behind the slick magazines of the 1990s. When companies learned that gay people were pumping $514 billion into the economy each year, they lined up to advertise in the glossy pages of *Genre* and *Deneuve*. Four decades after satin undershorts had won a foothold in the gay press, publications were overflowing with full-color ads for the objects of desire of the modern-day guppy.

▼ Ironically, it seems certain that the lesbian and gay press will benefit from the hard times facing general-interest news outlets, with the genre continuing to grow both in number of publications and total circulation. For as the captains of the American media shift from appealing to the masses to appealing to specialized audiences, affluent gay people clearly will be very desirable. What is not so clear is to what degree this phenomenon will benefit the movement. How much are gay civil rights hastened by gay people learning how to bleach their teeth and decorate their homes? Such material is not likely to persuade Congress to create federal protection for lesbians and gay men who have been fired from their jobs. What's more, as the lifestyle magazines lure major advertisers to their pages, they make life more difficult for local news-oriented publications that provide high-quality news content, as the big companies prefer to place their ads on slick paper than on newsprint. *Out* boasts a circulation of 100,000; the largest of the newspapers, the *Bay Area Reporter*, struggles to maintain a third of that figure. The competitive world of the media today, whether aiming for a broad audience or a narrow audience, continues to be defined by survival of the fattest.[6]

▼ The catalyst for creating an alternative press is the failure of mainstream media to provide a venue for outsiders. Phyllis Lyon, who founded the country's first widely circulated lesbian magazine in 1956, said: "*The Ladder* broke the silence. Finally. Before it came along, there was absolutely nothing about lesbians in the major press. We sent the papers press releases about our DOB meetings, but they wouldn't even print the times and meeting places—straight facts."[7]

Journalism graybeards who continue to swear unflinching allegiance to the

In 1994 FBI agents credited the Washington Blade with first suggesting that several murders along the East Coast may have been the work of a serial killer who targeted gay men. Courtesy of Don Michaels, *Washington Blade*.

establishment press will argue that things have changed and, with topics such as AIDS and gays in the military receiving front-page coverage, the lesbian and gay press is no longer needed. They are wrong. Mainstream media do *not* serve gay people well, as they filter the news of the day through mainstream eyes. For example, in June 1994 the *Washington Post* reported that the FBI was searching for a transient construction worker suspected of murdering four gay men. The *Post* did not mention, however, that FBI agents credited the *Washington Blade* for first suggesting that the murders were linked, as they had occurred in various East Coast cities. The murders were front-page news in the *Blade* for three months before the *Post* finally reported them. By that time, the *Blade* had already published half a dozen front-page articles as well as full-page public service announcements containing photos of the man. Six months later, police arrested him for the murders, which by that time had climbed to six.[8]

▼ The National Lesbian and Gay Journalists Association has an uneasy relationship with the lesbian and gay press. When founding the association early this decade, gay journalists who work for mainstream news media drafted membership criteria that would have excluded most journalists who work for the gay press. Those criteria specified that members had to be employed full-time as journalists; most gay papers still depend largely on freelancers and unpaid writers. It took some arguing to persuade the founders to modify their rules.

Many members of the association continue to have a patronizing attitude toward journalists who work for the gay press. It reads something like: "We real, professional journalists are in the driver's seat now. You amateurs go to the back of the bus." In a form of the internecine feuding that has plagued so much of the history of the lesbian and gay press, many gay people who work for mainstream news media show little gratitude for the role that founders of publications such as *Lesbian Tide* and *GAY* played in creating a "safe space" for mainstream gay journalists to come out.

▼ Despite the importance and ever-widening reach of the lesbian and gay press, the genre still has no national chronicle of the news of the day. Weekly tabloids committed to comprehensive news coverage serve many cities well, but people who live outside urban areas struggle to remain connected to the national movement. The only foray into daily gay journalism was by the *Montrose Voice* in 1986, which lasted nary a week. Will the twenty-first century be served by a national voice that combines the financial stability of lifestyle magazines, the wide geographic scope of electronic ventures, and the commitment to political leadership of weekly papers? The answer, unfortunately, is a resounding *no*. The magazines are succeeding quite well with their formula of nine parts fluff to one part substance, and the new technologies know that many of their youthful viewers, raised on a diet of MTV and videos, prefer to be entertained rather than informed. So it will be left to local newspapers to keep readers abreast of local issues and events, while providing enough entertainment content to amuse their readers and struggling to find enough local advertisers to stay afloat.

▼ The most important single contribution lesbian and gay journalism has made—and will continue to make—may be one most straight people simply are not able to fathom. For half a century, reading gay publications has served as a first tenuous step for men and women embarking on the very personal, and often profoundly difficult, journey toward acknowledging their homosexuality to themselves and the world around them. Readers detached from the realities of being gay in America may think the issue ended years ago. It did not. As long as readers blink when they think of one man sucking another man's cock or one woman licking another woman's clitoris, men and women will continue to struggle through the process of coming out.

I have, throughout this book, attempted to separate my own feelings from my work. Partaking of anonymous sex and losing friends to AIDS, for example, are not concepts I became familiar with through archival research. And I learned long ago that objectivity is a myth; everything we do and say is influenced by who we are and what we bring to the subject at hand. So, for the last point in this book, I choose to draw directly from my own experience.

I was late to recognize my sexual orientation. It was not until my thirties, and after being married and having two children, that I finally realized the urges I had been suppressing for twenty years meant that, yes, I was an unspeakable. To join a Gay Pride parade or walk into a gay bar was far too traumatic as a first step. To slip a copy of the *Washington Blade* into my briefcase, however, was manageable. Devouring every word gave me my first glimpse inside the world that I knew, somewhere deep inside my soul, I was destined to become part of.

Once again, I pose the question: "How much will the lesbian and gay press help in attaining the full freedom that lies somewhere in the future?" Reflecting on my own experience, which has been replicated by millions upon millions of other individuals who have read a gay or lesbian newspaper as a first tiny step into one of the most relentless social and political revolutions of the twentieth century, I know the answer has to be "A lot."

Notes

Introduction

1. *GAY,* "Bookshop Employees Arrested," 15 December 1969, 10; no coverage of the raid appeared in the *New York Times, New York Daily News,* or *Village Voice* between 15 November and 20 December 1969.

2. *GAY,* 15 December 1970, Dick Leitsch, "The Gay Vote," 9; Jack Nichols and Lige Clarke, "The Editors Speak," 2; Robert Amsel, "Homosexuals Weep While Hollywood Sucks!" 11.

3. Robert J. Glessing, *The Underground Press in America* (Bloomington: Indiana University Press, 1970), 15–16. The lesbian and gay press is not mentioned in such standard histories of journalism as Michael Emery and Edwin Emery, *The Press and America: An Interpretive History of the Mass Media,* 7th ed. (Englewood Cliffs, N.J.: Prentice-Hall, 1992) or Jean Folkerts and Dwight L. Teeter, Jr., *Voices of a Nation: A History of Mass Media in the United States,* 2nd ed. (New York: Macmillan, 1994). Nor is it considered in such histories of alternative journalism as Lauren Kessler, *The Dissident Press: Alternative Journalism in American History* (Beverly Hills, Calif.: Sage, 1984); or Laurence Leamer, *The Paper Revolutionaries: The Rise of the Underground Press* (New York: Simon and Schuster, 1972). It is the subject of one sentence in Glessing, *Underground Press in America,* 15–16; one paragraph in Roger Lewis, *Outlaws of America: The Underground Press and Its Content* (New York: Penguin, 1972), 41; four pages in Abe Peck, *Uncovering the Sixties: The Life and Times of the Underground Press* (New York: Citadel, 1985), 218–21; and six pages in David Armstrong, *A Trumpet to Arms: Alternative Media in America* (Los Angeles: J.P. Tarcher, 1981), 239–40, 249–53. The personal recollections of several lesbian and gay journalists are included in Ken Wachsberger, ed., *Voices from the Underground: Insider Histories of the Vietnam Era Underground Press* (Tempe, Ariz.: Mica, 1993). Two studies of the gay press, both from a sociological perspective, were undertaken in the 1970s but never published. They are Harold Corzine, Jr., "The Gay Press" (Ph.D. dissertation, Washington University, St. Louis, 1977) and Alan D. Winter, "The Gay Press: A History of the Gay Community and Its Publications" (M.A. thesis, University of Texas, Austin, 1976).

4. Rodger Streitmatter, *Raising Her Voice: African-American Women Journalists Who Changed History* (Lexington: University Press of Kentucky, 1994).

5. Alan V. Miller, compiler, *Our Own Voices: A Directory of Lesbian and Gay Periodicals, 1890–1990* (Toronto: Canadian Gay Archives, 1990). The bibliography lists 7,200 titles worldwide, including 2,678 periodicals published in the United States. A second important bibliography is Clare Potter, compiler and editor, *The Lesbian Periodicals Index* (Tallahassee, Fla.: Naiad Press, 1986), which is particularly rich in information about 1970s lesbian publications. A third bibliography is H. Robert Malinowsky, *International Directory of Gay and Lesbian Periodicals* (Phoenix: Oryx, 1987), which lists current publications.

6. On Henry Gerber and *Friendship and Freedom,* see Jonathan Katz, *Gay American History: Lesbians and Gay Men in the U.S.A.* (New York: Avon Books, 1976), 581–91.

7. Mary Katherine Goddard was a colonial printer and newspaper publisher who, in 1777, printed the official copy of the Declaration of Independence. John Peter Zenger was a colonial printer whose 1735 libel case helped establish truth as a defense against libel charges.

8. The most comprehensive examination of the major themes of the early African-American press is Bernell E. Tripp, *Origins of the Black Press: New York, 1827–1847* (Northport, Ala.: Vision, 1992), especially 82–91. Other important works on this topic include Lionel C. Barrow, Jr., "Our Own Cause: 'Freedom's Journal' and the Beginnings of the Black Press," *Journalism History* 4 (Winter 1977–78):118–22; Martin E. Dann, ed., *The Black Press, 1827–1890: The Quest for National Unity* (New York: G. P. Putnam's Sons, 1971), 16; Bella Gross, " 'Freedom's Journal' and the 'Rights of All,' " *Journal of Negro History* 17 (July 1932):245–62; Gunnar Mydral, *An American Dilemma: The Negro Problem and Modern Democracy* (New York: Harper and Brothers, 1944), especially 86; Kenneth Nordin, "In Search of Black Unity: An Interpretation of the Content and Function of 'Freedom's Journal,' " *Journalism History* 4 (Winter 1977–78): 123–28; Roland E. Wolseley, *The Black Press, U.S.A.,* 2nd ed. (Ames: Iowa State University Press, 1990), especially 3–42. The most comprehensive examinations of the major themes of the women's suffrage press are Sherilyn Cox Bennion, "Woman Suffrage Papers of the West, 1869–1914," *American Journalism* 3 (1986): 129–41; E. Claire Jerry, "The Role of Newspapers in the Nineteenth-Century Woman's Movement," in *A Voice of Their Own: The Woman Suffrage Press, 1840–1910,* Martha M. Solomon, ed., (Tuscaloosa: University of Alabama Press, 1991), especially 27–29; Linda Steiner, "Finding Community in Nineteenth Century Suffrage Periodicals," *American Journalism* 1 (1983): 1–15. The most comprehensive examinations of the major themes of the women's liberation press are Martha Leslie Allen, ed., *1989 Directory of Women's Media* (Washington, D.C.: Women's Institute for Freedom of the Press, 1989), especially 73; Maurine H. Beasley and Sheila J. Gibbons, *Taking Their Place: A Documentary History of Women and Journalism* (Washington, D.C.: American University Press, 1993), especially 192.

Chapter One

1. Lisa Ben, "In Explanation," *Vice Versa,* June 1947, 1.

2. Author's interview with Jim Kepner, 26 April 1993, in Washington, D.C.

3. Author's interview with Ben, 9 July 1993, in Studio City, California.

4. Author's telephone interview with Ben, 12 May 1993, during which Ben was in Burbank, California.

5. Author's interview with Ben, 12 May 1993.

6. Eric Marcus, *Making History: The Struggle for Gay and Lesbian Equal Rights, 1945–1990, An Oral History* (New York: HarperCollins, 1992), 7, 8.

7. Ben, "In Explanation," *Vice Versa,* June 1947, 2; author's interview with Ben, 12 May 1993.

8. Marcus, *Making History,* 9.

9. Ben, "Just Between Us Girls," *Vice Versa,* July 1947, 2; Leland Moss, "Interview with Lisa Ben," *Gaysweek,* 23 January 1978, 15.

10. Author's interview with Ben, 9 July 1993.

11. Ben, "Ring Out, Wild Belles!" *Vice Versa,* December 1947, 1.

12. Author's interview with Ben, 9 July 1993.

13. Author's interview with Ben, 12 May 1993.

14. Ben, *Vice Versa,* "Film Review," June 1947, 9; "Co-oper-8 in '48," January 1948, 1; "Hearty Greetings!" February 1948, 1; "Ring Out, Wild Belles!" December 1947, 1.

15. Ben, "The Hallowe'en Spirit," *Vice Versa,* October 1947, 1.

16. *Vice Versa*, "The Whatchama-Column," July 1947, 16, 17, 18.

17. Ben, "The Whatchama-Column," *Vice Versa*, November 1947, 12.

18. Author's interview with Ben, 12 May 1993; Marcus, *Making History*, 8.

19. Ben, "Commentary upon a Pertinent Article," *Vice Versa*, February 1948, 9, 10.

20. Moss, "Interview with Lisa Ben," 16; author's interviews with Ben, 12 May and 9 July 1993.

21. Ben, "Here To Stay," *Vice Versa*, September 1947, 4.

22. Ben, "Thanksgiving," *Vice Versa*, November 1947, 1.

23. Ben, "Here To Stay," *Vice Versa*, September 1947, 5.

24. Author's interview with Ben, 12 May 1993.

25. Ben, "New Year's Revolution," *Vice Versa*, January 1948, 8.

26. Ben, "The Whatchama-Column," *Vice Versa*, January 1948, 15.

27. Laurajean Ermayne, "The Night You Were Wed," *Vice Versa*, November 1947, 3; Moss, "Interview with Lisa Ben," 15.

28. Marcus, *Making History*, 6.

29. Ben, "Lesbian Lyrics," *Vice Versa*, January 1948, 14.

30. Author's interview with Ben, 9 July 1993.

31. Ben, "In Explanation," *Vice Versa*, June 1947, 1.

32. Ben, "In Explanation," *Vice Versa*, June 1947, 2.

33. Author's interview with Ben, 9 July 1993; Laurajean Ermayne, "The Night You Were Wed," *Vice Versa*, November 1947, 3.

34. Ben, "Editor's Reply," *Vice Versa*, July 1947, 17.

35. Author's interview with Ben, 9 July 1993. On Forrest J. Ackerman, see Martin Booe, "The Monster Maven," *Washington Post*, 28 May 1993, G-1.

36. "The Whatchama-Column," *Vice Versa*, June 1947, 18.

37. Ben, "The Whatchama-Column," *Vice Versa*, October 1947, 14.

38. Author's interview with Ben, 12 May 1993.

39. Ben, *Vice Versa*, "Unusual Records," October 1947, 13; "Bookworms' Burrow," November 1947, 7.

40. Ben, "Bookworm's Burrow," *Vice Versa*, July 1947, 9, 10.

41. *Vice Versa*, "The Whatchama-Column," August 1947, 16; November 1947, 9.

42. Ben, "Film Review," *Vice Versa*, June 1947, 10.

43. Ben, "Other Fiction on the Same Subject," *Vice Versa*, July 1947, 11.

44. "The Whatchama-Column," *Vice Versa*, September 1947, 12.

45. Author's interview with Ben, 12 May 1993; Ben, *The Ladder*, "What's in A Name?" March 1958, 6–9; "Masquerade," October 1958, 6; "Window Shopping," November 1958, 14; "The Secret Garden," August 1959, 4–22. The Daughters of Bilitis was founded in 1955 in San Francisco. Bilitis is the fictional heroine of the "Songs of Bilitis," erotic poems published in 1894 by Pierre Louys. In the verses, Bilitis is a contemporary of Sappho, who lived a lesbian lifestyle on the island of Lesbos in the seventh century B.C.

46. Author's interview with Ben, 12 May 1993.

47. Moss, "Interview with Lisa Ben," 16.

48. Author's interview with Ben, 12 May 1993; Moss, "Interview with Lisa Ben," 16.

49. Author's interview with Ben, 12 May 1993.

50. On alternative publications not valuing quality design and appearance, see Armstrong, *Trumpet to Arms*, 67; and Glessing, *Underground Press in America*, 47–48.

51. On the early African-American press expressing the hopes and wishes of black readers, see Gross, "'Freedom's Journal,'" 245–46, 262; and Tripp, *Origins of the Black Press*, 83.

52. On African-American newspapers providing an open forum, see Barrow, "Our Own Cause," 118–22; Dann, *Black Press*, 16; and Tripp, *Origins of the Black Press*, 88–89. On women's

suffrage newspapers providing an open forum, see Bennion, "Woman Suffrage Papers," 140. On women's liberation publications providing an open forum, see Allen, *Women's Media*, 73; and Beasley and Gibbons, *Taking Their Place*, 192.

53. Author's interview with Ben, 12 May 1993; Ben, "Here To Stay," *Vice Versa*, September 1947, 4.

Chapter Two

1. On Peurifoy's testimony, see William S. White, "Never Condoned Disloyalty, Says Acheson of Hiss Stand," *New York Times*, 1 March 1950, 1. On McCarthy's attacks on gays, see *New York Times*, "Perverts Called Government Peril," 19 April 1950, 25; William S. White, "Inquiry by Senate on Perverts Asked," 20 May 1950, 8. The Senate report was released 15 December 1950. Eisenhower issued Executive Order 10450 on 27 April 1953. On McCarthyism and gays, see John D'Emilio, *Sexual Politics, Sexual Communities: The Making of the Homosexual Minority in the United States, 1940–1970* (Chicago: University of Chicago Press, 1983), 40–53.

2. D'Emilio, *Sexual Politics*, 115.

3. Mattachines were court jesters who performed during medieval times and who today are thought to have been gay. *ONE* was published until 1969 and was briefly revived in 1972. *Mattachine Review* was published until 1967, and *The Ladder* until 1972. On the evolution of the content of *The Ladder* from a sociological perspective, see Kristin Gay Esterberg, "From Illness to Action: Conceptions of Homosexuality in *The Ladder*, 1956–1965," *Journal of Sex Research* 27 (1) (February 1990): 65–80.

4. Mr. G., "Letter," *ONE*, January 1958, 30.

5. Author's telephone interview with Dale Jennings, 21 January 1993, during which Jennings was in Glendale, California.

6. Author's telephone interview with Don Slater, 12 January 1993, during which Slater was in Los Angeles.

7. M. F., "Discussion, Anyone?" *ONE*, February 1954, 11.

8. Author's interview with Jennings, 21 January 1993; *ONE*, "I Am Glad I Am a Homosexual," August 1958, 1; *ONE*, "Six Years After," July 1959, 27; *ONE*, "Editorial," July 1959, 4.

9. *ONE*, "Editorial," July 1959, 55.

10. Author's telephone interview with Hal Call, 4 March 1993, during which Call was in San Francisco.

11. On the Homophile Movement, see Dennis Altman, *Homosexual: Oppression and Liberation* (New York: Outerbridge and Dienstfry, 1971); D'Emilio, *Sexual Politics*.

12. Laud Humphreys, *Out of the Closets! The Sociology of Gay Liberation* (Englewood Cliffs, N.J.: Prentice-Hall, 1972), 51. The Mattachine Society dissolved as a national organization in 1961, although some local societies, such as the Mattachine Society of Washington, continued to use the name.

13. Marcus, *Making History*, 62.

14. "Aims and Principles of the Mattachine Society," *Mattachine Review*, October 1962, 19–20; author's interview with Call, 4 March 1993.

15. Phyllis Lyon, "Once Upon a Time," *The Ladder*, October 1956, 3. Daughters of Bilitis was founded in September 1955. It changed into a federation of autonomous chapters in 1970.

16. D'Emilio, *Sexual Politics*, 104.

17. Kay Tobin (Lahusen) and Randy Wicker, *Gay Crusaders* (New York: Paperback Library, 1972), 50.

18. Author's telephone interview with Phyllis Lyon, 9 April 1993, during which Lyon was in San Francisco.

19. Letter signed "L.H.N." [Lorraine Hansberry Nemiroff], *The Ladder*, May 1957, 26.

20. *ONE*, November 1954.

21. Ernest Lenn, "Sex Deviate Ring Here," *San Francisco Examiner*, 24 September 1954, 10.

22. *ONE*, December 1953, back cover; *ONE*, October 1954, 31.

23. "About Those Ads," *ONE*, November 1954, 25.

24. "About Those Ads," *ONE*, November 1954, 25.

25. *The Ladder*, October 1957.

26. Dale Jennings, "To Be Accused, Is to Be Guilty," *ONE*, January 1953, 13.

27. *ONE*, "Annual Writing Competition," insert, January 1954; Norman Mailer, "The Homosexual Villain," January 1955, 8–12; Clarkson Crane, "Passing Stranger," April 1955, 24–27. Since the publication of *The Naked and the Dead* in 1948, Mailer has been regarded as one of America's most important contemporary writers. During the 1950s, he embraced a leftist philosophy and was associated with Marxist intellectuals. Crane's career as a novelist spanned the 1920s to the 1950s and included publication of *The Western Shore, Mother and Son*, and *Naomi Martin*.

28. Lisa Ben, *The Ladder*, "What's in A Name?" March 1958, 6–9; "Masquerade," October 1958, 6; "Window Shopping," November 1958, 14; "The Secret Garden," August 1959, 4–22.

29. W. Dorr Legg, "How *ONE* Began," *ONE*, February 1955, 12.

30. Dal McIntire (Jim Kepner), "Tangents: News & Views," *ONE*, April 1958, 18; December 1957, 23; November 1955, 8; February 1958, 18; June 1959, 13; December 1955, 10.

31. Marcus, *Making History*, 50–51.

32. Jim Kepner, "Miami Junks the Constitution," *ONE*, January 1954, 16.

33. Kepner, "News," *ONE*, September 1953, 17.

34. Winter, "Gay Press," 27; D'Emilio, *Sexual Politics*, 110; author's interviews with Kepner.

35. Letters signed "C.H., Pasadena, Calif.," *The Ladder*, March 1958, 20; "Anonymous," *The Ladder*, March 1957, 17.

36. David L. Freeman (Chuck Rowland), "For Courage: *ONE* Salutes Curtis White," *ONE*, May 1954, 27; *The Ladder*, "Attorney Stresses Nothing to Fear," April 1957, 15; Ann Ferguson (Phyllis Lyon), "Your Name Is Safe!" November 1956, 10.

37. Author's interview with Martin Block, 23 April 1993, in Washington, D.C.; *Mattachine Review*, "Readership and Reaction," September/October 1955, 23; "A 'Do-It-Yourself' Kit for Organizational Publications," Christmas 1955, 26–30; *ONE*, May 1954, inside front cover; "How Many Subscribers?" December 1954, 28.

38. Author's interview with Slater, 12 January 1993. ONE, Inc., began offering graduate degrees in homophile studies in 1981. Located on a three-acre estate, it also maintained an extensive library on homosexuality.

39. Author's interview with Kepner, 11 July 1993, in West Hollywood, California.

40. Author's interview with Block, 23 April 1993.

41. R. E. L. Masters, *The Homosexual Revolution* (New York: Belmont, 1964), 71; author's interviews with Legg, 13 January 1993, during which Legg was in Los Angeles; and Call, 4 March 1993.

42. Author's telephone interview with Del Martin, 9 April 1993, during which Martin was in her home in San Francisco.

43. Author's interview with Jennings, 21 January 1993.

44. Lyon, "Ann Ferguson Is Dead!" *The Ladder*, January 1957, 7.

45. Author's interview with Martin, 9 April 1993.

46. FBI field office reports, 21 May 1953, 6 July 1953, 14 July 1953, 7 and 10 February 1956, 19 November 1958, and 7 August 1959, Mattachine Society file, FBI Headquarters, Washington, D.C. The only person actively involved in the 1950s gay and lesbian press who had been affili-

ated with the Communist party was Kepner, who had been ejected from the party in 1948 because of his sexuality.

47. Author's interview with Kepner, 11 July 1993.

48. FBI field office reports, 6 July 1953, 9 September 1953, 15 February 1956, 28 March 1956, 13 April 1957, and 6 August 1959, Mattachine Society file, FBI Headquarters, Washington, D.C.; author's interview with Lyon, 9 April 1993.

49. FBI field office reports, 6 July 1953, 9 September 1953, 15 February 1956, 28 March 1956, 13 April 1957, and 6 August 1959, Mattachine Society file, FBI Headquarters, Washington, D.C.; author's interviews with Block, 23 April 1993; and Legg, 13 January 1993.

50. *ONE*, October 1953. front cover.

51. Alexander Wiley letter to Arthur Summerfield, 28 April 1954, Mattachine Society file, FBI Headquarters, Washington, D.C. Wiley represented Wisconsin in the U.S. Senate from 1939 to 1963.

52. "*ONE* & the U.S. Postoffice," *ONE*, March 1957, 6.

53. Author's interviews with Lyon, 9 April 1993; and Call, 4 March 1993. On J. Edgar Hoover's homosexuality, see Anthony Summers, *Official and Confidential: The Secret Life of J. Edgar Hoover* (New York: G. P. Putnam's Sons, 1993).

54. David L. Freeman (Chuck Rowland), "How Much Do We Know About the Homosexual Male?" *ONE*, November 1955, 5.

55. FBI field office report, 26 January 1956, Mattachine Society file, FBI Headquarters, Washington, D.C. Hoover and Tolson's relationship was legend beginning in the 1930s when the two men began forty years of dining with each other daily, vacationing together, and jointly attending social functions at the White House and elsewhere. See Summers, *Secret Life*, especially 75–86. On Hoover's scorn toward gays, see Summers, *Secret Life*, 189.

56. FBI field office report, 7 February 1956, Mattachine Society file, FBI Headquarters, Washington, D.C.

57. FBI field office reports, 1 and 15 February 1956, 9 April 1956, Mattachine Society file, FBI Headquarters, Washington, D.C.

58. Author's interview with Legg, 13 January 1993.

59. FBI field office reports, 2 and 10 February 1956, Mattachine Society file, FBI Headquarters, Washington, D.C.

60. FBI Headquarters memo to Los Angeles field office, 7 February 1956, Mattachine Society file, FBI Headquarters, Washington, D.C.

61. *ONE*, Dal McIntire (Jim Kepner), "Tangents: News & Views," February 1956, 10; March 1956, 6; FBI field office reports, 13 March 1956, 9 April 1956, and 24 May 1956, Mattachine Society file, FBI Headquarters, Washington, D.C.

62. *ONE*, W. Dorr Legg, "How *ONE* Began," February 1955, 8; Del Martin, "Editorial," January 1962, 8.

63. *ONE*, "Lord Samuel and Lord Montague," October 1954, 18; Jane Dahr, "Sappho Remembered," October 1954, 13; Los Angeles field office report dated 2 March 1956, Mattachine Society file, FBI Headquarters, Washington, D.C.

64. "*ONE* & the U.S. Postoffice," *ONE*, March 1957, 9, 10. The case went to the U.S. District Court Southern District of California, Central Division. The case was no. 18765, Civil Order on Motions for Summary Judgment, *ONE vs. Otto K. Oleson*. Otto K. Oleson was postmaster of Los Angeles. U.S. District Court Judge Thurmond Clarke delivered his opinion on 1 March 1956.

65. "*ONE* & the U.S. Postoffice," *ONE*, March 1957, 17. U.S. Appeals Court Judge Stanley Barnes delivered his decision on 27 February 1957.

66. The case considered by the U.S. Supreme Court was *ONE vs. Oleson*, 355 U.S. 371. The justices announced their decision on 13 January 1958. In siding with *ONE*, the justices

simply stated that the Court of Appeals decision was reversed, citing the decision in *Roth vs. United States,* which ruled that sexual-oriented material is not, per se, obscene. That earlier case, which the Supreme Court decided on 24 June 1957, involved a New York man who had advertised his publishing of erotic books, photographs, and magazines by sending circulars through the mail.

67. Don Slater, "Victory! Supreme Court Upholds Homosexual Rights," *ONE,* February 1958, 17.

68. "Supreme Court Decisions," *New York Times,* 14 January 1958, 37; Richard Lyons, "High Court Rules Out City Curb on Unions," *Washington Post,* 14 January 1958, A-8; "Supreme Court Lifts Ban on 2 Nudist Magazines," *Washington Evening Star,* 14 January 1958, A-3.

69. FBI Headquarters memo to Los Angeles Field Office, 21 March 1958, Mattachine Society file, FBI Headquarters, Washington, D.C.

70. Author's interviews with Jennings and Slater, 12 January 1993.

71. Geraldine Jackson (Betty Perdue), "As for me . . . ," *ONE,* January 1953, 16–17.

72. *ONE,* R. L. M., "As for me . . . ," July 1953, 17–18; James R. Steuart, "Homosexual Procreation," March 1961, 8; E. B. Saunders, "Marriage License or Just License?" August 1953, 12.

73. E. B. Saunders, "Marriage License or Just License?" *ONE,* August 1953, 11; author's interview with Block, 23 April 1993.

74. Author's interview with Block, 23 April 1993; Damon Pythias, "Take It from Me!" *ONE,* March 1954, 10.

75. Allison Hunter, "Editorial," *ONE,* February 1960, 4.

76. Steuart, "Homosexual Procreation," *ONE,* March 1961, 7–8.

77. Author's interview with Call, 4 March 1993.

78. *Mattachine Review,* January/February 1955, 2; Ken Burns, "A Problem," 25–26; Hal Call, "The Importance of You," 26.

79. *Mattachine Review,* Ken Burns, "A Problem," January/February 1955, 25–26; "A 'Do-It-Yourself' Kit for Organizational Publications," Christmas 1955, 32; George W. Henry, "Quote," March/April 1955, 23.

80. Hal Call, "Why Perpetuate This Barbarism," *Mattachine Review,* June 1960, 13.

81. Author's interview with Lyon, 9 April 1993.

82. *The Ladder,* D. Griffin, "President's Message," November 1956, 3; Suzanne Prosin, "The Concept of the Lesbian," July 1962, 5.

83. *The Ladder,* "ACLU Clashes with San Francisco Police on Vagrancy Arrests," June 1957, 19; "On Wearing Slacks," November 1957, 11; "Readers Respond," October 1958, 30.

84. Del Martin, "Is Our Editor BURLY?" *The Ladder,* January 1958, 16–17.

85. *The Ladder,* Sandra Pine, "Yes, I Am!" March 1958, 12; Jule Moray, "Open Letter to Sandra Pine," August 1958, 16–17.

86. Author's interview with Lyon, 9 April 1993; Del Martin, "The Positive Approach," *The Ladder,* November 1956, 9.

87. *The Ladder,* D. Griffin, "President's Message," January 1957, 8, 9; "DOB Questionnaire Reveals Some Facts about Lesbians," 26.

88. Letter signed "L.N." (Lorraine [Hansberry] Nemiroff), *The Ladder,* August 1957, 30.

89. *ONE,* "The Law," January 1953, 21–22; "Must I Answer That Cop?" October 1953, 3–6; "A Citizen's Rights in Case of Arrest," November 1955, 30; "Are You Now or Have You Ever Been a Homosexual?" April 1953, 5–13; "The Law," April 1953, 14–16.

90. *Mattachine Review,* Bob Bishop, "Discard the Mask," April 1958, 14; Carl B. Harding, "Whom Should We Tell?" August 1956, 9; Robert Kirk, "Fair Employment Practices and the Homosexual," April 1956, 12; John Logan (Hal Call), "You're Fired!" June 1956, 27.

91. J.O.I. Spoczynska, "The Experiment That Failed," *The Ladder,* June 1960, 7, 13.

92. *The Ladder,* Nancy Osbourne, "One Facet of Fear," June 1957, 7; Marion Zimmer Bradley, "Some Remarks on Marriage," July 1957, 15.

93. On lesbian pulp novels, see Fran Koski and Maida Tilchen, "Some Pulp Sappho," in Karla Jay and Allen Young, eds., *Lavender Culture* (New York: Jove, 1978), 262–74.

94. Del Martin, "The Positive Approach," *The Ladder,* November 1956, 8–9.

95. Sandra Pine, "Yes, I Am!" *The Ladder,* March 1958, 12–13.

96. Doris Lyles, "My Daughter Is a Lesbian," *The Ladder,* July 1958, 4.

97. "DOB Questionnaire Reveals Some Facts about Lesbians," *The Ladder,* September 1959, 4–26.

98. *Mattachine Review,* Evelyn Hooker, "Inverts Are Not a Distinct Personality Type," January/February 1955, 22; Alfred Kinsey, "Dr. Alfred Kinsey: Toward a Clarification of Homosexual Terminology," August 1956, 5; Havelock Ellis, "Havelock Ellis on Homosexuality," September/October 1955, 9.

99. Author's interview with Jennings, 21 January 1993; Paul W. Tappan, "Treatment of the Sex Offender in Denmark," *Mattachine Review,* March/April 1955, 12. The castration provision was removed in 1971.

100. *Mattachine Review,* James Phelan, "Sex Variants Find Their Own Answer," September/October 1955, 15; Albert Ellis, "On the Cure of Homosexuality," November/December 1955, 6; Mary Dorn, "A Psychologist Looks at Homosexuality," June 1960, 5. The American Psychiatric Association removed homosexuality from its list of diseases in 1973.

101. Kenneth Fink, "The Psychodynamics of the Homosexual," *Mattachine Review,* July 1960, 7, 9, 11.

102. Sten Russell, "The Personality Variables of Homosexual Women," *The Ladder,* May 1959, 4–7; Virginia Armon, "Some Personality Variables in Overt Female Homosexuality," *Journal of Projective Techniques* 24 (1960), 292–309.

103. "Editorial," *ONE,* July 1959, 55; Call, "The Importance of You," *Mattachine Review,* January/February 1955, 26.

104. *The Ladder,* October 1956, Lyon, "Once Upon a Time," 4; Martin, "President's Message," 7.

105. *The Ladder,* Helen Sanders, "Me vs. Taxes," May 1958, 10; Del Martin, "Me vs. Insurance," June 1958, 12–13; "DOB Questionnaire Reveals Some Facts About Lesbians," September 1959, 4–26.

106. "Wolden Charges Defiance of Law," *San Francisco Chronicle,* 8 October 1959, 4; "Sex Deviates Make S.F. Headquarters," *San Francisco Progress,* 14 October 1959, 1; "Wolden Is Praised for Fight on Vice," *San Francisco Progress,* 14 October 1959, 1.

107. Author's interview with Lyon, 9 April 1993; "'Organized Homosexuals' Issue in S.F. Election," *The Ladder,* November 1959, 5.

108. *San Francisco Chronicle,* George Draper, "Vice Issue Was Planted by a Wolden Supporter," 9 October 1959, 1; "Editorial: Wolden Should Withdraw," 10 October 1959, 1.

109. Earl C. Behrens, "All Incumbent Supervisors Win," *San Francisco Chronicle,* 4 November 1959, 1; Del Martin and Phyllis Lyon, *Lesbian/Woman* (San Francisco: Glide, 1972), 232.

110. *San Francisco Chronicle,* "How Mattachine Society Got Its Name," 10 October 1959, 4; "Key Strategy Decision for Wolden Due," 13 October 1959, 1; "Wolden Rips Newspapers, 'Won't Quit,'" 15 October 1959, 1; "Wolden Sued for Slander," 9 October 1959, 4.

111. Martin, "Editorial: The Homosexual Vote," *The Ladder,* July 1960, 4.

112. Author's interview with Kepner, 8 July 1993.

113. Phyllis Lyon and Del Martin did not know of Lisa Ben or *Vice Versa* when they founded *The Ladder,* but they later met her and saw her publication.

114. Author's interview with Lyon, 9 April 1993.

115. On African-American newspapers providing an open forum, see Barrow, "Our Own

Cause"; Dann, *Black Press,* 16; Kessler, *Dissident Press,* 89; and Tripp, *Origins of the Black Press,* 88-89. On women's suffrage publications providing an open forum, see Bennion, "Woman Suffrage Papers," 129, 140. On women's liberation newspapers providing an open forum, see Allen, *Women's Media,* 73; and Beasley and Gibbons, *Taking Their Place,* 192.

116. On women's suffrage newspapers spreading the ideology to a large and diverse audience, see Bennion, "Woman Suffrage Papers," 135, 140; Jerry, "Newspapers in the Woman's Movement," 27–28; and Steiner, "Finding Community," 5, 12.

117. Author's interview with Slater, 12 January 1993. On the founding of the black press marking the beginning of the movement for black civil rights, see Gross, "'Freedom's Journal,'" 245–46.

Chapter Three

1. On gay and lesbian militancy in the early and mid 1960s, see, for example, D'Emilio, *Sexual Politics,* 129–75.

2. Author's telephone interview with Barbara Gittings, 10 September 1993, during which Gittings was in Philadelphia. On the gay press in the early to mid-1960s, see Rodger Streitmatter, "Lesbian and Gay Press: Raising a Militant Voice in the 1960s," *American Journalism* 12 (2) (Spring 1995): 1–19.

3. Author's interview with Gittings, 10 September 1993.

4. Author's interview with Nichols, 10 March 1993.

5. *Drum*'s 10,000 circulation was larger than that of all the other publications combined. By 1965 *ONE*'s circulation had dwindled to 3,000 and *Mattachine Review*'s to 500, while *Tangents*'s was 2,000. *Citizens News* and *Cruise News & World Report* had a combined circulation of 2,000. *The Ladder*'s circulation had risen to 1,000, *Vector*'s was 600, and the *Homosexual Citizen*'s was 400. These figures are based on the author's interviews with Gittings, Kepner, May, Nichols, and Vincenz.

6. Author's interview with Gittings, 10 September 1993.

7. "Focus on Fashion," *The Ladder,* November 1964, 16.

8. Author's interview with Gittings, 10 September 1993.

9. Author's interview with Gittings, 10 September 1993.

10. Author's interview with Gittings, 10 September 1993.

11. Author's interview with Gittings, 10 September 1993.

12. Author's interview with Gittings, 10 September 1993; *The Ladder,* Franklin E. Kameny, "Does Research into Homosexuality Matter?" May 1965, 14; Florence Conrad, "Research Is Here to Stay," July/August 1965, 15; Franklin E. Kameny, "Emphasis on Research Has Had Its Day," October 1965, 10.

13. "Interview with Ernestine," *The Ladder,* June 1966, 8.

14. "Interview with Ernestine," *The Ladder,* June 1966, 7, 8.

15. Author's interview with Franklin E. Kameny, 24 January 1993, in Washington, D.C.; Washington Field Office report to FBI Assistant Director Clyde Tolson, 26 February 1957, Mattachine Society file, FBI Headquarters, Washington, D.C.

16. Kameny ran unsuccessfully for the first congressional delegate from the District of Columbia in 1971, receiving only 1.6 percent of the vote.

17. Author's interview with Gittings, 10 September 1993.

18. Author's interview with Kameny, 24 January 1993. Kameny and Jack Nichols founded the Mattachine Society of Washington in November 1961.

19. Marcus, *Making History,* 100; Tobin (Lahusen) and Wicker, *Gay Crusaders,* 100; Washington Field Office report to FBI Headquarters, 20 January 1966, Mattachine Society file, U.S. Department of Justice, FBI Headquarters, Washington, D.C.

20. Author's interview with Kameny, 24 January 1993.

21. Author's telephone interviews with Jack Nichols, 10 March 1993 and 21 February 1995, during which Nichols was in Cocoa Beach, Florida; Jack Nichols, "The Evangel Poem of Comrades and of Love," *GAY*, 7 May 1973, 7.

22. Warren D. Adkins (Jack Nichols), "Why Should I Join?" *Homosexual Citizen*, November 1966, 6.

23. Author's interviews with Kameny, 24 January 1993, and Lilli Vincenz, 7 September 1992, in Arlington, Virginia.

24. Lily Hansen (Lilli Vincenz), "Greetings to Our Readers," *Homosexual Citizen*, January 1966, 3.

25. Author's interview with Vincenz, 7 September 1992.

26. Clark P. Polak letter to the Janus Society membership, October 1966. The letter is held in the Janus Society file at the International Gay and Lesbian Archives in Los Angeles.

27. Author's interview with Kepner, 8 September 1993.

28. Author's interview with Kepner, 8 September 1993.

29. Polak, "The Issue," *Drum*, September 1966, 52; *For Members Only*, December 1966, 1. *For Members Only* was an internal publication of the Janus Society.

30. Polak, "The Failure," *Drum*, September 1965, 4.

31. The Vietnam War march took place on 17 April 1965. It was organized by Students for a Democratic Society.

32. Author's interview with Nichols, 10 March 1993; "Cross-Currents," *The Ladder*, May 1965, 22. The first picket by a group of individual gays, rather than a gay organization, was formed a year earlier at the Whitehall Induction Center in New York City to protest the draft board policy of releasing information on sexual orientation to employers.

33. Vincenz, "Marching for Gay Rights," *Program for Creative Self-Development Newsletter* 1 (3) (Spring 1993): 2.

34. Author's interviews with Lahusen, 15 September 1993, and Kameny, 24 January 1993.

35. *The Ladder*, October 1965, cover.

36. Field office reports to FBI Headquarters, 25 October 1965 and 23 May 1966, Mattachine Society file, FBI Headquarters, Washington, D.C.

37. Polak, "Homophile Puzzle," *Drum*, December 1965, 27; author's interview with Gittings, 10 September 1993.

38. *The Ladder*, "Homosexuals Picket in Nation's Capital," July/August 1965, 23; Tobin (Lahusen), "Picketing: The Impact & the Issues," September 1965, 4–6.

39. Tobin (Lahusen), "Picketing: The Impact & the Issues," *The Ladder*, September 1965, 8.

40. "Rusk Probed on Picketing," *The Ladder*, October 1965, 18; Kameny, "MSW Meets with Civil Service Commission," *Homosexual Citizen*, May 1966, 7. The U.S. Civil Service Commission ended its ban on gay employees in the federal government in 1975.

41. Martin Duberman, *Stonewall* (New York: Dutton, 1993), 99. *Vector* continued to be published until 1976.

42. Bill Beardemphl, "President Speaks," *Vector*, June 1966, 2; author's telephone interview with Bill May, 16 September 1993, during which May was in San Francisco.

43. *Vector*, "Grace Cathedral Picketed," October 1965, 1; "State Fair Booth Canceled," October 1966, 1.

44. Author's interview with May, 16 September 1993.

45. Bill Beardemphl, "President's Column," *Vector*, September 1966, 2.

46. "Mattachine Pickets White House," *Citizens News*, undated issue, the content of which indicates it was published in summer 1965, 16; "Pickets," *Cruise News & World Report*, October 1965.

47. Call, "Why Perpetuate This Barbarism," *Mattachine Review,* June 1964, 13.

48. Author's interview with Gittings, 10 September 1993.

49. Polak, "This Strange Eventful History Is Second Childishness," *Drum,* December 1964, 2.

50. Polak, *Drum,* "News," October 1965, 28; "The Issue," October 1966, 5; author's interview with Lahusen, 15 September 1993.

51. Polak, *Drum,* "The American Civil Liberties Union," October 1964, 15; "News: Asheville, N.C.," April 1965, 4.

52. *Homosexual Citizen,* Stephen Donaldson, "Gross Remarks in the House," September 1966, 16; Adkins (Nichols) and John Marshall, "Kansas City Results," April 1966, 8; Adkins (Nichols) and Michael Fox, "Echo 1965," January 1966, 5; David Wayne, "Illinois No Paradise for Homosexuals," August 1966, 12.

53. Tobin (Lahusen), "ECHO Report '64; Part Three: A Nazi Stunt Fails," *The Ladder,* January 1965, 21, 22.

54. Polak, *Drum,* "The Issue," October 1966, 5; "Editor's Note," November 1964, 33.

55. "Action in the Courts," *The Ladder,* June 1966, 13, 20; John Marshall, "Nationwide Attack on Draft Injustices," *Homosexual Citizen,* July 1966, 8.

56. *Homosexual Citizen,* Herman Slade, "Brooklyn Heights Mattachine Society," September 1966, 12; Adkins (Nichols), "A National Data Center for Government Snooping," November 1966, 18; "Mattachine Pickets White House," *Citizens News,* undated issue, the content of which indicates it was published in summer 1965, 16.

57. Kameny, "Hamilton Hotel Settles," *Homosexual Citizen,* June 1966, 3.

58. No articles about the 24–26 September 1965 New York conference were published in the *New York Times,* 24–30 September 1965. No articles about the 21 February 1965 Kansas City conference were published in the *Kansas City Star,* 21–25 February 1965. No articles about the 29 May 1965 White House picketing were published in the *Washington Post* or the *Washington Evening Star,* 29 May–4 June 1965. No articles about the 23 October 1965 White House picketing were published in the *Post* or *Star,* 23–27 October 1965. No articles about the 21 May 1966 White House and Pentagon demonstrations were published in the *Post* or *Star,* 21–25 May 1966. No mention of the bar raid was made in the *Los Angeles Times,* 1–4 January 1967.

59. Seattle Field Office report to FBI Director J. Edgar Hoover, 7 December 1962, Mattachine Society file, FBI Headquarters, Washington, D.C.

60. Robert C. Doty, "Growth of Overt Homosexuality in City Provokes Wide Concern," *New York Times,* 17 December 1963, 1; Paul Welch, "Homosexuality in America," *Life,* 26 June 1964, 66; *Washington Post,* Jean M. White, "Those Others: A Report on Homosexuality," 31 January 1965, E-1; Jean M. White, "Scientists Disagree on Basic Nature of Homosexuality, Chance of Cure," 1 February 1965, 1; Jean M. White, "Homosexuals Are in All Kinds of Jobs, Find Place in Many Levels of Society," *Washington Post,* 2 February, 1; Jean M. White, "49 States and the District Punish Overt Homosexual Acts as Crimes," 3 February 1965, 1; Jean M. White, "Homosexuals' Militancy Reflected in Attacks on Ouster from U.S. Jobs," 4 February 1965, 1; "The Homosexual in America," *Time,* 21 January 1966, 41.

61. *The Ladder,* Kameny, "Letters Time Didn't Print," April 1966, 23; Tobin (Lahusen), "Cross-currents," July 1964, 23.

62. Philip Gerard, "Symptom of The Times," *The Ladder,* December 1964, 10.

63. P. Arody, "Heterosexuality in America," *Drum,* October 1964, 18.

64. "LIFE Bigotry," *Citizens News,* undated issue, the content of which indicates it was published in the summer of 1965, 2.

65. Ernest G. Bormann, *The Force of Fantasy: Restoring the American Dream* (Carbondale: Southern Illinois University Press, 1985), 11; Altman, *Oppression and Liberation,* 41; Humphreys, *Out of the Closets!,* 131–34.

66. D'Emilio, *Sexual Politics*, 191.

67. Author's interview with May, 16 September 1992; Tequila Mockingbird, "Bar Tour," *Vector*, September 1967, 7.

68. *Vector*, "Special Groups Hold Interest," March 1965, 1; "Sir Camp-Out," May 1965, 1; Bill Beardemphl, "President's Corner," August 1965, 2; "Community House Proposed," May 1965, 1; "Community Center to be Discussed," August 1965, 1.

69. Polak, "Homophile Puzzle: Part Two," *Drum*, January 1966, 12.

70. *Drum*, Polak, "On Gay Bars," February 1966, 13, 15; Polak, "Homophile Puzzle: Part Two," January 1966, 11; George Marshall, "The Beginner's Guide to Cruising," March 1965, 12.

71. "Sex and the Land of Liberty," *Cruise News & World Report*, June 1965, 1.

72. Guy Wright, "Guy Wright," *San Francisco News-Call*, 25 July 1961, 15.

73. Hansen (Vincenz), "Viewpoints: Breaking the News to Our Parents," *Homosexual Citizen*, February 1966, 5.

74. *Homosexual Citizen*, Robert C. Hayden (Lige Clarke) and Adkins (Nichols), "In the Same Boat," January 1966, 19; Adkins (Nichols), "What Is Bieberism?" December 1966, 3; author's interview with Nichols, 10 March 1993. In 1971 Kameny and Vincenz were among the five homosexuals who testified before the American Psychiatric Association as a step toward the association's 1973 decision to cease classifying homosexuality as an illness.

75. Hansen (Vincenz), "Greetings to Our Readers," *Homosexual Citizen*, January 1966, 3.

76. Michael Fox, "How to Stop Blackmailers," *Homosexual Citizen*, July 1966, 3; Kameny, "If You Are Arrested," *Homosexual Citizen*, January 1967, 3; Kameny, "How to Handle a Federal Interrogation," *Homosexual Citizen*, January 1967, 5; " 'Pocket Lawyer' Ready," *Vector*, September 1965, 1.

77. *Drum*, "Woman's Way," October 1964, 23, 24.

78. *The Ladder*, Marilyn Barrow (Barbara Grier), "Living Propaganda," November 1963, 4; June 1963, 12.

79. Vincenz letter to "Ros," 22 February 1966, file marked "Homosexual Citizen Correspondence," Vincenz personal papers.

80. Author's interviews with Kepner, 8 September 1993, and Slater, 12 January 1993.

81. Author's interview with Slater, 12 January 1993; Kepner, "Toujours gai," *Pursuit & Symposium*, March/April 1966, 7, 23.

82. Author's interviews with Kepner, 8 September 1993, and Legg, 12 September 1993, during which Legg was in Los Angeles; Polak, *For Members Only*, June 1965, 2.

83. Author's interview with Gittings, 10 September 1993; D'Emilio, *Sexual Politics*, 171; Tobin (Lahusen) and Wicker, *Gay Crusaders*, 215. Martin and Lyon saw the dispute differently. Although they acknowledge that they differed with Gittings over the editorial philosophy of *The Ladder*, Martin said Gittings was chronically late sending copies of the magazine.

84. On the editorial dispute, see Vincenz memorandum to the Executive Board, Mattachine Society of Washington, 1 June 1967, file marked "Homophile Correspondence," Vincenz personal papers; undated manuscript marked "Astrology and the Homosexual," file marked "Homophile Correspondence," Vincenz personal papers; Richard A. Inman letter to Vincenz, 13 August 1967, file marked "Inman Correspondence," Vincenz personal papers.

85. Polak undated letter to Victor Studio, the content of which indicates it was written in late 1964; Polak memorandum to the Janus Society Board of Directors, 28 October 1964; Polak, *For Members Only*, June 1965, 2. The letter and memo are in the Janus Society file at the International Gay and Lesbian Archives in Los Angeles.

86. Polak, letter to the Janus Society membership, October 1966; "Editorial," *Citizens News*, 17 August 1964, 1; field office report to FBI Headquarters, 3 January 1966, Mattachine Society file, FBI Headquarters, Washington, D.C.; author's interview with Gittings, 10 September 1993.

87. Author's interview with Lahusen, 15 September 1993.

88. Author's interview with Kameny, 24 January 1993.

89. On early African-American newspapers serving as a catalyst to the rise of protests, see Mydral, *American Dilemma,* 86. On women's liberation publications being activist in orientation, see Allen, *Women's Media,* 73; and Beasley and Gibbons, *Taking Their Place,* 192. On editors of early black newspapers being activists, see Tripp, *Origins of the Black Press,* 10. On editors of women's suffrage journals doubling as leaders of the movement, see Bennion, "Woman Suffrage Papers," 130; Jerry, "Newspapers in the Woman's Movement," 29; and Steiner, "Finding Community," 6. On the staff members of women's liberation publications being activists in the movement, see Allen, *Women's Media,* 73; Beasley and Gibbons, *Taking Their Place,* 192. On women's suffrage and women's liberation presses offering specialized perspectives, see Steiner, "Finding Community," 4; Allen, *Women's Media,* 73; and Beasley and Gibbons, *Taking Their Place,* 192.

90. Author's interview with Legg, 12 September 1993.

Chapter Four

1. Author's telephone interview with Barbara Grier, 8 February 1994, during which Grier was in Tallahassee, Florida.

2. By mid-1969, the *Los Angeles Advocate* had a circulation of 23,000, *Drum* 10,000, and *Town Talk* 5,000; *Tangents* and *Vector* each 3,000; *Citizens News* and *Cruise News & World Report* a combined 2,000; *The Ladder* 1,200; and *Pursuit & Symposium* 400. These figures are based on statements in the publications and interviews with Gittings, Kepner, Lahusen, and Nichols.

3. Armstrong, *Trumpet to Arms,* 249.

4. Al Goldstein, "Screw You!" *Screw,* 2 May 1969, 2; Derek Miles, *Dirtiest Dozen* (New York: Midwood, 1970), 11–21. *Screw* is still being published today.

5. Author's telephone interview with Nichols, 10 March 1995, during which Nichols was in Cocoa Beach, Florida.

6. Nichols and Clarke, *Screw,* "Humping a Winner?" 29 November 1968, 12; "Homosexual Heritage," 20 June 1969, 16; "Hooker Holiday," 7 February 1969, 3; "Is Andy Warhol a Pimp?" 21 December 1968, 4; "Undecided Dicks," 30 May 1969, 19. In November 1969 Nichols and Clarke became editors of *GAY,* a biweekly newspaper also founded by Goldstein through his company Milky Way Productions. They continued writing the *Screw* column while editing *GAY* until June 1973, when they abandoned both.

7. Nichols and Clarke, "Stalls of Balls," *Screw,* 14 February 1969, 10.

8. Nichols and Clarke, *Screw,* "Off the Far End," 2 May 1969, 15; "Twilight Zone," 18 April 1969, 16.

9. Nichols and Clarke, "Do Homosexual Citizens Suck?" *Screw,* 20 June 1969, 16.

10. Author's interview with Nichols, 10 March 1995.

11. The driving force behind *The Advocate*'s transformation into a magazine was David B. Goodstein, a Wall Street investor. On the early history of the *Los Angeles Advocate,* see Niles Merton, "A Legacy of Victory," *The Advocate,* 6 October 1992, 10; Stephen J. Sansweet, "A Homosexual Paper, The Advocate Widens Readership, Influence," *Wall Street Journal,* 3 November 1975, 1; Rodger Streitmatter, "The *Advocate:* Setting the Standard for the Gay Liberation Press," *Journalism History* 19 (3) (Autumn 1993): 93. On the history of *The Advocate* from a staff member perspective, see Mark Thompson, ed., *Long Road to Freedom: The Advocate History of the Gay and Lesbian Movement,* (New York: St. Martin's, 1994).

12. *Los Angeles Advocate,* "Advocate Becomes Independent," February 1968, 3; *Los Angeles Times,* "Richard T. Mitch; Founder of National Gay Newsmagazine," 24 May 1991, A-47. PRIDE was founded in May 1966 and disbanded in July 1968.

13. Jeff Yarbrough, "We Are Born," *The Advocate*, 6 October 1992, 8; Tobin (Lahusen) and Wicker, *Gay Crusaders*, 79–80.

14. Sansweet, "Advocate Widens Readership," 1.

15. Bill Rau used the pseudonym "Bill Rand."

16. *Los Angeles Advocate*, "Editorial: Happy Birthday to Us!" September 1968, 14; Tobin (Lahusen) and Wicker, *Gay Crusaders*, 81–82; Sansweet, "Advocate Widens Readership," 1.

17. Tobin (Lahusen) and Wicker, *Gay Crusaders*, 81; Michaels, "Your Newspaper Gets Bigger, Bigger," *Los Angeles Advocate*, December 1968, 2.

18. Armstrong, *Trumpet to Arms*, 251; Lewis, *Outlaws of America*, 41; Peck, *Uncovering the Sixties*, 218; author's interview with Kepner, 26 April 1993.

19. Humphreys, *Out of the Closets!*, 113.

20. Author's interview with Nichols, 9 April 1993.

21. Nichols and Clarke, *Screw,* "Off the Far End," 2 May 1969, 15; "Old Boys: They Just Blow Away," 9 May 1969, 16; "Mattachine & Men," 16 May 1969, 16; "He-Man Horseshit," 23 May 1969, 20; "Undecided Dicks," 30 May 1969, 19.

22. Author's interview with Nichols, 9 April 1993.

23. Nichols and Clarke, *Screw,* "Bi or High," 7 March 1969, 6; "Four Star Fuck-Up," 4 April 1969, 14; "Off the Far End," 2 May 1969, 15.

24. Nichols and Clarke, "Four Star Fuck-up," *Screw,* 4 April 1969, 14.

25. Nichols and Clarke, "Humping a Winner?" *Screw,* 29 November 1968, 12.

26. Nichols and Clarke, *Screw,* "Off the Far End," 2 May 1969, 15; "Are Creamy Cunts Kosher?" 27 June 1969, 18.

27. *Los Angeles Advocate*, Sam Winston, "The Bead Reader," October 1967, 7; May 1968, 9; Michael Selber, "Get Your Rocks Off; Pull Your Pants Up," April 1969, 3.

28. William F. Damon, "Pot," *Drum*, January 1969, 12–13, 15.

29. Author's interview with Grier, 8 February 1994. The only women who knew the angel's identity were Shirley Willer and Marion Glass.

30. Author's telephone interview with Martha Shelley, 17 July 1994, during which Shelley was in Oakland, California.

31. *The Ladder*, June/July 1969; Lennox Strong (Barbara Grier), "In the Spotlight," April 1968, 15; Larry Mamiya, "Notes from the Underground: The Generation Gap," October/November 1967, 2–3.

32. On the intersection of the Lesbian and Gay Liberation Movement and the sexual revolution, see Ira L. Reiss, *An End to Shame: Shaping Our Next Sexual Revolution* (Buffalo, N.Y.: Prometheus, 1990), 99–102.

33. Nichols and Clarke, *Screw,* "Bi or High," 7 March 1969, 6; "Groping Around," 25 April 1969, 14; John Francis Hunter (John Paul Hudson), *The Gay Insider: USA* (New York: Stonehill, 1972), 171.

34. Nichols and Clarke, "Groping Around," *Screw,* 25 April 1969, 14.

35. George Marshall, "The Beginner's Guide to Cruising," *Drum*, March 1965, 12.

36. Polak, "Homophile Puzzle: Two," *Drum*, January 1966, 11; *For Members Only*, December 1966, 2.

37. *Drum*, "Sex in Prison," September 1966, 16; "Sex in Prison," October 1966, 49–50; William F. Damon, "Pot," January 1969, 13.

38. Larry Carlson, "The Homosexual in the Tenderloin," *Vector*, May/June 1968, 17.

39. Jim Kepner, "Toujours gai," *Pursuit & Symposium*, March/April 1966, 4. Issues of *Pursuit & Symposium* were published in April 1966 and June 1967.

40. Author's telephone interview with Kepner, 7 January 1994, during which Kepner was in Los Angeles. *Town Talk* was published from 1964 to 1966.

41. *The Ladder*, "Lifestyle of the Homosexual," February/March 1969, 17; Marty Ander-

son (Martha Shelley), "Is Heterosexuality Natural?" June/July 1969, 4; Jane Ogden, "Mono-Bi-and Polysexuality," June/July 1969, 32, 33, 34; author's interview with Shelley, 17 July 1994.

42. Armstrong, *Trumpet to Arms*, 250–51; Lewis, *Outlaws of America*, 41; Peck, *Uncovering the Sixties*, 220–21. On the importance of homoerotic images in the gay male culture, see John D. Glenn, "Gay Fantasies in Gay Publications," in James W. Chesebro, ed., *Gayspeak* (New York: Pilgrim Press, 1981), 104–13; Wayne Sage, "Inside the Colossal Closet," in Martin P. Levine, ed., *Gay Men: The Sociology of Male Homosexuality* (New York: Harper & Row, 1979), 148–63.

43. On the new attitudes toward nudity, see Armstrong, *Trumpet to Arms*, 52.

44. Author's interview with Kepner, 26 April 1993.

45. *Los Angeles Advocate*, October 1967, 8; September 1968, 1.

46. Author's interview with Kepner, 26 April 1993.

47. *Los Angeles Advocate*, January 1969, 20.

48. *Los Angeles Advocate*, July 1968, 20; October 1968, 25; author's interview with Kepner, 26 April 1993.

49. Polak, *For Members Only*, December 1966, 1; *Drum*, October 1964, cover, 29.

50. *Drum*, September 1966; J. L., "Dear Drum," April 1966, 36; Barbara Harris, *For Members Only*, March 1966, 1.

51. *Drum*, "Harry Chess," October 1965, 30; August 1965, 8.

52. Nichols and Clarke, "Groping Around," *Screw*, 25 April 1969, 14.

53. Al Goldstein, "A Man Loves a Man," *Screw*, 16 May 1969, 4–5.

54. *Vector*, April 1969, 1; April 1969, "It Feels So Good!" 3.

55. Leo Laurence, "Gay Revolution," *Vector*, April 1969, 11, 25; *Los Angeles Advocate*, "SIR Dumps Vector Editor," May 1969, 3.

56. *The Ladder*, April 1968; Lennox Strong (Barbara Grier), "In the Spotlight," April 1968, 15.

57. Don Slater, "Editorial," *Tangents*, January/March 1970, 30.

58. On the development of offset printing, see Armstrong, *Trumpet to Arms*, 32; Glessing, *Underground Press in America*, 39–43.

59. Between 1965 and 1969, for example, the *Berkeley Barb*'s circulation mushroomed from 5,000 to 100,000.

60. Author's interview with Nichols, 17 April 1993.

61. Nichols and Clarke, *Screw*, "Old Boys: They Just Blow Away," 9 May 1969, 16; "Undecided Dicks," 30 May 1969, 19; "Humping a Winner?" 29 November 1968, 12; "Do Homosexual Citizens Suck?" 20 June 1969, 16; "Are Creamy Cunts Kosher?" 27 June 1969, 18.

62. Author's interview with Nichols, 17 April 1993.

63. *Vector*, Jose Miguel Soriano, "Applause for Clap Clinic," April 1969, 22; Gale Whittington, "The Male Emergence," April 1969, 16.

64. Armstrong, *Trumpet to Arms*, 249–50; Chesebro, *Gayspeak*; Judy Grahn, *Another Mother Tongue: Gay Words, Gay Worlds* (Boston: Beacon, 1984); JoAnn Loulan, *The Lesbian Erotic Dance: Butch, Femme, Androgyny, and Other Rhythms* (San Francisco: Spinsters, 1990); Bruce Rodgers, *Gay Talk: A (Sometimes Outrageous) Dictionary of Gay Slang* (New York: G. P. Putnam's Sons, 1972).

65. Author's interview with Kepner, 26 April 1993.

66. *Los Angeles Advocate*, Corbet Grenshire, "It's the Heat, Baby," March 1968, 3; "1st L.A. Gay-in: Ultra High Camp," April 1968, 2; October 1967, 6.

67. *Los Angeles Advocate*, September 1967, 12; October 1967, 11; June 1968, 15.

68. *Drum*, "Harry Chess as Popperman!" October 1967, 3; "Sex in Prison," October 1966, 14; William F. Damon, "Sex in Prison," January 1969, 15.

69. Larry Carlson, "Sex in Public Places," *Vector*, May 1967, 14.

70. Lyn Pederson (Jim Kepner), "A Gay Camp Looks at the Camp Cult," *Pursuit & Symposium*, March/April 1966, 17.

71. Kepner, "The Life of the Lesbian," *The Ladder*, April 1967, 3.

72. Author's interview with Grier, 8 February 1994.

73. Anita Cornwell, "From a Soul Sister's Notebook," *The Ladder*, June/July 1969, 43. In 1983 Cornwell published *Black Lesbian in White America* (Tallahassee, Fla.: Naiad).

74. Hunter (Hudson), *Gay Insider*, 170.

75. Nichols and Clarke, "Stalls of Balls," *Screw*, 14 February 1969, 10.

76. *Town Talk*, "Vidi, Vici, Veni," 15 August 1965, 6; Hal Call, "Many People Work to Help Us, But . . ." 15 August 1965, 8.

77. *Los Angeles Advocate*, "Happy Birthday to Us," September 1967, 6.

78. Altman, *Oppression and Liberation*, 120.

79. "Harassment? Hell No!" *Los Angeles Advocate*, October 1967, 6; author's interview with Kepner, 26 April 1993.

80. *Los Angeles Advocate*, "Is the LAPD Working for Lamport?" March 1969, 1; "Using Our Strength," August 1969, 30.

81. *Los Angeles Advocate*, "Six of 21 Candidates Reply," March 1969, 2; Dick Michaels, "Cops Join Hoods in Harassing Bar," September 1968, 5; "Editorial: Courage Catches On," September 1968, 5.

82. *Los Angeles Advocate*, "All Join Hands 'n Dance," May 1968, 8; "Happy Birthday to Us!" September 1968, 4; "Not Hopeless Yet!" October 1968, 18; "Legal Defense Fund Takes Shape," November 1968, 3; "HELP Incorporates," December 1968, 3.

83. *Los Angeles Advocate*, Jim Kepner, "U.S. Capital Turns on to Gay Power," September 1967, 1; "Gay Power——$$$," October 1967, 8; "People Who Need People," November 1967, 6; Dick Michaels, "The World Is My Ashtray," January 1968, 4; "Unity and Action," April 1968, 6.

84. *Los Angeles Advocate*, "Happy Birthday to Us," September 1967, 6; Jack Foster, "Police OK Full Drag," February 1969, 1; "Pride Wins!!" November 1967, 1.

85. Del Martin, "History of S.F. Homophile Groups," *The Ladder*, October 1966, 9, 26.

86. Del Martin, "The Lesbian's Majority Status," *The Ladder*, June 1967, 23.

87. Author's interview with Grier, 8 February 1994.

88. Martha Shelley, "Homosexuality and Sexual Identity," *The Ladder*, August 1968, 7.

89. Nichols and Clarke, *Screw*, "Undecided Dicks," 30 May 1969, 19; "Off the Far End," 2 May 1969, 15; "Homo Is a No-No," 24 January 1969, 3.

90. *Drum*, "Philadelphia," November 1965, 5; "Op-op," September 1966, 34.

91. Leo Laurence, "Gay Revolution," *Vector*, April 1969, 11.

92. Author's interview with Call, 4 March 1993; Kepner, "Apology," *Pursuit & Symposium*, June 1967, 25.

93. Author's interviews with Kepner, 7 and 27 January 1994; Herb Caen, "Herb Caen," *San Francisco Chronicle*, 22 December 1966, 27; "U.S. News Wins a Small Battle," *Citizens News*, undated issue, the content of which indicates it was published in 1967.

94. "Polak Indicted," *Los Angeles Advocate*, March 1970, 5; author's interview with Kepner, 8 September 1993.

95. None of the themes are mentioned in the standard scholarly works on the three alternative presses: Tripp, *Origins of the Black Press*; Bennion, "Woman Suffrage Papers"; Jerry, "Newspapers in the Woman's Movement"; Steiner, "Suffrage Periodicals"; Allen, *Women's Media*; or Beasley and Gibbons, *Taking Their Place*.

96. Although the standard scholarly works on the early years of the African-American press have not examined the relationship between black newspapers and black-owned businesses (presumably because the number of businesses owned by African Americans was minuscule in the early nineteenth century), historians who have looked at the later stages of the

African-American press have made passing reference to this relationship. Those references suggest that the church/state line eventually blurred in the black press as it did in the gay press. See, for example, Lee Finkle, *Forum for Protest* (Cranbury, N.J.: Associated University Presses, 1975), 67; and Wolseley, *Black Press*, 317, 372, 381.

97. D'Emilio, *Sexual Politics*; Katz, *Gay American History*; Marcus, *Making History*; Altman, *Oppression and Liberation*, 120; Armstrong, *Trumpet to Arms*, 251; Lewis, *Outlaws of America*, 41; and Peck, *Uncovering the Sixties*, 218.

Chapter Five

1. Jim Rankin, "NACHO Upside Down," *Gay Sunshine*, October 1970, 4.

2. With a weekly figure of 25,000, *GAY* boasted the largest circulation. *The Advocate* followed with 23,000; *Come Out!* with 6,000; *Gay Sunshine* with 4,000; *The Ladder* with 3,800; *Gay Liberator* with 2,000; the *San Francisco Gay Free Press* with 1,500; *Gay Flames, Lavender Vision,* and *Vector* with 1,000 each; *Killer Dyke* with 700; and *Gay Times* with 500. These figures are based on statements in the publications and the author's interviews with Kepner, Grier, May, Mendenhall, O'Brien, and Shelley.

3. New York field office reports to FBI Headquarters dated 30 July 1969, 7 August 1969, 10 December 1969, 16 December 1969, and 31 March 1970, Gay Liberation Front file, FBI Headquarters, Washington, D.C.

4. Author's interview with Shelley, 17 July 1994.

5. *New York Times*, "4 Policemen Hurt in 'Village' Raid," 29 June 1969, 33; *New York Times*, "Police Again Rout 'Village' Youths," 30 June 1969, 22; "Hostile Crowd Dispersed Near Sheridan Square," 3 July 1969, 19; *New York Daily News*, "Homo Nest Raided; Queen Bees Are Stinging Mad," 29 June 1969, 1; Howard Smith, "Full Moon Over the Stonewall," *Village Voice*, 3 July 1969, 1; Lucian Truscott IV, "Gay Power Comes to Sheridan Square," *Village Voice*, 3 July 1969, 1; Jonathan Black, "Gay Power Hits Back," *Village Voice*, 31 July 1969, 1.

6. On details about the Stonewall Inn and the bar raid, see Duberman, *Stonewall*, 181–212.

7. Paul Berman, "Democracy and Homosexuality," *New Republic*, 20 December 1993, 22.

8. Dick Leitsch, "Police Raid on N.Y. Club Sets Off First Gay Riot," *Los Angeles Advocate*, September 1969, 3.

9. Leitsch, "Police Raid"; Berman, "Democracy and Homosexuality," 24.

10. Nichols and Clarke, "Pampered Perverts," *Screw*, 25 July 1969, 16.

11. Nichols and Clarke, "Pampered Perverts."

12. Nichols and Clarke, "The Editors Speak," *GAY*, 1 December 1969, 2; Hunter (Hudson) *Gay Insider*, 172; author's interview with Vincenz, 7 September 1992. Nichols and Clarke edited *GAY* while continuing the "Homosexual Citizen" column until June 1973. *GAY* ceased publication in February 1974.

13. "Bookshop Employees Arrested," *GAY*, 15 December 1970, 10.

14. *GAY*, Vincenz, "Where Have All the Lovers Gone?" 4 January 1971, 9; Hansen (Vincenz), "To Tell or Not To Tell," 15 March 1970, 15; Angelo d'Arcangelo, "Lustful Licks Cause Lily Livers," 11 May 1970, 12.

15. "Cross Currents," *The Ladder*, February/March 1970, 40.

16. Nichols and Clarke, "Editorial," *GAY*, 26 April 1971, 3.

17. Nichols and Clarke, "The Editors Speak," *GAY*, 31 December 1969, 2. *GAY* published weekly from April 1970 until October 1971, when it reverted to a biweekly schedule.

18. Corzine, "Gay Press," 100. The first issue of *Come Out!* was dated 14 November 1969 and the last September 1972.

19. "Come Out!," *Come Out!*, 14 November 1969, 1.

20. On the beginnings of the Gay Liberation Front, see D'Emilio, *Sexual Politics,* 233–35; Donn Teal, *The Gay Militants* (New York: Stein and Day, 1971), 38–60. The Gay Liberation Front took its name from the National Liberation Front, Algerian terrorists who had sought freedom from France a decade earlier.

21. Author's interview with Shelley, 17 July 1994.

22. *Come Out!,* Gay Commandoes, "The October Rebellion," 14 November 1969, 5; Mike Brown, Michael Tallman, and Leo Martello, "The Summer of Gay Power and the Village Voice Exposed!" 14 November 1969, 10; September/October 1970, "Out of the Dunes and into the Streets," 6; "Gay Liberation Heads South," September/October 1970, 13.

23. Joe Salata and Steve Gavin, "A Cocksucking Seminar," *Come Out!,* Winter 1972, 18.

24. Nichols and Clarke, "The Gay Press Meets," *GAY,* 4 May 1970, 2.

25. Staff, "Dear Contributor," *Come Out!,* June/July 1970, 3; Nichols and Clarke, "The Gay Press Meets," *GAY,* 4 May 1970, 2.

26. Teal, *Gay Militants,* 54–55.

27. *Come Out!,* "Come Out!," 14 November 1969, 1; Lois Hart, "Black Panthers Call a Revolutionary People's Constitutional Convention," September/October 1970, 15; Shelley, "The Young Lords Go to Church," April/May 1970, 10; Milani, "Mira, Young Lord," June/July 1970, 7; "Third World Gay Revolution," September/October 1970, 12.

28. Nick Benton, "Who Needs It?" *Gay Sunshine,* August/September 1970, 3. *Gay Sunshine* ceased publication in early 1971. After a staff reorganization, it reappeared in the spring as a literary journal published through the winter of 1982.

29. Author's telephone interview with Pat Brown, 6 July 1993, during which Brown was in Berkeley, California; *Gay Sunshine,* "Welcome Home Huey," August/September 1970, 6; Huey Newton, "Huey Newton on Gay Liberation," October 1970, 1.

30. Alycee J. Lane, "Newton's Law," *BLK,* March 1991, 11.

31. "Gay People Help Plan New Worlds," *Gay Flames,* 11 September 1970, 1. In the spring of 1971, *Gay Flames* began appearing as a pamphlet, continuing in that form until it ceased publication later in 1971.

32. Author's interview with John O'Brien, 16 July 1993, in Los Angeles. Three issues of *Gay Times* were printed in October and November 1970. Although it contained no names and was officially the voice of an organization called Red Butterfly, it was written, duplicated, and distributed by O'Brien.

33. Nichols and Clarke, "N.Y. Gays: Will the Spark Die?" *Los Angeles Advocate,* September 1969, 12.

34. Teal, *Gay Militants,* 88; Rob Cole, "The Leftists They Woo Call Them 'Faggots,'" *The Advocate,* 16–29 September 1970, 12.

35. Berman, "Democracy and Homosexuality," 25–26; Lois Hart, "Black Panthers Call a Revolutionary People's Constitutional Convention," *Come Out!,* September/October 1970, 15; "No Revolution Without Us," *Come Out!,* September/October 1970, 17.

36. Shelley, "Subversion in the Women's Movement," *Gay Sunshine,* December 1970, 14.

37. *Gay Flames,* "What We Want, What We Believe," March 1971, 1; Carl Wittman, "A Gay Manifesto," pamphlet no. 9, 1971; Steve Gavin, "Thoughts on the Movement," *Come Out!,* Winter 1972, 20.

38. *GAY,* Richard C. Wandel, "Kiss-in Staged by Young Men," 13 September 1971, 1; Nichols and Clarke, "Dancing Anyone?" 19 January 1970, 2; John Francis Hunter (John Paul Hudson), "The Rise of the New Conscience," 29 June 1970, 10–11; Nichols and Clarke, "The Editors Speak," 25 May 1970, 2.

39. Nichols and Clarke, *GAY,* "Editorial," 12 October 1970, 3; "Editorial," 21 September 1970, 3; "The Editors Speak," 10 August 1970, 3. The Lindsay zap took place at the centennial celebration of the Metropolitan Museum of Art, 13 April 1970, and the *Harper's* zap, 27 Octo-

ber 1970. See Joseph Epstein, "Homo/Hetero: Struggle for Sexual Identity," *Harper's,* September 1970, 37–51.

40. "Sorry, Huey," *The Advocate,* 14–27 October 1970, 20. The *Los Angeles Advocate*'s first biweekly issue was dated April 29-May 12, 1970. On the next issue, dated May 13–25, 1970, the flag read *The Advocate.*

41. Marilyn Barrow (Barbara Grier), "The Least of These," *The Ladder,* October/November 1968, 30; author's interview with Grier, 8 February 1994.

42. Rita Mae Brown, *The Ladder,* "Say It Isn't So," June/July 1970, 29; "The Woman-Identified Woman," August/September 1970, 6.

43. Author's interview with Pat Brown, 6 July 1993.

44. Charles Thorp, *Gay Sunshine,* December 1970, "Power/Liberate Create Theory," 9; "A Gay Liberation Manifesto," 8.

45. Author's interview with O'Brien, 16 July 1993.

46. New York Field Office reports to FBI Headquarters dated 30 July 1969, 31 March 1970, 3 December 1970, Gay Liberation Front file, FBI Headquarters, Washington, D.C.

47. *Killer Dyke,* September 1971, 3; "Killer Dykes," September 1971, 3. *Killer Dyke* was founded by a group of radical lesbians called Flippies. It ceased publication in 1972.

48. *Gay Flames,* 1 September 1970, "To Serve the Community," 4; "We're Fighting Back!" 2; "Views," 4.

49. *Come Out!,* Ronald Ballard and Bob Fontanella, "To the Gay Liberation Front," 14 November 1969, 4; Shelley, "Gays Riot Again!" September/October 1970, 3; "GLF News," June/July 1970, 22; "Lesbian Demands," September/October 1970, 16; Gay Commandoes, "The October Rebellion," 14 November 1969, 5.

50. *San Francisco Gay Free Press,* undated issue the content of which indicates it was published in December 1970, "Pigs Sty-me Stud," 10; "Editorial," 2; Charles Thorp, "Editor-Vendor Attacked by Closet," 5; Ralph Hall, "Rising Up Gay," 10. The *San Francisco Gay Free Press* was a spinoff of the *San Francisco Free Press,* an underground paper published from September 1969 to April 1970. Two issues of the *Gay Free Press* were published, one in December 1970 and one sometime in 1971.

51. Gay Guevara, "Gay Revos Strike," *San Francisco Gay Free Press,* undated issue, the content of which indicates it was published in December 1970, 15.

52. Michaels, "Sorry, Huey," *The Advocate,* 14–27 October 1970, 20.

53. Altman, *Homosexual Oppression and Liberation,* 177–78.

54. Teal, *Gay Militants,* 36; *Come Out! Selections from the Radical Gay Liberation Newspaper* (New York: Times Change Press, 1970), 5.

55. *Come Out!,* Ronald Ballard and Bob Fontanella, "To the Gay Liberation Front," 14 November 1969, 4; September/October 1970, 2; "GLF," April/May 1970, 2.

56. "Liberation? I Don't Need It!" *Gay Liberator,* July 1970, 3. *Gay Liberator* ceased publication with the dissolution of the Gay Liberation Front of Detroit in March 1971 but reappeared six months later as an independent newspaper published by a collective. It ceased publication in September 1976.

57. Corzine, "Gay Press," 99; *Come Out!,* April/May 1970, 2.

58. *Lavender Vision,* "Gay Community Is Consciousness," November 1970, 10; Katz, "On Messing with Straight Women," April 1971, 15. *Lavender Vision* ceased publication in April 1971.

59. Author's interview with Pat Brown, 6 July 1993; Craig Schoonmaker, "Separatists Forming Alliance," *Gay Sunshine,* January 1971, 3.

60. *Gay Flames,* "To Serve the Community," 1 September 1970, 4; "Views," 11 September 1970, 7; Carl Wittman, "A Gay Manifesto," pamphlet no. 9, 1971, 7.

61. "The Great Gay Conspiracy," *San Francisco Sunday Examiner and Chronicle,* 18 Octo-

ber 1970, 1; Leigh W. Rutledge, *The Gay Decades: From Stonewall to the Present* (New York: Plume, 1992), 13.

62. Don Jackson, "Alpine News Round-Up," *San Francisco Gay Free Press*, undated issue, the content of which indicates it was published in December 1970, 3.

63. Author's interview with Pat Brown, 6 July 1993; "Off the Snow Pigs," *Gay Sunshine*, February 1971, 4.

64. "'Circle the Wagons,'" *The Advocate*, 11–24 November 1970, 20.

65. "Stonewall," *Gay Flames*, 14 November 1970, 6; James Coleman, "Brother Don's Nightmare," *Gay Liberator*, December 1970, 16.

66. Author's interview with Shelley, 17 July 1994.

67. Craig Schoonmaker, "Separatists Forming Alliance," *Gay Sunshine*, January 1971, 3; Rutledge, *Gay Decades*, 13.

68. Lois Hart, "Some News and a Whole Lot of Opinion," *Come Out!*, April/May 1970, 3.

69. *The Ladder*, Rita Laporte, "Of What Use NACHO?" August/September 1969, 18; March/April 1972, 54; Wilda Chase, "*Men* Are the Second Sex!" August/September 1969, 34–35.

70. Del Martin, "Female Gay Blasts Men, Leaves Movement," *The Advocate*, 28 October/10 November 1970, 21–22.

71. "Cross Currents," *The Ladder*, October/November 1969, 40; author's interview with Grier, 8 February 1994.

72. Author's interview with Grier, 8 February 1994.

73. Gene Damon (Barbara Grier), "Women's Liberation Catches Up to *The Ladder*," *The Ladder*, August/September, 4; Grier, "Introduction," in Grier and Reid, *Lavender Herring*, 17.

74. "GLF Women," *Come Out!*, December 1969/January 1970, 10.

75. *Killer Dyke*, September 1971, Glif Twigger, "Liberation Front and Gay Revolutionaries," 5; "Woman-Identified Woman," 6.

76. Rita Laporte, "Of What Use NACHO?", 18.

77. Katz, "Smash Phallic Imperialism," *Lavender Vision*, November 1970, 5.

78. "Lesbians as Bogeywomen," *Come Out!*, June/July 1970, 10.

79. "Women's Movement and Lesbianism," *Lesbian Tide*, November 1972, 4; Rutledge, *Gay Decades*, 54–55; "Woman-Identified Woman," *Killer Dyke*, September 1971, 6. The National Organization for Women later softened its stand, and today lesbian rights is one of its top priorities.

80. Wade, "From My Collective Consciousness," *Lavender Vision*, November 1970, 9.

81. *GAY*, Hector Simms, "A Biopsy on Miss Thing," 1 June 1970, 15; Nichols and Clarke, "*GAY* and the Drag Queen," 22 June 1970, 2.

82. "We Might Like It," *The Advocate*, 11–24 November 1970, 20.

83. Pat Maxwell, "The Emperor's New Clothes," *Gay Sunshine*, January 1971, 16.

84. Angela Douglas, "Transvestite & Transsexual Liberation," *Come Out!*, September/October 1970, 21; author's interview with Shelley, 17 July 1994.

85. *San Francisco Gay Free Press*, undated issue, the content of which indicates it was published in December 1970, 1; "Free Angela Douglas!" 6.

86. *Gay Flames*, "Street Transvestite Murdered," undated issue, the content of which indicates it was published in late December 1970, 1; Sylvia Rivers and Arthur Bell, "Chris: Gay Prisoner in Bellevue," 14 November 1970, 2; 12 February 1971, "Jewel Box," 6; "Support Lesbian, Transvestite, & Gay Inmates," 1.

87. Shelley, "Gay Is Good," *Killer Dyke*, September 1971, 7.

88. Tip Hillary, "Viewpoint," *Vector*, May 1970, 12; author's telephone interview with George Mendenhall, 13 September 1993, during which Mendenhall was in San Francisco; *Gay Liberator*, A. Michael Weber, "Grease and Struggle," March 1971, 6; "Free Angela!" January 1971, 5; Angela Keyes Douglas, "No More Welfare for Transvestites," March 1971, 15.

89. Katz, "Macho and Monogamy," *Lavender Vision,* April 1971, 12.

90. Hansen (Vincenz), "The Bells Are Ringing," *GAY,* 16 February 1970, 18.

91. Author's interview with Grier, 8 February 1994; Wilda Chase, "*Men* Are the Second Sex!" *The Ladder,* August/September 1969, 34.

92. Nichols and Clarke, "Are You a Jealous Lover?" *GAY,* 15 June 1970, 5.

93. "What We Want, What We Believe," *Gay Flames,* March 1971, 1; *Come Out!,* Jim Foratt, "Word Thoughts," January 1970, 8; Joe Salata and Steve Gavin, "A Cocksucking Seminar," Winter 1972, 18; "What's Wrong with Sucking?" *Gay Flames,* pamphlet no. 3, 1971, 2; Gene Kittner, "How to Get Fucked (and like it)," *Gay Sunshine,* December 1970, 9.

94. Author's interview with Shelley, 17 July 1994; Bob Kohler, "I Can't Hear You—I Have a Carrot in My Ear," *Come Out!,* June/July 1970, 9.

95. "The Lavender Kid & Butch," *Gay Flames,* 11 September 1970, 4.

96. "Syzygoty, Diasporady and Amoebeity," *San Francisco Gay Free Press,* undated issue, the content of which indicates it was published in December 1970, 10.

97. "Platform," *Killer Dyke,* September 1971, 2.

98. Katz, "Smash Phallic Imperialism," *Lavender Vision,* November 1970, 5.

99. Author's interview with Mendenhall, 13 September 1993; *Gay Sunshine,* December 1970, 1.

100. Sharon DeLano, "An Interview with Barbara Grier," *Christopher Street,* October 1976, 44; Marilyn Barrow (Barbara Grier), "The Least of These," *The Ladder,* October/November 1968, 33.

101. "We Are Bleeding!" *The Advocate,* 3–16 February 1971, 22.

102. *GAY,* "Gay Couple Files Joint Tax Return," 1 June 1970, 3; Nichols and Clarke, "Congratulations to Dick and Bob," 1 June 1970, 2; "Two Men Apply for Marriage License," 15 June 1970, 12; Nichols and Clarke, "Congratulations to Jack and Jim," 15 June 1970, 2; "Cornell U. GLF Holds Sit-in," 21 December 1970, 1; Nichols and Clarke, "Editorial," 21 December 1970, 3.

103. *GAY,* Leitsch, "The Gay Vote," 15 December 1969, 9; Nichols and Clarke, "Bella Abzug for Congress," 8 June 1970, 2; "Bella Abzug's Victory," 13 July 1970, 2; "Editorial," 9 November 1970, 3.

104. *Come Out!,* Ellen Bedoz, Bernard Lewis, and Allan Warshawsky, "Dialogue," April/May 1970, 13; Allen Warshawsky, "Take Good Care of My Brother," April/May 1970, 4; Nichols and Clarke, "Let's End the News Blackout," *GAY,* 3 August 1970, 2. On the Goldberg incident, see Kay Tobin (Lahusen), "GAA confronts Goldberg, Blumenthal," *GAY,* 29 June 1970, 12.

105. Author's interview with Nichols, 12 November 1993.

106. *GAY,* John P. Leroy, "Beacon Lights on Bathing Beauties," 15 June 1970, 7; Nichols and Clarke, "Support GAY's Advertisers," 1 June 1970, 2.

107. *Come Out!,* "Come Out!," 14 November 1969, 1; "Joel Fabricant Perverts Gay Power," 14 November 1969, 3; "Gays Protest Police Raid on Bar after Young Man Is Impaled on Fence," April/May 1970, 4.

108. *Gay Flames,* "We're Fighting Back!" 1 September 1970, 1; "Who's on Top?" undated issue, the content of which indicates it was published in September 1970, 3; Carl Wittman, "A Gay Manifesto," pamphlet no. 9, 1971, 7; "Remember?!" 14 November 1970, 8.

109. John O'Brien, "Gay Bars," *Gay Times,* 27 October 1970, 1; author's interview with O'Brien, 16 July 1993.

110. Kathy Braun, "The Dance," *Come Out!,* April/May 1970, 3; *Gay Flames,* "Pigs Play It One Way," undated issue, the content of which indicates it was published in mid-September 1970, 3; "Join Us at Alternate U.," undated issue, the content of which indicates it was published in late September 1970, 2.

111. "Lesbian Demands," *Come Out!,* September/October 1970, 16; "We Demand," *Gay Flames,* 11 September 1970, 2; "What We Want, What We Believe," *Gay Flames,* March 1971, 1;

"Support Lesbian, Transvestite, & Gay Inmates," *Gay Flames*, 12 February 1971, 6; "Platform," *Killer Dyke*, September 1971, 2; Charles P. Thorp, "Power/Liberate Create Theory," *Gay Sunshine*, December 1970, 9.

112. O'Brien, "Critique of 'Gay Demands,' " undated flyer, the content of which indicates it was published in September 1970, 1.

113. Author's interview with Shelley, 17 July 1994.

114. The last issue of *Come Out!* was dated Winter 1972. *Gay Flames* ceased publication by the end of 1971, *Gay Liberator* in March 1971, *Gay Times* in November 1970, *Gay Sunshine* in February 1971, *Killer Dyke* by the end of 1972, the *San Francisco Gay Free Press* by the end of 1971, and *Lavender Vision* in April 1971.

115. Author's interview with Grier, 8 February 1994; Gene Damon (Barbara Grier), "Editorial," *The Ladder,* August/September 1972, 3.

116. Grier, "Introduction," in Grier and Reid, *Lavender Herring,* 17.

117. Author's interview with Pat Brown, 6 July 1993.

Chapter Six

1. Gilbert Choate, "Fag Mags," *Alternative Media*, 1978, vol. 10, 7–8.

2. "Gay Paper Sold," *Lesbian Tide,* January 1975, 24.

3. Author's interview with Jeanne Córdova, 13 July 1993, in Los Angeles.

4. Author's interview with Córdova, 13 July 1993; Marley Sooklaris, "In Retrospect," *Sisters,* June 1973, 14.

5. Collective Lesbian International Terrors, "CLIT Statement No. 3," *Dyke*, Spring 1976, 42; author's telephone interview with Gina Covina, 19 January 1995, during which Covina was in Vallecitos, New Mexico.

6. *Lavender Woman,* July 1972, 12; "Lavender Press Goes to the Big City," May 1974, 1; "Publications Workshop," August 1973, 4.

7. Author's interviews with Córdova, Covina, Grier, Kepner, Lyon, Martin, and Nestle.

8. Rita Mae Brown, " 'Gay Men Don't Understand Body Language of Women,' " *The Advocate,* 17 July 1974, 26.

9. *The Furies,* January 1972, Ginny Z. Berson, untitled essay, 1; Charlotte Bunch, "Lesbians in Revolt: Male Supremacy Quakes and Quivers," 9.

10. Ginny Z. Berson, "The Furies: Goddesses of Vengeance," in Wachsberger, *Voices from the Underground,* 319; Armstrong, *Trumpet to Arms,* 240.

11. Author's interview with Córdova, 13 July 1993.

12. Author's interview with Córdova, 13 July 1993. On lesbian feminism, see Lillian Faderman, *Odd Girls and Twilight Lovers: A History of Lesbian Life in Twentieth-Century America* (New York: Columbia University Press, 1991), 204–9; Ginny Vida, "The History of LFL," *Lesbian Feminist,* 25 August 1973, 2.

13. *Lesbian Tide,* Cynthia MacJeanne Córdova and Ann Doczi, "Celebrity Is a Death Rite: An Interview with Kate Millett," September/October 1975, 3; Jeanne Córdova, "Carter Aide Wants Nation to Hear What I Heard," May/June 1977, 12.

14. " 'Boys' in the Tide?" *Lesbian Tide,* September/October 1978, 24.

15. Maida Tilchen, "Ebb Tide," *Gay Community News,* 28 February 1981, 9; *Lesbian Tide,* "WE ARE FLAT BROKE! PLEASE SEND MONEY!" September/October 1975, 15.

16. Author's interview with Córdova, 13 July 1993; "From Us," *Lesbian Tide,* September/October 1977, 20.

17. Author's interview with Córdova, 13 July 1993.

18. Author's interview with Córdova, 13 July 1993.

33. *San Francisco Sentinel,* 1 June 1979, Charles Lee Morris, "Comments," 7; "The War on Castro," 1.

34. "The Sickness Spreads," *Los Angeles Times,* 24 May 1979, 6; "The 'Most Civilized' City," *Seattle Times,* 23 May 1979, A-12; Bill Gold, "The District Line," *Washington Post,* 25 May 1979, D-8; Dwight Gaut, "SF Gays Take to Streets," *Seattle Gay News,* 28 May 1979, 1; Larry Bush, "S.F. Gays Vent Outrage," *Washington Blade,* 24 May 1979, 1.

35. Jo Thomas, "75,000 March in Capital in Drive to Support Homosexual Rights," *New York Times,* 15 October 1979, A-14.

36. Bruce Stores, "March and Rally Electrify D.C.," *Seattle Gay News,* 26 October 1979, 8; Pat Wellner and Diane Gilliland, "Impressions from the Washington, D.C., March," *Lesbian News,* November 1979, 1; Charles Lee Morris, untitled article, *San Francisco Sentinel,* 19 October 1979, 1; "Gay Push into the 80's," *Lesbian Tide,* November/December 1979, 18.

37. *Washington Blade,* Lou Chibbaro Jr., "March Leaders Say Problems Are Resolved," 13 September 1979, 1; "Angela Davis Invitation Debated," 13 September 1979, 19; Don Leavitt, "The March!" 25 October 1979, 1.

38. Goodstein Papers, Box 2, folder 36, "Biography," 4; Stephen Fox, "Anita Bryant May Have Done More Than She Realizes," *Los Angeles Herald-Examiner,* 1 July 1977, A-8; "A Friend in the White House," *The Advocate,* 23 March 1977, 17.

39. "Advocate Publisher Goodstein Dead at 52," *Update,* 26 June 1985, 1; Duke Smith, "The Victory," *San Francisco Sentinel,* 17 November 1978, 2; Goodstein Papers, Box 2, folder 36, "Biography," 2–3.

40. "Advocate Publisher Goodstein Dead at 52," *Update,* 26 June 1985, 1.

41. *Gay Sunshine,* 8 March 1978; Bruce Blackadar, "Problems of a Gay Moderate," *Toronto Sun,* 31 May 1976, 6.

42. Sasha Gregory-Lewis, "Advocate Conference Creates Office: $66,000 Pledged," *The Advocate,* 21 April 1976, 6; "'Advocate' Conference Spawns Lobby Group," *Washington Blade,* April 1976, 1.

43. "'Advocate' Conference Spawns Lobby Group," *Washington Blade,* April 1976, 6.

44. Robert Chesley, *Gay Community News,* 5 March 1977, 1, "The Wit and Wisdom of Citizen Goodstein"; "Goodstein Faces 'Unkempt, Unemployable' Critics."

45. George Mendenhall, *The Advocate,* "The Question: Vote Pro-gay or Gay?"; "Involvement '76: A Special California Political Supplement," 2 June 1976, 4.

46. *Lesbian Tide,* Sharon McDonald, "9,500 March Against Bryant," July/August 1977, 6; Jeanne Córdova, "Gay, Feminist Coalition Sweeps IWY," July/August 1977, 8; Sharon McDonald, "National Lesbian Organization Born!" May/June 1978, 18; Jeanne Córdova, "From the Closets to the Stage," November/December 1978, 8.

47. *Bay Area Reporter,* "The Night They Drove Ol' Anita Down," 21 July 1977, 4; "Save Our Human Rights: Legislators, Bob Ross Honored by SOHR," 13 October 1977, 2; "Witnesses Needed," 24 May 1979, 1.

48. Karen Martin, "Demonstrators Ejected at City Council," *Philadelphia Gay News,* 3 January 1976, A-3; "Intro 384 Defeated in City Council," *Gaysweek,* 20 November 1978, 1.

49. Randy Shilts, "White House Meeting," *The Advocate,* 20 April 1977, 35.

50. Anderson, "Gay Press Proliferates," 22.

51. Anderson, "Gay Press Proliferates," 22.

52. "Gay Press Group Born At NYC Conference," *The Advocate,* 19 February 1981, 8; Jonathan Friendly, "Writers on Newspapers for Homosexuals Say Their Work Now Gains More Respect," *New York Times,* 12 January 1981, D-8.

53. Author's telephone interview with Joe DiSabato, 3 January 1989, during which DiSabato was in New York.

54. "Gay Press Group Born," *The Advocate*; author's interview with DiSabato, 3 January 1989.

55. Author's interview with Shilts, 11 August 1993.

56. Author's interview with Gregory-Lewis, 28 March 1994.

57. "Bryant Rants . . . No Sunshine for Gays in Florida," *Lesbian Tide*, May/June 1977, 16.

58. "Editorial," *Lesbian Tide*, July/August 1977, 22.

59. Jeanne Córdova, *Lesbian Tide*, September/October 1977, "Teachers May Face Initiative," 13; "Perspectives," 4.

60. *Seattle Gay News*, Mike Hughes and Bruce Stores, "Moral Majority Claims Big Win," 9 October 1981, 1; "Editorial: Keeping Track of the Moral Majority," 23 October 1981, 4.

61. *The Advocate*, 10 March 1976, Randy Shilts, "City Rights Laws—Are They Just Toothless Paper Tigers?" 6; Sasha Gregory-Lewis, "Editorial," 22.

62. Jackson and Persky, eds., *Flaunting It!*, 2.

63. *The Body Politic*, John D'Emilio, "Dreams Deferred: The Early American Homophile Movement," November 1978, 19; Mariana Valverde, "Taking over the House of Language," February 1979, 18; Gerald Hannon, "No Sorrow, No Pity: The Gay Disabled," February 1980, 19.

64. Gerald Hannon, "Men Loving Boys Loving Men," *The Body Politic*, December 1977/ January 1978, 30.

65. *The Body Politic*, G. Small, February 1978, 2; Michael Johnson, February 1978, 2.

66. Jackson and Persky, eds., *Flaunting It!*, 4–5. The raid took place on 30 December 1977. The charges were filed 5 January 1978.

67. Jackson and Persky, eds., *Flaunting It!*, 146.

68. Jackson and Persky, eds., *Flaunting It!*, 146.

69. Jackson and Persky, eds., *Flaunting It!*, 5–6, 238, 243.

70. Gayle Rubin, "Sexual Politics, the New Right, and the Sexual Fringe," *Leaping Lesbian*, February 1978, 13.

71. Harvey Milk, "Milk Forum: A Nation Finally Talks about . . . 'It,' " *Bay Area Reporter*, 9 June 1977, 17.

72. "Gay Men Beaten in Crane's Beach Incidents," *Gay Community News*, 13 August 1977, 1.

73. Allen White, "Attack on Divisadero Bus," *Bay Area Reporter*, 12 November 1981, 1.

74. Michael Fischer, "Two Gay Men Assaulted in Village; Pattern of Anti-Gay Violence Seen," *Gaysweek*, 31 July 1978, 10.

75. Author's telephone interview with Alan Bell, 9 June 1995, during which Bell was in Los Angeles; " 'Close Firetraps' Rally on Tuesday," *Gaysweek*, 1 June 1977, 2.

76. *Gaysweek*, "Long Fight for Everard Sprinklers," 1 June 1977, 2; " 'Close Firetraps' Rally on Tuesday," 1 June 1977, 2; "City Hall Site of Fire Violation Protest," 6 June 1977, 2.

77. *Philadelphia Gay News*, 16–29 October 1981, Richard Gajewski, "To Hell with the Humdrum," 9; J. DeMarco, "Better Living Through Chemistry? Not When Taken Internally," 13.

78. Shilts, "Hepatitis," *The Advocate*, 12 January 1977, 23.

79. Dave Heining, "Prisoners of the Queen's Tank," *Seattle Gay News*, 8 December 1978, 1; "State Police Admit Entrapment of Gays," *Philadelphia Gay News*, 7 February 1976, A-4.

80. Author's interview with Gregory-Lewis, 28 March 1994.

81. Sasha Gregory-Lewis, "Revelations of a Gay Informant," *The Advocate*, 9 March 1977, 13.

82. Gregory-Lewis, "Gay Informant," 13.

83. Gregory-Lewis, "Right Watch," *The Advocate*, 8 March 1978, 12.

84. Bridget Overton, "Sasha Gregory-Lewis, New Right Watchdog," *Lesbian Tide*, November/December 1978, 6.

85. Overton, "Sasha Gregory-Lewis," 6.

86. Shilts, "V.D.," *The Advocate,* 21 April 1976, 14.

87. Shilts, "V.D.," 14.

88. Author's telephone interview with Randy Shilts, 21 August 1993, during which Shilts was in Guerneville, California.

89. Christy Fisher, "Local Print Bumps into National Ad Walls," *Advertising Age,* 30 May 1994, S-2.

90. "A Sticky Face for Anita," *Gay Community News,* 29 October 1977, 1; "Why Anita Got Pied," *San Francisco Sentinel,* 20 October 1977, 8; "Anita Bryant Hit with 'Fruit' Pie," *Gaysweek,* 24 October 1977, 1.

91. "Anita Messes up Her Marriage," *San Francisco Sentinel,* 30 May 1980, 1; "A Sticky Face for Anita," *Gay Community News,* 29 October 1977, 1; "Why Anita Got Pied," *San Francisco Sentinel,* 20 October 1977, 8; "Anita Bryant Hit with 'Fruit' Pie," *Gaysweek,* 24 October 1977, 1.

92. "350,000 March World-Wide for Gay Pride," *Gay Community News,* 9 July 1977, 1; "Defeat of Intro 384 Spurs Angry Protest; 3000 March to Duffy Square," *Gaysweek,* 20 November 1978, 2; "Gay Push into the 80's," *Lesbian Tide,* November/December 1979, 18.

93. Allen White, "Attack on Divisadero Bus," *Bay Area Reporter,* 12 November 1981, 1; Eric Nadler, "Reported Anti-Gay Violence in White Plains Seen as 'Tip of Iceberg,'" *Gaysweek,* 31 July 1978, 10.

94. *Gaysweek,* 1 June 1977, 1.

95. *Bay Area Reporter,* "Missing Person," 29 July 1982, 3; "Murder South of Market," 16 February 1978, 4; "Straight Sought in Mass Gay Slayings," *San Francisco Sentinel,* 14 July 1977, 1.

96. "Pansies, Arise!" *Philadelphia Gay News,* 13–26 November 1981, 15; Bridget Overton, "We've Come a Long Way . . . Maybe," *Lesbian Tide,* May/June 1978, 14–15.

97. "Patent Office Refuses to Register 'Gaysweek' Name as Trademark," *Gaysweek,* 26 June 1978, 1; *Philadelphia Gay News,* "Newsbeat: Civil Rights," 18 September–1 October 1981, 4; "In the Media," 30 October-12 November 1981, 4.

98. Anderson, "Gay Press Proliferates," 22; Larry Goldsmith, "Fire Destroys GCN Office: Arson Suspected in Seven-Alarm Blaze," *Gay Community News,* 17 July 1982, 1; Charley Shively, "*Fag Rag*: The Most Loathsome Publication in the English Language," in Wachsberger, *Voices from the Underground,* 205.

99. Anderson, "Gay Press Proliferates," 22; author's interview with Bell, 9 June 1995. *Gaysweek* published its last issue in June 1979. On the *San Francisco Sentinel*'s financial difficulties, see "SF Paper May Fold," *The Advocate,* 29 October 1981, 12.

100. Author's interview with Shilts, 11 August 1993.

Chapter Nine

1. Lenny Giteck, "The Gay Pursuit of Muscle," *The Advocate,* 11 June 1981, 27.

2. Lawrence Mass, "Disease Rumors Largely Unfounded," *New York Native,* 18–31 May 1981, 7; "A Pneumonia That Strikes Gay Males," *San Francisco Chronicle,* 6 June 1981, 4; Lawrence K. Altman, "Rare Cancer Seen in 41 Homosexuals," *New York Times,* 3 July 1981, A-20.

3. Author's interview with Mendenhall, 13 September 1993.

4. Author's interview with Shilts, 21 August 1993.

5. Teresa Scannell, "AIDS: A Lesbian Perspective," *San Francisco Sentinel,* 13 October 1983, 15.

6. Author's interview with Shilts, 21 August 1993.

7. Steve Martz, "AIDS and the Gay Press," *Washington Blade,* 22 July 1983, 3.

8. Miller, *Our Own Voices.* The *Bay Area Reporter*'s circulation was 25,000, and the *Washington Blade*'s, *New York Native*'s, and *Christopher Street*'s all hovered around 20,000, ac-

cording to Allan F. Yoder, "Gay Publications Now," *Washington Blade,* 29 April 1983, 20. The total figure is based on the author's interviews with Kepner, Mendenhall, Nestle, and Shilts.

9. *New York Native,* untitled article 5–18 December 1980, 3. The first issue of the *New York Native* was dated 5–18 December 1980, and the newspaper continues to be published.

10. Author's interview with Lawrence Mass, 26 May 1994, in New York.

11. Mass, "Disease Rumors Largely Unfounded," *New York Native,* 18–31 May 1981, 7. The *New York Times's* first article about a new disease attacking gay men was Lawrence K. Altman, "Rare Cancer Seen in 41 Homosexuals," *New York Times,* 3 July 1981, A-20.

12. Mass, "Cancer in the Gay Community," *New York Native,* 27 July–9 August 1981, 1. The *Times* moved AIDS to page one with Robert Pear, "Health Chief Calls AIDS Battle 'No. 1 Priority,'" 25 May 1983.

13. Mass, *New York Native,* "Cancer in the Gay Community," 27 July–9 August 1981, 20–21; "The Epidemic Continues," 29 March–11 April 1982, 12.

14. Author's interview with Mass, 26 May 1994.

15. Author's interview with Mass, 26 May 1994; Mass, "An Epidemic Q & A," *New York Native,* 21 June–4 July 1982, 12.

16. Randy Shilts, *And the Band Played On: Politics, People, and the AIDS Epidemic* (New York: St. Martin's, 1987), 191.

17. Rodger Streitmatter, "AIDS: 'It's Just a Matter of Time,'" *The Quill,* May 1984, 22–27.

18. Yoder, "Gay Publications Now," 20; author's interview with Shilts, 11 August 1993.

19. Author's interview with Shilts, 21 August 1993.

20. "'Gay' Pneumonia? Not Really, Says Researcher," *The Advocate,* 23 July 1981, 7; Shilts, "Foreword," in Thompson, *Long Road to Freedom,* xv.

21. "POA Drops 'B.A.R.' Suit," *Bay Area Reporter,* 13 May 1982, 1; Paul Lorch, "Sleazy Rags," *Bay Area Reporter,* 21 October 1982, 6; W. E. Beardemphl, "Time for Facts, Not Fiction," *San Francisco Sentinel,* 17 February 1983, 5.

22. "Founder Purchases Sentinel," *San Francisco Sentinel,* 26 November 1981, 2.

23. Cindy Patton, "Gay Press: Advocacy versus Advertisements," *Gay Community News,* 14 May 1983, 3.

24. Author's interview with Mendenhall, 13 September 1993.

25. Mass, *New York Native,* "The Epidemic Continues," 29 March–11 April 1982, 13–14.

26. Randy R. Randall, "Brunch Causes 'Gay Cancer,'" *San Francisco Sentinel,* 1 April 1982, 7.

27. "The Caldron," *Bay Area Reporter,* 1 April 1982, 18.

28. *San Francisco Sentinel,* David Lester, "Most Tubs, Clubs Safe," 27 May 1982, 1; W. E. Beardemphl, "Safe and Responsible Baths," 27 May 1982, 5.

29. W. E. Beardemphl, "Destroying the Myth of AIDS," *San Francisco Sentinel,* 9 June 1983, 5.

30. Larry Kramer, "1,112 and Counting," *New York Native,* 14–27 March 1983, 1.

31. Author's interviews with Shilts, 21 August 1993; and Mendenhall, 13 September 1993.

32. Kramer, "1,112 and Counting," 1.

33. Kramer, "1,112 and Counting," 18.

34. *The Advocate,* "AIDS—A New Sexually Transmitted Disease," 28 April 1983, 10; Masha Gessen, "Twenty-Five Gay and Lesbian Years," 6 October 1992, "If It Takes 25 More" insert; Paul Lorch, "Gay Men Dying" *Bay Area Reporter,* 17 March 1983, 6.

35. Paul Lorch, "Gay Men Dying," *Bay Area Reporter,* 31 March 1983, 6.

36. "AIDS & Co. Strikes Back," *Bay Area Reporter,* 21 April 1983, 1.

37. Gary Schweikhart, "Angry AIDS Patients Organize"; Lorch Sends Blistering Response," *San Francisco Sentinel,* 28 April 1983, 1.

38. Shilts, *Band Played On,* 274.

39. *San Francisco Sentinel*, W. E. Beardemphl, "Time for Facts, Not Fiction," 17 February 1983, 5; Gary Schweikhart, "AIDS Gala Benefit Questioned," 1 September 1983, 1; Gary Schweikhart, "How the AIDS Benefit Report Is Flawed," 22 December 1983, 1.

40. Mike Hippler, "AIDS and the Baths," *Bay Area Reporter*, 15, 18.

41. "Garage Sale Marks Closing of Baths," *Gay Community News*, 10 September 1983, 2.

42. Author's interview with Mendenhall, 13 September 1993.

43. Mendenhall, "Sex Banned in Sex Palaces with Gay Backing," *Bay Area Reporter*, 12 April 1984, 1.

44. Paul Lorch, "Killing the Movement," *Bay Area Reporter*, 5 April 1984, 6–7.

45. *The Advocate*, 1 May 1984, David B. Goodstein, "Opening Space," 6; Nathan Fain, "Aftershocks from the Bay Area," 14, 15.

46. *Bay Area Reporter*, Allen White, "Small Turnout to Protest Sex Club Closing," 5 April 1984, 5; "New Editors for Bay Area Reporter," 28 June 1984, 11.

47. Author's interviews with Shilts, 21 August 1993; and Mendenhall, 13 September 1993.

48. Yoder, "Gay Publications Now," 20. Yoder was the Washington correspondent for the *Bergen* (New Jersey) *Record*.

49. Anderson, "Gay Press Proliferates," 19; John Jacobs, "Baby with AIDS Disease Raises Doubt about Blood Transfusions," *San Francisco Sunday Examiner and Chronicle*, 12 December 1982, 4; Lou Chibbaro Jr., "Hemophilia Group Urges Ban on Blood from Gays," *Washington Blade*, 21 January 1983, 1; "Potential AIDS Victims Urged Not to Donate Blood," *San Francisco Chronicle*, 4 March 1983, 39.

50. Shilts, *Band Played On*, 267.

51. Lisa M. Keen and Lou Chibbaro, Jr., "AIDS Funding," *Washington Blade*, 11 February 1983, 29.

52. Larry Bush, "Waxman Bill Would Speed up AIDS Research," *Washington Blade*, 25 February 1983, 1; Lou Chibbaro, Jr., "CDC Tightens Access on AIDS Records," *Washington Blade*, 3 August 1984, 1; Dave Walter, "House Report Blasts AIDS Response," *Washington Blade*, 9 December 1983, 1.

53. Dave Walter, "AIDS 'Probable Cause' Breakthrough Met with Cautious Optimism," *Washington Blade*, 27 April 1984, 1; Lawrence K. Altman, "Researchers Believe AIDS Virus Is Found; They Hope for Vaccine in Two Years," *San Francisco Chronicle*, 24 April 1984, 1; Cristine Russell, "Virus Discovery Could Lead to Test for AIDS," *Washington Post*, 24 April 1984, 1.

54. Dave Walter, "Brandt Asks HHS for More AIDS Money," *Washington Blade*, 13 July 1984, 1.

55. Susan Cavin, *Big Apple Dyke News*, "Unverified Theory: Is Aids Dioxin Related?" July 1983, 15; "Unverified Theory: Is Aids Dioxin Related?" (part 2), August/September 1983, 22.

56. On the *Journal of the American Medical Association* overstating the story, see Shilts, *Band Played On*, 300–1.

57. *New York Times*, "Family Contact Studied in Transmitting AIDS," 6 May 1983, 21; *20/20*, 26 May 1983; Patrick Buchanan, "Mother Nature Getting Even," *Seattle Post-Intelligencer*, 25 May 1983, A-15.

58. Paul Lorch, "Continuing Coverage," *Bay Area Reporter*, 4 August 1983, 6.

59. Bob Nelson, "'Casual Contact' Theories Incite AIDS Panic," *Gay Community News*, 18 June 1983, 3.

60. Bob Nelson, "AIDS Researcher Fights Eviction," *Gay Community News*, 22 October 1983, 6.

61. Peg Byron, "Complaint Filed for AIDS-Related Bias," *Gay Community News*, 3 September 1983, 1; Ray O'Laughlin, "United Airlines Removes Flight Attendants with AIDS," *New York Native*, 31 December 1984–13 January 1985, 11; "American Bar Association Lawyers

Oppose Homosexuals," *Big Apple Dyke News,* August/September 1983, 11; Craig Harris, "Corporate U.S. Looks at Workers with AIDS," *Gay Community News,* 1 March 1986, 3.

62. Jay C. Jones, "Official Makes Anti-Gay Remarks, Loses Position," *Gay Community News,* 6 August 1983, 1; "Pool Disinfected after Gay Group's Swimming Party," *Gay Community News,* 13 August 1983, 2; "AIDS Discrimination at Funeral Homes," *Big Apple Dyke News,* July 1983, 13; "Viewpoint," *Bay Area Reporter,* 4 August 1983, 6.

63. *Gay Community News,* "AIDS Employment Discrimination Case Resolved," 24 September 1983, 2; Jay C. Jones, "Official Makes Anti-Gay Remarks, Loses Position," 6 August 1983, 1.

64. Konstantin Berlandt, "Judge Bumps Juror with AIDS," *Bay Area Reporter,* 16 June 1983, 5.

65. Mass, "Cancer as Metaphor," *New York Native,* 24 August–6 September 1981, 13.

66. Bobbi Campbell, "I Will Survive," *San Francisco Sentinel,* 10 December 1981, 1.

67. Campbell, "I Will Survive," 1.

68. Campbell, "Gay Cancer Journal," *San Francisco Sentinel,* 7 January 1982, 1; 15 April 1982, 6; 27 May 1982, 12; 24 June 1982, 3. Campbell died in August 1984.

69. Gary Schweikhart, "AIDS Victim Speaks Out," *San Francisco Sentinel,* 11 November 1982, 4.

70. Philip Lanzaratta, "Surviving AIDS," *Christopher Street,* October 1984, 30–35.

71. Andrew Holleran, "Journal of the Plague Year," *Christopher Street,* November 1982, 15, 16, 18.

72. Mass, "Cancer in the Gay Community," *New York Native,* 27 July–9 August 1981, 21.

73. *New York Native,* Larry Kramer, "Personal Appeal from Larry Kramer," 24 August–6 September 1981, 13; Mass, "The Epidemic Continues," 29 March–11 April 1982, 15; "Thanks to You, We're a Hit!" 26 April–9 May 1982, 36.

74. Peg Byron, "AIDS and the Gay Men's Health Crisis of New York," *Gay Community News,* 30 July 1983, 8.

75. Rodger Streitmatter, "AIDS: 'It's Just a Matter of Time,'" *The Quill,* May 1984, 25.

76. Shilts, *Band Played On,* 91–92.

77. "AIDS Resource List," *Gay Community News,* 23 July 1983, 9.

78. *Washington Blade,* "Clinic's 'Safe Sex' Seminar Draws More Than 300 Men," 4 May 1984, 7; Jim Marks, "Having AIDS: The Pain, the Despair, and the Humor," 4 May 1984, 1; "Policy Set for House for People with AIDS," 7 September 1984, 11; Jeff Nackley, "AIDS and Preparing Your Legal Protections," 21 October 1983, 23; *Gay Community News,* "Social Security Benefits for People with AIDS," 20 August 1983, 2; "Housing Needed for Men with Aids," 20 August 1983, 2; George Mendenhall, "Gay Funeral Service Opens on Upper Market," *Bay Area Reporter,* 2 February 1984, 4.

79. Steve Martz, "A Concluding Word," *Washington Blade,* 25 February 1983, 21.

80. Pam Mitchell, "Dan White's Legacy Lives On," *Gay Community News,* 9 November 1985, 2; Roy Cohn died 2 August 1986.

81. Author's interview with Nestle, 12 January 1994.

82. "Breast Cancer among Lesbians," *Big Apple Dyke News,* July 1983, 12.

83. Author's interview with Nestle, 12 January 1994. *Lesbian Connection* was founded in the fall of 1974 by the Ambitious Lesbians collective in East Lansing, Michigan. It is still being published.

84. Untitled article, *Lesbian Connection,* April/May 1985, 2.

85. "Responses," *Lesbian Connection,* September 1982, 14.

86. *Lesbian Ethics* was founded in the fall of 1984 and ceased publication in 1990.

87. Jeanette Silveira, "Editor's Introduction," *Lesbian Ethics,* Fall 1984, 5.

88. *Lesbian Ethics,* "Non? Monogamy?" Spring 1985, 79; Anna Lee, "Tired Old Question of

Male Children," Spring 1985, 106; Jeanette Silveira, "Lesbian Feminist Therapy: A Report and Some Thoughts," Fall 1985, 23; Anonymous, "Malpractice," Fall 1985, 20; Mev Miller, "An Open Letter to an Abusive Therapist," Fall 1985, 19.

89. Susanna J. Sturgis, "Breaking Silence, Breaking Faith: The Promotion of Lesbian Nuns," *Lesbian Ethics*, Fall 1985, 99.

90. Joan Nestle, "My History with Censorship," *Bad Attitude*, Spring 1985, 4; author's interview with Nestle, 12 January 1994.

91. "Uncle Sam Doesn't Want You," *Lesbian Connection*, December 1982/January 1983, 11.

92. *Mom's Apple Pie* is still being published.

93. *Mom's Apple Pie*, Winter 1981, "CATCH 22 Alive & Well in Illinois," 3; "The Jarrett Decision," 3.

94. "On Choosing Publicity," *Mom's Apple Pie*, Winter 1981, 4–5.

95. Sue Zemel, "Legal Frontier: Donor Insemination of Lesbians," *San Francisco Sentinel*, 18 March 1982, 2.

96. Author's interview with Nestle, 12 January 1994.

97. Rima Shore, "Sisterhood—and My Brothers," *Conditions*, Spring 1983, 4. *Conditions* was founded in April 1977 and ceased publication in 1990.

98. Andrea Weiss, "Lesbian as Outlaw: New Forms and Fantasies in Women's Independent Cinema," *Conditions*, Spring 1985, 117–32.

99. Author's telephone interview with Elly Bulkin, 4 May 1994, during which Bulkin was in Jamaica Plain, Massachusetts.

100. Bunny A. King, "Bunny King," *Mom's Apple Pie*, Winter 1982, 9.

101. Barbara Macdonald, "A Call for an End to Ageism in Lesbian and Gay Services," *Lesbian Ethics*, Fall 1984, 57–63.

102. Author's interview with Nestle, 12 January 1994.

103. Joan Nestle, "The Bathroom Line," *Lesbian Connection*, September 1981, 3.

104. James Kinsella, *Covering the Plague: AIDS and the American Media* (New Brunswick, N.J.: Rutgers University Press, 1989), 32–33; Thomas Steele, "CDC Director Says Announcement of AIDS Cause Is Forthcoming," *New York Native*, 9–22 April 1984, 7; the *New York Times* did not publish the story about the virus being discovered until 22 April 1984.

105. Author's interviews with Thompson, 8 July 1993; and Sasha Gregory-Lewis, 28 March 1994; Goodstein Papers, Box 3, folder 16, 20; George Mendenhall, "David Goodstein Dies of Cancer," *Bay Area Reporter*, 27 June 1985, 2; "David Goodstein Dies at 53, Advocate for Homosexuals," *New York Times*, 26 June 1985, D-26.

Chapter Ten

1. Bob Woodward, "Gadhafi Target of Secret U.S. Deception Plan," *Washington Post*, 2 October 1986, A-13. Reagan first mentioned AIDS publicly in a 31 May 1987 speech.

2. "The Time for Gay Rage Is Now!" *The Advocate*, 5 August 1986, 18.

3. Michelangelo Signorile, "Newsflash: Outing Seizes America!" *OutWeek*, 16 May 1990, 40.

4. Sherman Hanke, "Are You Angry Yet?" *Gay Community News*, 19–25 July 1987, 5.

5. Miller, *Our Own Voices*; author's interviews with Kepner, McClurg, Nestle, and Shilts.

6. Otis Stuart, "Who Killed *OutWeek*?" *NYQ*, 1 March 1992, 28. *OutWeek* ceased publication in July 1991.

7. *OutWeek*, "What's Going on Here?" 11 September 1989, 4; "Beating the Bashers," 23 May 1990, 4; "Outspoken," 28 August 1989, 4.

8. Paul Rykoff Coleman, "ACT UP Takes on the Gay Press," *OutWeek*, 22 August 1990, 16.

9. John Umlaut, "Fright, Cameras, Action!" *OutWeek*, 28 August 1989, 35.

10. Donna Minkowitz, "Is It Disloyal to Insist on Fair Treatment from the Queer Press?" 21 April 1992, *The Advocate*, 33.

11. Otis Stuart, "Who Killed *OutWeek*?" *NYQ*, 1 March 1992, 32–33.

12. Deirdre Carmody, "Outweek, in a Shake-up, Ousts Its Editor," *New York Times*, 10 June 1991, D-10; Deirdre Carmody, "Outweek, Gay and Lesbian Magazine, Ceases Publication," *New York Times*, 28 June 1991, D-9; Stuart, "Who Killed *OutWeek*?" 30.

13. Sarah Pettit biographical statement provided by *Out* magazine, 22 June 1994.

14. *OutWeek*, Anne Rubenstein, "Designing Women," 30 May 1990, 45; Alison Bechdel, "Dykes to Watch Out For: Hell House," 26 June 1989, 5. The cartoon strip eventually was published in some two dozen lesbian and gay publications, and collections of the strips have been published in paperback and as calendars.

15. *OutWeek*, "What's in a Name?" 30 May 1990, 4; Signorile, "Gossip Watch," 14 August 1989, 47.

16. Jeanie Kasindorf, "Mr. Out: A Gay Journalist's Campaign to Expose Famous Homosexuals Prompts Charges of McCarthyism," *New York*, 14 May 1990, 88; author's interview with Signorile, 28 June 1994, in Washington, D.C. In 1993 Signorile published *Queer in America: Sex, the Media, and the Closets of Power* (New York: Random House), which recounted his experiences with outing.

17. *OutWeek*, "Peek-A-Boo," 7 August 1989, 44; 11 September 1989, 40.

18. Signorile, "The Secret Life of Malcolm Forbes," *OutWeek*, 18 March 1990, 40–45.

19. "Outspoken: Claiming Forbes for the Gay Nation," *OutWeek*, 18 March 1990, 4.

20. David Gelman, "'Outing': An Unexpected Assault on Sexual Privacy," *Newsweek*, 30 April 1990, 66; Dirk Johnson, "Privacy vs. the Pursuit of Gay Rights," *New York Times*, 27 March 1990, A-21; Eleanor Randolph, "The Media, at Odds Over 'Outing' of Gays: Deciding Whether to Publish Names of Alleged Homosexuals," *Washington Post*, 13 July 1990, C-1; William A. Henry III, "Forcing Gays out of the Closet," *Time*, 29 January 1990, 67; Kay Longcope, "Gays Divided on Tactic of Forcing Others out of the Closet," *Boston Globe*, 3 May 1990, 1; Michael Matza, "Out/Rage," *Philadelphia Inquioer*, 28 June 1990, E-1; Clarence Page, "Should the Closet Be Forced Open?" *Chicago Tribune*, 6 May 1990, D-3; Beth Ann Krier, "Whose Sex Secret Is It?" *Los Angeles Times*, 22 March 1990, E-1; David Tuller, "Uproar over Gays Booting Others out of the Closet," *San Francisco Chronicle*, 12 March 1990, A-9.

21. Signorile, "Gossip Watch," *OutWeek*, 18 April 1990, 55; Stuart, "Who Killed *OutWeek*?," 30.

22. Nina Reyes, "Gay Paper Fires Editor for Outing," *OutWeek*, 30 May 1990, 26; Benjamin Weiser, "Gay Activists Divided on Whether to 'Bring Out' Politicians," *Washington Post*, 19 September 1989, A-4; Randy Shilts, "The Nasty Business of 'Outing,'" *Los Angeles Times*, 7 August 1991, B-7.

23. Signorile, "Gossip Watch," *OutWeek*, 18 April 1990, 55; 18 July 1990, 45.

24. Signorile, "Gossip Watch," *OutWeek*, 22 August 1990, 51.

25. Signorile, "Gossip Watch," *OutWeek*, 20 February 1991, 64.

26. Stuart, "Who Killed *OutWeek*?" 28, 31.

27. Stuart, "Who Killed *OutWeek*?" 28, 31.

28. Stuart, "Who Killed *OutWeek*?" 30.

29. *The Advocate*, Stuart Byron, "Naming Names," 24 April 1990, 37; Signorile, "The Outing of Assistant Secretary of Defense Pete Williams," 27 August 1991, 43. *OutWeek*'s final issue was dated 3 July 1991.

30. *OutWeek*, Rex Wockner, "Activists Seize Stage at AIDS Conference," 26 June 1989, 8; Cliff O'Neill, "Activists and Artists Denounce Decision," 3 July 1989, 8; Andrew Miller, "Riot Erupts at Stonewall Faerie Gathering," 10 July 1989, 8; Cliff O'Neill, "Opposing Activists Clash

after Ruling," 17 July 1989, 9; Andrew Miller, "How to Fuck the Patriarchy," 31 July 1989, 25; Victoria A. Brownworth, "Reagan's Court, Bush's Sport," 31 July 1989, 24.

31. *Gay Community News,* Yoder, "Gay Publications Now," 23; Laurie Sherman, "Boston Protests Apartheid," 24 August 1985, 1; Joanne Brown, "5000 March Against Racism in Philadelphia," 8 March 1986, 1; Jennie McKnight, "150,000 Turn out for Abortion Rights March," 29 March 1986, 1.

32. *Lesbian Contradiction,* Jan Adams, "AIDS Is Getting to Us," Fall 1986, 20; "LesContortions," Spring 1986, 3. *Lesbian Contradiction* was founded in the winter of 1983 and is still being published, although it is now based only in San Francisco.

33. *Hag Rag,* "Lesbian Raped by Skinheads," May/June 1989, 16; "A Fucking Dress Code," September/October 1989, 25. *Hag Rag* was founded in July 1986 by the Hag Rag Collective. It ceased publication after the January/February 1993 issue.

34. *Lesbian Ethics,* Summer 1989, "Masked Women Disrupt Arraignment," 83; "Magazines Destroyed in Protest of Pornography, Rape," 81; "Vandals Leave Notes Protesting Pornography," 84; "When You Go Spray Painting, Remember . . . ," 88.

35. Sandy Dwyer, "ACT UP Targets Bush," *The News,* 10 June 1988, 1. *The News* was founded in 1986 and ceased publication in 1989.

36. *OutWeek,* 26 June 1989, Rex Wockner, "Activists Seize Stage at AIDS Conference," 8; Sandor Katz, "Whose Conference Was It, Anyway?" 18.

37. *OutWeek,* Rex Wockner, "ACT UP Demands AIDS Drug Release," 21 August 1989, 18; Cliff O'Neill, "AIDS Activists Shuts down D.C. Gov't Building," 24 July 1989, 20–21; Michael Abramowitz, "13 Arrested in AIDS Protest Blocking District Building," *Washington Post,* 12 July 1989, D-4.

38. John Zeh, "Protesters Pledge to Overturn Sodomy Laws," *Gay Community News,* 19–25 July 1987, 3.

39. Donna Minkowitz, "ACT UP Zaps Cosmo," *Gay Community News,* 24–30 January 1988, 1; Robert E. Gould, "Reassuring News About AIDS: A Doctor Tells Why You May Not Be at Risk," *Cosmopolitan,* January 1988, 146; "Reporting Bias Crimes," *OutWeek,* 6 June 1990, 4; James Barron, "Dinkins Calls for Racial Unity at 'Town Meeting,'" *New York Times,* 23 May 1990, B-1; Jim Whelan, "ACT UP Protest at NBC," *New York Native,* 28 November 1988, 7.

40. Cliff O'Neill, "The Mapplethorpe Mess," *OutWeek,* 3 July 1989, 8.

41. Author's interview with Mass, 26 May 1994.

42. Author's interview with Mass, 26 May 1994; Kinsella, *Covering the Plague,* 25, 32–33, 37.

43. *New York Native,* Charles L. Ortleb, "Publisher," 23 May 1988, 4; "AZT: Government-Approved Killer?" 28 March 1988, 1; "City Planning to Poison Prisoners," 30 May 1988, 1.

44. Kinsella, *Covering the Plague,* 40–43; James E. D'Eramo, "Is African Swine Fever Virus the Cause?" *New York Native,* 23 May–5 June 1983, 1; Charles L. Ortleb, "Antibodies to African Swine Fever Virus Found in City's Blood Bank," *New York Native,* 30 September 1985, 14.

45. Charles L. Ortleb, "AIDSGATE: The Medical Scandal of the Century," *New York Native,* 3–16 June 1985, 13; 17–30 June 1985, 7.

46. Kinsella, *Covering the Plague,* 46–47.

47. *New York Native,* 17 March 1986, 1; 23 June 1986, 1.

48. *OutWeek,* "Editorial," 26 June 1989, 4; Larry Kramer, "Xeroxed," 7 August 1989, 78.

49. Ann Giudici Fettner, "Going for the Gold: The New York Native's Personal Agenda," *OutWeek,* 17 July 1989, 31.

50. Author's interview with Mass, 26 May 1994.

51. "Safer Sex Guidelines," *OutWeek,* 26 June 1989, 37.

52. *Hag Rag,* "Lust Through Latex-Covered Glasses: Lesbians in the Age of AIDS,"

September/October 1989, 8–9; Lesly Winslow-Stanley and Kris Hermanns, "Guidelines for Protecting Ourselves—Safer Sex for Lesbians," September/October 1989, 9.

53. Author's telephone interview with Henry McClurg, 13 January 1989, during which McClurg was in Houston. The *Montrose Voice* was founded in 1980 and is published today as the *New Voice*.

54. Author's interview with McClurg, 13 January 1989.

55. *Montrose Voice*, 18 November 1988, "Cancer Drug May Stop Wasting in AIDS Patients," 9; "Treating HIV/ARC/AIDS," 3.

56. John S. James, "Itraconazole: Affordable Fluconazole Substitute," *OutWeek*, 26 June 1989, 30.

57. *Gay Community News*, "GCN and AIDS," 17–23 April 1988, 4; Chris Bull, "Newsletters Sustain Growing PWA Networks . . . ," 20–26 March 1988, 3; Chris Bull, " . . . But the Threat of Censorship Remains," 20–26 March 1988, 3.

58. Bruce Voeller, "Gay Papers Aid Lubricant Scam," *Gay Community News*, 19–25 July 1987, 4.

59. Author's interview with McClurg, 13 January 1989.

60. Author's interview with McClurg, 13 January 1989.

61. Author's interview with Grier, 8 February 1994.

62. Myrna Elana and Debi Sundahl, "Year of the Lustful Lesbian!" *On Our Backs*, Summer 1984, 4. *On Our Backs* continues to be published today.

63. "What's It All About . . . Alfreda?" *Yoni*, Fall 1986, 2. *Yoni* was founded in 1986 in Oakland. The last issue of *Yoni* at the Lesbian Herstory Archives or in the Human Sexuality Collection at the Cornell University Library is dated 1989.

64. Cindy Patton, "Editorials: Why I Write Porno," *Bad Attitude*, Fall 1984, 2. *Bad Attitude* was founded in the summer of 1984 and is still being published today.

65. Thompson, *Long Road to Freedom*, 184.

66. Nestle, "The Gift of Taking," *On Our Backs*, Summer 1984, 20.

67. "Proposition 64 Will Not Stop AIDS!" *Yoni*, Fall 1986, 14; "Lesbian Agenda for Action," *On Our Backs*, Fall 1987, 11. Proposition 64 was defeated.

68. Candy Cane, "One Woman's Foray on the Phallus," *Yoni*, Fall 1988, 14–16.

69. Susie Bright, "Toys for Us," *On Our Backs*, Summer 1984, 13.

70. Sue Hyde and J.J., "Dildo Envy," *Bad Attitude*, Fall 1984, 22, 24.

71. *Gay Community News*, Sue Hyde, "The Sexual Object as Peer," 8 March 1986, 9; Janice Irving, "Women's Bookstores Reject Lesbian Sex Magazines," 8 June 1985, 3.

72. Irving, "Women's Bookstores Reject Lesbian Sex Magazines," 3.

73. Nestle, "My History with Censorship," *Bad Attitude*, Spring 1985, 5.

74. Ellen Herman, "Lesbians & Kids: Community We Create," *Gay Community News*, 24 May 1986, 6, 12.

75. Norma Smith, "Mothers' Courage," *Lesbian Contradiction*, Fall 1987, 11–12.

76. Barb Wire, "Pursuing the Goal of Parenting," *Lesbian Contradiction*, Fall 1987, 14.

77. Richard Labonte, "Domes Partner Rights Proposed," *The News*, 10 June 1988, 1.

78. Stephanie Poggi, "Court Rules against Dykes in Kowalski Case," *Gay Community News*, 25 January 1986, 3.

79. Poggi, "Court Rules against Dykes in Kowalski Case," 3; Emily Klose, "The Fight to Free Sharon Kowalski Continues," *Windy City Times*, 4 August 1988, 16.

80. Rachel Lurie, "Victory for Sharon Kowalski," *OutWeek*, 17 July 1989, 15.

81. Lisa M. Keen, "The National March Takes Washington by Surprise," *Washington Blade*, 16 October 1987, 1; Karlyn Barker and Linda Wheeler, "Hundreds of Thousands March for Gay Rights," *Washington Post*, 12 October 1987, 1; Lena Williams, "200,000 March in Capital to Seek Gay Rights and Money for AIDS," *New York Times*, 12 October 1987, 1.

82. Peg Byron, "Thousands Watch as Hundreds of Gay Couples 'Marry,'" *Washington Blade*, 16 October 1987, 11.

83. "Obituary Policy," *The News*, 10 June 1988, 18.

84. "Obituaries," *The News*, 10 June 1988, 18.

85. Author's telephone interview with Jeff McCourt, 15 January 1989, during which McCourt was in Chicago.

86. "42% Rise in Harassment of Gays Found," *Los Angeles Times*, 7 June 1988, 2.

87. Author's interview with McCourt, 15 January 1989. McCourt founded the *Windy City Times* in September 1985. It is still being published.

88. Author's interview with McCourt, 15 January 1989.

89. *Windy City Times*, "L.A. Police Stand by Hate-Crimes Policy," 22 September 1988, 4; "Boston Gays Say D.A. Is Soft on Bashers," 10 November 1988, 4; "'Shut Up, Fag' Buttons Selling Briskly in California," 10 November 1988, 4.

90. Jeffrey McCourt, "From the Publisher," *Windy City Times*, 22 September 1988, 11.

91. *The News*, "Violence Hotline," 5 August 1988, 6; Aslan Brooke, "New KKK Head Attacks Gays, Blacks," 12 December 1986, 3.

92. Jane Meyerding, "Nonviolence," *Lesbian Contradiction*, September 1987, 15; "Call for Articles on Violence," *Hag Rag*, September/October 1989, 24.

93. *Lesbian Ethics*, "Lesbian Acts," Spring 1986, 90; Mary Sargent, "Women Rising in Resistance," Spring 1986, 93; "Guerrilla Feminism," Summer 1989, 89.

94. Kim Westheimer, "Lesbians Demonstrate at 'Dyke-Bashing' Hearing," *Gay Community News*, 23 November 1985, 1; *OutWeek*, Mark Chestnut, "AIDS Activists March up Sixth Avenue," 10 July 1989, 14; Andrew Miller and Duncan Osborne, "Bombing at Gay Bar Raises Community Ire," 16 May 1990, 12.

95. Cliff O'Neill, "Bush Signs Hate Crimes Bill into Law," *OutWeek*, 9 May 1990, 12–13.

96. *OutWeek* ceased publication in July 1991; the last issue of *Yoni* at the Lesbian Herstory Archives or in the Human Sexuality Collection at the Cornell University Library is dated 1989; *The News* ceased publication in 1989; *Hag Rag* began appearing irregularly in 1991 and ceased publication in early 1993.

97. Author's interview with McCourt, 15 January 1989.

Chapter Eleven

1. Glessing, Underground Press in America, 45.

2. Jeff Yarbrough, "Gays in the Glossies" panel discussion, National Lesbian and Gay Journalists Association convention, 24 September 1994, Minneapolis.

3. Kris Jensen, "Gay Journals Shun Pet Rock Status for a Solid Foundation," *Atlanta Journal and Constitution*, 30 May 1994, B-5.

4. "Alan Bell: BLK," *Victory!* April 1994, 5; author's telephone interview with Katie Cotter, 22 June 1994, during which Cotter was in Los Angeles.

5. Yarbrough, "Gays in the Glossies" discussion, 24 September 1994.

6. *Out* led the pack of slick magazines with a circulation of 100,000. *POZ* printed that same total, but many copies were distributed without charge to HIV-positive men and women who could not afford to subscribe. Other circulation leaders included *Lesbian News* with 90,000, *The Advocate* with 85,000, and *10 Percent* with 75,000. The total figure is based on the author's interviews with Córdova, Kepner, Kraft, Nestle, Shilts, and Stevens.

7. Arlene Stein, "All Dressed Up, But No Place to Go?" *OUT/LOOK*, Winter 1989, 36.

8. Deirdre Carmody, "New Gay Press Is Emerging, Claiming Place in Mainstream," *New York Times*, 2 March 1992, A-1.

9. Pat Guy, "'Out' Draws Advertisers to Magazine for Homosexuals," *USA Today*, 19 June 1992, B-4.

10. Jay E. Rosen, "The Media Business; Out Magazine's National Reach," *New York Times*, 7 March 1994, D-6.

11. Guy, "'Out' Draws Advertisers," B-4; Rosen, "Out Magazine's National Reach," D-6.

12. Cyndee Miller, "Mainstream Marketers Decide Time Is Right to Target Gays," *Marketing News*, 20 July 1992, 8.

13. Chiqui Cartagena, "Sex and the Single Girl," *Out*, May 1994, 100.

14. "Stone Soup," *Out*, February/March 1993, 8.

15. *Out*, Elise Harris, "Cowgirl Mystique," October/November 1993, 67; Michael Musto and Susie Bright, "GAYDAR," October/November 1993, 120; Brad Gooch, "Benefit Roulette," February/March 1994, 87; Kiki Mason, "Star Chasers," June 1994, 84.

16. Sarah Pettit, "Gays in the Glossies" panel discussion, National Lesbian and Gay Journalists Association convention, 24 September 1994, Minneapolis.

17. Michael Goff and Sarah Pettit, "Bronco Bucks," *Out*, October/November 1993, 14; Rosen, "Out Magazine's National Reach," D-6. Comedy Central's "Out There" aired 3 December 1993.

18. Rosen, "Out Magazine's National Reach," D-6.

19. Author's telephone interview with David Mulryan, 5 June 1993, during which Mulryan was in New York City; Paula Span, "ISO the Gay Consumer: Advertisers Are Coming Out in the Open and Finding a New Market," *Washington Post*, 19 May 1994, D-1.

20. Author's interview with Kraft, 10 June 1994, during which Kraft was in Los Angeles. *Genre*'s first issue was dated spring 1991, and it is still being published.

21. Author's telephone interview with Frances Stevens, 21 June 1994, during which Stevens was in San Francisco. *Deneuve* was founded in spring 1991 and is still being published.

22. Jensen, "Gay Journals," B-5. *10 Percent* was founded in October 1992 and is still being published today.

23. Miller, "Mainstream Marketers," 8; Andrea Adelson, "AT&T Increases Gay and Lesbian Ads," *New York Times*, 5 April 1994, D-21.

24. The Saab ad appeared in *Out*, November 1994, 5.

25. Christy Fisher, "Local Print Bumps into National Ad Walls," *Advertising Age*, 30 May 1994, S-2; Gary Levin, "Mainstream's Domino Effect," *Advertising Age*, 18 January 1993, 30; Martha T. Moore, "Courting the Gay Market: Business, Not Politics," *USA Today*, 23 April 1993, B-1, B-2; Guy, "'Out' draws Advertisers," B-4; Bradley Johnson, "The Gay Quandary," *Advertising Age*, 18 January 1993, 29.

26. Bradley Johnson, "Far Right Attacks Losing Out to $$," *Advertising Age*, 30 May 1994, S-7.

27. Johnson, "Far Right Attacks," S-7; Kara Swisher, "Targeting the Gay Market," *Washington Post*, 25 April 1993, H-1.

28. "Cheek to Chic," *Out*, October/November 1993, 88–93.

29. Jeanne Córdova, "Who Loves Ya, Baby?" *Square Peg*, May 1992, 5; Bradley Johnson, "Economics Holds Back Lesbian Ad Market," *Advertising Age*, 18 January 1993, 34. *Square Peg* was founded in March 1992 and ceased publication in August 1993.

30. Lindsy Van Gelder and Pamela Robin Brandt, "Surf Lesbos," *Out*, March 1993, 64–67; *Out*, March 1993, 89; Adam Block, "Undeniably Elton," *10 Percent*, Summer 1993, cover, 38; *10 Percent*, Summer 1993, 9; *Victory!* "Tim Gill: Quark," May 1994, 18; May 1994, 36. *Victory!* was founded in December 1993 in Sacramento and continues to be published today.

31. Richard Settles, "From the Chief," *Genre*, June 1994, 10.

32. *Genre*, Bruce Mirken, "Being Alive!" December 1992/January 1993, 42–43; "Community Prescription Service," June 1994, 77.

33. Kiki Mason, "Dating and HIV," *Out,* February/March 1994, 132; "Savvy Travelers," *Victory!,* June 1994, 11; Michael Szymanski, "Merrily Monroe," *Frontiers,* 25 March 1994, 100; Robert Patrick, "Pouf Positive," *OUT/LOOK,* Summer 1988, 53. *Frontiers* was founded in 1982 and continues to be published today. *OUT/LOOK* was founded in the spring of 1988 and ceased publication in 1992.

34. Sean O'Brien Strub, "S.O.S.: On Becoming a Survivor," *POZ,* June/July 1994, 6. *POZ* was founded in the spring of 1994 and continues to be published today.

35. *POZ,* Casey Davidson, "*Voila!* AIDS as Art," April/May 1994, 16; Casey Davidson, "*Philly,* the Sequel?" April/May 1994, 18; Karen Ocamb, "Home HIV Testing Is Near," June/July 1994, 48; "HIV Standard of Care," April/May 1994, 60–61.

36. *POZ,* Karen Ocamb, "Holistic Turnaround," April/May 1994, 47; Richard Perez-Feria, "Flex This," June/July 1994, 20; Casey Davidson, "C'est Magnifique!" June/July 1994, 23.

37. Sean O'Brien Strub, "The HIV Magazines: Help or Hindrance?" panel discussion, National Lesbian and Gay Journalists Association convention.

38. Strub, "HIV Magazines" panel discussion.

39. Leigh W. Rutledge, "Just the Facts," *10 Percent,* Winter 1992, 11. *BLK* was founded in Los Angeles in 1988 but was printed on newsprint until switching to slick paper and a glossy cover in 1991. It is still being published today.

40. Karen Ocamb, "On the Circuit," *Genre,* June 1994, 26; Emma Shera, "Lesbofile," *Deneuve,* March/April 1994, 30.

41. Val C. Phoenix, "Roseanne Tells and Kisses," *Deneuve,* May/June 1994, 43.

42. Brendan Lemon, "Virgin Territory: k.d. lang," *The Advocate,* 16 June 1992, 38, 44; *Square Peg,* Michael Szymanski, "Outing Oscar," May 1992, 21; Michael Szymanski, "Jodie Foster and Richard Gere," March/April 1993, 15, 29.

43. Jeanne Córdova, "Lesbian Comics Make Prime Time," *Square Peg,* May/June 1993, 19.

44. Jamoo, "RuPaul: The BLK Interview," *BLK,* December 1993, 9–14.

45. Mayer Rus, *Out,* "Pull up a Chair," July/August 1994, 138; "Love Seats," February/March 1993, 99; Sara Hunt, "Hollywood Hacienda," *10 Percent,* 33, 34.

46. Rachel Pepper, "Touring Toronto," *Deneuve,* March/April 1994, 56; "Hidden Provincetown," *Genre,* June 1994, 48; Eric Gutierrez, "Viva Barcelona!" *Out,* July/August 1994, 120; Mark Chestnut, "The Mile High Club," *10 Percent,* Winter 1992, 68.

47. *BLK,* December 1993, 4; "Zora," *Deneuve,* May/June 1994, 41.

48. Author's interview with Kraft, 10 June 1994.

49. Vincent Boucher, "Style Since Stonewall," *Out,* July/August 1994, 70–77.

50. "A Date with Spring," *Deneuve,* March/April 1994, 36–39.

51. Pettit, "Gays in the Glossies" panel discussion, 24 September 1994.

52. "Style," *Frontiers,* 25 March 1994, cover; 55–64.

53. Bryn Austin, "Field of Dreams," *Lesbian News,* May 1994, cover; 45.

54. *Genre,* Bobby Brite, "Hollywood Husbands," January 1994, 46; Jeffrey Marcus, "Sex, Lies and Silicone," April 1994, 40–41;

55. *Genre,* Brad Johns, "Hair Color To Be Proud Of," June 1994, 84; Jean Rosenbaum, "The Painless Face-Lift," February/March 1993, 82; Stanley Ely, "Open Wide and Smile," May 1993, 84.

56. Preston G. Guider, "Read My Lips," *BLK,* March 1991, 34; "Richard & Candy Farrell," *Victory!* May 1994, 30.

57. Wayne Hoffman, "*Victory!* Is a Success Story of Its Own," *Washington Blade,* 13 January 1995, 49.

58. Hoffman, "*Victory!*"

59. Hoffman, "*Victory!*"

60. Hoffman, "*Victory!*"

61. *Deneuve,* October 1994, Ann Wesley, "The Seasons of Life: Kay Gardner," 14–15; "Out in Front," 8; Victoria A. Brownworth, "I Want My Dyke TV!," 28.

62. Author's interview with Stevens, 21 June 1994.

63. Katie Brown, "Baby Dykes," *Deneuve,* September/October 1992, 9.

64. Bree Coven, "Hey, Baby!" *Deneuve,* March/April 1994, 47.

65. Sarah Pettit biographical statement provided by *Out* magazine, 22 June 1994.

66. Bob and Rod Jackson-Paris, "How We Met," *Out,* February/March 1994, 62. See Bob and Rod Jackson-Paris, *Straight from the Heart* (New York: Warner, 1994).

67. Pettit and Yarbrough, "Gays in the Glossies" discussion, 24 September 1994.

68. Joel Tan, "Memoirs of an Invisible Man," *Square Peg,* May 1992, 29; Meryl Cohn, "Northampton: 10,000 Cuddling, Kissing Lesbians," *10 Percent,* Spring 1993, 77; George Wayne, "Gaga for a Go-Go Boy," *Out,* July/August 1994, 16.

69. *Victory!* "Penetrating the Isolation," June 1994, 31; "Clinton Fein: Apollo Media," May 1994, 22. Randy Shilts, *Conduct Unbecoming: Lesbians and Gays in the U.S. Military* (New York: St. Martin's, 1993).

70. Steve Greenberg, "AIDS in the Next Generation," *10 Percent,* Summer 1993, 65, 66, 68.

71. Kevin Koffler, "Men We Love," *Genre,* December 1993/January 1994, 31–39.

72. Carmody, "New Gay Press," A-1; Heather Findlay, "Gay 101," *Out,* July/August 1994, 84–85.

73. *10 Percent,* Arie Schwartz, "Surpassing the Odds," June 1994, 66–67; Dee Mosbacher, "Right Answers," Spring 1993, 33.

74. *Deneuve,* June 1994, 18, 28.

75. *OUT/LOOK,* Spring 1988, 62, 90; "Premier Issue of Les/Gay Mag Censored," *Gay Community News,* 3–9 April 1988, 2; "Welcome," *OUT/LOOK,* Summer 1988, 3.

76. *OUT/LOOK,* Nayland Blake, "Tom of Finland: An Appreciation," Fall 1988, 36; "Tom: The Controversy," Winter 1989, 5; untitled editorial, Winter 1989, 1.

77. David Jernigan, "Why Gay Leaders Don't Last," *OUT/LOOK,* Summer 1988, 48.

78. *The Advocate,* Michelangelo Signorile, "Out at *The New York Times,"* 5 May 1992, 34; Donna Minkowitz, "Patricia Ireland Takes the Reins," 17 December 1991, 38; "Not Even Worth an Outing," 16 June 1992, 11; J.C. Janovy, "Melissa Etheridge," *10 Percent,* March/April 1994, 54.

79. Mark Chestnut, "D.C. Day Tripping," *10 Percent,* Spring 1993, 48; Chris Bull, "A Capital Idea," *The Advocate,* 1 June 1993, 25; CorboBal, "Moments from the March," *Square Peg,* May/June 1993, 12.

80. Janny Scott, "Gay Marchers Celebrate History in 2 Parades," *New York Times,* 27 June 1994, A-1; Eleanor Randolph, "Homosexuals Celebrate Protest at Stonewall 25," *Washington Post,* 27 June 1994, A-8.

81. "Outlook: Theater of Operations," *Frontiers,* 16 July 1993, 10.

82. Katie Brown, "Margarethe Cammermeyer," *Deneuve,* September/October 1992, 17.

83. Ian Young, "Coming out in Print," *Gay Sunshine,* Spring 1977, 13.

84. Jay Mathews, "From Closet to Mainstream," *Newsweek,* 1 June 1992, 62.

85. Fisher, "Local Print Bumps into National Ad Walls," S-2; Guy, "'Out' Draws Advertisers," B-4.

86. Yarbrough, "Gays in the Glossies" panel discussion, 24 September 1994.

87. Author's telephone interview with Jeanne Córdova, 28 June 1994, during which Córdova was in Los Angeles.

88. Deirdre Carmody, "The Media Business: Time Inc. Shelves a Gay Magazine," *New York Times,* 6 June 1994, D-7; Wayne Hoffman, "Time Pulls the Plug on Tribe," *Washington Blade,* 17 June 1994, 35.

89. Carmody, "Time Inc. Shelves a Gay Magazine," D-7; Hoffman, "Time Pulls the Plug," 35.

Chapter Twelve

1. Jackson and Persky, eds., *Flaunting It!*, 3.
2. Bonnie B. Ricca, "A Gay Frequency," *Deneuve*, March/April 1994, 10–11; David Noack, "A 'Gay Sensitive' News Service," *Editor & Publisher*, 15 January 1994, 12; Bonnie B. Ricca, "As Our World Turns," *Deneuve*, March/April 1994, 10; Charles Taylor, "KGAY: All Day, All Gay!" *Genre*, May 1993, 32; "King of the Gay Airwaves," *Victory!*, June 1994, 12; Robert Rodgers, "A Network of Our Own," *Genre*, May 1993, 80.
3. Author's interview with Jennings, 21 January 1993.
4. Author's interview with Block, 23 April 1993.
5. Author's interview with Shilts, 11 August 1993.
6. The *Bay Area Reporter* has a weekly circulation of 37,000.
7. Author's interview with Lyon, 9 April 1993.
8. Brian Mooar and Robert O'Harrow, Jr., "Slaying of Gay Man Linked to Fla. Suspect," *Washington Post*, 24 June 1994, D-1; *Washington Blade*, Lou Chibbaro, Jr., "Sixth Man Slain," 25 March 1994, 1; Lou Chibbaro, Jr., "Activists Alarmed by New Killings," 13 May 1994, 1; Lou Chibbaro, Jr., and Lisa Keen, "Murder Comes Knocking," 20 May 1994, 1; Lou Chibbaro, Jr., "Latest Total: 11 Murders, 11 Months," 3 June 1994, 1; Lisa Keen, "FBI Searching for Serial Killer," 17 June 1994, 1; "Looking for a Good Time?" 15 July 1994, 4; Lou Chibbaro, Jr., "Arrest Ends Eight-Month Killing Spree," 25 November 1994, 1.

Index

About the Author

Rodger Streitmatter is a professor of journalism at the School of Communication at American University. He is the author of *Raising Her Voice: African American Women Journalists Who Changed History,* as well as numerous articles on the history of journalism. He lives in Washington, D.C.